Seen and Unseen

Also by Kieran Flanagan

SOCIOLOGY AND LITURGY: Re-presentations of the Holy

THE ENCHANTMENT OF SOCIOLOGY: A Study of Theology and Culture

POSTMODERNITY, SOCIOLOGY AND RELIGION *(co-editor with Peter C. Jupp)*

VIRTUE ETHICS AND SOCIOLOGY: Issues of Modernity and Religion *(co-editor with Peter C. Jupp)*

Seen and Unseen

Visual Culture, Sociology and Theology

Kieran Flanagan

Reader in Sociology
University of Bristol

First published 2004 by
PALGRAVE MACMILLAN
Houndmills, Basingstoke, Hampshire RG21 6XS and
175 Fifth Avenue, New York, N.Y. 10010
Companies and representatives throughout the world

PALGRAVE MACMILLAN is the global academic imprint of the Palgrave Macmillan division of St. Martin's Press, LLC and of Palgrave Macmillan Ltd. Macmillan® is a registered trademark in the United States, United Kingdom and other countries. Palgrave is a registered trademark in the European Union and other countries.

ISBN 0–333–99854–5 hardback

This book is printed on paper suitable for recycling and made from fully managed and sustained forest sources.

A catalogue record for this book is available from the British Library.

Library of Congress Cataloging-in-Publication Data
Flanagan, Kieran, 1944–
    Seen and unseen : visual culture, sociology, and theology / Kieran Flanagan.
        p.   cm.
    Includes bibliographical references and index.
    ISBN 0–333–99854–5
    1. Christian sociology—Catholic Church.   2. Visual sociology.   I. Title

BX1753.F595 2004
306.6—dc22

2004042845

10   9   8   7   6   5   4   3   2   1
13   12   11   10   09   08   07   06   05   04

Printed and bound in Great Britain by
Antony Rowe Ltd, Chippenham and Eastbourne

In fond memory of John Farrell (1926–1998)
and Alix Farrell (1929–2003)

Contents

Preface   viii

Introduction   1

1   Sociology and Virtual Religion: Issues of Memory and Identity   14

2   Who Sees There? Tales of Character, Virtue and Trust   42

3   Visual Culture and the Virtual: The Internet
    and Religious Displays   73

4   To See or Not to See: The Plight of the Voyeur   102

5   Piety and Visual Culture: Seeking to See the Unseen   130

6   Dark into Light: A Sociological Navigation   158

Notes and References   194

Bibliography   223

Index   240

Preface

There is something almost portentous about presenting a third volume of reflections on how to link sociology to theology in ways that enhance mutual understandings. Why bother? To those in sociology such exercises seem futile; and to those in theology they seem unhelpful visitations from a discipline habitually hostile to its claims. Somehow, these studies of ambiguity in ritual, in the field of culture and in relation to the visual seem themselves ambiguous. They do not lie within the accepted contours of each discipline and so, standing outside, they seem affiliated to neither. Furthermore, the studies emerge in a long decline of institutional religion in England over the last two decades to the level where a realisation dawns that it is now a post-Christian society.

Yet, before sociology delivers its funeral oration on institutional religion – again – it might realise that the forces of secularisation that have fractured institutional religion now threaten to engulf the discipline itself. Sociology too lacks a mobilising vision and it too is affected by the disenchanting and fracturing powers of modernity as postmodernity came to indicate. Both sociology and theology seem to have arrived at a common sense of dissatisfaction with their place in the culture of postmodernity. For sociology, this culture signifies the burden of life without God; for theology, at least in England, it denotes a terrain peculiarly resistant to the planting of religious belief. Somehow theology lacks a grammar book to read culture in ways that might assuage sociology's growing fears about life without God. Few in either discipline seem to investigate what happens on the ground of culture, not so much where religion withers, as lazy references to secularisation would indicate, but how it flourishes – for despite the gloom, true believers still fill the pews even if their numbers are in slow decline.

Each volume is about working out into a vision, a sensibility of what lies beyond the cold analytical rhetoric of sociology. In the first volume that dealt with liturgy (religious ritual), the movements of representation and re-presentation led into concerns with the apophatic, the theology of post-modernity. The second volume addressed a nagging feeling that there was an implicit theology floating around sociology in its genesis whose implications have seldom been confronted. The more one thought the more it seemed that in the culture of postmodernity, sociology was sleep walking into theology. In peering at the field of culture, sociology did not seem able to see properly. Modernity had in some way disabled the sociological gaze, and postmodernity seemed to confirm its myopia. The need to look to see something beyond what disciplinary eyes can see led to this study.

It is a tale of the sociological gaze directed to the seen and the unseen, the earthly city and the heavenly city of St Augustine. Why might this disciplinary gaze look in that direction? This is to speak of a conversion of sight, a yielding to a wish to see in a particular way that suggests no entry points into sociology. Matters might so remain were it not for the increased recognition of the importance of reflexivity in sociology. This notion denotes the self-awareness peculiar to sociology of its position on the field of analysis and its ethical responsibilities for those so represented in its accounts. But the notion goes further. It relates to the inward facets of the sociologist, the self and its biographical dispositions. These bear amplification in relation to the spiritual dimensions of the self, facets so often neglected in sociology. Opening out these inner facets of reflexivity relates also to the visual sensibilities of the self, what it sees inwardly and without.

If what is seen is significant, the actor enters a realm of accountability for the act of seeing, one where moral inquests are held on the gaze. Culpability for seeing relates to social circumstances, dispositions and inclinations such as boredom and temptation and it is these that are set to lead off in a theological direction to face the issue of the study, how sociology comes to treat the seen and the unseen. In seeking to cope with the elusive properties of visual culture, sociology faces dilemmas of distinguishing between the forms of virtual religion and its theological prototype. These complicate the efforts of the sociological gaze to understand the dilemmas of the seen and the unseen that are central to theology but also to visual culture itself.

Visual culture reflects the advent of cyberspace, of powers to make virtual reality. These bring into focus wider issues of image and spectacle and questions of how things are seen and are arranged to be so viewed. Images matter, hence the concerns with their packaging. Not all that is seen with the eye of perception counts. The eye needs to attend to what it cannot see, what is left out, what is below the surface, and what is to be inferred. If it lacks this capacity, it has no means of surviving in a visual culture. Recognition of the limits of seeing, of what lies hidden, plays to theological advantage for it points to wider issues of how the unseen is to be seen. Seeing is an act with a narrative, a tale, and if sociology deals with the visual, it has to attend to this facet. As a study of the sociologist's dilemma in relation to the seen and the unseen, the tale or the narrative of the study becomes apparent. Yet, as the self becomes a project with tales and narratives, one encounters a peculiar paradox: those of sociology seem to have become muted in the public domain. Oddly, sociology seems to have become a victim of its own successes in characterising modernity.

Some fifty years ago, it seemed radical for the American sociologist C. Wright Mills to open out the prospect of a sociological imagination, one that articulated public sensibilities and anxieties. Now, the sociological voice is drowned out by many in the mass media, in quality newspapers and in television documentaries which articulate well tales that reflect public sensibilities. They seem to catch public anxieties better than many sociologists. It might appear as if sociology is now in a peculiarly Indian summer. For a brief period, Giddens placed sociology in a political ambit with the Third Way. The discipline seemed to have arrived as a sort of aide-de-camp to Blairism, but now the demand for messages from sociology appears to have dried up. Likewise, the discipline gained an enormous public profile in France with Pierre Bourdieu, a sociologist with almost priestly powers to consecrate the cultural heart of the nation in the shape of sociological expectation; but he died in 2003. Yet, sociology should not consider taking out retirement papers. It has become more not less important in characterising contemporary culture. It sees more than the public commentators whose utterances are packed into fifty minutes, or three pages of the colour supplements of the broadsheets. If it is to be useful and indispensable in dealing with con-temporary culture, sociology has to be able to take a longer view than the demands of weekly journalism can supply. But if it is to be of use, it needs to be radical in what it thinks even if, as Weber might suggest, this takes some inconvenient turns. Moving towards a consideration of the theological implications of sociology might be a case in point, one that this study explores.

The world seems changing utterly in ways those zealots of the late 1960s could never have envisaged. Decades since have marked changes from angry forms of feminism to ecological warriors, to global patriots, to what few expected, a realisation that the world as it enters a new century is facing divisions, not on the basis of class or gender or nationalism, but of religion. The rise of Islam has wonderfully concentrated minds of the West long habituated to secularity. The realisation is dawning that religion has not vanished, but also that something in the health of society is deficient. The missing ingredient is spirituality. Its lack seems all too evident not only in matters of civics and education but also in the realisation that public culture has become impoverished in ways that suggest a growing intolerance of forces of de-spiritualisation.

The present study was written between August 2001 and January 2004. In its writing, in dealings with visual culture, one felt like a performing flea hopping with abandon over chasms of scholarship in theology, philosophy, aesthetics and art history, to name a few disciplines one trespassed into. A number of difficulties emerged in the writing, not least that no particular image could be privileged though, as the study unfolds, the face of Christ becomes the end point of this sociological gaze. The absence of a definite image, a weakness, perhaps became a strength of the study. It permitted one to mark out a theme of opening to see as a matter of choice, but one cast in the expectations of sociology itself. All the time, one returned to the central issue of the study: the tale of sociology's dilemmas in endeavouring to see the unseen.

Dropping the authorial mask, I wish to thank a number of people who greatly helped in the writing of this study. My first and principal debt is to the Revd Dr Peter C. Jupp, an honorary fellow of the department and a co-editor with me on two collections of essays. Taking the manuscript for a couple of days to a retreat house, he cast a judicious, gimlet and charitable eye over it, marking up many infelicities and slips. What he caught was important, but what greatly affirmed was his critical positive response to what he read. He provided an enormous shot in the arm to finish up the study in a term of very heavy teaching. Needless to say, any mistakes left are my fault.

The reports of the two referees on the initial proposal were of great help. In particular, one should mention the highly detailed and helpful American report. It pointed me to a number of studies I might well have missed. More importantly, the report caught the essence of the proposed book and provided an inspiration as to how to proceed. The interested, sympathetic and critical responses to two papers from the study, presented at the BSA Sociology of Religion Study Group, were also highly helpful.

Over the course of writing the book, I am most grateful to my colleagues in the department of sociology at the University of Bristol. In particular, I would like to thank Professor Gregor McLennan, head of department from 2000 to 2003. Beset by demands for publication outputs, he trusted me to get on with the book and was a great source of encouragement for its completion. Jackie West, who took over the post, kept many emails marked urgent off my screen. Dr Tom Osborne provided some valuable suggestions as did a retired colleague Dr Willie Watts Miller. Despite a pending hip replacement operation, Dr Rohit Barot readily came up the stairs to deal with computer difficulties. He showed me great kindness. My colleagues in the Arts Faculty came generously to my aid with many valuable suggestions. Elaine Escott, the departmental administrator, Jackie Bee, the departmental secretary, and the Faculty Computing Service were ever patient in handling numerous daft queries. The undergraduate students who took my course on Social Theory and Visual Culture more than deserve mention. Aspects of the study were written in lecture form and they supplied many golden moments of insight that greatly aided its completion.

Occupying a sociological exile and being distinctly estranged from the liberal hegemony of English Catholicism, Clifton Catholic Cathedral, Bristol, supplied numerous compensations that kept my religious identity well rooted and pruned by the people there. In the course of writing the study, one was reminded of a higher calling, one well expressed in the professional dedication of Canon Robert Corrigan, Dean of Clifton Cathedral, parish priest and assistant priest, all in one, who currently ministers there to 1250 parishioners over a weekend with an intermittent supply from willing but badly over-stretched clergy. In particular, I want to thank the young men and boys who serve there. The brightest and best, a cheerful religiously focused band, they kept alive my hopes for the future of Catholicism. Fr Gordon Pavey helped me a lot with some arcane biblical queries. Finally, in this context, I would like to thank Fr Michael Robertson who managed to get the essence of the study faster than myself and who supplied me with a number of very handy hints on how to go forward.

My two editors at Palgrave Macmillan, Briar Towers and Jen Nelson, were most supportive and tactful in prodding me along to meet necessary deadlines. Richard Greatrex, manager of the SPCK bookshop in Park Street, kept gently reminding me that there was a place on his shelves for this new book. Finally, my thanks to my mother Mrs Maureen Flanagan and my brother Brian who keeps on eye on her, for asking with restraint when the wretched manuscript was going to be finished.

John and Alix Farrell, to whom the book is dedicated, were dear friends for twenty-five years. Both would have been greatly amused at the memoria the book was completed on.

Kieran Flanagan
Memoria of St Thomas Aquinas
28 January 2004

Introduction

Having often passed Shrewsbury on the train, the church spires and towers of this important Welsh Border town attracted attention. There seemed plenty to see for a visit. One particular tower that aroused interest was of the beautiful large Norman church of St Mary. Its interior is described by Jenkins as 'both majestic and intimate'. This Anglican church had lots of medieval glass to gaze at. After wandering around, one was greatly surprised to find that this was not a living church but a museum, in the care of a Conservation Trust since 1995.[1] It stood in the public square like a *Marie Celeste*, mysteriously abandoned and deserted. It seemed to give visual expression to the notion that English Christianity had expired.[2]

Abandoned churches, like abandoned railway stations, generate profound unsettlement. Their emptiness signifies the evaporation of their characterising social ambience. A redundant church invokes memories of times when babies brought to baptism yelped when the waters of life flowed cold on their brows, of the lovers who sealed marriage promises sacramentally and of the dead well commended to God by their clergy. One thinks of the past forms of fidelity to the liturgical cycle of Christmas to Easter, the observation of feasts and solemnities, heights of celebration that stand in contrast to the rhythms of ferial life. In this heritage museum, the liturgical cycle had stopped turning. The neatness and well-ordered appearance of St Mary's Church seemed to stand in marked contrast to the untidy clutter of its use in times past. Now it is a site where the unseen is no more sought. The symbols, artefacts and rituals that stood witness to the unseen are no longer seen in that light, for now there is nobody to look to see and possibly to believe. In some tragic way, the building had been assigned to a long Good Friday with no prospect of Easter Sunday deliverance. Served with a redundancy notice by those charged with its stewardship, the building had passed from the sacred into the custody of the secular.

As institutional Christianity seeks to accommodate itself to life on an increasingly hostile landscape, the path to the heavenly no longer follows a direct route. Instead, a labyrinth has been inadvertently constructed, one in

1

which dwindling numbers of the faithful have lost their way. The options for a return to a path that would lead to heavenly sights seem bleak. Few would look to academic theology to supply rungs to the heavenly.[3] It cannot be said that the mass media, particularly the BBC supply points of relief for institutional Christianity.[4] For many, England is a post-Christian society. Yet, that bland indifference to religious differences has a habit of cracking in the face of old prejudices liberal theologians thought had long vanished into memory.

Resuming its exemplary position in English society, Catholicism has been demonised and subject to moral panics in the past decade (1993–2003) by the BBC and some quality papers over a tiny number of ill-handled cases of child abuse. Efforts of the state to roll back prejudice in areas of race, sexuality, gender and discrimination seem to have left one exception: Catholicism.[5] As Anglicanism has sanctified inclusiveness, it has become caught divisively and irresolutely in sexual politics in ways that have generated massive public confusion as to where its authority lies: in revelation or in reason. In forging theological stances to sanctify public desires for the ordination of women and guilt-free homosexuality, Anglicanism has managed to rip itself apart. The weather forecasts from this experimental station set to feel the pulse on the ground of culture are dire. In all these crises, one can take comfort from the wry comment of the Catholic Scottish composer, James Macmillan, that 'the Catholic Church has been in crisis since the cock crew three times...'[6] Somehow, institutional religions (Catholicism and Anglicanism) have lost the capacity to effect and to sustain a mobilising vision of their theologies that would refract cultural sensibilities. The 'noble simplicity' of liturgy and its artistic styles, envisioned in the Vatican II documents, has collapsed into an ignoble chaos whose fractures postmodernity seems to amplify endlessly.

In English society, the making of Christianity over the past forty years has not worked. Like a large asteroid that exploded in the face of self-defeating efforts to modernise, bits and pieces of institutional religion have been scattered over the country. Churchgoing has been in continual decline since the 1960s, and there is no light at the end of the tunnel. This process of disengagement from commitment, characterised as secularisation, marks for some sociologists the death of God.[7] Although for others, it is the concept that is dead, not God.[8] A striking realisation that Christianity was not so much dead as buried in the UK came with the publication of the Census returns for 2001. It showed that 72 per cent of the population defined themselves as Christian. These figures suggested a massive disconnection from institutional Christianity.[9] From these figures, one conclusion is only possible: that strategies of renewal based on modernisation of the last four decades have been a grotesque failure. As sociologists had long suspected, the liberal Christianity that so sought to sanctify the spirit of the age has been nothing but an expedient effort in grave digging.[10] Those whom the mass media most loved as prophets of the age have been revealed as myopic practitioners, blind to the effects of their pronouncements: the disengagement of English society from Christianity. It was they who said difference did not matter and in the indifference so wrought, few could see the purpose of religious affiliation. In not seeing so, the need for a stable site to see has been lost. In these circumstances, it is not surprising that the unseen became clouded over.

Somehow, seen from the ground of culture, the economy of salvation operates in a deregulated manner. Structures for meshing earthly happenings with heavenly dealings are less characterised by estrangement than by anomie. The connection between norms (expectations) and structures to realise their basis has become unclear. In these disconnections of structure and regard, images of the heavenly have vaporised. Something has gone missing from the Churches: a capacity to supply testimonies for navigating from the seen to the unseen. Now there is no mobilising vision of how the unseen is to be seen and this lack has impoverished culture.

It must be confessed that sociology, for all its merits, hardly invokes confidence as a means for the recovery of dispositions to see the unseen. These are theological matters well removed from sociology's myopic gaze. Yet it is on the ground of culture, where capacities and incentives to distinguish the seen from the unseen are formulated and shaped, where things have gone awry. Dealing with the paradoxes of the seen and unseen are matters proper to theology, for they involve eyes of faith, but they also embody ways of seeing that are culturally contingent. Seeing involves ways and capacities, dispositions and outcomes that involve reference to visual culture. This division between the seen, as shaped in culture, and the unseen, as discerned through spiritual means, seems to denote antinomial properties peculiarly resistant to sociological characterisation. If so, why use sociology to understand such irresolvable dilemmas? In a peculiar way, the ground of culture has shifted in ways that attract sociological attention to these matters.

This is a study of the visual aspects of reflexivity as directed to an exercise in understanding how these dilemmas of the seen and the unseen are to be handled in ways that place sociological deliberations in theological ambits. Dealing with the seen and the unseen brings to the fore Turner's notions of 'liminality' and the 'liminoid'. This property of being in between has emerged with a vengeance as technology, notably through cyberspace, has blurred distinctions between the virtual and the real in images and icons difficult to decipher. These unsettlements beg questions about sociology's own way of seeing what belongs to religion. Its disciplinary dalliances with being a surrogate religion suggest that it has its own problems of distinguishing between the virtual and the real – what belongs to theology. Postmodernity signifies a confusion of sight, but also a sense of emptiness, a void, which causes a retreat into memory, a reaching back to times when refractions made more definite marks on the social. Often what is commemorated reflects a celebration of eras when seeing was clearer and society was structured to refract accordingly. What is now sought is an escape from the plenitude visual culture engenders in its present form, a plight that blurs sociology's own vision of itself.

It had not been intended to write this particular study. Another had been planned, but was abandoned for reasons detailed below. From the embers of this failed exercise in fieldwork, this study emerged as a response to three shifts in sociology that are incorporated in this book.

The first was stimulated by the successive publications of Zygmunt Bauman as he journeyed through postmodernity to the liquid modernity he discerns as following. Postmodernity emerged after 1989 and was a term of a moment that caught worries over how to live in mutuality when God had died and ideologies had failed. Although not writing in theology, many of Bauman's themes seemed directed to it. These related to the self, the seeking of an Other and a face to trust, if not to love. His sense of moral engagement suggested that sociology could not just live in itself in some disconnected manner, but that it had to find ways of looking past itself, hence his continued interest in Weber and Simmel. From his writings, one senses that there is a trajectory in sociology that points unexpectedly in a theological direction, not one he has followed but one which others could.

The second factor was the realisation that sociology occupied its own hermeneutic circles that turned and turned into imperatives to face the subjective. These turns had started slowly, with the return of the actor and the turn into concerns with culture. More radical turns for the discipline came with the advent of reflexivity and the implications it presented to sociology regarding its identity, and the ethical obligations these increasing concerns generated. The discipline had shifted in its expectations from distant professional relationships with its subject matter, to an urge to represent that oscillated between testimony and advocacy. This introspective turn was complemented and seemingly justified by shifts in culture itself towards recognition of confessions and tales as authentic accounts of lives of the excluded. This concern with amplifying such tales became very much part of the agenda of the politics of identity. The importance of these shifts was marked by the development of qualitative sociology.

The tales of identity politics, hitherto of the unvoiced and the excluded, are now heard all over the departments of sociology. Their utterances form part of the argot of much of contemporary sociology. By contrast, it is tales from theology that are deemed unrespectable and beyond the disciplinary pale. These are firmly *off* the sociological index. Sociology abhors displacements, and the imperative to restore other accounts, testimonies from theology, emerged as an ambition for this study.

The third factor that emerged was a growing awareness that oddly little sociological attention had been given to visual culture. As a term it buzzed around the edges of sociology. There were two reasons why sociology had to attend to visual culture. The first was the rise of the Internet. It posed a profound threat to sociology, by making possible interaction through images without apparent reference to social filters in ways Benjamin could never have envisaged. Secondly, there was a realisation that Foucault's gaze had connections with visual culture that had not been explored. The gaze has a wider remit than its use in Foucault where it was concerned with power and control. These shifts in sociology seemed worthy of exploration in ways that could build on facets of the two earlier books.

The first study, *Sociology and Liturgy*, might be regarded as a lengthy opaque study of the opaque.[11] It was concerned with what Rappaport termed the necessary fabrications of a symbolically constructed world and how within these could a touch of the Divine be found.[12] The study was liminal in many ways, not least in its concentration on the minor actors of the rite, those who are seen most but who counted least. One actor, the choirboy, has an unusual public significance in his capacity to incarnate the angelic, notably at Christmas. In his act, he seems to have one foot in the seen and the other in the unseen and so singing gives testimony to his citizenship of heaven and earth. The study had other ambitions, notably to explore the infelicitous frailties of ritual enactments and their redemption by reference to the apophatic (negative theology). The study was directed towards images and understandings of the Pseudo-Dionysius whose spiralling notion of the symbolic and angelic signified the linking of earth with heaven. Reference to the Pseudo-Dionysius provided a theological means of fleshing out the hermeneutic circle. Issues of the seen and the unseen floated around the book. Written between 1986 and 1990, postmodernity was in the unconsciousness of the study, not as an analytical liability but as an asset. In the chaos of judgement signified by postmodernity, religious rituals were no more ridiculous than other transactions in that culture. Even better, these rituals could find redemption for their own fractures. In an odd way, religious rituals seemed the beneficiaries of the advent of postmodernity. They could transcend the chaos.

Some of these themes were taken further in the second study, *The Enchantment of Sociology*, written between 1993 and 1995.[13] It was concerned with the centring of culture in sociological deliberations in ways that linked to the responsibilities for understanding generated by reflexivity (disciplinary self-awareness). Two themes emerged. One was related to worries over limitless curiosity and the other to the uses of ambiguity. Few sociologists have attended to the sociological significance of ambiguities, Bauman and the American sociologist Robert Merton being notable exceptions.[14] The study was an exercise in recovery of the sacred to its proper field in a culture dominated by notions of secularisation as a form of theft. Behind the study were ambitions to give this orthodox Catholic author a sociological legitimacy in the comfort station Weber so despised. As with the first study, sociology was pushed further into theology to follow a path others were pursuing.[15]

To offset the inward textual concerns of the first two studies with the persistence (not the demise) of religiosity, a qualitative venture was conceived in 1995. It was to be a study of the link between habitus and the ritual field in terms of a growth in expertise and sacerdotal disposition, one that linked the choirboy through to the priest in seven ages of liturgical man. It was hoped to link Suaud's *La Vocation*[16] to Dibie's *La Tribu Sacrée*[17] in ways that would reflect a recent Vatican document on the spiritual formation of the priesthood.[18] The aim of the study was to explore how these could be understood in English society, in both Catholicism and Anglicanism. The idea was to combine tales from the liturgical field in ways that would link virtue and vocation. It was to be a study in the reproduction and routinisation of a calling to ritual labour.

The study slipped at the first rung. Few of a potential sample lived in a culture so envisaged. Clerical life and those on the lower rungs were singularly uncontaminated by any form of sociological thought. To convert their tales to sociological rhetoric and expectations would involve an untenable ventriloquism. Their beliefs were constructed without reference to sociology and to re-construct these in the argot of the discipline seemed a wilful distortion. By 1998, hopes for the study faded. Somehow, the idea of a sociological study that sought to connect virtue to vocation in the ambit of clerical culture fell on stony ground. The massive publicity given to a tiny number of child abuse cases by the clergy suggested that these were not propitious times to launch such a study. Matters stood there until two breakthroughs came that sowed the seeds for this study.

The first was the providential arrival of the translation of eleven essays on religion by Georg Simmel that was published in 1997.[19] Somehow, one had not associated the study of religion with Georg Simmel, that brilliant polymath who forged sociology a century earlier in ways that eerily anticipated the analytical needs of a culture of postmodernity. His range was enormous and his formulations of a formal sociology have been unequalled. His status in sociology a century after he died is still in ascent. Uniquely, for a sociologist, he treated religion in ways that could be married to theology. His concern with religion was not as something dead, but as being defined by its vivid properties, a colouring that marked its content. Religiosity as it related to the spiritual opened out all manner of possibilities for understanding how the unseen could be seen from the inside of belief, but in ways that could be given sociological characterisations.

The second breakthrough, though not the concern of this study, arose from access, in 1999, to a translation of Marcel Mauss's famous but unfinished Ph.D. on the sociology of prayer. As Durkheim's nephew and best known for his study *The Gift*, Mauss's sociological credentials were impeccable for the study of a topic that seemed proper to theology. His appraisal of prayer as a social act indicated the way that what seemed a distinctively theological activity could be given a sociological characterisation and a defence of its utility.[20] Both Simmel and Mauss suggested that a socio-logical turn into matters of theology might not be a disciplinary misadventure into forbidden territory. Furthermore, both studies indicated that sociology's habitual treatment of theology normally marked with exit signs might not be as traditional as one might believe.

The original ambition to write a study of virtue and vocation was abandoned as it dawned that the advent of visual culture seemed to have sociological ramifications that had not been adequately considered, and certainly not properly in relation to religion.

Sociology has good reasons to treat the visual with the deepest of suspi-cions given the array of stakeholders and topics involved in its constitution. An intimidating array of philosophers, laden with dense secondary literatures, ranging from Plato to Kant to Lacan, to name a few, would require sociological attention. Likewise, psychology inserts itself into sociological deliberations on the visual with batteries of experimentation on perception that also claim notice. There are other factors that might seem to justify sociological hesitations about handling the visual. As a discipline, it might find the noble order of the Word far easier to handle than the ignoble disorders that scrutiny of the visual suggests. The visual seems surrounded with issues of the irrational that confirm sociology's worst nightmares. Magic and ocular powers lurk around in ways that sully sociological claims to be a discipline founded on the illumination of reason. Not surprisingly sociology seeks to consign matters of the visual to anthropology.

In so far as the visual has entered sociological deliberations, it seems marked by concerns with suspicion and distrust. Gender studies have gener-ated concerns with the male gaze, its intrusive and objectifying properties. In another setting, the gaze has emerged in the context of Foucault's work. Its use is disciplinary and its effects are to disaggregate the social, leaving the individual naked to the eye in the tower, whose gaze so controls and fixates. Yet, the agenda of visual culture points to wider concerns more friendly to sociological deliberations that one might expect.

Visual culture deals with the social relationships of seeing and being seen. The ingredients of the act of seeing, the gaze, the eye, the spectator and visual representations, all the property of visual culture, have profound sociological resonances. Dispositions and dilemmas of looking relate to matters of biog-raphy, where tales and justifications emerge. These relate not only to the social construction of identity, but also to an unexplored facet of reflexivity, disciplinary self-awareness, as it relates to the visual. Reflexivity bears on the sociological act of looking and the status of the sociologist as one who gazes. Unmasking the sociological gazer forms part of the remit of reflexivity, but in so doing, draws attention to the hidden nature of the spectator who operates in visual culture. The viewer has many names but all point to a property of the hidden: the lurker, the voyeur, the connoisseur who collects for privacy in looking. If the viewer has an embodiment that requires reflection, this inserts a crucial facet of visual culture into the expectations of reflexivity whose ethical basis sociology increasingly accepts. It is this moral and ethical basis of viewing as it translates into the religious realm that concerns the study so that what is in the social moves over into issues of a spiritual odyssey, a sort of pilgrim's progress of seeking to see the unseen. Issues of the seen and the unseen emerge in more familiar sociological territories.

The seen and the unseen are not only issues of methodology, but also of sociology's vision of itself. If in a scientific identity, sociology seeks to explain the seen; in its humanistic affiliation it searches for understandings and these often involve dealings with the unseen, particularly in the realm of culture, where the social and the spiritual display uneasy alliances. In times of disciplinary insecurity, sociology points to higher ideals and in so doing casts itself in a prophetic mode. Powers of prediction suggest a mastery of what is not yet seen. Sociology does not like to be burdened with the notion that some things are unseen and will remain so. This would impose an uncertainty on the discipline.

Ways of seeing not only point to capacities to see, but also to the intensity of the gaze and the right to look. Increasingly, the gaze and the visual are treated as entities that affect the social in ways that signify and that require recognition and response. Issues of microscopic detail emerge that seem beyond sociological remit, yet many of the notions so raised in visual culture occupy the terrains of Simmel who dealt with the eye and of Goffman who wrote elegantly on facework and sincerity. The eye itself has a symbolic and cultural significance. It takes on properties of power and danger that require social response and control. Thus, the wandering eye unsettles those who notice. Those looking into the eye seek to fix its gaze, so that social relationships can be returned to their customary tenor. The eye is easily unfixed in a culture where the gods of money can make any image shine – for profit. What is iconic, hallowed and singular in religion is mobilised to designate the passing fads of a culture that sees too much.

These theological images so profanely borrowed in popular culture point back to their prototypes. They beg questions about the right to make an image and such presumptions reach back into realms of theology. What might seem theological niceties form a hidden agenda for the ways Weber and Simmel approach the seen and the unseen. As subterranean tributaries these niceties present important implications for understanding how sociological responses to visual culture are shaped. If a theology underpins sociological approaches to visual culture, as it relates to religion and to handling the seen and the unseen, then at some point the transformative basis of the gaze requires attention. In such transformations, a change has occurred that links inner illumination to what the eye discerns and in some mysterious manner, some conversion of sight, some link is formed between the seen and the unseen and the social and the spiritual. It is in this terrain that the study operates, where character as a facet of visual culture is linked to transformation, hence the concentration on the face, but also on icons and pilgrimages as exemplary sites fit for sociological considerations. These are the sites where the tales of the seen and the unseen are to be found, at least in this study. Technology has greatly changed expectations of visual culture in ways that affect how the seen and the unseen are to be understood. Seeking to clarify these changes forms an ambition of the study.

Cyberspace has introduced notions of the virtual and the real. Issues surrounding the virtual form a dominant concern of the study. The virtual points to matters of resemblance that require deciphering. In matters of the seen and the unseen, deciphering what belongs to theology becomes complicated by sociology's own status as a virtual religion. This lends a myopic property to the sociological gaze. The notion of a virtual religion gives to sociology an illusory basis for proceeding to distinguish between the seen and the unseen. Powers of resemblance beg questions about the prototype and in turn this raises considerations that belong to theology. From its own disciplinary resources, sociology cannot authentically differentiate between the seen and the unseen, for this capacity does not arise from its remit. Sociology might be able to give a cultural contextualisation to approaches to the seen and the unseen; it can raise issues of character and disposition to see; but it has no analytical control over the conversion of sight to see. This is a matter of grace, one where sociology ends and theology begins. The issues of why some see the unseen and others do not haunt the study. These relate to another conundrum touched on in *Sociology and Liturgy*, of the blind seeing. More than anything this points to the mysterious link between the seen and the unseen.

In the film *Shadowlands*, a particularly poignant scene involved an American boy brought with his mother to Oxford to stay with C.S. Lewis. Uncertain and unhappy at the implications of a change in his mother's relationship in a strange land, Lewis takes the despondent boy up to an attic in his house. There amidst all the piles of old books, and furniture, stood a wardrobe, the one which Lewis indicated formed the basis of *The Lion, the Witch and Wardrobe*. The boy takes in the implication. When Lewis leaves him alone, the boy gazes sadly at the wardrobe. It looks terribly ordinary. Remembering the magic of the book, he fixes his eyes on its door. With a hesitant hand, and knowing that his disbelief will be confirmed, he opens the door. The wardrobe is bare. There is no magical vista to the unseen. Sadly, he goes back downstairs. His hopes had been dashed. He wanted to see, but could not. His plight is a parable for sociology's dealings with the seen and the unseen. Some gift, some additive, is needed, and this comes from theological reflection that leads to a quest for the grace to see.

Few sociological studies take as their characterising text the letter of Paul to the Hebrews. Its first verse stipulates that 'faith is the substance of things hoped for, the evidence of things not seen' (Heb. 11:1). The study seeks to understand from a sociological perspective a distinction of Paul that while we look not at the things which are seen, but at the things which are not seen: for the things which are seen are temporal; but the things which are not seen are eternal (2 Cor. 4:18).

The seen and the unseen denote differences between the material and the spiritual world where 'between the two, there opens up the existential space of man'.[21] The unseen refers to the heavenly and hellish, to angels and demons and to invisible principalities and powers.[22] Eye has not yet seen what is in the unseen yet it acts on the actor in an experiential way, one that generates religious emotions and sensibilities that have social effects.

Many facets of sociology already deal with what is unseen but not in ways that link directly to the theological. The unseen can refer to hopes for visions to be realised in a secularised eschatology. It can relate to ideas of utopia and to social arrangements radically re-cast in ways that bear on the unseen. Sociology has a respectable lineage of supplying visions that will lift its clients from the mire of the mundane. The visual hopes for this study come from St Augustine's *The City of God*.

Although Bauman touches on this study, few sociologists refer to it. This is a pity. Even more unfortunate is the neglect of the vast range of writings of St Augustine in sociology. As Besançon observes well, 'in reading Augustine, the Western European has the feeling he has come home'. In short, as he observes, his theology 'repatriates' us.[23] *The City of God* concerns the struggle to realise the heavenly city in the face of competition with the gods of the earthly city. St Augustine writes as 'a stranger among the ungodly, living by faith'.[24] This study is an effort to understand the plight of those who live as strangers away from their homeland. Using the seemingly alien language of sociology, the study addresses the aspirations of those who 'desire a better country, that is, an heavenly: wherefore God is not ashamed to be called their God: for he hath prepared for them a city' (Heb. 11:16). Even in this age this imperative persists, often in unexpected cultural circumstances.

Beaudoin has explored some of these issues in his influential account of the spirituality of Generation X. He has noticed how in the USA songs, music videos and movies are suffused with religious references, for instance to sin, salvation and redemption. This leads him to conclude that 'contrary to common perception, we appeared to have a very theological culture'.[25] He also notes the dark side of life, of a generation suffering what he aptly calls a 'meltdown of *meaning*'. This occurs where 'everything liquefies under the glare of a foundationless commercial culture...'[26] This insight can be related to Bauman's notion of liquid modernity, where nothing is solid. There is much in Beaudoin's comment that endless deconstruction eventually leads to the 'reconstruction' of religious alternatives.[27]

This study seeks to carry forward an ambition of the late great Swiss theologian, von Balthasar, who sought to restore eyes of faith to a world that has lost the capacity to see the unseen. This need to recover sight to the blind bears on Ratzinger's comments on art and images and their link to a renewal of faith. He argued that 'before all things it requires the gift of a new kind of seeing. And so it would be worth our while to regain a faith that sees'.[28] Gazing at a redundant church is not about an exercise in recovery, the re-filling of it with actors, an ambition few sociologists would discount. What is sought is for those who come again to see again, and it is this capacity that is lost that needs restoration. This relates to a point of Vattimo, that some seeking of a return to New Testament values is necessary as a means of reading the times. As he suggests,

> the need for forgiveness and the lived experience of mortality, of pain and prayer are characteristically 'positive' in as much as they are ways in which one encounters the radical contingency of existence, ways of experiencing a 'belonging' that is also a provenance and, in some almost ineffable sense that we none the less live out in the very experience of return, fallenness – at least in so far as the return also seems to be the recovery of a condition from which we have 'lapsed' (in the *regio dissimilitudinis* spoken of by the medieval mystics).[29]

Why this need for a return? At present there is a sense of drift into a future that seems fixed but surreal. The demise of postmodernity, a term that captured a moment of chaotic life after 1989, has left an enormous sense of vacancy. Those glittering prizes of life in 1968 that marked an eternal present now gleam no more as its pioneers decline into old age. Their heirs cast no prototypes and the mothers of invention breed no more. Resemblance becomes the basis of a culture where the virtual rules ruthlessly. This expansion of the virtual in ways that make its own reality affects the self, but also sociology in ways few have considered.[30] In an image-conscious age, the question of how sociology sees itself is not entirely redundant.

Sometimes, one feels sociology's own gaze at the looking-glass self operates in the vain manner of Snow White's Ugly stepmother. 'Mirror, mirror on the wall, who is the fairest discipline of them all' sociology says too often, so flattered is it by its own self-regard. Its gaze in the mirror bears a look of disdain towards other disciplines. Few of them are eligible to enter the academic ball, for few of them have sociology's perfection of scrutiny of the social. They only see it in bits and pieces, and are unable to decipher the patterns of the social sufficient to gain entry to that ball. Little escapes sociological scrutiny as Goffman observed, reflecting on his notion of role distance. For him, this concept 'helps to combat this touching tendency to keep a part of the world safe from sociology'.[31] This tendency refers to efforts to segregate the self according to the profane, the official world, and the sacred, that of one's circle of intimacy. But the mirror of modernity that fixes the sociological gaze is not all it is cracked up to be. Postmodernity has marked the mirror with fractures and fissures in abundance. What is the persona of the sociologist who looks at the looking glass? That is an issue of biography, but it also involves the search for an ideal visage to present to society, one that catches the essence of its tribulations. What does sociology so seek to see of itself?

In his contrast of Simmel and Goffman, Davis invokes two remarkably differing images for sociological self-regard. In a 'downward' image, Goffman appeals to the sceptical, to the comic and to life's cynics. A more 'upward' form appears in Simmel. Davis suggests he appeals to 'those with poetic or religious sensibility – life's spiritualists'.[32] In one model the sociological gaze is earthbound but muddy; in the other, it looks up and sees the stars. One cannot see the unseen, but the other aims to do so. It is curious the way sociology masks its own spiritual preferences.

For Simmel, the soul was central to his sociology. As one member of his circle observed 'the soul is the image of society and society the image of the soul'.[33] This seems near to Durkheim's notion of collective solidarity, but with a spiritual essence added, one adjacent to religion, but at a remove not too far from theology. The social mirrors some spiritual essence, some refraction that formed Simmel's ambitions and these suggest that efforts to seek to see the unseen are not in some parochial way 'unsociological'. These efforts to tread a liminal path between the seen and the unseen are not just some arbitrary pious insertions. They reflect the original dimensions of modernity that now seem well forgotten. After all, for Baudelaire, modernity dealt with 'the ephemeral, the fugitive, the contingent, the half of art whose other half is the eternal and the immutable'.[34] That other half of modernity seems to have vanished. Few notice its disappearance.

For Bauman, and others, the exemplary actor of modernity is to be found in Musil's novel, *The Man Without Qualities*. He is the hero of Bauman's excursion in *Liquid Love*.[35] He is a man without bonds of constraint. His plight is not admirable. His only solace is to wrest some dignity, some sense of mutuality from a dismal situation where refractions of hope are denied. His fate seems that of the sociologist as Weber prophesied in his famous essay 'Science as a Vocation'. Newman's series of lectures on the idea of a university is to academic culture what this essay is to sociology.

It is the tract of resuscitation for wearied sociologists whose ideals have fallen into the bureaucratic doldrums of academic life. The essay's stress on integrity, on the need for self-clarification and the endless affirmation of choice represents the essence of a sociological calling particularly when the night is dark and the sociologist is far from home. Having no powers to see in the dark, the sociologist wanders in emptiness in the remains of post-modernity. Weber's dismal vision seems to have come to pass. Oddly, towards the end of the essay Weber turns to the issue of the factual existence of theology and its relationship to science. This involves a question of choice Weber does not flinch from confronting. Unexpectedly, he inclines more towards the theological than some might realise.

What Weber despises is when science takes on the properties of academic prophecy, of a religion that involves playing at 'decorating a sort of domestic chapel with small sacred images...' Such descents into a virtual religion are to Weber 'humbug'. Unexpectedly, he argues that a religious return is higher than academic prophecy, for theology supplies what science cannot, a concern with ultimate meanings.[36] In this regard, the virtual religion of science generates a false consciousness over ways of seeing that marks a contrast with the forms available from theology. A choice over presuppositions is presented to sociology, which affects how the unseen is to be seen, and this issue forms the central concern of this study.

1
Sociology and Virtual Religion: Issues of Memory and Identity

The safe disposal of eight small aniseed balls, without breaking one's teeth, might not seem a matter of moment. To an eleven-year-old Irish boy it was, for their consumption was calibrated by ritual movements over the back streets of Limerick, not in the times of *Angela's Ashes*, but in those of the late Victorian Indian summer of the mid-1950s. The aniseed balls were purchased from Mrs Darcy's little shop half way up Chapel Street. It was not a busy shop. To each customer, Mrs Darcy gave a dedicated and full service, one where time scarcely intruded. The demands of service necessitated a nice little sit-down to observe the world passing by before the next customer might come. Her shop was near Cornmarket Row, where one's grandparents occupied a tall Georgian house.

The house had seen more graceful days. On the ground floor, grandfather would sit at the door of a shop smoking a pipe whose tobacco lasted an eternity. No customers seemed to come. This puzzled a young mind as to what he was expecting, for he seemed happily just to gaze out on the street and watch life pass by. As in Mrs Darcy's little emporium, the advent of a customer seemed an unwarranted intrusion from the outside world. 'Why was he there?' was a question posed to one's very sharp English grandmother whose response was that he had to be put somewhere, so that sitting at the door combined a façade of usefulness with an expulsion from her terrain upstairs. Understanding dawned slow on the young mind.

The time taken to suck one aniseed ball took one to William Street, two melted descending the seemingly steep Chapel Street to the church below and three vanished in ambling around to Cornmarket Row. The house of the grandparents overlooked a nineteenth-century French-style covered market. In retrospect, it seemed filled with redundant extras from *The Quiet Man*. Vendors cried aloud in the market, donkeys neighed and lots of old little ladies in black shawls bustled busily about the place. It was like a warren of ants, the sort found when lifting up a large stone. If Thackery were to return for more Irish travels, he might have seen a familiar sight. For the rest of the time it was deserted. Quite correctly, it returned to its proper use as a venue for sending a balsa wood glider off to sail in and out of the pillars of the covered way that ran around the walls of the market. Such aeronautical labours involved running over the market, over the straw-strewn muddy cobblestones and in such endeavours the few remaining aniseed balls were barely sufficient to stoke one's energy. This was a world of the definite, vivid in its presence, unripe for memory and unforeseeable in any future.

Inhabiting a discipline profoundly unfixed in present cultural circum-stances, even sociologists have an urge to go back to inspect sites of memory and to re-fix the compass points of identity. In returning, one hoped that this site of childhood so intensely felt would be virtually the same and that some resemblance to what was remembered would be found. Unfortunately, in going back to Limerick in 2001, the scenery shifters of time had done a cleansing job. Bizarrely, what one saw seemed littered with sociological tags. Chapel Street was now a pedestrianised space littered with pseudo-Victorian bollards. Squatting incongruously, the bollards seemed to signify some obscure postmodern point yet at the same time they stood in testimony to the needs of the heritage industry. Mrs Darcy's shop was now a *Subway Salad Bar* and a branch of Pizza Hut had replaced grandfather's shop. The take-away culture of globalisation had hit Cornmarket Row. The house of one's childhood had been demolished to make way for a red bricked multi-storied car park, with its own fretted twirls of green iron work replacing the shabby Georgian windows that used to look out on the market. The tumbling down house that faced on to the farrier's yard had been demolished to make way for a concrete piece of modernism. On the left side of the former yard was a concrete hut that proclaimed itself as the best Adult Store in Limerick. Turning up into the High Street, one found at the top a bright red shop front that was an Internet café.

The sudden change from this late Victorian twilight zone lodged in the 1950s into the ordered disorder of a culture of postmodernity seemed unfor-tunate. It was not to be expected that the burghers of Limerick would slap a preservation order on the sites of one's childhood. The surprise of the shift in perception of the landscape was less its re-ordering than the way it had been re-cast to reflect all too accurately sociological expectations of seeing. This bears on a point of Giddens that sociology moves easily in and out of the modernity it constitutes.[1] Oddly, sociology has become a victim of some ill-earned success where a gap between its forging of concepts and their cultural use has narrowed incredibly. Public discourse is increasingly framed in the argot of sociology. As the rhetoric of sociology is so appropriated, so also are its dilemmas, the ones it has barely formulated and certainly not resolved. One problem increasingly looming is the need to distinguish between the virtual and the real. This points to rather a forbidding territory.

Times move on, and the sights of the 1950s and of 2001 of the same place could not but be different. What was seen related to more than shifts in ageing. The landscape of childhood had been re-cast to make it seem more authentic than what had gone before. Neater, more ordered and more sensitive to heritage, what was now seen had been re-arranged to be read in a particular way. Pastiche, imitation and resemblance underwrote what was available to the eye. The gaze now saw what was re-arranged not for biography, but to service the needs of cultural memory. Individual biography might need servicing, but so does society. It has its own deposit of memory. As time goes by, society needs to re-inspect its relationships to the field of culture whose gleanings require re-inspection to see what is still rooted and what has been uprooted in the ploughing.

That accident of personal biography that clashed with the outcome of the needs of cultural memory drew into focus a tension between the virtual and the real. What was seen in the present was virtually like that remembered, but not enough to convince, for the sense of childhood memory formed a more formidable witness to the real, what the area was authentically like. What was seen in 2001 was a plausible resemblance, an imitation, almost counterfeit of what one had gazed at in the early 1950s. Experience of the prototype gives one a jaundiced eye towards what is presented as the virtual, whether to serve the needs of the heritage industry or cultural memory. One can spot the difference in ways that undermine confining what is seen to sight. The eye needs memory to re-call what it did see but sees no more.

As the needs of cultural memory increase, so do expectations for the virtual. Strangely, the capacity to expand the virtual, through technology and historical research, can make the past seem inauthentic to those who actually inhabited it. But as these powers of the virtual increase to meet the expectations of contemporary cultural representation and recognition, the question of the prototype, the original template, returns to cast a long shadow. The virtual always begs question about the prototype, its ethos, its mentalities now lost to time. One is curious about life in the prototype, for the virtual presents matters in a light that is too transparent. Somehow, the powers of the virtual insufficiently satisfy. They refract inadequately in ways that return the gaze to the issue of their prototypes. These issues become poignantly cast in relation to religion.

In English society, the cultural landscape is increasingly littered with redundant churches no longer able to fulfil their stipulated designations of giving witness to the unseen. Standing devoid of purpose, they give reproachful witness to a culture devoid of powers of recognition of their original purpose. As Evangelical traditions gain ascent in English Anglicanism, a sense of detachment from memory increases. These traditions do not need such buildings, cast as they are for the needs of the medieval world of Catholicism that the Reformation was set to displace. For Evangelicals, rituals bear superstitious baggage; they service the needs of the eye not the Word.

As these buildings are increasingly transferred to civic and secular custody, these redundant churches occupy a place in the heritage industry. They also have a place in the wider issues generated by culture and memory. Even if religious memory fades, society needs some form of memorialisation, even through the virtual, to remember in culture what is best not forgotten.

The need to attend to memorialisation has been advanced very much in French sociology. The politics of commemoration have a more evident significance in France than in England. This arises from the radical displacement of religion from French cultural memory. The capacities to sacralise have been transferred from religion to civil and secular orders. In the march of reason, the virtual triumphed over the real in matters of religion and the light of reason given to citizens precluded them from caring to notice the difference. This legacy of the French Revolution marks a divide in memory between religion and culture whose equivalent in England is the Reformation. In both settings, Catholicism has a displaced existence, being somewhat outside memory and yet being oddly within it. Catholicism hovers uncertainly before the virtual, undecided over whether to claim back what has been misappropriated for profane imitations.

The culture and politics of memory have their own edifice complex where the unconscious of society needs to be given visible representation in some image or mobilising symbol. Now, it might be said that sociology is able to sustain a grand indifference to these matters of memorialisation, especially as they bear on matters of religion. After all, as a child of modernity, it is the beneficiary of a spirit of secularisation and as such, sociology has a vested interest in preserving religion in the unconsciousness of society. But this generates an unsettling question. If institutional religion is disappearing and the sociological tradition is to confirm its departures in analytical pieces, what has replaced it? This relates to a profoundly uncomfortable question for sociology. As a surrogate for religion, sociology faces a risk that some myopic parties might seek to cast it in virtual terms. In so casting sociology as a virtual religion, might confusion emerge that would cause some to see it as a real one? In more innocent times, religion could be treated as a form of false consciousness or a deception. Now matters have changed. There are so many virtual forms of religion about that sociology risks being taken in by the forgeries that loom in ways unseen before.

This chapter is concerned with how sociology is situated as a discipline in relation to the virtual. In the first section, it is argued that some form of choice between the virtual and the real emerges in the politics of memory. For its realisation, memory requires forms of recollection and re-presentation in the present. Its duty is to invoke a sense of the unseen, what is lost to time, which needs to be re-seen in the present. This begs questions when memory deals less with what is unseen, than how those in the past dealt with the seen and the unseen. Some entry point is required, and the door is the metaphor for this. It fulfils theological and sociological needs for an idea of opening. In the second section, sociology's need to choose between the virtual and the real in relation to religion is explored. This relates to the risks of blindness peculiar to sociology when it does *not* attend to differences between the virtual and the real and becomes misidentified. Sociology might have an interest in not attending to deciphering these differences if one finds a claim to being a virtual religion in its traditions. Virtual religion comes into focus in present society in two specific areas: the concert hall and the Internet, whose powers of calling up a virtual reality seem god-like.

The third section returns to the degree to which sociology persists as a virtual religion in its misappropriations of the language of religion that belong to the real – Catholicism. When sociology needs to summon up its visionary powers, it lapses into the rhetoric of a virtual religion. In France, to render this virtual religion vivid, Catholicism is plundered for metaphors, images and rhetorical flourishes that supply a higher order of appeal than mere analysis can deliver. The fourth section argues that when sociology faces a need to inspect its disciplinary identity for the purposes of formulating protocols for its novices, it falls further into issues of virtual religion. Finally, the fifth section suggests that notions of civil religion are similar to those of virtual religion, but with a crucial distinction. Notions of virtual religion do not require reference to theological distinctions, but this is not the case with civil religion. It is decidedly Protestant in its borrowings. This leaves the study with an unsatisfactory division in its theological leanings. Catholicism lurks incredibility in French efforts to formulate a virtual religion as the apex of aspiration for the discipline. Protestantism hovers around civil religion, one that points to the way American society is shaped to the command of a virtual religion. From these points, one can discern the genesis of what is to come in the study. Theological assumptions are buried in sociology's dealings with culture to a greater degree than it has confronted. These assumptions generate matters of theological choice sociology has been reluctant to consider.

I

Mr Mandelson's 'Siamese twin' elegantly resolved a delicate problem of representation in a neutered manner. Distinctions between virtual and real forms of religion might seem a form of sociological navel watching yet the advent of the millennium forced English society to pass a practical test in arbitrating between these distinctions. The need to make a monumental mark in time, for the recent millennium, concentrated political minds wonderfully. It also occasioned a delicate issue of what was to be the domain symbol of this monumental endeavour. Given that English society was post-Christian, multi-faith and inclusive, some all-embracing mobilising symbol had to be found. Despite state rights of patronage over Anglican episcopal appointments, the idea of erecting a cross inside the Dome would have been political suicide. It would have denied all the aspirations of New Labour for an inclusive society. On similar grounds, other religious emblems had to be rejected.

Initially, it would seem that a £90,000 long legged redheaded woman with a small head would be the most suitable candidate for memorialisation on top of the Dome.[2] The government minister then responsible for the Dome, Mr Mandleson, thought that this model was too gender-specific. Instead, he settled for a giant half-man, half-woman, a 'Siamese twin' that transcended differences of gender. Who the twin was or where he or she came from was beside the point. This androgynous figure aroused much controversy. It was described by the less charitable as a 'genetic monstrosity'.[3] For others, it symbolised the curse of the Dome and the dangers of playing with cultural memory. In short, the issue of the figure exposed a crisis in how English society represented itself to itself in a post-Christian fashion.

Christianity was ghettoised in the Spirit Level section of the Dome, an appropriately entitled area for the calibration of all religions, virtual or real. This circular Dome lost lots of money, never fulfilled its projections for visitors, and its opening night was a disaster. As an exercise in virtual religion, it never caught the public imagination. The Dome came to reflect the spiritual and cultural vacuity of Blairism. For sociologists, it brought into focus the cultural importance of memory and commemoration, a concern that mattered greatly to the discipline's founder and the virtual religion he instituted. Wernick suggests that Comte's church of humanity was 'one vast exercise in memorialisation'. Festivals, calendars, shrines and parks, all culminated in a festival for all the dead.[4] Sociology was involved in the memorialisation business more than many of its practitioners realised.

Although English concerns with memorialisation became evident at the time of the millennium celebrations, in France they had arisen decades earlier in response to the need to mark in cultural memory the Revolution of 1789. This led to a culture of commemoration in the 1960s and 1970s that was concerned with marking dates, symbols, civic gatherings and rituals that would link past and present.[5] Nora's notion of *lieu de mémoire* refers to the vestiges, symbols, artefacts, and the embodiments of commemorative consciousness that survive history, which need resuscitation. It represents the loss of something sacred that requires rituals of re-presentation in a ritual-less society. Central to the notion of *lieu de mémoire* is that memory is not something spontaneous; it requires 'commemorative vigilance', the staging of interventions such as the marking of anniversaries, the organisation of ritual celebrations and spectacles.[6] This relates to an important facet of memory: the way the visual governs its re-construction. Nora introduces a term 'mirror-memory' to show the way that what is drawn from the past serves to reflect present identities. It is through differences that the elusive basis of identity emerges. The issue is not about origins, but 'a way of figuring out what we are from what we are no longer'.[7] This involves a radical re-casting of history.

Watts Miller draws attention to another notion of Nora, *milieux de mémoire*. This concerns sites of memory and in this regard, there has been an explosion of these. But the problem is that these are no longer about sharing in mutuality. As sites of memory, they are concerned with 'how there can be solidarity among a mass of mutually anonymous individuals. They are a route, in our large-scale world to what has been called a "community of strangers"'.[8] From these notions of the past emerge a loss of solidarity but also a sense of estrangement, where memory stands accusingly against the present. It is the unravelling of these threads of memory that underpins a sense of disconnection in the present. Memory begs a question of restoration, and it is this imperative to re-thread and to re-memorialise that forms the ambitions of this study. If memory is to be of use, it requires some coherent focus, some capacity of re-call to enable what is of the dead, what lies unseen, to be seen again by the living. Rituals and symbols fulfil this need. They facilitate not only the knowing of memory but also its restoration as living and vivid.

The central thrust of Halbwachs' approach to collective memory is that it requires a social construction if the tales and stories so embodied are to live on in a present far removed from a past wherein they were conceived and formulated. The social is the means of sustaining recollection by marking symbols and rituals to be re-presented as representations.[9] Thus, for Halbwachs,

> every religion is a survival. It is only the commemoration of events that terminated or sacred personalities who disappeared long ago. There is no religious practice that must not be accompanied, at least for the officiating priest, and if possible, for the believer, by a belief in divine or sacred persons who have manifested their presence in the past and exercised their influence in defined places and periods, and whose gestures, words, and thoughts are reproduced through practices in a more or less symbolic form.

In this context, 'religious thoughts are concrete images that have imperative force and generality of ideas . . . that represent unique persons and events'.[10]

Political and cultural events conspire to cause these images to lose their force. Removed from their contexts of recollection, they no longer vitalise and so the link between the past and the present is broken. The French Revolution and the English Reformation ruptured the continuities of memory of Catholicism and broke its powers of continuity. In France, the cultural and symbolic capital of Catholicism was dispersed after the French Revolution. The god of reason and humanity replaced the God of Catholicism. The state took to itself rights of sacralisation of memory, and sought to re-cast the civil in ways that betokened a virtual religion of commemoration of the heroic and exemplary virtues of the French Revolution.

In the English Reformation, Nora's 'mirror-memory' in relation to Catholicism was broken by state decree. The orderings of relationships between the earthly city and the heavenly city that so marked the genius of late medieval Catholicism were shattered in an iconoclastic revolt that left a mark of profound guilt on the English mind. Memories of these events have faded and constitutional niceties of Establishment have cemented over recollections of what those former times were like, before the fall into the Reformation. Only in Northern Ireland do sensibilities of difference over doctrine and liturgical practice still persist. These tribal divisions that keep alive such forms of religious memory seem incomprehensible to those for whom such differences are matters of indifference on mainland Britain.[11] Secularism and ecumenism have conspired to suggest that these religious differences are of no consequence. What has faded from memory is the realisation of what has been lost to view of liturgical life as lived before the Reformation. A sense of this loss can be felt when visiting a late medieval church now in Anglican possession where discomforting archaeological evidences lie around the building as bare reminders of the imaginative powers of the liturgies used before the Reformation. Such little churches provide a microcosm of great events. Hervieu-Léger has suggested that 'for centuries the parish represented *the* society of memory' in a chain that linked its inhabitants back through time and the expression of this was found in the church.[12] The Reformation broke these chains and often Protestant forms of recollection of such parishes tell an incomplete story.[13] It is only when an historian provides an imaginative account of what life might have been like in a small parish before the Reformation that one realises what has been unlinked from memory and what the other tales might be.

Duffy has provided a unique insight into the effects of the Reformation on a small Devon parish and its church.[14] The account reveals the cult of images that linked the world of the seen with the unseen in a community where everybody had a stewarding part and where piety was given its fullest of visual expression. Public and private forms of religious life were intermingled. In the church, the pious knew where to look to discern representations of a world yet unseen. Chantries serviced the notion of intercession where priests, or sometimes choirboys, were given endowments to pray and sing for the departed.

The Reformation ruptured the notion that the visible actions of those in the earthly city could have an impact on the heavenly city. With the abolition of purgatory in the Reformation, the intercessory powers of the clergy were lost. Links with the heavenly collapsed, and in the present it is the funeral directors who come to manage death with earthly effect.[15] A whole religious imagination was closed and as Duffy graphically indicates, the visual piety of Morebath was dismantled.[16] This process of iconoclasm that coincided with the genesis of modernity marked the beginning of the secularisation of visual culture. One edifice the Reformers hesitated to raze was the cathedral. It stands enigmatically in relation to cultural memory illustrating to a society what it had forgotten. As Vauchez has suggested, 'the cathedral was in every way an illustration of the Christian conception of time: time not as mere flux but as preparation, within each individual as well as in the world, for the coming reign of God'. The cathedral now stands as an architectural emblem of the link between the seen and the unseen, a 'symbol of the holy city and anticipation of the heavenly Jerusalem'.[17] As von Balthasar suggested, the 'cathedrals were the visible expression of contemplation and could only be understood by those prepared to devote themselves to the contemplation of the things of heaven'.[18] The trouble is that few in present culture devote themselves sufficiently to seeing the unseen to be able to discern the cultural and symbolic capital of these richly laden edifices. Re-reading their basis depends on an eye of appraisal, a re-seeing that grasps their enduring significance.[19] Too much of cultural memory and capital is embodied in these buildings to let them drift into decay. Too many chains of memory might be uncoupled if this were to happen. Although the cultural relevance of the cathedral, even in a post-Christian society such as England, might be conceded, its place in sociology might be less clear-cut.

The cathedral has been an important but underrated resource for sociological thought. It was the source of Bourdieu's notion of habitus. What was seen in the cathedral could be merged into the unseen, a scaffolding signified in Thomist philosophy. Habitus represented the disposition to merge both.[20] But for Simmel, it supplied the metaphor of the door. For Simmel, the door marks a notion of entering and exiting. It suggests a property of looking in, one expressed in the ornateness of the door of the Gothic cathedral. The structure of the door 'leads the person entering with certainty and with a gentle, natural compulsion on the right way'. The journey is from the outward to the inward in a fixed direction. The basis of the value of door and the bridge (the other metaphor, one that links the seen and the unseen in a liminal manner) 'for the visual arts lies in the general aesthetic significance which they gain through this visualization of something metaphysical, this stabilization of something merely functional'. Thus, Simmel argues that the actor must always separate but cannot connect without separating, but the door offers the prospect 'of stepping out of this limitation into freedom'.[21] The door is the enabling device for the liminally bound, to see between the seen and the unseen, to visualise in some imperfect manner what is beyond mere perception. Pointing beyond, the door also orders what is in the realm of the social. It not only marks entitlements to entry, thresholds, surveillance of those who pass through, trust and distrust, and etiquettes of greeting and departing; it also carries a notion of petition. The notion of knocking at the door is implicit in the property of prayer, where seeking and openings are to be found in Matt. 7:7. The door stands not only for those who seek, but it also expresses the self-imposed plight of God, for it is written: 'behold I stand at the door, and knock: if any man hear my voice, and open the door, I will come in to him, and will sup with him, and he with me' (Rev. 3:20). The door occasions a curiosity about what cannot be seen.

Journeying back to Catholicism, Huysmans displayed an almost forensic ethnographic brilliance in recording liturgies he gazed at from the back of Parisian churches. One particular ceremony fascinated him. This was the clothing ceremony of a Benedictine novice. These ceremonies aroused a fullness of horror in the Gothic imagination in the nineteenth century. Gazing at the whole event, Huysmans felt transported back to the Middle Ages. Part of the ceremony involved the novice knocking on the door leading to the enclosure and petitioning in Latin to be admitted. The door opened and she vanished from the world presumably never to return. Durtal (a fictitious front for Huysmans) gazed stupefied. The whole event seemed as a tableau.[22] The door points to a seeking to see, but also to a property of awareness of its necessity. This impulse can be found in notions of reflexivity.

When expectations of reflexivity are applied to particular areas, such as those of religion, matters become more complex but in ways that give comfort to Christian practitioners seeking to reconcile their sociology with their theology.[23] Increasingly, the demands of reflexivity call those dealing with religion to treat it on the inside of belief, and not in some disembodied manner of the outsider.[24] As Stark and Finke argue, the human side of religion as a form of belief is increasingly being opened out in sociology in ways that avoid old-time reductionisms. Approaching the study of the religion from the inside, they argue that

> social scientists are unlikely even to grasp the human side of phenomena for which they have no empathy. While it is not necessary that social scientists who want to understand religion be religious, it is necessary that they be able sufficiently to suspend their unbelief so as to gain some sense of the phenomenology of faith and worship.

They go on to cite a comment of Durkheim that those who do not bring a religious sentiment to the study of religion cannot speak of it. They are like the blind trying to speak of colour.[25] In one of the earliest linkings of ritual and reflexivity, Rappaport pointed to something vital, but obvious, that 'in performing a ritual one *participates* in it. To participate is, by definition, *to become part of* something larger than the self'. In performing, the actor comes to accept what he realises. To understand this process, the sociologist has to understand it from the inside, at the level of understanding of the actor and the meanings sought – an orthodox Weberian stipulation.[26] There is a definite theological property to Rappaport's characterisation of ritual. For him, 'ritual, then, is possibly the furnace within which the image of God is forged by a mystified reflexivity out of the powers of language and of emotion'.[27] In so entering, disciplinary self-awareness becomes implicated in religious awareness as the sociologist engages with what the actor seeks.

It is one thing to proffer reflexivity as a form of empathy to the other or even the Other, but this notion of being part of something greater than the sociologist might signify the risk of being acted on from outside the field of inquiry. One might accept that religion needs to be studied from the inside, but it becomes perilous to suggest that this might involve a vulnerability to what comes from outside. Muscular sociology does not entertain visions that come in the night. Sociology is a discipline of the day; its duty is to bring matters to its light. Dealings with the night are unfamiliar terrain. Whatever its other ambitions, sociology has no desire to emulate Daniel's dream: 'I saw in my vision by night, and behold the four winds of the heaven strove upon the great sea' (Daniel 7:1–2). Dealing with visions might not seem part of the disciplinary duties of sociology.

II

At the end of his lecture, 'Science as a Vocation', Weber observed that those who wait for new prophets and saviours are in the same position as indicated in the Edomite watchman's song included among Isaiah's oracles:

> He calleth to me out of Seir, Watchman, what of the night? The watchman said, The morning cometh, and also the night: if ye will enquire, enquire ye: return, come.[28]

Weber's biblical excerpt is from 'a grievous vision' where Isaiah is enjoined to set a watchman who foretells what he sees. Set to see in day and night, he sees a chariot of men who come to say that Babylon has fallen and that all 'the graven images of her gods he hath broken unto the ground'. Somebody other than the prophet asks the watchman 'what of the night?' (Isaiah 21:5–12) This seems a curious query in a complex set of verses that speaks volumes about Weber's perspicacity regarding Biblical knowledge.[29] What Weber laid down was the necessity of choice, one that lay between religion and science. Being religiously unmusical, he could not quite make a leap of faith himself.[30] Yet, oddly, given Weber's disdain for the visual in his sociology, this affirmation of the duty of choice occurs in settings of Isaiah that ask the oracle what is seen. The account goes on to speak of the 'valley of vision' that leads back to Jerusalem (Isaiah 22:1). Again, matters return to the seen and the unseen.

Between light and dark is a twilight zone where the virtual is easily confused with the actual. Where is the sociologist to look, given these equivocations about what the night might hold? Weber's injunction at the end of 'Science as a Vocation' is perverse. The issue of the visual is abandoned for concern with the interior, for the sociological calling is to look *away* from the social and to look within, to 'find and obey the demon who holds the fibres of his very life'. Thus, the fulfilment of a duty to integrity lies within the chamber of private judgement, a very Protestant injunction that speaks suspicion of what lies outside in orderings of the social and the visual implications it bears. But what if the conscience of the self is stifled, and the eye is presumptuously blind to what it *should* fear in the social? After all, all sorts of mirages, fantasies, masquerades and illusory visions can loom as spectres in a culture marked by suspicion. Even if Weber's injunction not to play the prophet is accepted, sociologists still encounter legions of false prophets with no such inhibiting calls to integrity. In *not* attending to the visual, to what lies in the social, sociology for all its inward attention might be blind to the consequences of its analytical stance, however worthy. These issues emerge in a splendid satire on sociological sensibilities.

Festinger's *When Prophecy Fails* pursues an impeccably orthodox sociological question: how does a group respond when their belief systems become untenable? Paradoxically, failures effect their re-affirmation.[31] This issue forms the basis of Lurie's comedy of analytical errors, *Imaginary Friends*. This is an account of a study of a small rural sect, known as the Truth seekers, by Tom McMann, the author of a classic of descriptive sociology, and by his assistant, who chronicled everything. Admirably reflecting the methodological fissures of sociology, the study leans heavily on McMann's faith in the strengths of observation studies rather than those of quantitative methods. Whereas quantitative methods facilitate a disembodiment of the self on the field of enquiry, observer participation leaves the sociologist vulnerable to an embodiment, an empathy with the tribe under study that risks disaffiliation from the protocols of disciplinary identity and its ethics of detached enquiry. The study foreshadows the emergence of reflexivity and some of the dilemmas that emerge when its concerns are attached to the field of religion where prophets rule.

Reflecting on the disaster this study effected, where McMann went mad, Zimmer, his assistant felt the whole experience seemed an ironic version of the means-justifying-ends type of argument. Their means of entry had been based on the excuse that 'we were seeking Truth, we were proposing to lie ourselves blind to the Truth Seekers'.[32] The book oscillates around the issue of who was observing who and, in the course of the account, McMann, so believing in the sect as a basis of a large study, comes to fulfil its needs by becoming the visitor they had prophesied would come from outer space. The whole study made Zimmer nervous. Listening to the scribble of the pencil taking down notes from Outer space, Zimmer 'sent up a half serious request for the spirits of Max Weber, C. Wright Mills and Nicolo Machiavelli to get me through what lay ahead'.[33] At the end of the book, Zimmer reflected that he and the professor were never 'just observers'. Social scientists, he noted, often spoke about the effects of participant observation on the group studied, but rarely about the effects on the participant himself. From the events surrounding the study of the sect, Zimmer had 'begun to wonder occasionally if sociology itself is absolutely sane',[34] a question many sociologists have asked themselves. Somehow, in dealing with issues of religion, sociology comes unstuck. In this tale, of *not* being able to tell of the difference between the real and the virtual, the sociologist was propelled into being the answer to the prayers of the group. A prophetic mantle was bestowed and even if the sociologist did not see its necessity, others did. D'Agostino's observation seems prophetically exemplified in this tale, when he noted that 'while the sociology of religion is an important enterprise, it is also certainly a perilous one, not for the faint of heart'.[35]

Coming closest to the religious flank of sociology, those in the sociology of religion (who often fled theological ambits) are forced into proximity with virtual forms that unsettle. These forms still contain embers that signify what the fire of faith might look like if lit up. The powers of prophecy still attract even if the obligations of religious belief do not. As one commentator observed, when sociology takes on the mantle of prophetic utterance about the directions of social change, at least in America, there are 'roaring sounds of silence' surrounding religion.[36] The notion of the virtual in religion suggests something more than the dismissal notices of false consciousness. Lurie's parable of misrepresentation seems to suggest that there is something of religion in sociology that makes it prone to misrecognitions of the seen and the unseen, even if these mix in dangerous ways. In seeking motes of religion in society, sociology has its own myopia of not seeing the beam of religion in its own disciplinary eye. This selectivity of sight bears on the virtual in religion but more particularly on the way sociology has ill-disguised ambitions to be a virtual religion.

The virtual in relation to religion takes on three contrasting sociological meanings. The first highlights the propensity of sociology to become a virtual religion. The second relates to issues of misappropriation and performance so that what is of the sacred becomes attached to what is purely secular. The third form of the virtual bears on the image-making powers found in cyber-space that greatly complicate sociological efforts to understand the links between visual culture and religion. In relation to religion, the advent of cyberspace as a way of dealing with the seen and the unseen is both an asset and a liability.

The dalliances of sociology with virtual religion start with Comte. He had made strenuous efforts to form what Petit terms a 'super-Catholicism', a religion of positivism. This religion is 'dogmatic, cultist and highly ritualistic'. As a religion of humanity, she suggests, it seeks 'to bind together the human community here on earth, instead of promising to each of us an individual salvation in the another world'. To illustrate her concluding points, she cites the comment of Etienne Gilson that 'Comte had in mind an atheist Augustine whose City of God descends to Heaven on earth'.[37] The unseen was part of this virtual religion, but imperialised and reduced to the seen, to the canons of Positivism that were to govern the advance of sociology. It was the theology of this virtual religion, the instrument for a faith seeking understanding of the cult of humanity, in which man is the god. This property of deification not only percolates down to recent sociology, notably that of Goffman, but it also emerges in the religions of the self so characteristic of the stresses and strains of life in a culture of postmodernity.

Stedman Jones argues well that religion was the quintessential social institution for Durkheim, the testing ground for his theories.[38] For him, religion 'involves forces, symbols, representations and the conscience collective, but above all beliefs'.[39] By attaching collective representations to beliefs, Durkheim paved the way for the formulation of a question sociology has treated ever since with equivocation. Was his cult of man, his religion of humanity a virtual religion in its own rites of analysis? Did it escape the clutches of the Catholicism it sought to replace or was it a doomed exercise? This is a question difficult to answer, but what is clear is that the claims of sociology stand at odds with those of the real theologies of Catholicism, which the discipline was founded to supersede. Some sociological bodies that dealt with religion, especially in the late 1960s, sought to secularise the basis of their affiliations and to move away from the ambit of Catholicism.[40] The use of the term 'vocation', inserted by Weber in its ambitions, suggests an appeal to something more than what comes from mere perception. There is a property of prophecy, of the oracle, in the calling of sociology, to see what the laity cannot discern.[41] In this regard, settling for imitations and plausible resemblances will hardly suffice. To fulfil its vocation with integrity, sociology has to find some sensibility of self-regard, some image that gives focus to its claims to see what others cannot.

Back in 1977, before the rise of reflexivity, Carroll argued that it 'should be demanded of every sociologist that he comes to know the idealized self-image in terms of which he judges the world'.[42] This points to what the sociologist identifies with and seeks to embody. One idealised image is the privatised angst Weber bequeaths to sociology, but a more general set arises from a god-like property of enduring scientific scrutiny and scepticism under the inconvenient burden the discipline brings to social affairs. Postmodernity has destroyed this Olympian sense of engagement with the gods of science. Ironically, the forces of secularisation that destroyed real religion have acted in a similarly destructive manner on the virtual religion of Positivism. Capacities for self-description by reference to some god-like powers of narrative are no longer credible. As Luhmann aptly suggested, 'the proclamation of the "postmodern" has at least one virtue. It has clarified that contemporary society has lost faith in the correctness of its self-description'.[43] As sociology seeks to mirror society, its domestic doubts are also refracted in its subject matter. God might have died,[44] but so also have the gods of sociology. This leaves sociology with a need to find an idealised self-image that is credible, and the increased recognition of reflexivity accentuates that imperative to so search. Sociology needs something credible to invoke to visualise. Somehow the virtual gods of the cult of humanity seem inadequate for the task.

The second strand of the virtual refers to forms of religion, the sacred or liturgical, which are imitations of real religions. Bergeron coined the term 'virtual religion' to refer to an explosion of interest in Gregorian chant in the mid-1990s. Her notion of virtual religion emerged from the contrast between the authenticity of an ensemble production of chant in a cathedral, and the rugged, less exact performance of the monks for whom this was the daily work of giving worth to God. Somehow the virtual form, the concert, seemed more authentic than the real thing, the actual forms of monastic chant. As she suggested,

> the concert presented a virtual liturgy, one in which we were invited to participate, but also one that required nothing of us whatsoever. It is the condition of being between two realities, both of which are denied, that creates the desired effect of this music.

This liminal property invites a choice of staying in the virtual space the concert music invokes, and adhering to its criteria for the sacred, or of moving to another definition, one that belongs to the real, its lineage and forms of cultural and symbolic capital.[45] Choral music takes on an image that moves from the archive to the public arena, from settings of ruin to restoration in an evolution of appreciation that has been rarely studied.[46] In the concert hall, performance is given the liturgical support of a virtual religion, which claims access to notions of the sacred that serve aesthetics. The performance bears an interest that simply requires acceptance rather than negotiation. Similar music performed in a cathedral as part of a liturgical event reflects a property of disinterest of giving worship to God and what is done is sacred only to that end. Postmodernity has accelerated permutations of virtual religion.

The concept has been expanded creatively by Beaudoin to characterise the ambiguous attitudes of GenX (those born between 1961 and 1981) to religion. Beaudoin argues that simulations, the making of the virtual, can lead to a more thorough religious practice. In a perverse way, the virtual can become the gauge of real forms of liturgy. The basis of the gaze shifts from the expectations of the real to the virtual. He suggests that 'GenX's culture of virtuality, of both reality and its imitation, uses irony to communicate religious ideas'.[47] Pastiche, playfulness and imitations suggest that virtual religion is *the* religion of a culture of postmodernity. It is self-made religion, where cultural props are assembled in a highly individualised manner to make one's own church. This property of play and disconnection can become tiresome. It can create an urge to connect that is an outcome of an overuse of the virtual. Flory and Miller make a good point that Generation X do not perceive their religion in terms of disputations over written texts 'but on narrative, image and experience in religious belief'.[48] It is this property of directness that underpins a seeking of connection and validation in relation to religiosity. In this second form, the virtual is a double-edged weapon. At one level, it signifies the capacity to simulate to render imitations of religion more credible in their virtuality than what they imitate, but in another way it signifies a need to restore relationships with the real, the prototype. Efforts to wrest the real from the virtual suffer charges of being conservative, when in actual effect they are radical forms of restoration.

The third facet of the virtual bears on Lurie's parable of sociology having to exercise a prophecy in terms of discerning what comes out of the air. It relates to consideration of what emerges from cyberspace and its fragmented and de-contextualised experiments with cultural forms. In this miraculous expansion of image, icon and representation, the virtual and the real have become mixed up in ways that exceed even sociology's powers of arbitration. Sin, grace, pilgrimage, altars, icons and images can be represented in virtual terms in the religions of cyberspace.[49] This form of the virtual working through the Internet gives diverse and disconnected believers a chance to fulfil a complete identity as a religion through the Internet.[50] The Internet and digital technology provide simulations and forms of experience seemingly more authentic, in a virtual space more intensely felt and more individually crafted than anything to be found in social reality.[51] The field of culture is no longer required to fertilise the visual; it can now appear in a tidier disembodied form in ways that make social reality seem untidy, cluttered and disabling, and to that degree it shares something in common with the second version. In the third version, the powers of Faust have been democratised; they are the rights of all who inhabit a visual culture.

The manifold, confusing and contradictory relationships between the virtual and the real in these three settings might generate a paralysis, a sense that there is no way of distinguishing between these. Yet, each form of the virtual suggests an accentuation of choice. The gods of Comte's virtual religion might elicit questions about God; the virtual form in the concert hall might simply echo Benjamin and demand that choral music be returned to its nexus of tradition, its forms of memory; and the virtual that emerges in the third form points to the need to cultivate more trustworthy visual forms of arbitration between the seen and the unseen. In approaching the virtual, the issue of the self-image of the sociologist returns, for after all it is his vision that governs the account. If this is the case, then it would seem that sociology also has its own ways of seeing. Sociology has a field for looking and its disciplinary eye suffers the embodiment that afflicts others. As a discipline, it can think that its plight of regard is peculiar to the times and forget that in other times, similar difficulties of characterisation arose over the fraught relationships between the seen and the unseen where there were also many gods to be distinguished by the learned.

Appraising the researches of the Roman antiquarian Marcus Varro, St Augustine characterises these as 'the kind of learning which we Christians call secular'. Varro's *Antiquities* expressed 'the fear that the gods may perish, not through an attack of the enemy, but through the indifference of Roman citizens'. They too feared the forces of what has become embodied in the notion of secularisation. Cicero looked to Varro to change things, in an expectation that might seem to be that of the contemporary sociologist of religion. Thus, Cicero wrote of him:

> we were like strangers in our own city, visitors who had lost their way. It was your books that, as it were, brought us back home, so that at last we could recognize who we were, and where we were. It was you who revealed to us the age of our country, the sequence of events, the laws of religious ceremonies and of the priesthoods, the traditional customs of private and public life, the position of geographical areas and of particular places, and the terminology of all matters, human and divine, with their various kinds, and functions, and causes.[52]

Like Varro, the sociologist faces the contradictory task of chronicling forms of religion but in ways that overcome the indifference so accentuated in a culture of postmodernity, where finding the difference that matters turns out to be highly elusive. This is possibly because virtual religion still operates in the aspirations and the identity of sociology more than one might realise.

III

The degree to which the ambience of French Catholicism seeps into the formulations of its sociology has gone unchronicled in its reception in English and American academic life. Comte's mission statement to sociology embraced rituals, catechisms, a sacred calendar, its own priesthood and altars, an apparatus of a virtual religion, one made in imitation and likeness of Catholicism. This virtual religion had its articles of faith bound into a collective consensus that set the contexts of sociological values in ways that anticipated later notions of paradigms. As Oliver suggested in relation to Durkheim, 'faith in science does not differ in its essentials from faith in religion'.[53] In his treatment of society as god, Durkheim might be said to have sacralised sociology.[54] This tradition was nobly carried forward by Bourdieu. An expression of the aspiration that sustains the sacralisation of sociology in a Durkheimian manner appears at the end of his pretentiously titled collection of essays, *Pascalian Meditations*, where Bourdieu finishes with a creedal flourish. He states unequivocally:

> sociology thus leads to a kind of theology of the last instance: invested, like Kafka's court, with an absolute power of truth-telling and creative perception, the State, like the divine *intuitus originarius* according to Kant, brings into existence by naming and distinguishing. Durkheim was, it can be seen, not so naïve as is claimed when he said, as Kafka might have, that 'society is God'.[55]

The issue of Comtean borrowings from Catholicism comes into clear focus when efforts were made to import his teachings into nineteenth-century Ireland. This posed an acute problem for liberal Irish Protestants who sought to use a religion of Positivism to transcend religious differences. Irish Catholics were unlikely to exchange their faith in God for one in humanity when the 'new' religion virtually borrowed all the trappings of Catholicism. If lapsing, they were hardly likely to settle for such a virtual religion.[56] Some Protestants, however, were attracted to the properties of memorialisation in Comte's positivist religion, a point mentioned above. The religion of Comte fitted admirably to the religion of nationalism. As Pelling suggests, 'in Comte's religion of humanity, remembrance of the dead, symbolising worship of humanity was central. The heroes of the national past were a particular object of reverence . . .'[57] In Ireland, nationalism and Catholicism were interwoven in forms of memorialisation that Comte's virtual religion could only aspire to imitate.

The religion of positivism still flourishes, notably in France and in Brazil, where it had sufficient impact for one of its sayings to be placed on the national flag. Although no liturgical order was found for the Paris chapel, one was uncovered for the Positivist Church, a Humanity Temple, in Rio de Janeiro. The order of service started with the officiant in front of the humanity altar making the positivist sign. Then came a hymn in humanity's name, after which came 'a classical music execution'. The sermon extolled vegetality and animality laws and noted that biology prepares sociology and moral(s) to form a link between sciences and the cosmology group. Another 'classical music execution' followed. At the end, the officiant (stands up looking to the public) and gives the final invocation that starts with a call – 'let's put our hearts up to HUMANITY and confirm to it the recognizing that we feel full by the education we have received'. The text of the website encourages all to read Comte's Positivist Catechism. From the website, the building seemed to have all the accoutrements of a church, a nave, altar, candles and pulpit. Presiding over all this is a bust of Auguste Comte, presumably there as a mere human and not as a god (www.arras.com/br/igrposit/foto2html). Why should sociology blur the line between a virtual religion and the real thing – Catholicism?

Borrowings from theology endow sociology with a legitimacy, a right to use the language of Divinity to enhance, to embellish and to secure the credibility of its insights.[58] This recourse to theology enables sociology to speak of what it cannot utter from within its own rhetorical resources. The extensive writings of Bourdieu are littered with theological concepts appropriated to characterise the basis of power on the field of culture. The constitution of the field and its control relates to powers of consecration, but also to habitus, the capacity to play the game with a flair that comes from the realisation of a disposition. The roots of habitus lie in theology, notably in Aquinas (with debts to Aristotle). These appropriated theological notions are central to Bourdieu's sociology of culture. For him, sociology has terrifying powers in its exposure of contingency but also in the exercise of its prophetic tasks. Thus, Bourdieu wrote of the

> wretchedness of man without God, or any hope of grace – a wretchedness that the sociologist merely reveals and brings to light, and for which he is made responsible, like all prophets of evil tidings.[59]

Bourdieu's famous inaugural lecture, 'a lecture on a lecture', awarded a god-like power to the sociologist to bring to light deeds that thrived in darkness. Above all, through reflexivity the sociologist had powers of redemption derived from a self-awareness of position on the field but also a capacity to stand outside it. Resolution of this antinomy gave the sociologist powers of a divinity. In this lecture, Bourdieu returns to this Pascalian theme of the wretchedness of man without God. But in the lecture, he argues that 'what is expected of God is only ever obtained from society'. The basis of the resolution of wretchedness lies in the social, not in God. The social is the domain that ultimately matters. Again, the language of theology is appropriated to sociological ends, when he asserts that 'the judgement of others is the last judgement; and social exclusion is the concrete form of hell and damnation. It is also because man is a God unto man that man is a wolf unto man'.[60] The reflexive sociologist seems to hold the keys of the kingdom of the social. As Duncan suggests, 'in this lecture, which uses religious language so liberally, sociology takes on an almost mystical character'. He is also correct to point to the religious character of Bourdieu's vision.[61] But it is one that veers off so close to the virtual in the service of sociological prophecy, its power of antinomy of standing inside but also outside society, that few inspect the borrowings from the real thing. This points to an issue seldom explored: sociology's implicit theology.[62] It points to a dilemma of sociology. How does it recognise where the shadings of virtual religion merge into those of real religion? The discipline might shake off its borrowings, its metaphors and rhetoric that give it a property of a virtual religion, but there are points where it reverts to an inspection of the real thing to resolve what it cannot from its own analytical resources.

Few doubt the influence of Michel Foucault, yet fewer would wish to pay attention to the Early Church borrowings that underwrote his complex attitudes to sexuality and the identity politics that marked the later parts of his life. His attitudes to theology and Catholicism in particular are complex and seldom confronted.[63] Like Weber, and also an intellectual polymath, Foucault had a deep interest in the technologies of the self and its regulation. His concerns with confession are familiar; less so is his interest in the regulation of the self in relation to sexuality, and this brought him to the study of the genesis of monasticism in early Christianity and to the writings of the theologian John Cassian (c. 360–430). Cassian formulated the basis of monasticism, upon which St Benedict later built. He also developed a rigorous approach to sexual purity and the virtues of virginity that are treated as fundamental to the realisation of monastic aspirations.[64] A similar escape back to Early Christianity occurs in Maffesoli's notion of the tribe.

This concept arises in response to the fractures of affiliation of modern life. Tribes represent properties of vitality, an ambience of connection sought in the public square by disparate emotional communities. His treatment of the individual and the collective owes much to Durkheim and his efforts to sacralise humanity. For him, 'religion . . . is the matrix of all social life'. It is the crucible for the creation of 'being together', a mysterious *puissance* or vitality that requires sociological inspection.[65] To find a template for this 'social divine', Maffesoli turns to studies of Early Christianity and its capacities for an 'elective sociality' that involve the networking of tribes of believers.[66] Like habit, which is fraught with boring overtones, but which has releasing properties, custom is denoted as the unspoken residue of being together. The double process of 'social *reliance* and of negotiation with the holy characteristic of the early Christian communities' form the working hypotheses of what he wishes to understand about tribes in the present. These communities operating against the Pagan societies of Late Antiquity supply models of vitalisation for his contemporary tribes.[67] These communities also provide examples of networking in small groups. In looking at the paradoxical power of modernity to effect unity through blurring of differences, he observes that 'the master craftsmen of the Middle Ages knew a thing or two about this, and built our cathedrals on this principle'.[68] This need to attend to what divides, what might effect social solidarity but also transcend it, points to the functions of the unseen, their transcending power over seen differences. Thus, efforts to see the unseen have healing functions in the forms of hope they service and supply.

Use of metaphors that are distinctly Christian not only arises in recollections of past forms of communal bonding, but also is a means of characterising a future as yet undisclosed. These dalliances with theology persist and are given unexpected expression in English society in the writings of Bauman. These are considered in the next chapter. In this context, however, it is interesting to note the way that theological borrowings creep into Bauman's vision of things unseen. This particularly emerges in relation to the virtue of hope.

Reflecting on Bauman's deepening critique of socialism, Smith notes that 'the object of hope should be a high ideal, whose achievement is way beyond the distant horizon'. He descends on Bauman's last sentence in *Socialism: the active utopia*, where St Paul wrote 'hope that is seen is not hope. For who hopes for what he sees?' But the verse which follows is equally important: 'if we hope for that we see not, then do we with patience wait for it' (Romans 8:24–5).[69] The answer to the waiting lies in the context of the verse so cited. It refers to the groaning of creation and its waiting for redemption. It is about hope in an unseen force, the Spirit sent to console, a Trinitarian solution

Bauman would hardly avow as a Jew. What lies in scripture and is cast under the light of the heavenly city is often re-cast for use in the virtual religion of sociology. Thus, the metaphors of the organic that underpin a Durkheimian approach to social structure can be traced to Paul's metaphor of the body, its weakest parts and their mutual concern and interdependence. The metaphor is used to characterise the hierarchy and community of the Church presented as a model of the social and the need for the utilisation of gifts and talents of all (1 Cor. 12:12–31).

Notions of virtual religion as part of the ideal self-image of sociology persist. They particularly arise in terms of the protocols laid down for novices aspiring to be sociologists. Issues of dealing with the seen and the unseen emerge in fieldwork, but also in confronting the pantheon of ideal type figures that have dominated and shaped the genesis of the discipline. These figures are its heroes and its disciplinary exemplars.

IV

Whaling has argued that all major religions have the following eight characteristics: religious community, ritual, ethics, social involvement, scripture, myth, concepts, aesthetics and spirituality.[70] Some of these elements can be found in the ethos of sociology itself. Sociology has an exalted notion of community, and as a discipline it aspires to a prophetic mode in its highest estimations of itself. Endowed with its own code of ethics of enquiry, sociology aspires to maximise autonomy and human dignity free from social constraint. Appealing to more than can be seen, sociology's visions are emancipatory as it seeks to lead the blind, the entrapped, to kingdoms ordered and lit by lamps of reason sociologists are given to bear for entry into darkened territories governed by unreason. Sociology has its own canonical texts that are virtually scriptural in the reverence awarded to them. To use Bourdieu's phraseology, sociology forms its own oblates and novices to be fit to bear analytical burdens.

In a highly imaginative speculative essay, Richard J. Martin explored the degree to which sociology has the characteristics of a virtual religion. His concern was with the nature of sociology and the degree to which it took on cultic elements when considered as an occupation. Published in 1974, the essay drew on the self-scrutiny of sociology and the way its disciplinary orientation was realised in forms of piety, prayer and mystique. These theological notions were metaphors to understand how sociology understood itself. Piety related to disciplinary proprieties and prayer was given a location in the ritual round of sociological life, conferences and graduate training. Prayer had a mimetic property, for it shaped the sociological character of graduate students. It enabled them to fulfil the disciplinary powers they sought.[71] Conversion of view was also part of the training of the student, a change of orientation that moved the novice from a non-sociological perspective to a sociological one. Martin gets nearest to the notion of sociology as a virtual religion in his discussion of mystique. This anticipates Bourdieu's notions of habitus. Mystique refers to the unrecognised knowledge under-pinning sociology, its language and style of enactment that takes on a sacerdotal property to the laity, to outsiders on the discipline.[72] Concern with the instillation of values in the training of postgraduates bears on the need to instil an ethical dimension, an awareness of calling.[73] The mantle of a virtual religion that sociology takes on in its treatment of its novices serves to socialise them into treating with reverence the higher ideals of the discipline, its vision, its ideals, its protocols and its obligations. Images require a social construction, a point sociologists make to others but seldom to themselves. The image making of anthropology particularly occurs in fieldwork where there is a need to reconcile what is seen in fieldwork with what is inscribed.

Margaret Mead's famous work *Coming of Age in Samoa*, published in 1928, was subject to two decades of criticism by Derek Freeman that she had been hoaxed and that the image she had drawn was a distortion. The controversy surrounding Mead's fieldwork points to a wider issue of its construction. Traditionally, fieldwork in anthropology has been treated as a rite of passage, an encounter with tribal customs, whose properties are translated into text in some 'magical' process of conversion. The power of anthropology derives from this capacity to transfer from one context to another in a manner that secures a brand image for the tribe, one that becomes associated with the anthropologist who performed this process of re-imaging. In her study of fieldworkers in anthropology, Jackson has explored the liminal quality of fieldnotes as they lie between memory and encounter and between private sentiment and their re-casting in public disclosure in a professional account. The fieldnotes mark an effort to reconcile the self of the anthropologist with the tribe to be represented. The self of the fieldworker comes into play as discrepancies between memory and what is recorded in the notes emerge. Thus, she notes that many of those interviewed spoke of the kind of person revealed in the notes. Their moral character emerged as they worked with a process of creating something from the fieldnotes, the major physical remain of the study. As she suggests, fieldnotes had a heavy emotional valence and sacredness because they are objects crucial to the performance of the rite.[74] This rite refers to the process in which the tribe comes into being illustrating the way anthropologists come to their own consecrations, their antinomies of the seen and the unseen. It is what is brought to the event to be characterised that enables it to come into life. Conceptual pre-suppositions are brought to social reality to shape it.

In Weber's context, they are ideal types, exaggerations of social reality used to shape and to characterise it. The necessity of dealing in abstract pictures or images entails strict adherence to reading empirical matters in hand. The seen and the unseen emerge in the unbridgeable gulf between 'is' and 'ought'. These methodological necessities can mask biographical imaginings and dispositions, the habitus of the sociologist himself in playing the game of analysis, what he is disposed to wish to see. These fieldwork matters point to worlds of imagining of what was seen, what might never have been and what becomes decidedly unseen.

To an unexpected degree, sociology is governed by deference to exemplary actors or types. These occupy the pantheons of sociological imagination. Devoid of an actual context of gestation, these imaginings hold a powerful sway on the proprieties of the discipline. Weber's Calvinist has no corporeal existence yet his personality exercises a bleak hold over the discipline. It would be a foolish sociologist who sought his plaque in Amsterdam, Philadelphia or Geneva. Likewise, Durkheim's notion of ritual was based on imaginative readings of the fieldwork of Spencer and Gillen in Australia. Then there are Goffman's actors. Although they enter sociological existence through being based on interviews and observations, his inmates, waiters, the stigmatised and the grotesque form tribes whose territory resides in the sociological imagination. Their lack of place in reality disturbs few sociologists who seek entry to Goffman's country. This relates to an important point of Waksler that Goffman's analysis 'recognizes the ultimate impossibility of making absolute distinctions between the "real" and the "as if" – both for members of society and for sociologists – and moves analysis to spheres where such impossibility does not fetter sociological inquiry'. Goffman's concern is with one way 'that the social world *can be seen* to work...'[75] This property of the 'as if' provides a vital means of entry for this study into the relationships between the seen and the unseen.

There is a fine line between hypotheses and imaginings that Goffman crosses with impunity. In reading Goffman, nobody could seriously think that these sociological actors exist in a real world with personalities and character (the absence of these is one of his weaknesses). They are largely the figments of a brilliant sociological imagination that has re-cast the way the discipline sees the world. The unseen status of those so invoked is beside the point. The fact that they are imagined adds to their allure. Building on the notion that nations are invented, Anderson coined the idea of imagined communities to characterise the growth of nationalism. In this regard, the political community is

> *imagined* because the members of even the smallest nation will never know most of their fellow-members, meet them, or even hear of them, yet in the minds of each lives the image of their communion.[76]

The building of disciplinary affiliation bears a similarity to the properties of edification in religion. Some texts are regarded as canonical; some founding fathers are treated as exemplary prophets; and some concepts are enduring in their authoritative range. In their use, reverence builds up a sense of image of communion in a common vocation, whose exemplary sermon is Weber's

'Science as a Vocation'. After a long period of asceticism in lonely preparation, the sociological novice comes to his Ph.D. viva to seek consecration to
distribute the communion of knowledge to undergraduate followers likely
to believe in his powers. The way sociology comes to be established as a
virtual religion can be found in Bourdieu's *Homo Academicus*. Disciplinary
boundaries are kept in creedal formations, hierarchies elicit deference, heretics
are dispatched and oblates assert their loyalty to their patron, the professor, but
also to their discipline of affiliation.[77]

Although Christianity might have slipped away from English cultural
consciousness, notions of virtual religion abound in Durkheimian versions
too conspicuous to ignore. Commentators reached for the notion of a virtual religion to describe the World Cup and Jubilee celebrations in 2002. The
term had floated around as a puzzled response to the mass mourning for
Princess Diana. There was something in the order of a culture of postmodernity that meant that the public, if not sociologists, reached for the rhetoric of
virtual religion to describe what they saw. Thus, shopping malls are described
as cathedrals of consumerism, icons are the terms of reverence for the images
of mega-stars, and charisma denotes the surreal gifts of highly skilled football
players.

V

In France and the USA virtual religion has had wide currency in notions of
civil and secular forms of religion. These refer to the political need to hallow
what is deemed as sacred in forms of memorialisation, the reverential marking
of symbols of national endeavour, and the provision of rituals of commemoration that express the values of republicanism, and the freedom and
democratic rights of its citizenry. Civil and secular religions have their own
feast days, Bastille Day and Thanksgiving Day being examples. Some symbols
become highly sacred. Thus, prohibitions exist on the use and the disposal
of the US flag, when it has become worn out. This flag is endowed with
a religious status, one confirmed by the pledges recited to it in classrooms.
The Bill of Rights, the moral template of the nation, is lodged in a mausoleum
in Washington. Its architecture is Classical Grecian, and it has the aura of
a cathedral, a site of pilgrimage for the citizenry to inspect their documents
of liberation. Protestant in origin and in its stress on liberty, toleration and
separation of powers, civil religion marks well the divide between the virtual
and the real. Lacking any dogma, and being non-sectarian, it binds everybody
to a generality of memory. As Bellah wrote,

> the words and acts of the founding fathers, especially the first new
> presidents, shaped the form and tone of the civil religion as it has been
> maintained since. Though much is selectively derived from Christianity,
> this religion is clearly not itself Christianity.[78]

Wuthnow denoted civil religion, narrowly conceived, as 'the use of God language with reference to the nation'.[79]

Public religion is a means of speaking of the sacred in the realm of society. In its public or civil forms, this virtual religion services a sphere for the regulation and production of the sacred outside the nexus of institutional religions. In American society, the constitution strictly prohibits the use of religion in public spheres.[80] In the UK, the established church supplies the needs fulfilled by civil religion. It does so in ways that reflect a Protestant Settlement for the monarchy and a nation whose identity is built on fidelity to the values it incorporates. In matters of cultural memory, Protestantism controls the account, for Catholicism, in this regard, is not deemed creditworthy.

Whatever its demerits, the notion of a civil religion has important implications for issues of religion and visual culture. The power of display in architectural forms, whether in Babylon, Xanadu, Athens or Rome, serves to mark positions of legitimacy and status. These forms are to be seen in ways that render the inferior docile. Commandeering public space, they speak much of the contours of sacred geography and what its arrangements present as a basis of emulation.[81]

Anticipating many later sociological formulations, Varro treated religion in terms of the needs of the citizens of the commonwealth it serviced. He divided his theology into the 'mythical', the 'natural' and the 'civil'. 'Mythical' or 'fabulous' (in terms of fable) theology is peculiarly suited to the theatre, to performance and spectacle; the 'natural' relates to the world; and the 'civil' to the needs of the city. St Augustine spends much time demolishing these distinctions in *The City of God*.[82] The notion of virtual religion arises in the context of Seneca's criticisms of the rites of civil theology where the role chosen for wise men 'is to simulate conformity in the act while having no religious attachment'.[83] Varro's central interest was in 'natural' theology. This produced a mob of deities whose naming Augustine satirises. They served to alleviate the worries of the citizens of the Roman commonwealth. Finding a fit object for worship posed numerous pitfalls. Gods were invented to provide an honourable explanation for obscene ceremonies. Thus, St Augustine argues that

> the men of antiquity invented images of gods and their attributes and ornaments, so that those who had been initiated into the mysteries of the teaching could fix their eyes on them, and then apprehend with their mind the true gods, namely the Soul of the World and its manifestations.[84]

In his writings, Varro treated human affairs before those of the divine, on the basis that the latter dealt not with something in nature but with purely human institutions.[85]

Something similar can be found in Durkheim's notion of religion as the image of real society. As Durkheim argued, 'if religion has given birth to all that is essential in society, it is because the idea of society is the soul of religion. Religious forces are therefore human forces, moral forces'.[86] Stedman Jones cites a central facet of Durkheim that 'divinity is the symbolic expression of the collectivity' and adds that for him 'the gods...are conceived not perceived'.[87] The mistake of the Romans was to name these gods in an anthropomorphic manner, which St Augustine tears to pieces. Varro and Durkheim would concur on the conception of the gods and the social needs they fulfil. But for both, the truth or falsity of religion was beside the point. Varro, it is claimed, asserted that 'it is an advantage to communities that brave men should believe themselves to be sons of gods, even if it is not true'. This also accounts for the invention of ostensibly religious rites 'where lies about the gods were thought to bring advantage to the citizens'.[88] Gods that are projections of the citizens can effect infamy and degradation as shown in the activities of those who followed the Great Mother as mentioned in *The City of God*. Thus, St Augustine argues that '"civil" theology has invited wicked demons and unclean spirits to take up residence in those senseless images and by this means to gain possession of the hearts of the stupid'.[89] Failure to distinguish between the virtual and the real in religion can generate mass mayhem and times have not changed much since St Augustine wrote so acidly of Varro.

Something more than the dignity of man is reflected in these criticisms of Varro that also point to a flaw in Durkheim that Stedman Jones has noticed. Rituals serve to confirm beliefs. They enable society to be conscious of itself yet, as Stedman Jones suggests, there is a circularity here whereby what is social and what is of religion affirm each other. She goes on to add that

> the republican problematic was to turn the object of faith from God to society; it was to harness the power of belief to make and underwrite society. So society can be compared to the gods; it too will die if no longer believed in.[90]

Even if religion does flourish in virtual form as something sacred, it risks doing so in a diminished and restricted form, even if it is the worshipper that is sacralised, a point which Watts Miller raises. When man becomes god, there is a scaling-down of the sacred environment. Referring to Nora's work on memory, Watts Miller writes that 'where they see the rituals of a more or less flourishing secular religion, he sees what are nowadays empty shells of the sacred, "the rituals of a ritual-less society"'.[91] In his conclusion, he states that secular religion 'still needs to live off some such spirituality in the environment around it, in order to give meaning to its own ideas of our limited unsuperhuman world'.[92] In short, the virtual needs the real. This form of living off the real relates to Davie's notion of the vicarious, where a minority exercise traditional beliefs on behalf of a majority who settle for virtual forms of religion, those dispersed and treated as the fruits of secularisation.[93]

Virtual religion comes to signify what the actor needs to gain from the deification of the social, even it no longer seems either necessary or useful. As Goffman observed 'in the contacts between such deities there is no need for middlemen; each of these gods is able to serve as his own priest'.[94] This self-consecration has expanded in the context of postmodernity, where spiritual powers are treated as capacities to be unlocked, often in a mixing of therapy and New Age values. Thus, a book entitled *Rituals for Sacred Living* sets down advice on the management of the sacred areas of the home, mealtime rituals, spiritual cleansing and the sacralisation of sexuality. Rituals are devised as techniques for coping with stress and 'negative energy'. Advice on posture, spiritual and aura cleansing, rituals for cutting ties and the decoration of altars for domestic use are also given.[95] Comte's little altars that serviced a cult of humanity have now been domesticated to serve the expressive needs of individualism in postmodernity, where the self ministers to itself as its own god. This new priesthood that mirrors its own divinity suffers the conceit of seeking to look more widely, and in so doing, its gaze returns to the social. In so looking, it finds inadequacies reflected that cause it to examine again templates and imitations, things missing in the mirror. Unfortunately, the self finds itself returning to an interest in the prototype and to its interconnection with virtual versions.

The notion of virtual forms of religion living off the real versions finds expression in Séguy's idea of metaphorical religion. This metaphorisation, a property of modernity, effects a form of symbolic violence on traditional religion (to use Bourdieu's term). In seeking to modernise, traditional religions collude in their own peripheralisation. As Séguy observes, traditional religions become seduced into deference to the reconstitutive powers of modernity. Secular or virtual religions become indices of the world, the false consciousness of religiosity and also the illusory reference points for theological connection. This is why liberal theologies are always doomed to fail, for they base their insights on the virtual religions the populace use as surrogates for what institutional religions do not supply. Virtual religions are religions of compensation that can never excel their prototype. In so legitimising these secular religions, theologians become false to their own forms of memorialisations.[96]

Arguments for a secular religion are rare. Fenn has recently argued for the demystification of the sacred, which is mysterious and set apart. His critiques are based on the authoritarian and corrupting power of religion and its idolatrous properties. For him, idolatry is a sign of the sacred. It takes to itself powers of exclusion that render the marginalised and the inarticulate dumb. The sacred facilitates a repression of what belongs to the memory of those on the margin. In its sacralisation of texts, civil religion carries a Protestant property of nostalgia, its form of sacramentalism.[97] The edicts of the Founding Fathers, and thanksgiving for their memory, effect a flow of grace into the civil order of American society, but in ways where some are deemed to be more eligible to receive than others.

Few sociologists think of their calling in terms of servicing a public theology that understands the truth of tradition that Bellah seeks to restore.[98] Public theology is certainly not part of Giddens' notion of the Third Way. Fenn makes a good point that as various political groups lay claim to the sacred, a war over idolatrous claims occurs in the public market. For whatever reason, Prime Minister Blair has found it convenient to emulate the terms of civil religion in English society, and to sacralise the rhetoric of his party, its manifesto and its claim to speak for the nation, albeit in a multi-faith inclusive manner, where the rights of all are enshrined, but in a peculiarly authoritarian way. The civil rights of those marginalised are affirmed but in ways that render dumb those foolish enough to still wish to make religious and moral distinctions about matters of sexuality. It is this misappropriation of the language of the sacred in the public arena for idolatrous purposes of dominance that Fenn deplores. But there is another deception abroad.

Virtual religion seems the beneficiary of a false memory syndrome. It manages to abolish a sense of recollection of how real religion might be seen. Those who deal in the spectacles of real religion might feel a form of symbolic violence that Bourdieu has coined, that the culture they inhabit suggests they ought to collude in *not* seeing what they believe they see. Few might bother to attend to distinctions between the virtual and the real in matters of religion, writing these off as speculative manners and as conundrums of little analytical consequence. Yet, as culture has taken a visual turn, and matters of transparency have become of decided importance, the need to secure distinctions between the virtual and the real have increased not decreased. As this visual turn accelerates, it does so as concerns increase with testimonies, stories and tales. The visual has merged with tale telling in ways that would not been envisaged in the late 1980s. In the next chapter, the way this tale telling has emerged is linked with the growth of visual expectations of testimonies. These yield concerns with trust, but also with the issues of who sees and to what end?

2
Who Sees There? Tales of Character, Virtue and Trust

A legacy of postmodernity is that the collapse of belief in grand narratives has left space for many little tales to be told. Numerous outlets exist for such disclosures in the mass media, in chat rooms on the Internet, in advice columns in magazines and on television chat shows. The advent of Jerry Springer marked the indefinite expansion of membership of the chattering classes. The expectation of having a tale to tell and of being heard has lent a confessional property to culture. Absolutions are granted by talk-show hosts or by a sympathetic audience taken in by the tales disclosed. Oddly, this shift in cultural consciousness and expectation has occurred as levels of confessional practice have fallen dramatically in Catholicism. As the sacrament loses its credibility, virtual forms spring up elsewhere all over culture. This culture of disclosure forms a basis for entertainment where the viewers of some shows vote whether or not to believe the tales. As the visual provides endless opportunities for the showing of testimonies, the need to query these in terms of trust or distrust has also expanded. These terms increasingly emerge as part of the expectations of a culture where what is seen matters intensely. The reflexivity sociology tinkers with is nothing compared to the levels of self-awareness and disclosure that have come to mark the expectations of contemporary culture. In this regard, sociological practices regarding disclosure lag behind public expectations of tale telling in other areas of culture.

The democratisation of tale telling emerges from the unfettered growth of individualism in life after postmodernity. These rights to declaration might be based on self-delusion. The Enlightenment endowed the self with seemingly god-like powers of disclosure. Unfortunately, this deification coincides with the growth of suspicion about all these tales told. Scepticism and surveillance is the lot of these many gods and their testimonies. A god may trust himself, but other deities might not. In these galaxies of divinity, idols try to pass on the basis of face value. Because false gods can move about with impunity, claims to divinity need to be checked and re-checked. Technology now provides endless means for doing so. If untruths pass unchecked, then few will trust sufficiently to invest in the making of social bonds.

These trends occur in a culture that is highly image-conscious. There is a considerable growth in understandings of images, their powers, the relationships they effect and the transformations they can yield.[1] Advertising, fashion and the media, all play their part in manipulating images in ways that raise complex issues for sociological understandings of visual culture and its moral implications. The powers of images that often were only available to private collectors have now moved into public expectations of the right to gaze. A consciousness of images, the emotions they invoke and the claims they can make propel sociology into a worried concern with matters of visual culture. Icons, brands, sponsorship and the aura of association with the famous, all point to the importance of the visual but also to worries about its illusory basis. Public distrust over the notion of spin, famously attached to Blairism in Britain, has generated a cynicism about politics and its dark arts of presentation and manipulation. This has generated indifference amongst voters and an increasing number are disinclined to vote. This has had a devastating effect on the health of democracy and political culture. The forces of disenchantment that hit organised religion have now turned to politics. Both find strategies for inventing credible forms of enchantment highly elusive. To remedy the situation, increased attention has been turned to the status and curriculum of civics in schools. Trust in the political apparatus needs to be restored amongst the young, who see but do not believe in anything they are told by politicians. Somewhere in the rise of testimonies and issues of trust and distrust, matters of the visual emerge in sociologically significant ways. Exploring these issues form the concern of this chapter. It suggests that trust and distrust are distinctly linked together in the visual in ways that have implications for how the seen and the unseen are to be understood in present cultural circumstances. Furthermore, as the visual accelerates in cultural significance, the need to attend to the virtual and the real can only increase in importance.

To understand how sociology comes to some of these questions, the chapter starts with a comparison of two highly original thinkers seldom compared: Zygmunt Bauman and Alasdair MacIntyre.[2] Each has made profoundly important contributions to understanding the implications of the Enlightenment and the degree to which its legacy is by no means benign. These unsettlements have implications for reflexivity in ways that force sociology radically to re-think its destiny and its relationships to understanding the human condition whose dilemmas it is called to articulate in shifting cultural circumstances.

For a half a century, Bauman, a Polish Jewish exile living in Leeds, has calibrated shifts in the theoretical expectations and moral concerns of sociology over a half a century. With rare insight, he has chronicled the evolution of sociology from a discipline subservient to reason and a zealot of the legislative ambitions of modernity to one doomed to cope with the fractures and disorders of postmodernity. For him, sociology has been forced to confront its limitations as modernity has matured into postmodernity. The questions modernity has uncovered have simply been carried forward without answer or rupture into postmodernity. In his distancing from an unqualified faith in reason, Bauman comes to focus on issues of ethics, on how makings of mutual understandings have become distinctly hazardous in the face of increased sensibilities of contingency. Unusually, for a sociologist whose mature work was largely written in the UK, one finds an awareness of matters that belong to theology emerging in his work as it evolves. This will be discussed in the first section of the chapter.

MacIntyre, a Scottish-Irish philosopher, a convert to Catholicism, living in North Carolina, shared with Bauman worries over the classificatory powers of the Enlightenment. He offered a more explicit form of resistance to these powers by seeking the rehabilitation of notions of virtue, based on re-casting links with narratives and stories of heroism. His concerns are related to memory, to what culture had forgotten. It is in the past that he finds solutions. These issues will be discussed in the second section of the chapter.

In the third section of the chapter, the fragmentation and fractures signified by the notion of postmodernity are considered in the way these necessitate attention to narratives. Attention to these narratives has generated a shift towards qualitative methods in sociology, but in the acceptance of testimonies some curious inconsistencies emerge. As reflexivity is linked to biography a curious omission emerges: the reluctance of sociologists to speak of themselves and their own private lives. This silence regarding biographical dispositions suggests that sociologists often off-load problems of contingency on to others but seldom apply these to themselves. This relates to another inconsistency over the sort of groups sociologists tend to endorse as having tales deserving of hearing. Testimonies that form part of gender and sexual politics are deemed to have a 'natural' ascendancy over those emerging from religious spheres. Tales and testimonies spark interest in Goffman's notion of a moral career that begs question about narratives of the self. These have an obvious place in religious understanding and suggest that issues of reflexivity arise in a particular way in the study of rituals. These considerations lead on to questions of trust, a crucial ingredient in late modernity. These form the fourth section of the chapter.

If the self cannot trust, it cannot make itself, for it has nothing to root in that which is safe. If it cannot trust its own story, how can it trust the tales of others? Trust points to expectations of performance and its fulfilment. It relates to beliefs secure enough for the self to venture forward, for what it distrusts it retreats from. Trust relates to the ordering of society in terms of what it fears and the suspicions it generates. These questions of trust form a means of linking visual culture to sociology. This leads on to the fifth section of the chapter.

The notion of being seen has been famously explored in Orwell's *Nineteen Eighty-Four* and in Foucault's notion of the gaze. Yet, these two accounts have had a distorting influence on sociology's relationships to visual culture, for they are primarily geared to circumstances of distrust. The moral agenda of surveillance is tilted towards a denial of trust, and it operates on the basis of a fallen character. There are few virtuous testimonies in these approaches and the actor so seen is denied a means of edification – and escape. So seen, he is left with no tale to tell. Clearly, sociology cannot tolerate a situation where its domain concerns disappear: the self, its tales and its social ambit. Distrust destroys the social bond; it undermines incentives to recognise and be recognised; and it leads to nihilism and destruction. If sociology should have no interest in affirming forms of seeing that destroy what are matters of its stewardship then it needs to turn to inspect the opposite, circumstances of trust that facilitate a flourishing in the social. Something more from the visual is required than a mirroring of a fate of self-destruction.

I

Few current sociologists can match the prolificacy and the astuteness of understandings that Zygmunt Bauman has supplied in his chronicling of the human condition as its site of identity has shifted from modernity to postmodernity. His productivity was very much realised only after his retirement from academic life and might generate plaudits, but that is not where his value to sociology lies. His significance comes from a depth of readings in disciplines ranging from aesthetics, ethics, architecture, to philosophy and theology. Sociology is very much the fulcrum point of this wide-ranging European mind that pursues, with exemplary rigour, Weber's notion of an intellectual vocation where choices are always to be starkly laid out if not stoically cast. Many facets of his writings deal with issues of coming to terms with the incompleteness of the project of modernity, whose debris has floated as fragments into the culture of postmodernity. This culture presents itself as a mosaic whose patterns are marked as pastiches, for playful deliberation in a game of interpretation where there are no consensual rules or agreed compass points for journeying. The postmodernity he so propagated is no longer an adequate term, one which he has replaced with the notion of liquid modernity, the melting down and lack of solidification of what passes in contemporary culture.[3]

The incompleteness of modernity has ambiguous properties for Bauman. At one level, modernity embodies properties of freedom, but at another it poses acute dangers regarding limits on these. These dangers emerge when reason is treated in terms of a fundamentalism that can become tyrannical in its absolute claims. Because of these dangers, Bauman wishes to preserve an opening, a property of incompleteness in the project of modernity and the postmodernity it grows into. In this regard, ambiguity forms a crucial ground for defence of the human condition by Bauman. Ambiguity preserves the issue of choice, but it does so in ways that preclude arbitrary classifications and exclusions by what he terms the gardening state.[4] The need to order and to legislate with the powers of reason, when applied to culture, generates profound dangers for the 'uncultivated', those who do not 'fit' on the field. To preclude such arbitrary exclusions that can reach an end point in the manufacture of death, through the instruments of calculation that define a civility, Bauman, writing as a Jew, has a vested interest in making matters indeterminate. It is best to keep the agenda of culture open to preclude tyrannical closures. To that degree, there is a providential property to postmodernity, an interest in indeterminacy that runs as a thread through Bauman's writings.

Understanding realised through the application of hermeneutics becomes a charter for his sociology. The legitimate concerns with the irresistible forces of reason coincide with the advent of postmodernity, a state of mind that arises from the disconnections wrought by modernity. In this state of mind, the actor has to learn to live with contingency. This leads to what Bauman terms the ethical paradox of postmodernism, 'that it restores to agents the fullness of moral choice and responsibility while simultaneously depriving them of the comfort of the universal guidance that modern self-confidence once promised'.[5] Postmodernity involves finding a consensus, a strategy for life, which the maturation of modernity has destroyed. Thus, postmodernity signifies a continuity with modernity, but also a discontinuity, a property of estrangement from its effects, notably contingency, disenchantment with reason and the dislocation of the individual from community and credible forms of commitment. The uncoupling of the self from communal engagement is not the only worrisome facet of postmodernity. More disturbing are the dangerous Faustian powers of modernity that postmodernity has unmasked. Even the self has become an object of manufacture, or rather believes it has powers to do so. Yet, in the face of these opportunities for self-actualisation, individualism reigns but in ways that accentuate a nagging dissatisfaction with what has been realised. The self lacks powers to create an enduring individualism, one based on a distinctive character. These efforts of the self to find itself in the face of endless opportunities to mirror what it wants, reflect the wider point that postmodernity has brought Simmel's tragedy of culture to an unexpected maturity. This tragedy refers to the limitless amplification of objective means of fulfilling desires that is not matched by an equivalent growth in subjective powers for their assimilation. It is against this background that Bauman conceives of 'sociology as a cultural activity *par excellence*. It is the exercise of human spirituality, the constant reinterpreting of human activity in the course of activity itself'. This gives sociology an important task of maintaining a self-reflective, self-monitoring quality of human action.[6]

In the present struggle for understanding, Bauman argues that sociology has never been more needed. These times are sociology's moment of necessity where it has to take sides. Thus, for him 'there is no choice between "engaged" and "neutral" ways of doing sociology. A non-committal sociology is an impossibility'.[7] This does not make its tasks any easier. Sociology has to start with the social to effect forms of manifestation but these cause the discipline to collide with human impulses of the individual that seek to rise above the need to order. This reflects a theme that runs through Simmel and one that leads Bauman to suggest that sociology is a 'schizophrenic discipline, organically dual, at war with itself'.[8] In this trench warfare, sociology often has to reach outside itself to find some ultimate focus. This need emerges in Bauman's use of Levinas's approach to the Other. Instead of taking a theological detour, Bauman sidetracks the issues so generated into ethics and politics.

Bauman has written little directly on postmodernity and religion. In his one essay, discussed below, Bauman comes to the issue of self-sufficiency in relation to God in a re-formulation of the notions of independence and dependence. Notions of self-sufficiency and its limits form his defining traits of religion. Self-sufficiency becomes unstuck over issues of the basis of existence and death. There is a masking, a repression of knowledge of death and mortality in a culture that promises an illusion of unending life that deeply concerned Bauman in another study.[9] Bauman argues that modernity rebuffed concerns with the afterlife and masked the horror of death. These concerns haunt his essay on religion. Actors afflicted with the uncertainties of postmodernity turn not to preachers for a vision of life, but to identity experts to aid in the development of tailored strategies for coping more with the immediate than the eternal. These experts supply a virtual religion that seeks to maximise the powers of the self in ways where there is gain but no pain, and no barriers to the pursuit of what is wanted.[10] But the most unexpected facet of this essay is its defence of fundamentalism as a specific response to the necessities of postmodernity. Fundamentalism relieves the burden of choice. It provides an alternative form of rationality that meets the needs of a constituency of the dispossessed, those for whom the burden of self-sufficiency is too great.[11]

In Bauman's case it is difficult to separate out biography from his theoretical shifts. A military career in state socialism, expulsion from Poland in 1968 and migration to a chair of sociology in England cannot but have subterranean implications for his relationship to disciplinary reflexivity. In three of his most notable books, *Modernity and Ambivalence*, *Legislators and Interpreters* and, most notably in, *Modernity and the Holocaust*, Smith observes that Bauman discovered his spiritual ancestors, Jewish intellectuals who advanced understanding of a civilised culture of modernity that yielded forces that ordained their destruction. The effects of their fate must have had some impact on Bauman's disenchantment regarding modernity and his hopes for enchantment with the advent of postmodernity in the late 1980s. It represented what Smith terms 'a new unpromised land. This is the State of Ambivalence, a home for all postmodern exiles'. These are Jewish intellectuals, such as Freud, Simmel and Kafka. Again, to follow Smith, the above three works are not the narrow products of a professional sociologist, but are personal testimonies and all the more valuable for the integrity of thought they express.[12] In his rediscovery of his Jewishness, Smith suggests that Bauman came to the issue as an outsider, one who had to 'get inside his outsiderness...'[13] This imperative of biography gave Bauman a licence to incorporate and to confront theological matters that arose from his Judaism in ways that seem denied by unwritten convention to other sociologists, not least those with Catholic inclinations.

Stuck in this conundrum, and although not quite a card-carrying believer, in his later writings Bauman comes to matters of theology in an unexpectedly sympathetic way. For instance, commenting on Levinas's ethics, Bauman gives fullsome praise to John Paul II, describing him as 'perhaps the greatest, the most wholesome and outspoken *ethical philosopher* in the history of the Papacy'.[14] In the same extended interview, Bauman indicates that he is increasingly turning to biblical metaphors, all others, he asserts, being pale by comparison. He goes on to add that 'if the ethicality of the human predicament stands in the focus of sociological inquiry, biblical stories have amply proved their unfading potency'.[15]

Beilharz has suggested that Bauman has found 'a hole in the heart of modernity. It is called ethics. Moderns fill this hole with order, with rules and regulations'.[16] Modernity does not merely mask its nefarious powers; it sows conditions for the misrecognition of good and evil. The capacity of the Holocaust to order mass murder in a bureaucratic manner gave this monumental evil a veneer of civility, one that begs questions about how a capacity uncovered in modernity to routinise nefarious activities could do so in ways that mask their grotesque basis. Bauman confronts sociology with the moral implications of a stance that lent it a degree of respectability. This disciplinary stance of value-free pronouncement comes from Weber, as does the notion of the rise of a bureaucracy solely concerned with the rational ordering of means to ends that are not in its remit to question. In the case of the Holocaust, bureaucracy, as the exemplary mode of calculation of modernity, stands morally indicted for its blindness towards what it should have seen: evil on an unimaginable scale. Again, to follow Beilharz, in his study, *Modernity and the Holocaust*, Bauman uncovered an uncomfortable issue: good and evil had become bound into the social in ways that sociology had to clarify. The power of the collective to crush the voice of conscience points to wider concerns of social collusions with evil.[17] What is uncovered is the price of an ordered world built where powers of making moral distinctions had become lost. In ethical terms, those who should have seen with the light of reason did not. Living without God had a price. As Beilharz suggests:

the death of God has left us unable to discern the distinction between what is possible and what we ought to do: again, we allow the technical capacities to generate their own ends as well as the means which might be appropriate to them.[18]

Somehow, sociology had become entrapped in legitimising what modernity had masked: the antinomies of the Garden of Eden, where the tree of knowledge seemed to afford the solution of endless curiosity, powers proper to God and not to man. This was a theme of *The Enchantment of Sociology*. The issue of Good and Evil appears in many facets of Bauman's writings. As Bauman observes in his introductory chapter, 'Lives told and stories lived: an overture':

> whatever it is, society 'manipulates it', much as it manipulates that other knowledge, of good and evil – but its freedom of manoeuvre in this case is greater, and its responsibility more grave, since humans ate from the Tree of Good and Evil, but only heard of the Tree of Life and have no memory of tasting its fruit.[19]

Oddly, a reminder of this point to the inhabitants of the culture of postmodernity occurs in ritual form in the reading of the Book of Genesis by a choirboy in the Service of Lessons and Carols at Christmas. The dangers of a cultural amnesia become all too evident. This gives sociology a strange task of vigilance, of conserving the memory of what was seen and what should be seen but which present day culture treats as unseen.

Modernity is a project laden with imperfections that the gifts of the Enlightenment cannot redeem. These imperfections leave the self as naked, disconnected and isolated. Trust has become hazardous in the social, yet only by reference to an Other can completeness be found. Yet, here a most interesting point arises. This seeking of an Other occurs where God is dead and when the god of the social has also gone. As Bauman expresses it,

> after *Deus absconditus*, which started off the modern confidence in the powers of the human *species*, came *Societas abscondita*, which triggered the postmodern confidence in the powers of human *individuals*.[20]

The crisis of self-sufficiency the individual suffers under, accentuated in the setting of a culture of postmodernity, can only be alleviated through relationships that generate a dependence and that require a giving and a seeking of the face of the Other. This imperative leads to an ethical domain but it also gives rise to theological considerations. Asked why Levinas pointed him towards politics rather than theology, Bauman gives a somewhat nebulous reply. For him, the Other and God are in each other's company and their human necessity derives from the combined impact of insufficiency and desire in the human condition.[21] For Levinas, the face of the Other is the original site of the sensible. It involves an imperative to go beyond what might be masked, or what appears in plastic forms. To gaze at the naked face is to find a vulnerability, a place for the exercise of responsibility. His notion carries a property of obligation before the Other, but in ways whose relational dimension is not sketched.[22]

Unlike, the eclectic concerns of sociology's attachments to virtual religion, in rhetorical borrowings and metaphors, one finds in Bauman's later writings, a turning in the direction of theology in ways that seem alien in the conventions of British sociology. It is this turning towards issues of real theology as against its virtual imitation that lend a potency to Bauman's intellectual journeying in sociology over a half a century. It is this seeking of a face, even of the faceless Other, which provides the thinnest of links between sociology, visual culture and the imperatives of religiosity. It is this testimony to a seeking that gives Bauman's work a value for this study.

One of Bauman's most perceptive metaphors is the use of the pilgrim to describe journeying in the context of modernity and of the tourist wandering without compass points in the culture of postmodernity. These provide marked contrasts of journeying in circumstances of the definite and indefinite. His discussion emerges in the context of a treatment of the broken middle, as the seat of ambiguity, where anxiety, choice and the need for responsibility emerge. This notion of the broken middle, a term of Gillian Rose, is used to describe what Bauman marks as a spiral of disenchantment. For Rose, it represented the failure of the human to replace the Divine. At her end she made a choice to move from Judaism to Christianity on her deathbed.[23]

Bauman's concerns are with the question of the quality of life and its corresponding modern invention, identity. It is treated as '*an oblique assertion of the inadequacy or incompleteness of the "what is"*'(his italics).[24] This forms the background for the important section of his chapter on broken lives and strategies. One of these strategies is his notion of pilgrimage. This notion is derived from *The City of God*, where it reflects journeying towards the heavenly city. Other means of escape are available apart from that vision, the desert being one.

Here, Bauman makes a very important turn in his argument, one where theological stances have sociological implications. What he confronts is the Protestant template that marks relationships with modernity, where the seeking is inward and not in the social. Bauman goes to Weber to make the argument that Protestants became '*inner-worldly pilgrims*' (his italics), who 'invented the way of embarking on pilgrimage without leaving home'. Their earthly dwelling, inwardly and outwardly was the desert. It is also the site for identity building. In this regard the pilgrim is the metaphor for the modern man but that world of the desert has become inhospitable. Identity is not so much an act of construction as of preservation. This allegory of modernity, of seeking fixedness in the world, bears properties of a belief in something definite.[25] As Beilharz notes, this brilliant engagement of Bauman with the *Protestant Ethic* marks the way that what is worthy of sociological emulation slides into the dilemmas of Weber's iron cage, of disenchantment. The ideal presented to sociology is an instrument of entrapment.[26] In that sense, postmodernity represents an evolution of that entrapment within, whose prime casualty is the social. The self-sufficiency of modernity has collapsed into the insufficiency of postmodernity. There are now no footprints to follow in the desert. This leads Bauman into concerns with the metaphors that follow for life in postmodernity and these deal with necessary circumstances of wandering.

In the world of postmodernity, as matters become more indefinite, the characterising metaphors of the stroller, the vagabond, the tourist and player, replace the pilgrim. If the pilgrim journeys to find a point of fixation, the tourist travels with an abiding fear of being fixed.[27] The life of one is to seek attachments and the other is to preserve detachment. Tourists accommodate to life in fragments, free in their disconnections and their denial of obligation to act on what they see. Bauman has astutely noted that freedom and security go together and this antinomy is well exemplified in the notion of community. The identities so cast in a liquid modernity stand outside notions of community, something sought but something that eludes, hence his recourse to Tantalus.[28] In the context of the issue of the practical ethical commitments he seeks, Bauman worries over the loss of the art of love. Thus, he suggests that

> morality may stop short of saintliness. But I am deeply worried that loving may well be on the way to becoming a forgotten and seldom practised art. Without that art, there is little hope for morality; and even less for a just society.[29]

The value of Bauman lies in his originality, in the grandness of his rigorous re-casting of sociology in the setting of an era where narratives and traditions no longer bind. His thinking is forged in concerns with plights of disconnection; hence the needs to re-set, to re-articulate what is forgotten, which are so endemic in his writings. For him postmodernity is modernity without illusions, and sites for self-understanding have changed radically. The overspilling of his sociology into ethics, philosophy and theology is not some vocational neglect, some failure to guard disciplinary boundaries – his vision of the discipline and its debts to Weber and Simmel are too broad for such petty concerns. He writes as a sociologist coming from a European tradition whose theological ambit is part of the setting of debate in ways that have vanished in English and American sociology. Few who read Bauman's writings seem to attend to the theological resonances that surround his sociology. Yet, these are also endemic in the discipline and its links with modernity.

Going back to Baudelaire's notion of capturing the eternal in the fleeting, Bauman cites with approval an insight of Arendt that he writes in the following way, the resonances for the sociological pursuit of the seen and the unseen being obvious. He comments:

> Arendt suggested that the sole criterion of the greatness of art is its eternal power to impress and arouse. The Gothic cathedrals built to outlast any other human constructions, the frescoes covering the walls of baroque churches, engraving the fragile beauty of mortal faces in un-ageing marble, the Impressionists' obsession with ultimate truth of human vision – all met these demands and criteria.[30]

There is a sociological prejudice, a vulgarised Weberian notion, that entering the discipline into the pursuit of theological issues is a sort of cheap escape from stoical responsibilities. It is in the métiers of theology, however, where sociology finds its burning issues. Somebody, much ignored within sociology, who took such a theological route in his critiques of the Enlightenment and its arrogance of classification, points he shares with Bauman, is Alasdair MacIntyre. It is his concerns with virtue and with tales that point in a direction fruitful for this study.

II

Sociologists might have good reasons for neglecting MacIntyre. He comes laden with a dispiriting baggage of philosophy and theology remarkably difficult for sociology to grapple with. He has received enormous recognition, particularly in theology, and also philosophy, but scant regard in sociology.[31] There are perhaps four facets of MacIntyre that might account for an unwarranted sociological neglect of his works.

First is an unfortunate matter of timing that his seminal work, *After Virtue*, was published too early, in 1981, well before its relevance could be grasped for later debates on postmodernity. Many of its themes, of virtue, character, memory and tradition and the rehabilitation of narrative emerged later in debates on postmodernity, not so much as its characteristics, but as facets of a desirable agenda for a sociology of resistance to its fated fracturing powers. The book anticipated many of the concerns of communitarianism which had such an impact in politics, but less so in sociology.

Secondly, there were only peripheral concerns with matters of sociology in *After Virtue* and these were highly critical. These criticisms are to be found in MacIntyre's notion of emotivism. It suggested that moral judgements are statements of preference sustained in worlds of bureaucracy and therapy. Goffman and Weber were charged with advancing this notion of emotivism in their sociology. Goffman was criticised for liquidating the self, and Weber was charged with promulgating a notion of bureaucracy that eradicated distinctions between the manipulative and the non-manipulative in social relations.[32] This charge of propagating a moral blindness, devoid of character and of insensitivity to its consequences also appeared in Bauman's devastating critique of Weber in *Modernity and the Holocaust*.[33] There is a defence of MacIntyre's charges against Weber of moral indifference but this relates very much to facets of his essay on 'Science as a Vocation'.[34]

Thirdly, there is an estranging property of nostalgia in MacIntyre's *After Virtue* which some of his critics have found off-putting.[35] MacIntyre's notion of virtue related to tales of Irish lore, about heroes and exemplars. These form part of the rich stock of memory that underpins Irish nationalism. Forming a living tradition, the revival of what seemed antiquarian underlay the rise of Irish Romanticism and its effects in the 1916 Rising where a terrible beauty was born into the culture of Ireland. The other strand of the charge of nostalgia might relate to the Catholicism that underpins *After Virtue*. It was written at the time of his conversion into Catholicism and, here again, biography is of crucial importance. MacIntyre moved from a Presbyterian background through to Marxism and then to Catholicism. Like many other converts, MacIntyre found this the beginning of intellectual movement, not its end.

Fourthly, there is an inescapable theological dimension to MacIntyre's work in its approach to virtue ethics, a concern with traits of character rather than an ethics, such as in Kantianism or utilitarianism, where outcomes based on calculation count. In its reliance on Aristotle, but also on Aquinas, virtue ethics has always had a definite Catholic dimension to it. The revival of interest in virtue ethics emerges in a charter essay written by Elizabeth Anscombe, a radically orthodox Catholic. In asking the question of how goodness can be understood outside the tradition that gave it legitimacy, she anticipates problems that Bauman encounters as the distinctive outcomes of postmodernity but which he cannot resolve. She is looking at survivals of ethics or virtue that lie outside the framework of thought that renders them intelligible.[36] Echoing Bauman, but in a formulation he would not write, she notes that

> those who recognize the origins of the notions of 'obligation' and of the emphatic, 'moral', *ought*, in the divine-law conception of ethics, but who reject the notion of a divine legislator, sometimes look about for the possibility of retaining a law conception without a divine legislator.[37]

Her concern was with a huge gap in philosophy, at present unfillable, a concern with human nature and action, with what is characterised as of virtue and of human flourishing.[38] This reconnecting back to traditions that give continuity to issues of virtue governs MacIntyre's concerns. They echo also a comment of Iris Murdoch on the will as the creator of value, a point she derives from post-Kantian moral philosophy. She claimed that values which were previously in some sense inscribed in the heavens and guaranteed by God collapse into the human will. There is no transcendent reality. The idea of the good remains indefinable and empty so that human choice may fill it.[39]

A concern with the good, with what is linked to tradition, marks a contrast between Bauman and MacIntyre. Bauman's encounters with the Holocaust forced him to insert the issue of evil into his sociological deliberations, but in seeking to characterise its basis, he spends little time on its opposite: good. On the other hand, MacIntyre spends only a small amount of time on the issue of evil. His concerns are with the good, with virtue. These are embodied in a tradition but also in settings of practice set for their realisation. Like Anscombe, for him, the loss of religion is a loss of the justification of philosophy. The same might be said of sociology itself. There are three highly important facets to MacIntyre's approach to virtues.

First, virtue is '*an acquired human quality the possession and exercise of which tends to enable us to achieve those goods which are internal to practices and the lack of which effectively prevents us from achieving any such goods*' (his italics).[40] Earlier, practices were described as 'any coherent and complex form of socially established cooperative human activity through which goods internal to that form of activity are realized...' They relate to the realisation of powers of excellence.[41] Deeds and acts of courage are properties of virtue that concern MacIntyre. Thus, he asserts 'a man in heroic society is what he does'. Performance forms the basis of judgement.[42] Virtue relates to properties incarnate in performance that realise a tradition but also embody its virtuous basis.

Secondly, the concern with the practice of virtue, with what is relational, is what realises happiness and prosperity. This brings in a property of discernment, for what is done in practice needs to be so identified as virtuous. Traits of character require a transmission, a manifestation to secure their just recognition. It is in this area that virtue acquires a complex relationship to the seen. On the one hand, the display of virtue renders the virtuous vulnerable to demolition by the cynical, but on the other, they risk the vice of pride in their parading of a moral superiority. Those laden with vice lust to sink their teeth into the virtuous, to break their façade and to place them firmly amongst the fallen. Virtues relate to dispositions that sustain practices, capacities to overcome harm, but also to the furnishing of an increase in self-knowledge of what is good.[43] It is in this regard that virtue can be linked to the possibilities visual culture presents. It might seem that having dismissed the heroes of sociological narratives, Weber and Goffman, MacIntyre has provided an account of virtue that is immune to interventions from sociology, yet he opens out a vast range of possibilities that have been seriously neglected.

By seeing virtues in the context of the traditions they embody, MacIntyre links the exemplification of virtue to memory. More importantly, by linking virtue to dispositions, he opens out a connection to the way fields of culture are reproduced according to the capacities of the actor. For MacIntyre, 'virtues are dispositions not only to act in particular ways, but also to feel in particular ways'. These are based on the capacity 'to act from inclination formed by the cultivation of the virtues. Moral education is an "education sentimentale"'.[44] This understanding arises in Bourdieu's term habitus. MacIntyre's stress on the contextualisation of virtues can be related to Weber's concerns with the routinisation of religion. The linking of virtue to practice and the realisation of memory points to capacities for re-invention of character, properties of which relate to the nurturing of inclinations to seek to see the unseen.

Thirdly, virtue relates to what MacIntyre has termed the narrative character of human life.[45] Virtues arise in the sociology of sport. Thus, Alt has explored well the moral culture of sport in terms of fairness, the heroic and the public display of character. As a ritual and a spectacle, the game is presented for moral inspection, of how endeavour is conducted and won. Sponsorship, artifice and image making might corrupt the beautiful games, yet, there is enough of virtue and the heroic to maintain massive public interest.[46]

For this study, MacIntyre's value lies in his rehabilitation of narratives, not of the grand kind that postmodernism despises, but of those with little testimonies of their reach into properties that transcend their virtuous practices. These properties relate to the aesthetic, and the spiritual, but also to sensibilities of seeing peculiar to the virtuous. These issues of how they come to see in forms of embodiment beg questions about how the founding fathers of sociology had visions that stemmed from strange states of disembodiment.

III

The expansion of autobiography into being accounts of the practice of everyday life[47] marks a contrast with the strange reticence surrounding the personal lives of the founding fathers of sociology. It is only recently that an interest in sociological biography has emerged. Efforts to place the biography of the sociologist in the analysis, to write his tale into the account form part of a sociology of sociology, a sociology of knowledge applied to itself.[48] Masking biography facilitates a sense of disembodiment, of objectivity in the accounts, suggesting that great sociologists lived as gods far removed from the untidiness of everyday life. This property of removal seems to confirm their status as oracles gazing on the social but who do not inhabit its milieu.

It could be said that part of the reason for under-estimations of Simmel relates not only to his versatility, but also his proximity to the cosmopolitan culture whose social construction he sought to capture in his sociology.[49] By contrast, attitudes to Durkheim and Weber border on the reverential. These were god-like in what they sought and saw. Somehow, one does not wish accounts of ordinary life to intrude to sully their reputations. One gets slightly embarrassed but pleased to discover facets of the human emerging in their lives. Why is one amused by a photograph of Durkheim snoozing on a deck chair on the beach on family holidays, or instructing Mrs Durkheim to cease playing the piano so loudly?[50] Likewise one's faith in the man who invoked the Edomite watchman is jolted by the account (and the thoughts it invokes) of Weber leaving town in the Wild West for fear of a gun fight breaking out between the editors of two Oklahoma newspapers. This was in 1904, the year when one of the essays on the Protestant ethic and the spirit of capitalism was published.[51] This sense of texts produced in disembodiment, where personal lives are masked, continues.

In the case of Bourdieu, his reflexivity is geared to recognising structural and intellectual determinants that might distort the sociologist's relationship to the field. It is seldom geared to reveal anything of the private, or what can be deemed 'egocentric and logocentric'. In his assessment of Bourdieu's contributions, Wacquant suggests that 'it is not the individual unconsciousness of the researcher but the epistemological unconsciousness of his discipline that must be unearthed'.[52] In his approach to reflexivity, the inward is cancelled in a form of self-knowing geared to maintaining disciplinary integrity.[53] But this leaves open more questions than are answered when applied to Bourdieu himself. What in his biography caused him to reach for so many Catholic metaphors? How did Catholicism, if at all, influence his work? In his work, there is continuity of the practice of removing from Catholicism a terminology that exalts his sociological vision. Thus, Bourdieu writes,

> at the risk of shocking both the rigorous methodologist and the inspired hermeneutic scholar, I would say that the interview can be considered a sort of *spiritual exercise* that, through *forgetfulness of self*, aims at a true *conversion of the way we look at* other people in the ordinary circumstances of life.

Whereas Foucault usurps the gaze of God, Bourdieu's usurpation is equally grand. The interviewer is to repose 'a sort of *intellectual love*', a gaze on the interviewed similar to that on God, so that in a totality of love, a totality of response is given to the interviewer.[54] Are these proper questions to ask regarding his relationships to Catholicism, or do they subtract from the vision of his work, its sweep and grand scale? This sociologist took on himself powers of distance, anonymity and disembodiment to deconstruct the disembodiment of others, yet as a god he absolved himself from turning these processes on himself. The masking of his own biography seemed to facilitate his sociological deification. Because it suggests something private, subjective and perhaps of wish-fulfilment, there is a tendency to affirm that the sociologist's own story is *not* part of the sociological tale, a case in point being Bauman's own biographical trajectory.[55]

Every form of sociology, however objectively cast, bears an interest, hidden or otherwise. Thus, appeals to the disinterested basis of survey research are undermined when social settings, expectations of use and its politics are taken into account, an example being explorations of sexuality. Findings take on properties of legitimisation of trends and mandates for education, public funds and claims of recognition in sexual politics.[56] By intention or default, sociology has a consciousness raising property in modernity, a point C. Wright Mills well understood.[57] The sociologist is part of the account and is one voice amongst many, but one with a distinctive task of facilitating the telling of stories untold. To hear better, the sociologist has to turn back on the self, the biography and his own story, if the tale is to be told authentically.[58] This gives rise to issues of personal preference and of what type of sociology the sociologist is inclined to affiliate with.

In the meltdown wrought by postmodernity, sociology increasingly faces choices over the forms of faith used to hold sway over the discipline. Sztompka is correct to argue that two forms of sociology have now emerged. He argues that the 'hard' version dealing with instrumental notions of social ties based on interest and calculation, and on an individualistic, egoistic rationality has given way to concerns with 'soft' issues those of the 'us' that relate to the moral obligations of social relationships. In these reside questions of trust, friendship and, one can add, properties of virtue, those of esteem in forms of moral recognition.[59] This softening marks an opening out of sociology to a concern with reception, with receiving and the hearing of tales from a diversity of groups claiming to be unvoiced in contemporary society. Recognition of a right to be heard is a fundamental facet of the agenda of identity politics. This opening out of sociology to hear tales of the world as lived has been marked by three interrelated changes that affect the style and practice of the discipline.

The first shift relates to the way a hermeneutic dimension has entered the practice of sociology, one that carries forward issues of symbolic interaction,[60] but also a concern with deeper and more authentic forms of understanding. Postmodernity has facilitated the rise of a diversity of schools or interest groups, especially those working from sexual and gender politics. These have stories, narratives and tales to tell whose chronicling demands a humanist commitment in the eyes of Plummer. Sociology becomes an instrument for their amplification.[61] The second shift marks the growth of qualitative methodologies that rely on transcripts, diaries, life histories, and narratives of biographies and autobiographies in a variety of social conditions. This humanist methodology is specifically geared to dealings with culture, particularly the habits and belief systems of a community. Seeking these in an authentic form of expression necessitates a reliance on what Alasuutari regards as testimonies, tales and accounts elicited through a rapport with the respondents.[62] The third strand relates to a link between narrative, the self and reflexivity, where identity is a social construction. In articulating the narrative of the self, its own justifications are to be found.[63]

All these movements involve sociology hearing many tales, autobiographies and biographies, all with claims for a hearing. As Holstein and Gubrium observe, 'the grand narrative of the self is now replete with the small tales of myriad distinct storytelling occasions, which leap out of diverse and variegated discourses and texts'.[64] The price of this shift is that the self is increasingly responsible for the stewardship of its own narrative, its choices and the shapes these take.

If, as Maines has argued, sociology's narrative moment has arrived, is he correct to argue that this begs questions about *what* stories are to be told?[65] More importantly, what is the community of narrative in which these stories are to be told? This raises issues about the personal identity of the sociologist. Hiding behind the impersonality of the genealogist no long suffices and attachment to some form of community needs to be realised.[66] But if such connections are to be made, then some form of character, some exemplary traits and virtues are required to flesh out the identity of the sociologist. If communal recognition is sought, then attention needs to be given to a neglected facet of culture: character, a property that links to virtue.[67] If sociology is not to be stuck telling tales to imaginary friends, then some seeking of an 'us' is required.

In seeking an 'us', the sociologist has to choose from a babble of tales, testimonies and narratives. Which testimony of the unvoiced is to be heard?[68] To retrieve some initiative, the most obvious question to ask is who is most prone to want to tell a tale? All these tales differ in their exits and entries. Whereas sexual politics is characterised by tales of entry to its domain of dignified self-proclamation, those surrounding Catholicism are of exiting roles. Often they were tales of departures, and their justifications for leaving religious life in the 1980s.[69]

Some groups have been the 'natural' beneficiaries of this move towards qualitative sociology. Feeling unrecognised, their narratives reflect broken or disrupted or estranged lives, and some healing is to be found in being heard. Their narratives are statements of dislodgement, ones which some in sociology want to hear. Stress on tales and narratives are to be found in issues of gender, disability, medical sociology, ethnicity and, indeed, worlds of common-sense accounts whose scrutiny ethnomethodologists pioneered in the 1970s and 1980s. Postmodernity seems to facilitate the telling of tales of displacement, a case in point being provided by Sarrup. His is a tale of being an Indian in England, facing the double bind of cultural disconnection as an immigrant but also of being estranged in a culture of postmodernity whose rules of affiliation seemed contradictory.[70] Correctly, he argues that identity presupposes identification. It presupposes some focal point of connection where a narrative can be told.

Tales are told for a purpose, of empowerment, of legitimation, but also as testimonies of some hurt. They serve to attract others with similar tales so that community and solidarity can be effected in the telling. In sexual politics, particularly those affecting homosexuals, tales of coming out serve to strengthen solidarity and to that degree they bear a quality of 'us'. These are tales of justification, of retrieval of dignity, but also of assertion of sexual autonomy told for the community to strengthen its resistance to a culture of exclusion. These tales try to secure a truth of affairs, as Plummer notes. They move what might seem proper to the private to the realm of the public where authenticity always requires attention. For Plummer, stories enable essences of the self to be found and communities to be built around these narratives. These stories build up community.[71] In these accounts are notions of mutuality and edification, though hardly in a religious sense.

It is a commonplace criticism of Goffman that he paid little attention to actual stories and narratives of actors and their characters in constructions of his worlds. Indeed, it is usually claimed that the self melted in the role in his accounts. Yet, in his analysis, of necessity, the self had to construct a tale for himself. This emerges in the notion of a moral career. This points to the self-accounting of the actor's movements between the public and the private in *Asylums*. A moral career refers to the self and its significant society. The issue of morality arises in 'the regular sequence of changes that a career entails in the person's self and in his framework of imagery for judging himself and others'. In a footnote, Goffman links the genesis of the term to ceremonies of status transition. Thus, for him, moral careers have a bearing on 'spectacular changes in one's view of self' in forms that accompany participation in social movements and sects.[72] The value of the term is that it links to ceremonies and status transitions that involve moving between private and public realms. The notion of a moral career also forms a significant section of *Stigma*.

In *Stigma*, the term is used to refer to the learning experiences regarding the plight of the stigmatised. It is 'both the cause and effect of commitment to a sequence of personal adjustments'.[73] In short, the term relates to how the stigmatised adapt to the consequences of possessing a stigma. Although Goffman is using the term in regard to groups who clearly are not religious, some of his points apply to those who are. The moral career forms part of the way the stigmatised individual

> may single out and retrospectively elaborate experiences which serve for
> him to account for his coming to the beliefs and practices that he now
> has regarding his own kind and normals.[74]

There is a property of an inquest in the tales involved in a moral career. These are accounts of changes in recognition. Yet, what sociology chooses to recognise as tales worthy of hearing is remarkably arbitrary.

In the case of sexual tales, sociology turns on the hearing aid; in the case of religious outings, it is switched off. Tales of homosexuals outing as Christians and to a life of celibacy would occasion deep unsettlement in classes on the sociology of sexuality. Any tales told are supposed to go in the opposite direction, for there is no sociological grammar to account for those who commit themselves to lives of sexual inactivity. Such pious tales would undermine the basis of the course where sexuality is treated as a leisure activity or a fundamental right of self-actualisation. Notions of self-denial or chastity do not 'fit' the expectations of courses on the sociology of sexuality. Somehow, it is permitted to use sociology to nurture sensibilities regarding sexuality and all its permutations, but not those of religiosity.

In matters of religion, the conventions of academic life are easily unsettled, particularly in a secular university. The subjectivity that might be tolerated on a course on sexuality is treated as intolerable or, in some unarticulated way, improper, when matters expressed are those of religion. Such worries are well expressed in the title of an essay by Chris Anderson on 'The Description of an Embarrassment: When Students Write about Religion'.[75] While a large amount of the sociology of sexuality is based on student samples, only a tiny amount on their religiosity exists, even in North America.[76] Religious rhetoric is the forbidden language of the secular and civic academy. It is ruled out of the cultural field of the university. This poses some singular problems when teaching a course on the sociology of religion. A conversion of view permitted on a course on the sociology of sexuality is acceptable; on a course on the sociology of religion it is deemed profoundly unacceptable.

The ethical implications of teaching the sociology of religion emerged on a course taught by the author. Only a tiny number of students went to church weekly. For the majority of the students, religiosity was something they had long discarded; few went to rituals to soak up their ethos and feel it as insiders; and even, worse, few would know what to look for if they attended a rite. Given these circumstances, how was one to teach a way of seeing rituals and symbols so central to sociological understandings of religion as a form of practice? The telling of tales is not only a matter of recognition; it is also about a capacity to recognise, to distinguish and to see what those who routinely attend rituals glimpse of the unseen.

To get around these difficulties, a fieldwork exercise was established, where all students had to attend a religious ritual. The vast majority elected to attend Christian rituals, even though a minority of the class over the years are non-Christians. Rituals were to be studied in their context of enactment and, as an exercise in ethnography, students were to record, afterwards, all they saw. An aim of the exercise was to force students to think reflexively in ways where they had to reconcile what they saw with what 'official' socio-logical accounts suggested they should have seen and categorised. To some extent, the fieldwork exercise had ambitions to fulfil Bourdieu's notion, cited above, and to find a 'true *conversion of the way we look at* other people'. This expectation for reflexivity takes on a slight different meaning when related to an exercise studying how people believe in the liturgies they enact and participate in.[77]

Do the narrators of tales heard for sociological use recognise themselves in the account?[78] Answering this question posed numerous difficulties for the students, for few had access to the belief systems that governed the activities of the participants in the rituals studied. Another issue that perplexed them was over how far they had to go inside the belief system to understand the way its adherents understood it. All of these students took the exercise on ritual and reflexivity very seriously. Some treated the exercise as their rite of passage into sociological understanding. Very few went to mock, and virtually all sought to understand. In these efforts to understand religious rituals through sociological lens, believing and non-believing students came to contrasting dilemmas. Each faced a sort of squint in the sociological looking.

Believing students found it hard to reconcile their inner sensibilities of rites they habitually attended with expectations of seeing these in the unfamiliar perceptions and expectations of sociology. They could see with the inner eye, but what emerged from use of a sociological eye seemed estranging and misleading. They felt they should see as an outsider, but they had insufficient sociological knowledge or self-confidence to get to this outside stance where they were supposed to see more. In the face of such dilemmas, many students just ditched sociological expectations and wrote as true believers. For them, their theology came first. Sociology became part of the baggage train of the exercise, a clumsy burden borne for course credit. Wearing sociological lens to view the rites seems profoundly estranging, for their religious beliefs habituated them to discern these in other more inwardly directed ways.

The dilemmas of the non-believing students were equally poignant. They found they could provide a deadly accurate piece of ethnography, marking ritual movements, responses, symbols and texts with considerable ability. As outsiders, they could see well, for the lack of an inner eye found compensation in the eye of perception. What frustrated them was the realisation that they were outsiders to the inner forms of the ritual. Somehow they could not get access through sociological means to what gave the ritual its living property. They found it hard to see the rituals through the eyes of the believers who had spiritual eyes to see the unseen. To see as they did involved a conversion of sight, which for many of the students seemed a sociological price too high. They felt this left their sociological tales in some ways incomplete. This issue of a conversion of sight bears on a point of Plummer that

> over and over again, then, in life history research we find the straining towards 'a catharsis of comprehension', to overcome that 'certain blindness' of which all human beings are victims.[79]

One of the puzzles of life is why some people are blind to the obvious. This does not refer to matters of perception, but to inner discernment of what is obvious to others. Pig-headedness, denseness, failure of attention, self-centredness, all relate to charges of blindness, to insensitivity to what ought to be seen but is not. Testimonies serve to help others to see what they cannot. William James has helpfully pointed to the discrepancy between visions of inner significance and the realisation that what was seen was done in a dead external way. This emerges in the context of the worth of something different in perspective, status or an action. Something rises up in sensibility, where the inner eye captures what might not seem available to others blind to similar stances. James suggests that what might seem for the spectator an unfruitful idleness, a useless empty communing, might be confused with a sense of stillness, one that permits the watched to feel a state of suspense of heightened watchfulness of nature in the heat of the day on the hill.[80]

Shifts in capacities to see are tales of conversion worth telling. Increasingly, it is the ethnographer who has to prove what he has seen if his tale is to be believed. This points to an added dimension of reflexivity. It relates to Geertz's notion of 'being there'. What is required is not only a witness of authenticity, but also a capacity to penetrate the recesses.[81] Accounts based on 'being there' derive their validity from the capacity to have seen with an ethnographic eye. Hine amplifies this expectation so that it refers also to the notion of a sense of ethnographic presence, the account of one who was there and who intermingled with the tribe.[82] The ethnographer has participated in what Geertz describes as a 'thick description' and what is brought back is a tale constructed from the experiences of being on the inside. This property of being on the inside and of interrogating to understand better makes the tale not so much authentic as more trustworthy. Thus, as Hine notes, 'ethnography can be a process of self-discovery and reflexivity can be a strategic element in developing insight'.[83]

Shifts in expectations of how ethnographic accounts are to be rendered in the field and the acceptance of advocacy in relation to reflexivity, all point to the need for integrity of witness by the ethnographer. These elements all conspire to change how religious belief is to be understood. Thin reductionist accounts are insufficient. Furthermore, some notions acceptable in anthropology take on differing meanings when set in the context of religious rituals. Testimony and presence point to properties of availability, of openings to what is believed. Sociological reasons for not hearing the voice of the believers have dissolved, and efforts to keep the witness mute seem untenable in the light of permissions given to almost everybody else to speak. Tales and testimonies bear questions regarding their trustworthy nature.

IV

In her insightful study of lying, Bok observes that social life without minimum conditions of trust would be impossible.[84] Everything would have to be checked; no investment in social interaction would take place because of endemic deceptions; and expectations for future actions could not be formulated because there would be no basis to believe that they would be realised in agreed terms. Lack of trust in social affairs would mean they would never cement sufficiently to facilitate moving forward. Fears and anxieties about being misled make many hesitant about forging social bonds. Nobody wishes to be taken in by what is solely available to perception. A capacity to see astutely protects trust. Such seeing expresses the virtue of wisdom but also a gift of inward illumination. It points not so much to what is seen but to what should be seen if the eye is wise. But trust bears not only on the seen; it relates to hopes for the unseen.

The precariousness of trust, of dealing in conditions of uncertainty, where something has to be taken for granted, has a religious quality. Möllering has noted the quasi-religious property of trust in Simmel's writings. Relating to an earlier point of Sztompka on two sociologies of action, Möllering notes the division Simmel makes between strong and weak facets of trust. Calculation that minimises risk and circumstances of loss of trust is a hard version. It relates to money, to trust as expressed in credit-worthiness. The softer version has a more indeterminate quasi-religious property. It is a process that involves a suspension of suspicion, a leap-like entry into trust. This lends an 'as if' property to trust. It points to proceeding in faith and the bracketing of inhibiting doubt. The movement from hard to soft is one of moving from 'good reasons' to what Möllering has termed expectation, interpretation and suspension that involve a 'mental leap'.[85]

The issue of trust appears occasionally in Bauman's works and most substantially in *Postmodern Ethics*, in the setting of the Other. It is where the face becomes like a mask that the question of trust emerges. In the face of a multiplicity of Others, trust becomes related to anxiety, but not to disposing of it. Society is the resource for ethics with strangers, and it supplies the rules.[86] This relates to a weakness in reliance on Levinas that his Other is of a one with a face. It involves a duo that pays little attention to the seeking of responsibilities in a trio of relationships, those in a community.[87] In Bauman's approach antinomial issues of security and freedom fuel suspicions regarding communitarianism.[88] The reason why the issue of trust is of more importance than its passing references in Bauman might indicate is that it lies at the root of the social bond between strangers. It is the exemplary site of mutuality in community, in forms of life, a sort of 'paradise'.[89] To trust is to be affirmed, for trusting is a form of recognition of worth.

In her Reith Lectures for the BBC, Onora O'Neill draws out well those who play on issues of trust, such as spin doctors, those in public relations and in the mass media. In her lectures, she brings into focus a paradox that

> high enthusiasm for ever more complete openness and transparency has done little to build or restore public trust. On the contrary, trust seemingly has receded as transparency has advanced.[90]

The technology of checking has expanded possibilities for misinformation and deception. Ironically, the growth of a culture of accountability has lowered expectations of trust and has generated a society that orders its affairs increasingly on the basis of suspicion and surveillance. Rules that minimise discretion in areas of sexuality and disability confirm that agents who serve those affected are to be distrusted, and that they are incapable of moral discretion. Easy access to litigation has deepened sensibilities of distrust and awareness of the risks of relying on trust alone. Oddly, protective devices for securing trust have rendered it a more elusive proposition than before the advent of this culture of accountability. Procedures for certifying trust have replaced the need for judgement of virtues of character. To win, one assimilates the rules or procedures for the certification of trust and plays these accordingly. Virtues of character are deemed antique. They necessitate recourse to judgement of moral difference that a culture of political correctness seeks to smother. Not unexpectedly, these restrictions on judgement amplify circumstances of distrust whilst at the same time nullifying any means of resistance to its growth.

The pursuit of performance indicators, mission statements, freedom of information and data protection acts, all have increased a distrust of the activities of many occupations. As they are distrusted and deemed to be corrupt and lazy, university lecturers in the UK have been subject to forms of surveillance in research rating and teaching quality exercises, where explicit ordering of information takes on a brilliance of masking the true state of affairs. It is assumed that the efficacy of the procedures for certifying trust is coterminous with the effectiveness of their use. The paper landscapes that have reshaped higher education in the UK fooled few except the politicians who sanctioned these.

O'Neill makes a notable point that trust 'is valuable social capital not be squandered'.[91] Not unexpectedly, she asks who certifies the certifiers of trust, a highly topical question in the light of the accountancy scandals that rocked American finance in 2002. If trust is so valuable, who acts as its conservators? Trust is based on duties not rights. Concentration on the legal enforcement of rights has obscured expectations of duty and the obligations its exercise entails.[92] Trust involves estimations of status, honour and esteem. Even if public culture limits judgement in social interaction, the same cannot be said of its use in the certification of credit-worthiness (for loans), childcare, employment, dating agencies and so on. The search for trust covers a wide facet of culture and relates to practices, occupations, rituals and representations.[93] To be well trusted is to be well recognised. It is clear that the cultural ground for the making of trust has changed greatly. It is now a crucial property of social relationships in ways Giddens has well explored in the context of late modernity.

For him, the notion of trust facilitates exchange in the context of the disembedding effects of globalisation. Trust in expertise relates to issues of confidence and faith. Contingency increases sensibilities of risk and anxiety, hence increased concerns with matters of trust. For Giddens, reliability is a crucial dimension of trust.[94] Giddens distinguishes between facework commitments and faceless forms, the former referring to relationships of co-presence, and the latter to the development of faith in 'symbolic tokens or expert systems' or abstract systems. These interact in an ambiguous manner. His concern is how trust is to be exercised in the absence of facework as exercised in tradition and in pre-modern societies.

This absence of facework relates to a concept of Goffman: civil inattention. This links trust to a visual realm, in particular the forms of exchange facilitated in chatrooms and on the Internet. This point relates to issues pursued in the next chapter. At this point, one can start to discern issues of morality and trust that form part of the emergence of visual culture as an increasingly dominant form of expression. The form of visual exchange, of seeing or not, relates to notions of agency that Goffman has illuminated in regard to civil inattention. It refers to the paradox of recognising but not signifying that one has seen.[95] It refers to forms of interaction that are partial. Where relationships take on deeper implications unsuited to notions of civil inattention, notions of trust change. Intimacy of exchange and interaction require different considerations of trust and the uses it is to fill.[96] This generates some inconsistencies in Giddens' approach not least in relation to religion.

The notion of trust has to be seen in the context of a quest for ontological security that is a continuity of identity in environments of action. For Giddens, religion belongs to the pre-modern and its cosmologies. In his view, it is not part of modernity. In a curiously naïve point, he claims that reflexively organised knowledge, governed by empirical observation and logical thought, has undermined the need to attend to religious cosmologies.[97] Implicit in his approach is the belief that trust is something that can be ordered. Yet, in the case of religion, this not possible for a God that permits being ordered is no God but a projection of human vanity. One should not trust such a God. Anyhow, the domain properties of culture in relation to ordering relate to matters of distrust, hence the concern with increasing uses of technologies of the visual to exercise surveillance. What is entrapped confirms grounds for treating what is seen in a culture with suspicion. Looking, being seen, spectacle and surveillance, all point to a growing consciousness of the implications of living in a culture where values of transparency sit at odds, as O'Neill indicates, with deepening levels of suspicion about who sees. A rather more delicate question emerges: who would like to see with an all-seeing eye?

V

Weber's Edomite watchman is not the only seer of sociological significance to be found on the city walls or on one of its towers in the Old Testament. Other prophets stood and stared, Habakkuk being a case in point. Unlike the antinomial ditherings of the Edomite over night and day, Habakkuk's vision had deep resonances for visual culture. He had a deep worry over a God 'of purer eyes than to behold evil, and canst not look on iniquity' (Hab. 1:13) that could gaze idly over the chaos and the oppression of his prophets and people. God could see but not in a way that connected to their plight. Relief came in a vision. Five woes were to fall on Nebuchadrezzar, who had built a town with blood and established a city by iniquity (Hab. 2:12). The fifth woe was of prescriptions against the worship of false gods. Thus it was written:

> What profiteth the graven image that the maker thereof hath graven it, the molten image, and a teacher of lies, that the maker of his work trusteth therein, to make dumb idols? (Hab. 2:18).

False gods sowed distrust, being guilty of not fulfilling their promises. Claiming to see all, their metallic eyes saw nothing. The powers of discernment of these gods were a function of what their followers believed they could see. By imputing capacities to see, their followers were strengthened in their beliefs over what should be seen. But giving worship to false gods betrayed a trust between God and his people. It was to confuse differences between the virtual and the real and the only reward was a condition of myopia. Disavowals of idolatry can be found in Act II of Handel's oratorio, *Judas Maccabaeus*, which ends with the chorus of men and boys earnestly proclaiming:

> We never, never will bow down
> To the rude stock or sculptur'd stone
> We worship God and God alone

What they wanted is well expressed by the priest in Act III who famously petitions:

> Father of Heav'n From Thy eternal throne
> Look with an eye of blessing down
> While we prepare with holy rites
> To solemnise the feast of lights

Those of more profane dispositions do not wish to have 'an eye of blessing' coming down on their activities. For them, other eyes can be manufactured in image or idea that fulfil the all-seeing capacities of this God. These artificial eyes are set for those with pride who saunter with impunity in the cultural circumstances of Bauman's liquid modernity. They quaff happily without regard to Divine scrutiny. Unlike the virtuous, they hope that 'our eyes may be the servants of our desires'.[98] For all they care, the eye of God can go on a permanent blink as they stroll through the marketplace to catch new sightings for worshipful gaze on idols, icons of pleasure and glittering celebrities. Not for them is the notion that 'the Lord is in his holy temple, the Lord's throne *is* in heaven, his eyes behold, his eyelids try, the children of men' (Ps. 11:4). But if they stroll obliviously to the eye of God, and hide not, who does the watching? If the eye of God is on the blink, what might come to pass unnoticed?

The notion of God not seeing permits other testimonies to flourish, those that emerge from life under artificial eyes. Unfortunately, these eyes too can become deified and, far from liberating, their gaze can be pernicious, entrapping in ways that shape culture to conform to expectations of profound distrust of those so seen. Secularisation of the ocular sows seeds of doubt. Somehow, the issue of the gaze has become narrowed in ways that unsettle those seen. Far from flourishing, those so seen wither. In their witherings, sociology is expelled from the field of view. God and sociology are the prime casualties of the artificial eye and its gaze.

The notion of the 'gaze' has become associated with Foucault and, indeed, seems his invention if not his intellectual property. It is a term that underpins many facets of visual culture. His notion of the gaze arises in two contexts. The first emerges in his paradox of the invisible visibility. This affects the perceptual and epistemological basis of clinical anatomy. Foucault argues that 'truth, which, by right of nature, is made for the eye, is taken from her, but at once surreptitiously revealed by that which tries to evade it'. Thus, knowledge unravels layers of the hidden, as in opening envelopes. The absolute eye of knowledge in clinical settings, particularly those of anatomy, controls what is visible by hijacking it into the invisible. Death becomes a means of reading life. The visible is subject to suspicion and clinical control.[99]

The second setting of the gaze, and perhaps the best known, emerges in his use of Bentham's *Panopticon*. This was a fantasy, an 'as if' but one that underwrote Foucault's famous discussion of Panopticism. This refers to the power of the visual applied through reason to classify, to discipline and to control in universalising forms of experimentation on the actor. The process starts with prisons and ends with them, for as Foucault asks 'is it surprising that prisons resemble factories, schools, barracks, hospitals, which all resemble prisons?'[100] Seldom has the visual been given such a power to structure and to reproduce types or inmates who need discipline and change of character. This capacity of power is illustrated in the case of instructions on the state control of mechanisms of discipline envisaged in eighteenth-century Russia. What emerges is a power of surveillance, one that is omnipresent and permanent. It is

capable of making all visible, as long as it could itself remain invisible. It had to be like a faceless gaze that transformed the whole social body into a field of perception: thousands of eyes posed everywhere.[101]

When set against the expectations of visual culture, Foucault poses two reversals of expectation. First, the light of the Panopticon is a means of entrapment. The light in the darkness is not one of hope, for as Foucault indicated in an interview, 'the principle of the dungeon is reversed; daylight and the overseer's gaze capture the inmate more effectively than darkness, which afforded after all a sort of protection'.[102] Secondly, and more importantly, spectacle is made redundant in this new form of power of sight. What belonged to the public in ritual forms of punishment is shifted into the private in a more pernicious all the more encompassing structure whose power is accomplished through the gaze that penetrates all. Far from enlivening, the gaze in the Panopticon kills the commonwealth. It is a gaze that coagulates by contrast with what went before in times of spectacle. Thus, Foucault suggests that

> with spectacle, there was a predominance of public life, the intensity of festivals, sensual proximity. In these rituals in which blood flowed, society found new vigour and formed for a moment a single great body.

In the new gaze, the power of spectacle is hijacked, for he goes on to observe:

> we are much less Greeks than we believe. We are neither in the amphi-theatre, nor on the stage, but in the panoptic machine, invested by its effects of power, which we bring to ourselves, since we are part of its mechanism.[103]

It might seem that Foucault has excelled himself, not so much in celebrating the closing of the eye of God, but also in effecting the death of god, the one of Durkheim. The eye in the tower, in seeing all, effects far more than even Goffman could have envisaged in *Asylums* where 'every total institution can be seen as a kind of dead sea in which little islands of vivid, encapturing activity appear'.[104] In Foucault's world of visibility, no encapturing activities appear, save of bondage to a light that freezes and certainly does not offer the hope of liberation. In this setting the prisoner fears to show his face lest the light of surveillance shows up something that would blemish the record. Indeed, in the Panopticon, the inmate has no wish to show his face, for the unseen in the tower would see too much. In this setting there is no social face or a basis of regulation of it.

In his essay on facework, Goffman had noted that

> approved attributes and their relation to face make of every man his own jailer; this is a fundamental social constraint even though each man may like his cell.[105]

In Foucault's world, the inmate is own jailer to the degree to which he does *not* show his face and so denying disclosure denies himself. He has no mirror to see himself and he certainly does not trust the refracting gaze of the eye of the tower to find himself. The little god with no face to show dies in the light.

On reflection, even Foucault got worried about what was lurking in these issues of the seen and the unseen. Looking at the central tower, Foucault wondered who Bentham had made its occupant? Foucault asks:

> is it the eye of God? But God is hardly present in the text; religion only plays a role of utility. Then who is it? In the last analysis one is forced to conclude that Bentham himself has no clear idea to whom power is to be entrusted.[106]

Foucault's query directs attention to Paul's comment on the all-seeing surveillance of God, where 'neither is there any creature that is not manifest in his sight: but all things are naked and opened unto the eyes of him with whom we have to do' (Heb. 4:13). Bentham's fantasy formed part of the project of the Enlightenment in regard to visual culture. This project sought to secularise the basis of surveillance and to escape the all-seeing eye of God. The effect of this secular ambition, as expressed in Foucault, marks not only the death of God, but also the 'death of man'.[107] The gaze from the tower that exemplifies the eye of reason becomes a substitute for the unseen God. This eye of reason offers no hope of reciprocity – ever. The power of this substitute for the Divine derives from a form of projection that is more complete in effect and more beyond redress than Feurbach could have envisaged. Powers of projection have given man a god whose reflection back assassinates him.

The seer in the tower controls what is to be seen and unseen in ways that affect and effect the self. But for the self, there is no reciprocity, no possible response back. The gaze is total in its enveloping power. In so looking, those so seen have no will, no agency, autonomy or sense of regard. They are seen to be diminished by this god; not enlarged as in the case of God. Distrust governs the gaze of the god of the tower of the *Panopticon*. It services no solidarity. The architectural arrangements mark a segregation, an isolation of individuals, to render them compliant before the all-seeing gaze that encompasses all to be seen. The gaze penetrates its objects of domination who can but re-cast their selves to mirror what they cannot see.

The genius of the *Panopticon* is the economy of power it exercises on the basis of deference to the unseen. In this emblem of the values of the illumination of reason, the light shines brightly to dazzle and to immobilise in servitude to the unseen gazer. Sometimes it is better *not* to know who is watching in a world of counterfeit scrutinisers where everything is noticed.

Like Foucault's figure in the tower, the Big Brother of Orwell's *Nineteen Eighty-Four* has no identifiable existence, a failing that oddly enhances the power of his all-encompassing gaze. He is a symbol of one who sees everything and gives the party its focal point of deference. Unlike in Bentham's

Panopticon, his all-seeing image marks him as an object of love displayed to all his subjects. These willing victims collude in total affirmation of the ethos that governs all facets of their lives, public and private. In this regime, there is no truth, for all is doublespeak. As with the inhabitants of the *Panopticon*, the ruled live lives under assumptions of distrust. They inhabit conditions where their will is to be denied. Unlike in Bentham's paradise for the fallen, the gaze is individualised so that each subject is rendered servile by the gaze from the telescreen that sees all and disciplines all. Those who do not comply are to be 'cured' or vaporised, that is deemed never to have existed.

The manipulation of memory is a crucial ingredient in this world where the capacity to forget is an instrument of social recognition. Reflecting on this absolute control of a world where everything of the seen and the unseen is so rigorously regulated, Winston, the 'cured' hero, thought it all seemed like a chess game. Looking at the portrait of Big Brother (posted everywhere and thus intensifying the sense of being watched), Winston mused:

> white always mates, he thought with a sort of cloudy mysticism. Always, without exception, it is so arranged. In no chess problem, since the beginning of the world has black ever won. Did it not symbolise the eternal, unvarying triumph of Good over Evil? The huge face gazed back at him, full of calm power. White always mates.[108]

The issue of Big Brother might have faded into literary history, were it not for a television programme of the same name that seemed to grab the attention of a significant section of the English in 2002. The eye of God, long displaced by the eye of the Enlightenment, is now replaced by the democratisation of the eye. Millions of viewers fit into the television eye and become voyeurs of the moment. Looking into the activities of night and day of eight or so young men and women, the millions have powers of ejection as they view this experiment in virtual living, where no detail of privacy is spared public exposure. The occupants of the house speak ill of each other before the camera (but not to each other). The last one to stay wins, a judgement based on the verdict of millions of watching voyeurs, who see but are not seen by the occupants of the house.

Those selected go through a very selective exercise, and they have to face the manipulations of other Big Brothers, the show's producers who set tasks for the housemates. An enormous amount of confessional material appeared on the edited nightly versions of the show, which the housemates would not tell their friends, but felt free to confide to a nation. The house, described as 'penal chic' on the first show, 'cabin fever' on the second and 'urban Zen' on the third, facilitates a sense of disembodiment, for the housemates are on a doomed cruise whose only purpose is to provide spectator sport for voyeurs.[109] Because there is no script, the world so seen has a property of authenticity, of disclosure of the unexpected that gives viewers something to gossip about, without consequence. Like virtual religion, they can look on, but without the boring effort of having to forge commitments to those whose lives they watch in all their intimacies. Reflecting on the popularity of the show, one of the psychologists who interpreted events nightly said:

> we have the illusion that we are seeing everything, which gives us a Godlike sense. I believe it empowers us as viewers more than any interactive tech-nology. It gives us a sense of superiority, which comforts us and enhances our self-esteem.[110]

Portrayed as reality television, an enormous amount of manipulation of what is seen is unevenly concealed. The manoeuvrings of the producers and the tests on the relationships of the household seem natural in a world that is profoundly artificial and unnatural, for in the end only one occupant wins the plaudits of the viewers who vote in this macabre drama. The eviction process bears a resemblance to the vaporisation processes of *Nineteen Eighty-Four*. The power of extinction has been granted to the viewing audience. This capacity of selection and rejection gives to all voyeurs the realisation of a god-like property to govern the fate of those observed. It underlines the degree to which the visual has become a vital ingredient of popular culture and the means through which many transactions can be made or unmade.

These sensibilities of the visual as a crucial ingredient of culture mark the way it is shaped by reference to what is seen and unseen. Within the visual, not only issues of spectacle, but also social relationships that reflect and respond to seeing and being seen, emerge. The power of the visual might have an illusory basis. It might be based on paranoia, myopia or wishful thinking, but this does not matter, for the visual as an entity itself increasingly governs the shape of culture and what it values. It is the belief that the visual has effects that matter and the prudent adjust their activities accordingly. Increasingly, they act as 'as if' seen, and so adjust their patterns of behaviour to confirm this expectation but also to conform to it. In regard to the visual, beliefs about its basis are increasingly deemed real in their consequences. In responding to what one believes to be the visual and what lurks behind it, the actor comes to exercise a self-surveillance. He is how he is seen.

Given the risks involved in this area of myopia, of fantasy and fiction, the need to attend to matters of trust and distrust are understandable. As the visual expands, suspicion and surveillance might mark many forms, but another side is that this accentuates a need to find a basis for trust, so that one can believe in what is seen. In all this, the self has to find a credible response to this expansion of the seen in a visual culture. The need to attend to ways of seeing have fallen on every citizen, every spectator and every voyeur, for spectacle has inescapable degrees of implication for those who see, particularly when technology permits the virtual and the real to be really mixed up. Daniel might have seen visions in the night whose apocalyptic basis frightened many since. Artists, theologians and liturgists have dwelt on these visions. Now computer technology can make many-sided monsters with more than ten heads for all to see. Cyberspace seems to have shoved visual allegories out of the way by showing a capacity to sketch visions in ways undreamt of before. It is not that issues of the seen and the unseen are irrelevant fantasies; it is that technology seems to have taken on powers to visualise them in sketches without limit. In cyberspace, all now can mix the seen and the unseen in any image they want. This power has shifted the basis of the morality of seeing. With these newly found powers, a danger emerges that the social is no longer necessary. Even worse, this expansion of visual culture seems to serve sociologists with redundancy notices.

3
Visual Culture and the Virtual: The Internet and Religious Displays

Between television and the home computer, an increased amount of work and leisure activity is devoted to looking at the screen and deciphering what is seen on it. With so many visual outlets available, the contingency of post-modernity has invaded the gaze, for with so much to see there is confusion about what to see and how to see it. Sometimes, the activity of looking can be passive, but in other forms it can be interactive. Increasingly the camera lens supplies the means of being there for all who view. Visual technology seems to supply *the* window through which many facets of culture are to be seen. This technology also affects expectations of authentic fieldwork. No longer is it sufficient for the anthropologist to convey in text his two years in the field; a video is expected as well to supply a visual basis to what people will read later in other forms of academic communication. The enormous expansion of access to the visual, to worlds hitherto unseen, is a much-remarked miracle of technology. This ocular turn to the making of culture has been surprisingly under-researched in sociology. Visual culture, the inchoate discipline that signifies this turn, has been kept at a sociological distance. This suspicion is curious, for concerns with the implications of visual culture are to be found in the formation of the mental life of the metropolis that Simmel so well chronicled. He supplied grounds for thinking that this expansion of visual opportunity was not entirely beneficial.

Writing on the growth of 'mere visual impression' in modern social life, Simmel pointed to the way seeing can effect its own estrangement as emotional life become attenuated before the ocular plenitude found in cosmopolitan life. The visual generates a sense of entrapment stemming from 'the lack of orientation in the collective life, the sense of utter lonesomeness, and the feeling that the individual is surrounded on all sides by closed doors'.[1] It is doubtful if Simmel could have envisaged the almost endless expansion of image making permitted by technology and the privatisation of seeing this facilitates. As Cooper suggests, 'subjective experience is now framed by technological processes in a manner previously unimaginable'. Unfortunately, as he goes on to suggest, 'the lure of VR (virtual reality) is all too often the promise of unbounded autonomy, a promise which can only lead to disenchantment'.[2] This disenchantment can be linked to a sense of disembodiment, of not seeing from any social context. In the face of such visual excess, the self can seek a return to embodiment. Such shifts seem endlessly complex and bewilder the mind endeavouring to assimilate so much image making.

Images, spectacles and cultural icons have become instantaneously available in cyberspace, a term first coined in 1984. Mobile phones now permit face-to-face conversations. Expectations to see instantly and everything have greatly expanded. These changes draw attention to acts of looking and the technological forms through which a myriad of images are seen. These give rise to capacities to see what is forbidden: images in child pornography. As the visual expands through technology, ways of seeing become enormously diffused. The contingency attached to the visual combined with the endless images to be seen makes sociological characterisations of acts of seeing highly problematic. The response of those who view might be fleeting or deeply transformative in ways that simply reflect subjective preference. Socio-logical accounts of the visual risk being engulfed in the ocular excess now provided through technological means. It is difficult to know what to include or what to exclude in any sociological analysis, for all images have claims for inclusion. This limitless expansion of the visual in a multitude of cultural forms has no precedent. There are no templates in sociology for understanding the dilemmas that the advance of visual culture now generates. In dealing with the visual, sociology faces some added complications.

Technology not only facilitates the endless de-contextualisation of images; it also makes possible forms that need no original, the visual basis being located in the digital and in cyberspace. These images do not so much mirror social reality as make their own refractions. The virtual takes on powers of resemblance that seem more real than their prototypes. In the making of images, the viewer sees with no inhibition, no morality and no presumption. The miracle of technology in the making of images in a virtual reality absolves the viewer from such antique inhibitions. Yet, the screen can become a desert, a site for mirages, illusions and figments and as the making of the visual expands, the need to differentiate between the virtual and the real becomes undermined. As Holmes has suggested:

> pluralism on the Internet may be entirely generated through a play of masks in which difference does not actually have to be confronted because it can be manipulated.[3]

Although material on the Internet can be manipulated, the use of websites enables groups unheard in the mass media to present their own stories with integrity and without distortion by editorial filters. These groups hire web-masters to set out their tales illustrated in ways that authenticate their beliefs. Search engines such as Google enable websites to be found on almost all topics. Religious groups have been particular beneficiaries of the democratic access offered by the Internet. Cyberspace permits the unfolding of religious tales in ways denied in terrestrial outlets. This is not to suggest that the theological and enigmatic bases of the seen and the unseen are resolved in their presentation on cyberspace. Rather, it is to suggest that the resources of visual culture, as they bear on religious memory, can be exploited in virtual form to amplify a disposition to look at dilemmas raised by the conundrums of the seen and the unseen and to seek to see these in a new light in the estranging circumstances of postmodernity. The Internet has expanded the significance of the seen and the unseen in visual culture in ways that would seem unimaginable to the medieval mind.

The first two sections of this chapter deal with consideration of the pedigree of visual culture and move on to explore the making of images through technology, particularly photography. It forms the basis for understanding the expansion of image making on the Internet. More than making images is involved in life on the Internet, for it has communal and interactive dimensions that blur distinctions between the virtual and the real. The capacity of the Internet to manufacture a virtual reality seems to amplify the notions of the virtual mentioned earlier. This issue is discussed in the third section of the chapter. In the fourth section, the impact of the Internet on religion is examined, where loss and gain are explored. In the final section of the chapter, the complexities of the virtual are re-examined with a view to finding a *fourth* form.

Three forms of the virtual as bearing on religion were mentioned in Chapter 1. The first was used to refer to sociology's dalliances with virtual religion, where on some occasions the discipline became one. The first form also links to civil religion and in that regard incorporates facets of Durkheim's approach to the sacred and its collective and sustaining functions. In origin and replication, sociology stands equivocally to virtual religion.

The second form of the virtual in religion extends this notion of imitation into matters of performance, where what is purely aesthetic and secular is weighted with borrowings from traditional religions. These borrowings permit the ritual of the concert hall to appear in the aura of a virtual religion, one whose appeal to the aesthetic rises above the narrow and sectarian distortions of institutional religions for whom the music was originally written. The symbolic and cultural capital of Catholicism is recognised for its power but is re-appropriated to service the needs of a virtual religion. Its claim to disinterest in performance permits it to deny the obligation to commitment that Catholicism enjoins for such sacred music and its ritual use.

It is the third form of the virtual as it relates to the power of image making that forms a crucial concern of the study and this chapter in particular. The parable of *Imaginary Friends* anticipates, perhaps in tragic form, the visual dimensions of reflexivity, the failure of a self-awareness to realise that the sociologist is part of the religious field, and even if he does not make a choice of what to recognise, others will. This third form of the virtual, of dubious powers of endlessly amplifying images, has been accentuated with the Internet in ways that have profound implications for how matters of the seen and the unseen are to be handled. Not only ways of seeing, but also expectations of what can be seen underline the significance of visual culture, but in links with religion that have been barely recognised in sociology. The notion of the virtual carries many pitfalls. It bears a notion of resemblance but also disconnection from some prototype or original. Memory and curiosity creep into the virtual, for there is always a wonder about the original, what did it mean, what did it look like? The trouble with cyberspace and the virtual reality it produces is that both seem to imperialise visual culture. The Internet has come to dominate expectations of the visual so that excursions to see the prototype of what is virtually produced have a property of novelty.

A paralysis in the ocular plenitude so wrought through technology erodes the need to view in a social context. Increasingly, it risks taking on artificial and estranging properties. Thus, images presented in cyberspace increasingly disguise their terrestrial origins. More potently they suggest a licence to view that requires a slight regard for etiquette. The problem that emerges is that viewing in cyberspace seems devoid of social implication and accountability. Somehow, dealing with the virtual requires virtuous properties of restraint sociology has an interest in amplifying.

The Internet generates an expectation that everything can be seen without restraint and that all forms of curiosity regarding the visual can be resolved. The need to refer to assumption and presumption is no longer self-evident in dealings with cyberspace. No patience, no prudence, no fortitude of searching is required, for the search engine will provide instantaneous answers to any query. The effects of the Internet can be overplayed, yet it has radically changed expectations of visual culture and the relationships between the viewer and viewed. The need to cultivate virtues of regard and to view with inhibition seems to have dropped into disuse. This means that the ways of seeing and cultural forms of spectacle for handling the seen and the unseen have become redundant, not because these matters are incredible, but because the procedures for approach seem to have fallen into decay in the wider visual culture. The need for reverence for the antinomy between the seen and the unseen lacks a cultural mechanism for expression or, indeed, awareness of its necessity. This lack also obscures the wider implications of the seen and the unseen and the radical claims these make.

The unseen might express the heavenly, what is yet to be seen, what will be revealed at the Last Judgment. But what is of the unseen has been seen. It is revealed in the Incarnation of Christ who is 'the image of the invisible God' (Col. 1:15). This stark theological assertion stands ill with the tendency of sociology either to ignore choices of belief, or to postpone them by zealous adherence to notions of pluralism. Yet, if a theological stand is not made, sociology is crippled in the way it can handle the seen and the unseen. It has thrown away its ticket of entry to the paradigm.

The first three forms of the virtual can be treated as myopic mirrorings, misrepresentations that pass on the basis of imitation in ways that distract attention from the need to attend to the prototypes, those that come from theology, from the real, as of faith and orthodoxy. Now, liberal theologians would regard such stipulations as the product of a simple-minded sociology. Leaving aside the arrogance of stipulating differences in such a cavalier manner, what returns is the notion of 'as if'. This is where a humble sociology can spurn the theologically proud. What sociology is concerned with is the seeking of an understanding of how one acts on the notions of the virtual in a virtuous manner 'as if' they were true. A fourth dimension of the virtual is required, one that links disposition, virtue and visualisations as they seek to discern the seen and the unseen. It is these accommodations to the antinomies of the seen and the unseen that form the hermeneutics of the study.

I

Great uncertainty surrounds the content, significance and use of the term visual culture. Perhaps the most straightforward definition of visual culture available, and the one that is very sociological, is Mitchell's that it is 'the study of the social construction of visual experience'.[4] Still in a state of envisagement, visual culture is a disciplinary oxymoron dealing with a prospectus of topics. An advertisement for a new *Journal of Visual Culture*, published by Sage, whose first issue appeared in April 2002, provides a useful prospectus of the area. Technologies of seeing, gazes and glances, public and private spheres, performance, the eye, iconoclasm and idolatry, displays and images are listed along with concerns over the hidden, aesthetics, appearances and colours. Indicating that there was no systematic critique of visual culture upon which to construct a curriculum, let alone agreement as to what was in the discipline, Mitchell bravely provided a syllabus for a single-year course. The first term dealt with signs, images and visuality, iconography, aesthetics and spectacle, their decipherment, representation and reproduction. The second term concentrated on bodies in terms of sacred and profane images, character, the gaze and the glance, and invisibility and blindness. That term was to include issues of display in terms of sexuality and death. The last term was to deal with worlds that related to issues of power, visual regimes, media, nations, spaces, and the ownership of the image.[5] The breadth of topics that potentially can be included within the ambit of visual culture is matched by the range of disciplines to which it is potentially aligned. Walker and Chaplain list 34 disciplines upon which visual culture draws, ranging from design history, heritage studies, to queer theory, social history, and second last on the list – sociology.[6]

This property of being multi-disciplinary, inchoate and recent gives to visual culture a status of being outside the regular academic milieu. There are few degrees in the UK in visual culture and it is rarely a unit on the socio-logical curriculum. Its natural habitation seems in feminism, film, media and cultural studies. Being outside disciplinary accountability, visual culture thrives on a free-floating property that facilitates its concerns with the transgressive and the suspicious. Outside the conventions of culture, some adherents of visual culture mask their sectional interests by exercising their rights to unsettle conventional ways of seeing, religion being a particular target for transgression. But visual culture relates to wider issues proper to sociology. Labelling, stereotyping and categorising solely on the basis of what is seen have long attracted sociological distaste. The issue of how one is seen is part of the agenda of identity politics and its concerns with rights of representation and recognition. These ambitions underline a selectivity of sight, a disposition to mark what *should* be seen and is not. The eye of indifference that identity politics nurtures to secure an inclusion of the excluded carries a price that in matters of sexuality distinctions of judgement are not made, and indeed, are not to be. The result is the nurture of a certain blindness for reasons of civil purposes of inclusion of all with dignity, a conferral based on the denial of moral distinctions.

Mizroeff draws attention to an important facet of visual culture that it 'does not depend on pictures themselves but the modern tendency to picture or visualise existence'.[7] In dealing with visuality, he argues that the central concerns of visual culture are with forms of 'interaction between viewer and viewed, which may be termed the visual event'.[8] These events have distinct sociological resonances, as they point to matters of spectacle and open out understandings of the way forms of seeing are arranged in particular and stipulated ways. What is so arranged presupposes that those who gaze know how to look, not only in their use of the visuality but also in their capacity to discern and distinguish. It is assumed that those who see know what to look for.

Sight requires a visual literacy not merely to see but also to view an image in a manner that accords with the expectations of its creator and the mode through which it is presented. Thus, the painter has magical powers to capture images on canvas in ways that make for subtle viewing of light and shadow whose hues form not only a means of evaluating char-acter but also inferences of beauty in nature. The making of images involves the painter in drawing on an imagination to represent an image that bears comparison with an original. Each form in its highest state of excellence has the power to capture the essence of an image. This power is set to naught if those who gaze do not know what to look for. Forms of visual appreciation presuppose cultural forms of looking and in that way affect what the eye *elects* to constitute. In some ways, it is not difficult to link sociology to the visual.

Given sociology's concerns with representations, rituals, appearances, symbols and the commodification of cultural artefacts with brand names whose image makes them immediately identifiable, it might be said that visual culture adds little to what is already being done in the discipline. Clothing, fashion and styles of appearing have purposes of display and recognition that betray an awareness of the power of the visual and concerns with how entities are seen. Facets of visual culture are embedded in Veblen's notion of conspicuous consumption. Yet, notions of visual culture attenuate expectations of how sociology is to approach what is seen. As Mitchell has correctly observed,

> whatever visual culture is, it must be grounded not just in the interpretation of images, but also in the description of the social field of the gaze, the construction of subjectivity, identity, desire, memory and imagination.[9]

What is also new for sociological consideration is the way the visual has become a vital ingredient of self-consciousness, a sense of awareness, but above all a mode of cultural expression, expectation and exchange. Increasingly culture is ordered according to expectations of the visual. Even more importantly, styles and manners of looking have taken on ethical and moral concerns, issues discussed in Chapter 4. In this milieu that promotes the significance of visual culture, the processes of seeing, the gaze, the eye itself, and the protocols for handling the visual, generate a contingency that complicates greatly sociological approaches. Realisation of the significance of these processes marks a response to shifts in the ordering of culture itself to handle matters of surveillance where distrust emerges as endemic in matters relating to the visual. The actor's duties and expectations of how to act, as indicated earlier, have changed markedly. Increasingly, being so seen renders the actor part of a documentary account. At one level, this expansion of the visual for the purpose of surveillance is for the actor's own protection, but at another level such pervasive seeing has an intrusive, estranging property. It begs questions about where the image so caught on camera might go, who will see it and to what end?

As actors adjust their appearances to expectations of the visual, seeing and being seen have accentuated the coquettish properties of impression management in ways Goffman is unlikely to have envisaged. As the visual expands in cultural significance, so too do the arts of simulation and dissimulation. These do so in a culture increasingly interested in masquerades and imitations that are virtual in resemblance. If myopia is not to rule and the gaze is not to be vacuous, then spotting ploys of manipulation that confuse the unseen with the seen are necessary devices. What starts to emerge is that the seen and the unseen are not the strange antique concerns of theology, but form the manners and morals of social exchange in a culture increasingly predicated on the visual. As the visual becomes attached to the cultural, the issue of which discipline has brand ownership starts to emerge, and as suggested above there are many with claims.

In disciplinary terms, visual culture bears a Janus-faced property. One facet claims to be rooted in aesthetics and art history, whilst another seeks more immediate uses in film studies, and studies of gender, ethnicity and sexuality. The multi-disciplinary nature of visual culture enables some more than others to be 'the natural' beneficiary of this academic inchoateness. As Mitchell observed, 'cultural studies might be thought of as the awful truth that was concealed for so long under the euphemism of inter-disciplinarity'.[10] These divisions of disciplinary affiliation pose dilemmas for sociology.

As a discipline, it can say little about aesthetics, a bit more about art history, perhaps, but it certainly does not want any dalliances with cultural studies. It is seen as a rival to sociology, and is certainly not to be regarded as providing an authentic voice for understanding the basis of culture.[11] Nor is sociology enamoured with how cultural studies uses its relationships to visual culture. Innovation, transgression and the invocation of postmodernity to endorse a breakdown in a consensus of taste form the basis of a marriage between visual culture and cultural studies.[12] Sociology might accept the significance of the visual, but questions are begged about what form of culture is to govern its reading. This is the weak flank of visual culture for it faces numerous stakeholders with claims on its constituting powers. The importance of images, their packaging and rights of representation suggest there is no neutral dimension to visual culture. Images can be manipulated on the basis that changes in their shape can adjust the social basis of what they refract. This belief points to powers of refraction and also to a belief that what is unseen should be seen in some credible way. More importantly, the purpose of the visual emerges as a crucial cultural issue.

In his discussion of culture, Mirzoeff notes worries of those in history of art that many aspects of visual culture are de-stabilising, not least in the relativism they generate, where any image, embodied or disembodied, is licensed for view. There are no boundaries to display. Perversely, although he genuflects to Arnold, Mirzoeff's concern with culture is with its racialised inheritance.[13] The trouble is that hesitations about securing a definition of culture enable visual culture to become a creature of identity politics in its particularising and sectional ways. If, as Eagleton argues, culture can be treated as a normative way of imaging society,[14] the hijacking of visual culture by cultural studies and the zealots of the politics of identity has reductionist consequences. A descent from the universal to the particular in culture follows, but also a narrowing of vision and spirit that also worried Bauman. As Eagleton observes, in a 'three way interaction, culture as spirituality is eroded by culture as the commodity, to give birth to culture as identity'.[15] In a rather radical move, he argues that both modernism and postmodernism have medieval roots.[16] What seems of the immediate, which can be seen now, betrays lineages of culture memory that go back to forms of visualisation in the past that somehow saw more of what ultimately mattered.

Images become de-spiritualised in the pursuit of the particular. Transgressions are permitted in the absence of universalising claims of culture. At the same time a victim status is claimed for such capacities to transgress. These range from sterile efforts at blasphemy by the visually challenged, to forms of bodily modifications that mark a thin line between artistic conceit and hard pornography, to the re-setting of gender and sexuality in images that can be best described as ambiguous and transient. Although such cultural re-packagings derive their mandates from the opportunities generated by contingency and their rhetoric from notions of the immorality of discrimination, what they mask is the reductionism of such special pleadings. They exemplify the paradox Jay has explored, of the way illumination based on reason leads to a narrowing of the visual and its closure into disenchantment.[17] This stands at odds with an expectation that culture should yield an enchantment of spirit and vision. Acts of seeing that oscillate between the risks of disenchantment and the wonders of enchantment require the cultivation of a capacity to distinguish between both, lest those who gaze be misled.

The notion of knowing what to see relates to Berger's well-known stipulation that 'every image embodies a way of seeing. Even a photograph.' A selectivity of what is to be seen can be masked in the form of reproduction of the image. In a society besotted with images, it is important to note a crucial point. These serve to conjure in appearance what is absent. The seen and the unseen become interlinked in issues of images, and these lie at the heart of the makings of contemporary culture.[18] What lies below the surface, what belongs to inference rather than perception, what is of symbol rather than sign point to the need to cultivate ways of seeing that can distinguish. The secularity of visual culture seldom adds in a dimension of the unseen that bears on the spiritual, or a recognition of the impact of the invisible on the mundane circumstances of life where too much is of the visible. Here, the virtual and the real in matters of religion are easily confused.

Berger argued that in dealing with the value of an object, often a religious image, something other than market forces should dictate the basis of appraisal. Thus, he asserted that 'the spiritual value of an object, as distinct from a message or an example, can only be explained in terms of magic or religion'. Yet, since these are no longer living forces, the object takes on an 'entirely bogus religiosity' where it is treated like a holy relic.[19] This condemns works of religious art to the endorsing values of virtual religion of the art gallery. Their original use becomes obscured in ways nearly lost to history.[20]

In the course he sketched on visual culture, Mitchell felt that it was unthinkable without reference to Benjamin's famous essay on art and technology.[21] For Benjamin, 'the uniqueness of a work of art is inseparable from its being imbedded in the fabric of tradition'. He went on to add that many works of art operated in ritual orders. These supplied the unique 'authentic' value of the work of art. In a point that anticipates the second form of the virtual religion used above, he suggests 'this ritualistic basis, however remote, is still recognizable as secularized ritual even in the most profane forms of the cult of beauty'.[22] But is the virtual sufficient, especially when it so well masks its borrowings from the original? The protocols for seeing the original no longer make claims, and in such liberties of view, is it any wonder that the eye wanders, seeking but not connecting, for the counterfeit permits no other outcome?

In a way that anticipates Bourdieu's notion of habitus, Benjamin observes that 'a man who concentrates before a work of art is absorbed by it'. The gaze on a work of art in ritual is sustained by a collective sense of others looking, and colluding to see. But in the mechanical reproduction of art, the viewer might not notice the hidden cost of its facile capacity to produce images. In this context of the mechanical, as Benjamin suggests, 'reception is a state of distraction'. Everybody is an art critic simply because movies require no critical attention. In short, 'the public is an examiner, but an absent-minded one'.[23] This state of perception and reception becomes especially problematic in a culture described as taking 'a pictorial turn'.[24] When spectacle was sealed into religious rituals in eras where no rival forms of display were on offer, the incentive to see to believe had at least an authoritative context. With the advent of de-contextualisation and erosion of aura and authority, the capacity to see in former ways has become lost, a point that applies particularly to dealings with the seen and the unseen. In this regard, a hermeneutic consideration arises in relation to the visual. Antique objects seen, such as angels carved in the roof of a medieval church, have a property of survival against vicissitude and hostile circumstance. Seen now, their visual reception is radically different to how they were viewed when originally commissioned. Reconciling these differing contexts of gazing forms a sociological ambition of the study.

It is too sweeping to suggest that an era of the mechanical reproduction of art carries some germ that nibbles away at aura. In the setting of religion, there is always hope for a healing of the eyes to secure sensibilities of aura. Such viewing is not a function of cultural circumstances of production and reception of objects. What has changed is the loss of inhibition in the construction of images. The facility with which these can be made has obscured the need to attend to protocols for viewing images, particularly those that would benefit from an eye cast with a diffidence and a humility of regard. The technology that so easily makes images distracts attention from the need to service rituals of regard, where what is seen is venerated for what it points to beyond, to the unseen. In a peculiar way, mobilisation of the social to understand the construction of images facilitates their hallowing. The social not only assists in effecting recollection of what is important to notice but also in marking out images designated as doors that might open to see the unseen.

The invention of photography enabled images to be made in ways that dissolved lingering spiritual inhibitions about the freeness of their manufacture. In modernity, a lot of redundancy notices have been served, and it might seem that the artist, the painter, also received one. Photography permitted the apparently exact making of images in a democratising process available to all. No special spiritual, aesthetic or creative powers were required, no virtuous humility in the task of creating an image was necessary, for modernity had sprung the gift of rendering the visual in culture unproblematic. This gift further confirmed the god-like status of man that he could make any image, at any time, instantly, could collect these indefinitely and could have a monopoly of pleasure in what he saw. More worrisomely, the endless capacity to reproduce images without reference to the original (the photographic negative has no artistic value) might signify miraculous powers that distract from the need to attend to the prototype.

II

The making of images lies at the root of Baudelaire's account of modernity. In his famous essay, the *flâneur*, observer, philosopher, sometimes dealing in heroic or religious subjects, sometimes closer to the novelist or the moralist, is the 'painter of the passing moment and of all the suggestions of eternity that it contains'.[25] Attitudes to the seen and the unseen (in partial resemblance to their theological visualisations) emerge in the attitudes of the *flâneur* in the genesis of modernity. His gaze is not idle, nor is it vacant. The painter, the newly recovered convalescent, has a childlike curiosity about the world he sees going by in the city. He is dazzled by what he sees. Seeking to chronicle in visual form what he saw, he sketches, but like a draughtsman and as one who draws from memory.[26] In seeking to transfer into the realm of visual culture, the painter anticipates the photographer. As Sontag observed, 'photography first comes into its own as an extension of the eye of the middle class *flâneur*, whose sensibility was so accurately charted by Baudelaire'.[27] There is, however, one crucial difference. The photographer needs no memory to draw on to make an image; the eye of the camera captures it effortlessly, instantly and accurately. The arrival of the photographer to rival the artist raises three important issues.

First, the photographer has an almost miraculous power to intervene and capture a moment of time. He can freeze the fleeting in the transient and immortalise it. In the exercise of these powers he becomes god-like in his capacity to capture the essence of modernity. Thus, as Barthes indicated, 'what the Photograph reproduces to infinity has occurred only once; the Photograph mechanically repeats what could never be repeated existentially'.[28] The living moment of actually seeing is different to what is seen in the photograph. It can capture an essence, but not the radiance of the personality of the sitter. What is caught is a surface on the face. Lighting makes its own language of inference in the picture so shot. This bears on a point of Benjamin that the camera gets close to the subject, but at a price. The distancing properties of aura become overridden in the powers of proximity the camera realises. The necessary magicing of distance is easily sacrificed. The opportunity for use of this technology enables the claims of a reverential distance to be ignored, resulting in the sacrifice of the aura so necessary for a work of art.

Though it has shortcomings, photography has claims to be a form of art. It offers sights deeper and more exact than the naked eye can see.[29] Indeed, it can capture what the eye cannot see, and to that degree the camera makes its own dimensions of the seen and the unseen – through the miracle of technology. At the time of its invention, as Slater indicates, the camera revolutionised access to worlds that were unseen and that could not be seen. This capacity to expand the agenda of the visual lent a property of magicing to its powers in relation to spectacle.[30] The enlargement of visual opportunities with the invention of the camera formed part of a wider movement of concern with spectacle in the late eighteenth and nineteenth centuries that Jervis has noted. More than anything, this expanded puzzles over the seen and the unseen, the absent and the present, the surface and the depth of appearances, issues that have become infinitely more complex in an era of virtual reality, where image and reality have become hopelessly confused.[31] What was miraculous in technology has been secularised by endless use in a culture of postmodernity where the significance of what is seen is often confused with its availability. In that expansion, the need to attend to a wisdom of discernment seems to have fallen into disrepute.

The second issue relates to the assumptions and presumptions surrounding the social construction of images. These are illustrated in the differing routes the photographer and the icon painter follow in assembling their images. The photographer does not require recourse to memory to make his image; the shutter does this for him. On the other hand, the icon painter reflects deeply into memory to find an image within that his inner eye sees but which needs to be framed without. His ambitions are unoriginal, for the icon follows stipulated forms, whereas for the photographer, originality is the name of his game. One prays and the other preys. One petitions for his image to unfold; the other stalks, predatory, waiting to snatch the shot. One fears idolatry; the other seeks it. One is humble before what he paints, lest he be guilty of presumption, for the image of God is not to be cast lightly. For the photographer, no such humble petition for access to the unseen seems necessary, bar restrictions of the law on privacy. His ambitions are to render seen what has not been seen before, and to hunt for images that reflect his powers. In so seeking, he trespasses with impunity, for as Sontag suggests to photograph people is to violate them, by seeing them as they never see themselves, by having knowledge of them they can never have; it turns people into objects that can be symbolically possessed.[32]

The right of possession of the image photographically appropriated is alien to the icon painter. He draws what he cannot possess, and sketches what he wishes to be possessed by. Whereas the photographer seeks to render the unseen seen exactly, the icon painter settles for a glimmer of the unseen in the image he imperfectly strives to make. Their attitude to the eternal and the transient is entirely different. The photographer wishes to freeze the eternal in the present and to render it transient no more. In so fixing, he makes his fame. He wishes to possess what he shoots. As Sontag has observed, 'photographs are a way of imprisoning reality, understood as recalcitrant, inaccessible; of making it stand still'.[33]

The icon painter, on the other hand, has no such ambitions to make God still. Instead what he seeks is to paint an image that reflects the serene stillness of a Divinity that radiates for those with eyes of faith to see. Whereas the photographer has aspirations to be original in all the frames, the icon painter deals with images in different circumstances. The humility that governs inscriptions of the Divine carries a price of denial of ambition to see all and to paint all, but the reward is a strange power of refraction, to mirror an aura of the Divine in images, deeply unoriginal, but profoundly original in what they disclose. The path of the icon painter is the exemplary route for coming to the antinomies of the seen and the unseen.

The third issue relates to the status of those who make a photographic image. It would be spurious to argue that the camera denies a role for the operative. The photographer arranges what is to be seen or not, and in the angle and in the frame draws out implications. As Sontag well observes, 'photography is the paradigm of an inherently equivocal connection between the self and the world'.[34] This is where the self can be effaced or celebrated, can be seen or unseen as part of the photographic act. She also makes a striking point on the moral powers of the camera. On one hand, in its portrayals, it can affirm virtue, qualities of heroism and fortitude, or moments of compassion, but on the other hand it can savage in its framing by chronicling acts of barbarity that cause viewers to turn away their face. Referring ingeniously to Feurbach, Sontag points to a dilemma, a slight of hand that photographic art effects. Feurbach drew attention to the way expectations of his era deemed images to be more authentic than the originals as representations of life. Images become the gauge of reality and not just representations of its form.[35] In the making of images, the democratisation wrought by photography and endlessly amplified in the Internet makes all viewers gods. They effect their own deification in the images and likenesses they make, and in so doing they effect their own divinities. A hope is expressed that the self can see a better picture of itself, one that reflects its desires and ambitions.

Every picture tells a tale and often it is one of the personality of the photographer himself. By manipulating camera angles, by using soft or hard focus, and in the art of framing, the photographer sets the contours of the narrative as he seeks to capture an essence of the sitter. It is what eludes in the picture that generates a curiosity and that makes a photograph worthy of a second look. Some essence might be caught of the sitter, some characterising property that requires a closer look. The camera has a power to render apparent that which the eye cannot see. It has a capacity to render something visible from the invisible; thus, through mechanical means aspects of the unseen can be seen, though in a different sense to the social efforts required to realise these in a theological realm of understanding. This power of the camera relates to Foucault's notion of invisible visibility.

The paradoxical link between the visible and the invisible that Foucault raised has been put to use to understand the medical gaze. It is the power of the gaze to embody the sensory but also an epistemological capacity to structure what is not seen that Foucault terms invisible visibility. This not only refers to what is seen, but also to what can be treated as an invisible truth, one revealed by the eye of knowledge. To see at both levels of the visible and the invisible marks the clinical gaze and its power to see and discern. In the end it is the fate to die that combines the visible and the invisible. As Foucault writes: 'death left its old tragic heaven and became the lyrical core of man: his invisible truth; his visible secret'.[36] Again, Foucault stumbles across the theology of the seen and the unseen – and runs.

The visual, the camera and the eye in the tower, refract back in ways that affect and effect social arrangements and the adjustments to be made whether the actor is seen or not. The camera penetrates a nexus of relationships and if it succeeds, it manages to tell of these in an image that reflects their totality. It does so as a witness by providing an indisputable record of having been there. In itself, the camera has an impact on the social, not only as a means of validation of what was seen, but also to solemnise what *should* be seen. In an imaginative manner, invoking Durkheim, Bourdieu explores photography in terms of its social function and illustrates the way the camera generates its own rituals. It becomes an instrument of self-description for the group and a means of adding to its social memory. Elaborately set up, the photograph enables a group to make a visual statement of their own definition and form of integration.[37] The layout of a group photograph expresses a hierarchical arrangement, the allocation of a field of positions laid out in the manner of a sociogram, where a nexus of relationships is to be read into the image. Bourdieu suggests that this power of image making is why photographic practice, acting as

a ritual of solemnization and consecration of the group and the world, perfectly fulfils the deeper intentions of the 'popular aesthetic', the festive aesthetic, that is, the aesthetic of communication with others and communion with the world.[38]

Despite these powers of sacralisation, the vividness of the camera and its facility of use, there are illusory considerations hovering around the camera and its image-making powers. As Sontag points out, 'the camera's rendering of reality must always hide more than it discloses'. She goes on to argue that the

> omnipresence of photographs has incalculable effect on our ethical sensibility. By furnishing this already crowded world with a duplicate one of images, photography makes us feel that the world is more available than it really is.[39]

It is this property of availability that worries Sontag, where the photograph governs indices of reality; the camera is the calibration of all that is seen and all that ought to be. As Balzac observed, 'the whole of a life can be summed up in a momentary appearance'.[40] This is to echo the notion that the medium, the camera, governs what is to be deemed visual. It is the authority for what is seen and can be. It supplies a moral account of what is seen in an instance. The camera offers the possibility of making an image that will resolve the needs of a personal identity. Again, to cite Sontag, 'photography is seen as an acute manifestation of the individualised "I", the homeless private self astray in an overwhelming world – mastering reality by a fast visual anthologizing of it'.[41]

The Internet has speeded up this whole process in ways that make necessary sociological attention to facets of visual culture. These advances mark an enormous distance from Benjamin's worries about the mechanical reproduction of art. Images now float off into the global village for viewing by lurkers and voyeurs entirely unaccountable for what they see, with no sense of commitment of obligation to their objects of gaze, and no reverence for the social ambience of their local circumstances of representation and reception. Far from mitigating the need to distinguish between the seen and the unseen, the facility in which images can be de-contextualised has accentuated the need to attend to what lies below their surfaces.

Jervis draws attention to two useful facets of visual culture: the notion of image and of allegory. First, his reference to Flem's characterisation of image is useful. He has argued that 'the image exists somewhere between imagination and reality', inhabiting 'a symbolic space where the past merges with the present, the visible and with invisible'. In what can be described as the 'frenzy of the visible', Jervis points to the increased concern from the late eighteenth century with spectacle, mass entertainment and the display of events increasingly dominating cultural sensibilities and expectations.[42] In the second point, Jervis goes on to make a striking reference to Baudelaire's stress on the notion of allegory as a property that feeds on the imagination. Allegory raises issues not only of depth, but also of deciphering. The notion of allegory involves a looking back, a property of nostalgia to make sense of something that has disappeared from view.[43] This concern with the allegorical shapes the imagination of modernity as it seeks for needs that lie below the surface of the *flâneur's* existence. The arrival of the Internet intensifies these properties of allegory. Never before has the urge to see the unseen been better serviced.

Computer games, graphics and the visual wonders to be found in virtual reality, all feed the imagination. These conjure up all manner of imaginary worlds that permit frontiers to be crossed, images to be re-arranged and tales to be re-cast, for one of the unexpected outcomes of digital culture is the rehabilitation of stories and narratives. Mythologies, symbols, tales and heroes, and battles with good and evil have taken on a new visual life. Ironically, cyberspace has facilitated the return of what modernity cast as incredible. This technology, far from giving comfort to the amnesia of modernity about such matters, seems to have supplied a means for their resuscitation. On the screen, the need for enchantment is given a visual plenitude. The pre-modern has returned. The enchantment postmodernity marked as its distance from the endemic disenchantment of modernity, fuels this need to look back past its amnesia. Great themes are re-written in visual form that galvanise the masses who seek an ocular liberation in fantasy. The ghosts of virtual religions have returned as a societal unconsciousness is stirred to see what it forgot. The shock of delight that greeted the cinematic trilogy of the *Lord of the Rings* illustrates the point well.

Dark, deep struggles over the ring mark the return of fascination with issues of good and its triumph over evil. To see such tales is to see human destiny re-written. Although there might be a property of virtual religion to the *Lord of the Rings*, elements of the prototype, the Catholicism of Tolkein, lurk in issues of seeking and redemption, in apocalyptic struggles between good and evil. Technology has presented in vivid and imaginative form issues of the seen and the forces of the unseen that require attention if what is fated is not to transpire. These rehabilitations form part of an urge of an age hungry for the spiritual and enchantment. New Age religions in the 1990s marked further turns in concerns with the countercultural that emerged in the late 1960s. This is not to suggest that seeing the unseen in theological expectations is the unproblematic beneficiary of these shifts in technology and its relationship to visual culture. Rather it is to suggest that cultural needs in regard to the visual are not adequately recognised in contemporary theology. It still does not feel the need to write a grammar for discerning the visual. Some of the charges made by sociologists in the late 1960s that modernisation was taking down the scaffolding between the seen and the unseen have taken on a new plausibility. The stark colours in which sagas and mythologies are cast in virtual reality mark an unfortunate contrast with the apologetic and pallid paintings of heaven and earth that liberal theologians have sought so assiduously to supply in their endemic misreadings of the expectations of contemporary culture.

In some way, digital culture has undermined the reticence of the eye to look. New ways of seeing salvation have to be formulated, for the times are changing and the sites for sights are shifting. Unexpectedly, in the light of technology, new twilight zones hover for the eye to glimpse in glimmers. These might incline in a theological direction. The issue of virtual reality has changed the way the seen and the unseen are to be seen.

III

For some, the unseen God of religion from whom all images emanate has been replaced by tiny computer chips that seem to have similar powers of creativity. It is not transparent to those with a slight technological mind as to how this plenitude of visual gifts appears from what might as well be nothing. As options to see expand, the source contracts, but in the case of the Internet in rather different circumstances. Unlike the eye in the tower that uses its power to shrivel the actor into a disciplined image, life in the Internet offers exactly the opposite. Active rather than passive, the actor interacts and exchanges with what the unseen produces as images that incarnate a virtual reality. This endless expansion of virtual reality, where anything can be seen points to a paradox Bauman has well expressed about life in liquid modernity. Things become more hidden with the expansion of opportunity to see. Thus, he suggests that 'when the Other dissolves in the Many, the first thing to be washed away is the Face. The Other(s) is (are) now faceless. They are *persons* ("persona" means mask, and masks hide not disclose faces)'.[44] This echoes some paradoxes noted earlier that increased transparency of trust seems to lead to a greater sense of distrust and the effect of the light of reason managed to generate forces of darkness in Panopticism.

The issues raised by virtual reality are complex, recent and still unravelling. In its most complete use, the term refers to forms of visual technology that control sensory perception and that insulate the self entirely from contact with the social. Such advances in technology that simulate new worlds of experience are exceptional and are often associated with laboratory experimentation, particularly in psychology. In its advanced form, virtual reality comes near a hyper-reality where what is experienced is part of a physical reality. It refers to what comes after the Internet and marks a capacity for radical disembodiment of self and sensibility. Its concerns are with what can be seen of people and objects in three-dimensional forms. The viewer sees these as if inhabiting a social reality, but one produced in digital or computer-based forms.[45] The spaces so opened out through technology seem revolutionary in their capacities to make images, to render the seen in simulations that a decade ago would have been unimaginable. Virtual reality realises a property of 'as if' on a scale that transcends problems of time and space. As Rheingold indicated, virtual reality 'is a magical world onto other worlds, from molecules to minds', where reality disappears behind the screen.[46] Cranford supplies an equally succinct definition of virtual reality as '*a human-computer interface that immerses the user in an illusory world created by the system to enjoin the greatest degree of participation possible within that world*' (his italics). For him, virtual reality is the final stop on a trajectory in the desire to create and engender the sense that *we are there*.[47] Virtual reality relates to forms of technology that completely envelop the self, or that leave it with degrees of detachment as a viewer with space to retreat.

The military origins of the Internet in the USA as a secure means of communication conveyed the notion that it was a purely technological invention, one without a cultural image. As its domestic use expanded, a cultural image was developed in negotiations between producers and users. As a reaction to its military origins, the Internet took on libertarian and populist properties, being designated as a site for unfettered expression and a realm of free exchange.[48] Its image was shaped to mark its capacity to circulate the communication of moral and social ideals. In its newly cast cultural shape, the Internet was endowed with a pioneering image, one that signified its capacity to open out new frontiers. These came to reflect utopian possibilities. From its beginnings, the Internet offered a radical democratisation of access to images, but also their individualised manufacture. The use of this technological invention seemed to fulfil imagination in ways that bordered on science fiction. The instructions for use are direct, images and information can be very rapidly retrieved, and instantaneous satisfactions are offered. Although the technology is changing, and interactive viewing of television is becoming widespread, the Internet is still an exemplary site, one with its own claims to a community of users who interact through chatrooms, websites and other forms for the posting of messages. The literatures on the Internet and the virtual reality it produces are vast but are on the boundaries of sociological recognition.

Despite its disclaimers, the Internet seeks to replicate the necessities of a social world and its efforts to civilise exchanges. Procedures have to be found to bring an order to a technology where disorder is all too possible. This gives rise to what is known as *netiquette*, the conventions for working in cyberspace, where anarchy is all too possible. Although the Internet offers endless individualised access to the visual, some forms of social ordering are required and these have not been well explored. The Internet involves an unexpected amount of social collusion to secure a common effect, where the viewer is not just an isolated gazer. But as Coates indicates, little research has been undertaken on this *being together*. This sense of being together lacks one crucial ingredient that Coates draws attention to – Goffman's notion of co-presence. It is this sense of being before an image, but not in its living ambience, that limits life in cyberspace. It can mimic social reality, but cannot reproduce it as felt. To that degree, the Internet produces images whose surface demands further excavation and retrieval in some authentic ambience that only the social can supply. The issue of co-presence indicates how an interaction order is established through a language of inference based on textual exchange, one with its own distinctive forms and morality.[49]

The exchanges of the chatroom might involve a presentation of self, but not in Goffman's notion, one based on face-to-face interaction. In the chatroom, a form of disembodied communal affiliation is possible that is but an aggregate of viewers not co-present to each other.[50] A face can be presented that has no occupying self. On chatrooms, the face appears as a mask, an avatar, an icon-based image that becomes symbolic of the self so displaced. It can be changed about at whim. This gives rise to a crucial weakness of life in cyberspace that Coates catches well. He argues that 'the possibility of an infinite community because the lack of face-to-face sight heralds simultaneously a kind of death to "difference" and a closing off of the social'.[51] The freedom and liberty the Internet offers, its property of frontier work, can lead to the eradication of the social and to an escape from obligations to its sustenance. This escape can be illusory. At some point, however addictive viewing of virtual reality becomes, some re-entry into the social is required, however hazardous the prospect of return may be. This return can be difficult, for the social appears as disordered and difficult to navigate. It is not surprising that disenchantment over the Internet should come, and it did, in two stages.

The first stage came sometime between the autumn of 1996 and the spring of 1997, when the Internet gained an image problem in the traditional press. It became a sign of 'millennial paranoia'.[52] Oddly, these fears suggested that this form of technology could not handle the sacred ordering of time and its consequences. The second stage reflected the feeling that the allures of the Internet had been oversold. This disillusion led to a collapse in share values of facets of the dot-com industry between 2001 and 2002.[53]

The Internet provides a unique means of escaping from social reality, but it also a means of re-ordering it, a point Holmes has noted.[54] Rather prophetically, Cranford suggested that 'as VR technologies improve, the distinction between "real life" and virtual experiences will blur'.[55] The worlds so presented require no constraints and the opportunities for searching for these are limitless. Virtual reality might offer endless pleasures of searching and finding images to the point that the viewer comes to believe in his own disembodiment. He might feel that there should be no limits to the pleasures he seeks. These ambitions become the basis of deceptions easy to carry off, given the anonymity of viewing the Internet offers. Adults can pretend to be children talking to other children for nefarious purposes. The viewer can have the status of being a lurker,[56] a sort of super voyeur, who scrolls without being seen and whose gaze leaves no identifying marks. Lurkers can shop around indefinitely. All manner of sexual fantasies can be fed in ways that can become addictive, as more and more images are ruthlessly collected. The Internet offers not only ultimate forms of escapism, but also endless re-inventions of the self that never need to be confronted or scrutinised. As Coates writes well,

> no matter how chaotic the world beyond the screen becomes, users can return to the safety of their terminal and the disembodied relationships these imply. Here accounts can be terminated when those they interact with become 'too real'. The use of free email services are crucial here as individuals can simply terminate one *Identity* and create another.[57]

Hine offers one of the few studies that supplies an ethnography of the Internet, one with its own form of reflexivity and social construction. Her study is based on the link between the Internet and the trial of Louise Woodward, who was charged with second-degree murder of a child in her care in 1998. The case aroused considerable public interest in the USA and in the UK and was noteworthy for the judge's deliberations being posted on the Internet. Many websites offering support for her emerged and these formed the basis of Hine's study.

The value of her study lies in its chronicling of the social factors shaping the use of the Internet when mobilised to deal with a particular issue. This gets around the indefinite randomness often associated with studies of virtual reality whose basis seems violated by any notion of selectivity. Her concern is with studying ideas of strategic relevance rather than seeking objective characterisation. For her, 'the challenge of virtual ethnography is to explore the making of boundaries and the making of connections, especially between the "virtual" and the "real"'.[58] Given the focus of her concerns, it is not surprising that she treats websites as forms of social action.[59] Using Clifford's notion of a 'connective ethnography', she suggests that this provides a means of treating the Internet not so much in terms of 'being there' as that of 'getting there'.[60] It is this property of searching to find a 'being there' that marks the allure of surfing on the Internet.

Although it can be used for random viewing, most users are likely to surf with a purpose, to seek some connection, some image unseen in social reality, but one that can be found somewhere on the screen. The almost limitless expansion of websites makes sociological characterisations of the Internet hazardous. Leaving aside those who use the Internet as an engine for sexual gratification, there are some serious users, and some of these searches are for sites that offer prospects for religious affiliation. There are more religious seekers than the image of the Internet would suggest. As Brasher observes, 'one of the best-kept secrets of cyberspace is the surprising amount of religious practice that takes place there'.[61] A startling array of religious sites can be found. Instead of treating the Internet as some vehicle for pioneering social experimentation into the realms of science fiction, it should be regarded as a marketplace with websites for prophecy, all displaying a message that ultimately matters. The significance of the Internet can be overrated and some come to believe its own propaganda that it is *the* site for cultural expression. Whether this is true or false is beside the point. For the purposes of this study the Internet provides material for understanding the way seeing is related to believing. More importantly, the Internet points to the need to attend to the visual dimensions of religion where websites become channels for conversion and transformation. What goes on the Internet opens out wider questions for understanding the link between sociology and visual culture in matters of religion.

IV

The Heaven's Gate cult was like many others around California that some sociologists of religion love to chronicle for their archives. Small in size, formed in the 1970s, its leader, Marshall Applewhite, named 'Do', a former Catholic, had a small, highly dedicated following of men and women. It had concerns with the apocalypse and played on fears about the end of time. Its beliefs were much influenced by science fiction, UFOs, *The X-files* and New Age religions. Disembodiment was a domain value, for they treated their bodies as 'shells' or 'containers' that frustrated efforts to realise the next level of life. As a number of its members were website designers, it became noted as a sect that sought to recruit through the Internet. This reflected its efforts to form a religion fit for life in cyberspace. Heaven's Gate might have just been one odd cult amongst many but for the circumstances of its self-extinction.

Its core of 39 members committed suicide in San Diego, California, in March 1997, and of these eight of the men including 'Do' had had themselves castrated. The website collapsed in the face of the massive public and mass media interest in such bizarre events. The precipitating event for their mass exodus as 'the away' team was the arrival of the Hale-Bopp comet, and the belief that behind it was a flying saucer that would take them to another level. A survivor of the 'exit' sought to maintain the memory of Heaven's Gate on a website still to be found on the Internet, but public interest in the cult rapidly waned.[62]

In one way they were part of a lineage of exclusive inward looking cults whose isolation from the world enhanced the powers of their charismatic leaders and facilitated mass suicides.[63] Yet they left some awkward questions, not so much over their claims to be a religion but their relationship to the Internet which, for some, became demonised after the event. In her comprehensive essay on the link between the cult and cyberspace, Robinson notes that 'it comes as no surprise that the people who joined Heaven's Gate would be attracted to the Net and digital culture in which it can be difficult to distinguish real life from virtual life'.[64] The dangers of exploring too far into virtual reality in what might be termed a virtual religion were all too evident. It generated what Potz felt 'promises to be the first great Internet mystery'.[65] The movement did not resolve age-old issues of final destinations. The lesson to be learnt is that technology could not resolve issues of the frailty of the human condition; rather it accentuated them.

While the sociological significance of Heaven's Gate might lie in the use of the Internet to recruit,[66] more worrisome issues arise over the capacity of its websites to blur distinctions between the virtual and the real in relation to religion. In the case of the Internet, judgements had to be made on the basis of the visual. In her assessment of the Heaven Gate departures, Brasher rightly indicates that 'as the boundaries between religion and other cultural creeds thin, the ability of traditional religions to adjudicate interpretation of their myths and symbols is diminished'.[67] In the case of Heaven's Gate, the lack of a coherent self laid the seed beds for a self-annihilation.[68] As a cult, Heaven's Gate had its own internal culture, but one disembodied from a wider social ambit. The emergence of such cults, as in the case of funda-mentalism, represents a vote of no confidence in modernity. As Maniscalco suggests, such killer sects can be seen as an extreme reaction to the disaggre-gation, disembedding and dislocation of a globalised culture. These sects expressed an urge to effect a distance from the world and to generate a radical new agenda of difference. In their effort to escape from the entrapment of authority in traditional religions, they themselves become highly authoritarian in practice and as Maniscalco indicates, these sects are often characterised by sexual abuse.[69]

The fate of the Heaven's Gate movement points to a curiosity: the way Weber's choice of elective affinity between this world and the next re-emerges in cyberspace. It comes to replicate a sociological dilemma for dealing with the seen and the unseen. Images of cyberspace present a fantasy world of escape where the virtual is manifested in ways that absolve reference to the social and to the divisions of the human condition. This forms part of its mythology, of being a free space, where all can see without restriction. Unsurprisingly, the Internet offers endless possibilities for proselytisation and even if the outcomes for recruitment are problematic, the scope for reli-gious propaganda is enormous.[70] More than might be realised, cyberspace is missionary territory. Cyberspace provides a marketplace of images and texts that reflect the divisions of religion on the ground of culture where matters of belief have to be constructed. In this regard, the issues of the seen and the unseen become amplified and are placed in a sharper focus than was ever the case before. This becomes apparent in the division effected by the opportunities cyberspace offers between issues of religion-on-line, items that relate to information about religious belief and their organisation and on-line-religion, where viewers participate in what might be termed a virtual liturgy. Helland points to the way on-line-religion provides a site of practice for a church of cyberspace.[71]

In one of the few efforts to examine virtual church services, Schroeder *et al.* examined the form that an interactive ritual takes on the Internet.

Although co-presence is lacking, a symbolic and textual order is presented in a tight and structured manner. Despite their small size, 'virtual services, by analogy with a "normal" church service, take place within a relatively public context'. The informal, interactive style of services studied on the E-Church tended to be charismatic in form. The respondents felt that they were co-present to each other, although not in a face-to-face form.[72]

In Catholicism, the validity of a sacrament's conferral depends on the co-presence of its recipients. This issue recently emerged over 'on-line confessions'. Co-presence relates to culpability, hence the need for the presence of the sinner and for him or her to see that their sins are forgiven.[73] Prohibitions on virtual sacraments relate to matters of validity; that those receiving the sacrament have to be present at its point of conferral. Thus, a recent Vatican document on the Internet made the definite point that

> virtual reality is no substitute for the Real Presence of Christ in the Eucharist, the sacramental reality of the other sacraments, and shared worship in a flesh-and-blood human community. There are no sacraments on the Internet; and even the religious experiences possible there by the grace of God are insufficient apart from real-world interaction with other persons of faith.[74]

The position of the Vatican regarding the Internet would reflect Helland's distinction above between religion-on-line that it would mark as acceptable and on-line-religion which it would treat as theologically unacceptable. The Vatican defended religion-on-line on the basis that websites could overcome distance and isolation of its believers. Websites were commended for effecting social solidarity. They could enable viewers to keep in touch with each other in virtual communities that compensate for what could not be accomplished in off-line social circumstances.[75] This is illustrated in the alien field of Gothic culture, where a dispersed membership realises an identity through a virtual community on the Internet. This gives them a focal point for the construction of an identity. Their virtual community proclaims a standard for identification marking how they ought to appear.[76] The Internet facilitates a sense of solidarity amongst fundamentalist groups who use virtual communities to regroup. They become the beneficiaries of a global technology, where the local is given universal powers of representation.[77] All this contributes to the vitality of religion and opens out possibilities hitherto unavailable. In this context, Lyon is right to suggest that 'much secularization theory produced earlier in the twentieth century mistook the deregulation of religion for the decline of religion'.[78]

Cyberspace and the Internet have accentuated religious differences, not eradicated them. Far from entrapping religion, cyberspace enlarges its possibilities and offers new opportunities for the self to find itself in new ways of mirroring the reality it desires. No longer restricted by local prejudice, those seeking a religiosity can find it in images wrought in cyberspace. Religious forms of life need not be airbrushed out of existence in the malicious actions of the ungodly who govern newspapers and television; true believers can post their own accounts on the Internet and tell their own stories. Far from locking everything in an eternal present, cyberspace plays its own distinctive part in rehabilitating tradition and memory. It permits funda-mentalists to reconnect to notions of tradition that can be presented in visual form through the Internet. Yet the use of the Internet does not get around endemic problems of observing religions and putting them to domestic use in contexts alien to those of their sacred gestation. Narayan has pursued these issues well in his essay on Indian ascetics and the traffic in their images between India and North America that give rise to much perplexed reflexivity.

Reflecting on the popularity of Indian ascetics, he argues that the popular-isation of these ascetic images in an alien culture drains them of their religious overtones. They come to represent the needs and illusions of the importing culture. It treats these images with scant regard for the issues he felt had emerged in his fieldwork, of finding an understanding of the 'hierarchical relations of the observing Self and observed Other'. The imperi-alising gaze of the importers was little concerned with these matters. For him the notion of 'being there', which so characterises fieldwork accounts, has to be offset by 'being here', in the university or scholarly nexus one inhabits. He raises an important question: 'what happens to anthropological knowledge if the boundary between "the field" and "the home" is rendered porous?'[79] For him, there is no segregation between the self and the Other, and between the field and the social existence of the anthropologist. This gen-erates particular difficulties when there is a religious dimension to 'the field' and 'the home'. A choice has to be made between the two if sociology is not to be disembodied. This issue of choice was well expressed by William James who noted that

the science of religions may not be an equivalent for living religion; and if we turn to the inner difficulties of such a science, we see that a point comes when she must drop the purely theoretic attitude, and either let her knots remain uncut, or have them cut by active faith.[80]

The breadth of religious websites available on the Internet gives witness to the degree to which a partial picture emerges in other media forms. Thus, in a surprising way, the Internet fills in enormous gaps in knowledge about religion, more particularly in its specific facets. There is much in Brasher's comment that 'the computer craze of the last decades exacerbates Americans' loss of the past'. This is because it locks them in a 'perpetual present'. As she suggests, 'cyberspace offers the ideal public space for a people without a history'. Cyberspace enables viewers to construct a history and to re-invent images of the past in ways that make them vivid.[81] Chains of memory can be re-linked, so that what is of the past seems vibrant and new in the present, all the more so because it appears in cyberspace. A vivid example of this is provided by Dagenais, of how a virtual pilgrimage to Compostela was generated for his students.[82] The technology supplies an aura and makes vivid that which other media forms deem lifeless or unworthy of notice. It is these magical powers of transformation that effect a rehabilitation of memory and give to the Internet peculiarly facilitating powers for religion.

Websites supply windows on worlds hidden from view. Thus, on the Internet, one can find the witty website of some Dutch Poor Clares, on clarissen. eindhoven@inter.nl.net, where a nun answers a query 'why am I here?' Coming from an entirely non-religious background, she always had a desire for God. Pressed with questions on all sides, and feeling an emptiness as she watched drugs devour more and more of her friends, this young woman felt chosen by God to live as a symbol of Divine Love. Clad in a full traditional Franciscan habit, this young nun gets up at night to pray. She fasts and abstains from all that the world affirms as of value. Seeming to retreat to the antique, she supplies a good response to charges of escapism from the world. She writes on the website:

> only that which is eternal is forever new. And the unchanging language of love is totality. Insofar as monastic tradition speaks that tongue of total self-donation is it forever new. New wine in young hearts made increasingly capacious as tradition tutors them in love's native tongue. Such totality knows no limits of time or place. Unencumbered by the codes of comfortable conformism, it can span entire oceans as well as centuries.

In this setting, the Internet can supply a link between image and its rationale in ways that are unique. Those engaged on the inside of religion, as liturgical workers, choirs, servers, priests, or those in religious life can post their own tales in ways that link biography to the expectations of visual culture in ways hitherto unavailable.

Religious orders seem to have found a natural outlet for their talents on the Internet. Those of the Dominicans and the Benedictines particularly stand out. Their websites are often works of art, laden with beautiful calligraphy and with lots of information about their founders and their distinctive charisms. On the website of Stanbrook Abbey, England, one clicks and enters a marvellous set of graphics that describes their day of prayer and work. The hands of a large clock rotate marking points where a plenitude of information emerges on their liturgical offices and their round of life. Websites for religious orders enable the young, as postulants or novices, to tell their tales about coming in with a view to encouraging others to follow. These tales are frank, and smack of authenticity. So far little is known of the effects of websites on recruitment to religious orders. One senses that those with a definite image, habit and a communal and structured life, present the most credible websites and it is to these that the young are turning to re-invent a tradition and to rehabilitate a memory. What emerges from these accounts is the unexpected way the Internet facilitates a contextualisation and gives witness to its basis.

In an overview on researching religion in cyberspace, Dawson draws attention to a number of important points. First, for her the Internet '*is, simultaneously, a product of this age of uncertainty, a promoting agent of this uncertainty, and a cultural response to this uncertainty*' (her italics).[83] Secondly, she draws attention to the link between the Internet and the formation of identity and the strong desire it facilitates for a connection between on-line and off-line social relations.[84] She suggests that interactive websites that link on-line and off-line sites might form true virtual communities, a building up that could be expanded.[85] This reflects a particular capacity of the Internet, one which the Vatican document on the Internet and ethics mentioned above particularly endorsed. There are indications of virtual communities of faith emerging on the Internet that serve to link with off-line life. Brasher provides a useful example of the use of the Internet to find a monastery to visit.[86] Many monastic websites, besides giving information on their way of life and on how to join, provide the basis for a virtual community for oblates, and for collaborative prayer between those who live in the monastery and those whose connections with it are largely made on the Internet. This bringing together into a virtual community of prayer is well illustrated by the success of the Jesuit-run website, *Sacred Space*.[87]

V

Sociological inhibitions about distinguishing between the virtual and real forms of religion, discussed in Chapter 1, have taken on a new existence in relation to dealings with what comes from cyberspace and other forms of electronic imaging. There is no point in saying that the need to distinguish between the virtual and the real does not matter. Images surrounding sexuality and violence might be kept locked in virtual reality, but there is always the risk that responses to these might be taken into social life with evil consequences. Appropriations of these images might reflect a failure to distinguish between the virtual and the real. In law and in common morality, the viewer is culpable for this failure to distinguish. The risk is that the virtual becomes a surrogate for real life. This might be to forget a distinction Goffman makes in *Stigma* between actual and virtual social identity. The former refers to characterisations proved to be possessed and the latter to those imputed in potential retrospect. Some form of negotiation, some career of looking is required to reconcile both.[88] If, as suggested above, the seen and the unseen have antinomial properties, then in strict terms they are irreconcilable. But this would be to render the distinction between them unprofitable in theological *and* sociological terms. Far from paralysing and cutting the self into two, responses to antinomies can effect an enlargement as the actor seeks to cope with their contradictory implications. In this regard, Shields provides an innovative twist on the notion of the virtual.

For him, the virtual has a property of the almost, of some nearness or proximity to the original. First, Shields indicates that in its Latin derivation the virtual relates to what is of virtue, that is powers, strengths, personal qualities and capacities to produce effects. It is this transformative property of the virtual to complete in some credible or tolerable way what is incomplete that interests this study. This notion of the virtual arises in his brief mention of the relationship of the man to the angel. The value of his insight is that it permits the introduction of issues of agency into the notion of the virtual. Secondly, he draws attention to the theological overtones of the term, notably around issues of transubstantiation. Is the bread and wine in the Eucharist changed into a Real Presence or is it something virtual? In both cases, the virtual is pointing to what is above reality but also to what transcends it. The powers and traits combine to effect a radical transformation.[89] These insights shape the way the virtual might be explored for the issues of social transformation it opens up rather than closes down in some tyrannical form of visual false consciousness.

The viewing of endless images through the Internet has brought into focus issues that would have been deemed insignificant a decade or so ago. As the Internet expands in use, for shopping, recreational and educational purposes, the relational aspects of the visual take on an unforeseen significance. Use of the Internet generates a whole host of questions about the disembodiment of the viewer, his co-presence with the object of sight, and the community and identity that result from viewing, that forces a choice between the virtual and the real. In these complexities and as images do not require contexts of realisation, the social as a medium of visual expression takes on an unexpected vulnerability. These powers to wrest any image from any context might seem new, yet they carry forward old dilemmas, some of which extend back to the growth of printing.

Before printing, sacred texts were copied by hand and largely confined to the libraries of cathedrals and monasteries. This rarity served to signify the sacred qualities of these texts whose viewing and reading were exceptional. The rise of printing of the Bible facilitated individual and private appreciation without regard to ritual setting. This democratisation of use was greatly facilitated by the translation of the Bible into the vernacular. Study of scripture became a private activity, one where individual judgement and conscience was to be formed and this right formed a crucial plank of the Protestant call for Reformation. The difficulty was that stress on private readings made it unclear why public readings in ritual settings were so necessary. Stress on private rights for reading made ritual public readings seem redundant. It is true that Protestantism laid great stress on the primacy of the Word in rituals and in sermons, but it did so in ways that were isolated from the visual. These props were removed but as they were the magic surrounding the proclamation of the Word evaporated. Its public utterance gripped less and less as the slow slide of Protestantism into secularisation indicates, especially in Northern Europe.

Vulnerability to abuse or destruction has always been the fate of religious images. This reflects their power, not only for transformation, but also for division. Efforts to break the link between faith and its visual manifestation in images are not new. In the seventeenth century, Japanese missionaries were given a cruel choice of either walking on an image of Christ, thus apostatising in the eyes of their persecutors, or refusing and being staked on the shore to be drowned by the incoming tide and so abandoning their flocks.[90] The sea of faith had a different set of meanings on those shores.

The recent Vatican document on the Internet observed that it is neither good nor evil. The moral status of the Internet depends on the uses made of it and the choices to be realised. The question of virtual reality simply accentuates these stakes, most particularly in relation to religion.[91] In this setting, the virtual bears on the almost, what might be realised in heroic struggle, a point Shields recognises in his comments on the link between the angelic and the pursuit of chastity. Rightly, Shields regards the virtual as a metaphor-making device. It has a property of escape from the confines of the material. Lying in his uses are properties of re-capturing, admittedly in digital form, and this is the property the Internet opens out.[92] This leads him to consider a term he coins: liminoid virtualities. These refer to zones and spaces that are virtual but also temporary in their contrasts to everyday life. They can be related to a wider culture, but also to the re-introduction of possibilities of transformations. It is this property of not only escaping but also of re-capturing that suggests the way the virtual as related to the liminal opens out a means of characterising the theological endeavour of seeing the unseen.

Shields draws attention to the 'betwixt and between' property of the liminal as Turner conceived it. The liminal denotes notions of threshold and in this context it relates to the sense the actor realises of gazing through the seen into the unseen and almost seeing it, but in ways difficult to articulate. It is not that one has seen the unseen; it is that one has come so close to seeing it that what is seen seems radically different. For Turner, the liminoid refers to what is individualised and artistic. It has a ritual property for it is a commodity that one plays with. In Turner's account, both the liminal and the liminoid relate to studying symbols in social action.[93] In this regard, the social is mobilised as a means of transformation of seeing.

Liminoid virtualities are the *fourth* version of the virtual. They mark the virtuous struggle to see the unseen, one that involves a gaze with grace of relief. They involve accepting what is temporary and artificial as virtual in terms of representations of the unseen. These supply contrasts to the material, the mundane and the everyday. It is the liberating aspect of the visionary that gives the term its use. In this way, a linkage can be made to some themes in *The City of God*. A value of liminoid virtualities is that they open out questions of who sees and to what end. Electing to see points to issues of embodiment, culpability and circumstance, but also the cultural milieu where the act of seeing the unseen flourishes or withers. Formulating links between virtue and the virtual builds on not only the morality of the gaze, but also its social construction and the inescapable implications of looking that can occur as the visual relentlessly expands. Increasingly, identity is based on what is seen and this generates moral implications for the gaze.

4
To See or Not to See: The Plight of the Voyeur

The notion of giving an arm and a leg for a good dinner took a literal turn in a court case in Germany, where it emerged that the guest at a dinner had offered himself as the main course. Apparently, the host took him at his word. This unexpected emergence of cannibalism signified an unpleasant void in the mortal expectations of a culture of postmodernity. The guest eaten had signified consent, so a defence was mounted on the basis of sexual taste and also euthanasia. What seemed a private matter took on unavoidable public dimensions. In the end, the cannibal was found guilty of manslaughter in January 2004.

Something dangerous, something primitive had emerged for the taboos surrounding such forms of bodily disposal had disappeared. Doubtless such aberrations had occurred before, yet there was something unique about this peculiar case that has ramifications for this study. The man who had presented himself for eating had been recruited through the Internet. Many others had offered themselves to the accused as the stream of emails read in court indicated. Dangerous fantasies had been given scope for expression through the Internet and these mirrored the limitless basis of sexual taste in the real world. The issue was not about images of cannibalism, but about the wish of some to be cannibalised. Some perverted urge for self-sacrifice had emerged, one that crossed a line between the civilised and the uncivilised. Instead of marking an escape from the divisions of the human condition, the Internet became an instrument for mirroring its most debased properties. Far from offering an outlet for bizarre forms of sexual perversity that could be formulated in images in cyberspace, the Internet was used as a means of recruiting clients to fulfil their desires in the real world. While it might be possible to regard the activities of a peculiar sexual niche as being perverse and exceptional, the case had wider ramifications, especially when it was indicated that a video of the victim being carved up had been made for the Internet and that a number of film directors were starting to queue up to secure the rights of the case.

The case brings into focus the extraordinary powers of technology when applied to visual culture to find and to manifest almost any image whose intensity, detail and depth generate possibly dangerous fascinations. Visual awareness and expectations of what can be seen have been radically transformed. Thus, the mobile phone with a lens (camphone) can be used to stock pornographic websites. The worries are such that swimming pools used by children now insist that all mobile phones be left outside the pool, lest images be posted on websites. A new crime of voyeurism has been added to the Sexual Offences Act 2003 to punish those who post on the Internet without consent private sexual activities surreptitiously caught on camera. A new world of intrusiveness has opened up and as Rowan suggests, visual privacy has ended.[1] A climate of fear increasingly surrounds the limitless advance of visual culture where the powers and limits of the visual know no boundaries. There is a prophetic cast to the comment of Morris, writing earlier, that the present world is obscene in its 'hypervisibility, the terror of the all-too-visible, the voracity, the total promiscuity, the pure concupiscence of the gaze'. The urge and expectation to see all seem to denote what Jay terms a postmodern hysteria of the visual.[2]

No taboos, no boundaries, no limits to seeing appear to exist, and the roving eye so freed is uniquely presented with dangerous sights, ones that transfix and transform. The lurker or voyeur has moved from the tower to the front of the computer screen to scroll as a god through all the scenes of life in a totality of seeing without cultural precedent. Yet, these god-like ocular powers have a downside. In the encircling gloom of postmodernity, the eye of inhibition has become unfixed. It sees too much for the actor to assimilate and in its ocular conceit, the eye risks damaging the self of the actor. Times when the medieval pilgrim crossed path, river and mountain to journey to see now seem antique to the eye accustomed to roving about in cyberspace looking for any image that will please. Yet, this is to forget that what the eye sees implicates the gazer in ways that effect undesirable transformations of appetite. In the seeing, the identity risks being changed radically as unexpected urges and inclinations are stimulated. Some forms of seeing can generate unwanted passions.

Walking around a church, one might find a statue of St Augustine. Cast in plaster, gaudy in colour, venerable and aloof, he seems a saint who never lived. Yet, he saw the effects of seeing what was best not seen in the case of one of his childhood friends, Alypius. His tale is curious but salutary. Despite a nobility of character, St Augustine observed, 'the whirlpool of Carthaginian immoral amusements sucked him in; it was aboil with frivolous shows'. Unfortunately, Alypius loved the circuses. He also dabbled in Manicheism. It 'captivated precious souls who were still too ignorant to penetrate the depth of virtue and liable to be deceived by the superficial appearance of a virtue that was but feigned and faked'. When he went to Rome, he was assailed by 'an entirely unexpected craving for gladiatorial entertainments'. This came about because of a failure to guard his eyes.

Having hitherto resisted such displays of butchery, his friends drew him by force to attend this 'cruel and murderous sport'. He went, but boasted 'you may drag my body into that place and fix me there, but can you direct my mind and my eyes to the show?' He would be present but absent to get the better of his friends and the performance. When there, he kept 'the gateways of his eyes closed'. Unfortunately, overwhelmed by curiosity at the noise, 'he opened his eyes, and suffered a more grievous wound in his soul than the gladiator he wished to see had received in the body'. He saw the blood and gulped the brutality along with it. He could not turn away,

> but fixed his gaze there and drank in the frenzy, not aware of what he was doing, revelling in the wicked contest and intoxicated on sanguinary pleasure. No longer was he the man who had joined the crowd; he was now one of the crowd he had joined, and a genuine companion of those who had led him there.

In becoming part of the crowd, he got carried away in their madness. A failure to guard his eyes had changed his relationships to the social. The moral basis of his gaze had been reconstituted in ways perhaps neither desired nor intended.[3]

Alypius left a tale for St Augustine to reflect on which is more than what can be said of the lurker and the voyeur who see in disembodied mode, locked in anonymity and who are strangely mute about what they see. This exposes a peculiar conundrum ripe for sociological reflection. As the technological applications and image making of the Internet expand expectations for seeing, those who see vanish into anonymity. Lurkers and voyeurs leave few tales or testimonies about what they saw. In the seeing, it would seem that not only has the social vanished in the disembodiment of seeing, but that the self has also disappeared. It mirrors nothing in the plenitude of seeing. Is this the dilemma of the voyeur? How does he stop seeing so much? His plight is peculiar because as his capacity to see expands in a limitless fashion, he becomes blind to his plight.

In a peculiar way, the voyeur marks the dangers of what St Augustine invoked from scripture as the 'concupiscence of the eyes'. Only the very pious shield their eyes. Others less holy have to live in this world of endless visual opportunity. Anyhow, an imprudent guarding of the eyes might leave those with pious aspirations stumbling, when a more serpentine approach to the ocular might keep the jocular at a healthy distance. Besides, St Augustine's expectations regarding custody of the eye were based on fears over idle curiosity. Useless spectacles and unselective seeing worried him greatly. Realistically, how is one to discipline a 'lust of the eyes' in a visual culture so replete with useless spectacle?[4]

Disembodiment of viewing marks the redundancy of a context for viewing, but also a sense of utilising the social as a looking glass to calibrate the morality of what is seen. If theology seeks a selectivity of viewing, so does sociology. Both have a common interest in the rehabilitation of the cultural ground of seeing. Protocols for seeing restore an inhibition and make sensitive the realisation that acts of seeing and being seen have moral dimensions that govern and shape social interaction. The restoration of the ritual surround to seeing is not just a matter of re-contextualisation; it is a means of the actor finding an estimation of himself that accords with shifts in self-understanding of the human condition.

Reflexivity has destroyed the notion of the sociologist as a disembodied spectator on the social, a voyeur endlessly polishing his disciplinary credentials. If the sociologist is now grounded in the demands of embodiment, then his gaze, likewise embodied, has to attend to the present cultural circumstances of seeing. In so doing, the malaise surrounding the visual in contemporary culture requires attention. Is it fated that distrust, surveillance and suspicion should govern the gaze, or are other forms around that need to be taken into account that would permit a visual emancipation?

In this chapter, the disciplinary eye of sociology is given attention, for it has expectations that require shaping. Its own ways of seeing are also malleable according to context. It is suggested that Simmel supplies sociology with an alternative version of looking to the somewhat pernicious form of gazing supplied by Foucault. Simmel's form of seeing opens out issues of trust and enlargement. If the actor is to realise a selectivity of regard, then some means of distinction needs to be made between glittering sights that are false, and those worthy of regard that mirror better things, not least the unseen. The inclination to see and to grasp what is false might be due to a visual myopia. But this misapprehension might be due to something more unfashionable: temptation. The secularisation of temptation and its displacement by notions of addiction are characteristic of the expectations of modernity, but these processes collide with one of its distinctive traits: boredom. Modernity signifies the freeing of the sociological eye, but as it roves with increasing dissatisfaction it becomes disinclined to look. Its plight mirrors in visual form Simmel's tragedy of culture. Too many images are presented to the eye of perception for the inner eye to grasp, and in this disjunction, the inclination to seek to see the unseen becomes a prime casualty. This crisis of the visual, of indifference, has an inner dimension, one expressed in a term allied with boredom: 'acedia'. This form of melancholy marks a disincentive to look at matters of the spiritual where a vision of relief might be found. Unfortunately, issues of the gaze are dominated by questions of gender and pornography. These reduce the issue of the gaze to the sectional and the diminishing. To offset this reductionism, the chapter turns to forms of seeing or not being seen in settings of social action, where agency is restored and a ritual surround is rehabilitated. Somehow, the identity, the soul of those who see, needs to be re-cast so that the act of seeing comes to mirror not the vacuity of the voyeur locked in his pleasurable anonymity, but that which can be caught in the act of looking that points to a contagion of seeing, a collusion that accomplishes liminoid virtualities. As the actor shines in the seeing, the unseen is mysteriously mirrored back. It is what clouds this shining that concerns this chapter.

I

Sociology has suffered a continued failure to attend to its theological debts. Its dalliances with virtual religion cast a property of false consciousness on the discipline that seems to confirm that it does not need to attend to its theological archaeology. Present suspicions regarding the visual are doubtless well grounded in the limitless expansion of images and spectacles. Yet, these suspicions spring also from not only theological considerations that stipulate ways of seeing but also prohibitions on what is to be seen, a point Jay has noted.

He indicates that an interest in Levinas and Judaism developed in France in the 1970s and the 1980s that reflected concerns about the status of images and their representation in a culture of postmodernity. Jay suggests that the Jewish taboo on making of images was used by Lyotard to make sense of 'the pain of unrepresentability'. What should *not* be seen and what should *not* be represented come into focus as the dilemmas of postmodernity.[5] Such a reading seems to affirm suspicions not only about the making of images, but also about the presumption in so doing. From a Jewish theological tradition, prohibitions on making images of the unseen God are invoked to give solace to a culture of postmodernity insecure about its dealings with the seen. This unexpected invocation of an iconoclastic tradition to make sense of what cannot be represented needs to be related to another distinctive theological tradition also invoked to make sense of the plight of life in postmodernity. Apophatic theology seemed to turn the screw on the plight of the actor in postmodernity. Not merely was a solace of representation denied, but God had become absent, so that there was no basis for an image to be invoked, for there was nothing to be seen of the unseen. Blind, hopeless and mirroring nothing save his own vacuity, Pascal's coin spun as a wager seems to have fallen into the good eye damaging its capacity to see. Yet, is this theological turn of Judaism to be naturalised as *the* mandatory turn for sociology? Why is the solace, the sacramental means of seeing the unseen of Catholicism, to be ruled out of court? This presents sociology with an unusual dilemma of making a theological choice, of what to invoke in theology that would permit a maximisation of understandings of visual culture. Unexpectedly, understandings of its calibrations are to be found in theological hinterlands. What also becomes apparent is that there is more to the eye than that meets the eye.

The eye is more than an optical instrument, a mere fleshly means of perception. As Illich has argued, 'the Information Age incarnates itself in the eye'.[6] It has its own cultural and symbolic properties, ones that affect and effect implication in the act of seeing. Eyeing has a form of accountability. To eye somebody is to make a demand, warranted or otherwise. The eye has its own language of purpose. Asking somebody to keep an eye on a property denotes its accountability. Keeping an eye fixed on an object fulfils trust. Acts of seeing have a legal status. For example, as a witness, one is responsible for having seen. The power of regard of the eye is indicated by its intensity of use. Hostile staring can be denoted as a form of sexual harassment. As a site for designations and dispositions, the eye signifies powers for good and evil. Casting an eye invokes powers of the spiritual and in some paradoxical way this instrument of perception permits access to the unseen. This power is well expressed in Yeats' poem 'Under Ben Bulben':

> On limestone quarried near the spot
> By his command these words are cut:
>
> Cast a cold eye
> On life, on death.
> Horseman, pass by![7]

Given its link to vision, it is not surprising that the eye should have many adjectival designations that express social and spiritual states. These reflect the contradictions embodied in the eye, of longing, of lingering and of roving. The unfixed eye unsettles. Like the self, the eye needs something to focus on and this involves deciding what to see or not to see. If the eye is a way of looking that has its own symbolic and cultural properties, then sociology has its own ocular instrument, its own set of visual expectations.

In the notion of a sociological eye is a disciplinary gaze.[8] Sociologists are trained to be alert to what they see. As Gary Marx observed, in his reflection on the nature of the disciplinary tasks for fledgling sociologists, they should 'be passionate! Social observation, ideas and communication are our life blood'. He goes on to cite from Walker Evans: 'Stare. It is the way to educate your eye and more. Stare, pry, listen... Die knowing something'.[9] Fieldwork, observation and participation, all mark properties of seeing that are peculiar to sociology. What is seen is gathered into some narrative that forms the basis of a text or article. The rhetoric of a way of looking at the world takes on its own gloss in sociology. Thus one can point to Goffman's view of the world. It bears a cynical property, one of calculation, artifice and manipulation of what is seen and what is not to be seen. Yet in all this, sociology does not wish to be captive to the visual. It has its own social constructions of what should be seen and what lies beyond perception.[10] Explicit concern with a visual sociology is recent.[11] Disciplinary forms of seeing emerge also in anthropology, not only in the descriptions of cultures but in the way images are represented. In her aptly titled work, *The Ethnographer's Eye,*

Grimshaw has pointed to the importance of film and television in constructing images of cultures in attempts to visualise their basis.[12] The results of seeing required a certain testimony but also the need to persuade the reader or the audience of what one has seen. A cultural and social construction operates in regard to the visual that invites sociology to attend to its own ocular considerations.

Foster has touched on these requirements in his notion of social visuality. This has its own rhetoric of representation and its own properties of social fact. It also relates to scopic regimes that deal with paradoxes and differences in regard to the visual.[13] Frank has supplied another approach to visuality, one that fits closer to this study. She regards visuality as a 'reconstructive process, one that considers how language, symbols, myths, and values become attached to the act of seeing'.[14] Oscillating between the wistful and the empirical, the mind is never bound by what the eye merely sees, yet it is compromised within its visions. It nurtures expectations of what might be seen but then is not. As the self and identity of the sociologist becomes more accountable to forms of identity and identification, the issue of their ethical ends comes to the fore.[15] Fantasy, wish-fulfilment and ideological myopia afflict the sociologist's view of the world, what is seen and what is unseen. Reflexivity affirms embodiment, but it also draws attention to the moral implications of sociology's own scopic regimes. Combing reflexivity with ethics and the visual generates a knotty problem for sociologists in dealing with religion. They point to the issue of what the sociologist *should* see in the field. Likewise this points to the converse, a concern with what the sociologist did *not* see. In some way, the visual attached to reflexivity opens out moral issues sociology has not really confronted.

In his vision of a reflexive sociology, one that reflects on itself, Gouldner suggests that 'to a theorist there are two kinds of social worlds: permitted (or "normal") worlds, and unpermitted (or "abnormal") ones'. His vision of a reflexive sociology involves seeking a goodness, a moral value. In this regard, '*un*permitted worlds are those where (1) good objects are seen to be weak, or (2) bad objects are seen to be strong'. For him, social theorising is a symbolic effort to overcome and to transform these unpermitted worlds.[16] This means that 'we sociologists must – at the very least – acquire the ingrained *habit* of viewing our own beliefs as we now view those held by others'.[17] When these expectations are moved over to matters of theology, the implications are deeply radical. One of the very few sociologists who even mentioned the term 'evil', Gouldner betrayed a certain discomfort at the exclusion of religion from sociological deliberations. His concerns touched on the issue of something ultimate.[18] Sociology has its own ways of seeing the world but as these are examined, the reflexive implications of its gaze become more apparent. More importantly, sociology comes to have its own expectations as to what can be gained from visual culture, what form it desires, and the ends to which understanding of its basis are to be put.

Barnard has made a useful distinction between the strong and the weak sense of visual culture. The latter refers to forms and entities of the visual, produced and consumed in the cultural arena, whereas the former, relates to what he terms 'values and identities that are constructed in and through visual culture'.[19] The strong version is the concern of this study. If values and identities are to be secured, then the need to see in distinctions is a necessary part of ways of seeing, for as Berger indicated, some lead to the false surface glamour of the images of publicity and others to the depths portrayed in art.[20] Seeing in distinctions requires the actor to look below the surface, and to service the inner eye where the depths of sight are to be found that refract back sensibilities of the unseen that are mysteriously linked to the eye of perception. In a peculiar way, both eyes see together, what is seen and what is unseen.

II

As suggested in Chapter 2, there is a pernicious property to Foucault's approach to the gaze. Its illumination is an instrument for entrapment and for the dissolving of social bonds. Gazing into the light, the actor cannot see, and anyhow there is nothing to see. Designations are pointless. Tales of those so seen are few in Foucault's world, for the eye in the tower eradicates everything of the social, even testimonies of the lives of those who shrivel under the gaze. Despair not hope, compliance not freedom, distrust not trust are their untold tales of living under the power of the eye in the tower, all seeing but all uncaring.

By contrast, Simmel's concern with the eye, part of his sociology of the senses, points in an entirely opposite direction. For him,

> the eye of a person discloses his own soul when he seeks to uncover that of another. What occurs in this direct mutual glance represents the most perfect reciprocity in the entire field of human relationships.

The use of the eye in the glance serves to effect trust. At its highest ambition, the eye seeks a mutuality of edification and a perfection of reciprocity.[21] In these issues, subtle distinctions between the gaze and the glance matter.[22] Unlike in Foucault's gaze, where the actor is disciplined into becoming an object of surveillance detached from the social, for Simmel he is freed to be implicated in it and to enact very much as a subject. In Simmel, seeing is linked to the spiritual in ways few other sociologists would admit. This has obvious sociological implications for dealing with how the seen connects to the unseen. But in Simmel's case, matters are more complex, for his concerns are with the ways the unseen is seen in the seen.

Unlike other sociologists, Simmel was concerned with the soul of culture and its place in cosmopolitan life. In this setting of strangers, money is the god. It achieves its power through its colourlessness. The very opposite arises in Simmel's approach to religion. His concern is with the colour of religion. In the colour of religion are to be found its vibrancy and its property of light. This begs a question: how do some see this colour and others do not? An obvious answer relates to the eligibility to so see, a point reflected in the promise of Christ, 'blessed are the pure in heart; for they shall see God' (Matt. 5:8). Such seeing requires moral and spiritual credentials whose necessity seems no longer necessary. Nowadays there are few equivalents to the Syrian ascetics Brown uncovered, whose control of the body meant that 'only a thin veil separated the world of the seen from the unseen realities that glowed beneath its surface'. This gave them a capacity to bring 'the vibrant energy of the angels through the half-translucent curtain that separated the unseen hosts of Heaven from the present world'.[23] Such reachings into unseen are truly exceptional, but it is what they signify that is more important, that there is an integrity in seeing. This bears on a point of von Balthasar that in the novels of Bernanos, '*truth lies in the saint's way of seeing*' (his italics). This gives sociological comfort, for what is emphasised is that 'sanctity' is something lived existentially and communicated. It has a social dimension.[24] It also leads to a point Debord noted that 'spectacle is not a collection of images, rather it is a social relationship between people that is mediated by images'.[25] Unfortunately, the truth of affairs can become distorted in their mode of constitution, so that what is seen can be illusory and in this regard, Debord makes some grand claims.

For Debord, spectacle is a systematic misrepresentation of culture, an ideological masking of its true basis that operates as 'a permanent opium war waged to make it impossible to distinguish goods from commodities....'.[26] In short, for him, the spectacle is 'a specious form of the sacred',[27] and as a visual form of false consciousness it relates to the illusory projections of religion to be found in Marx's notion of commodity fetishism. What is in the visual is to be treated with the deepest of suspicion. In the first lines of an introduction to a collection of his essays, Jameson provides a similar suspicion of the visual, suggesting that it 'is *essentially* pornographic, which is to say that it has its end in rapt, mindless fascination'.[28] Almost as a revolt against its Catholic hinterland, there were conspicuous efforts, not least by Sartre and Foucault, to deconstruct the visual and to treat it in terms of a form of entrapment, a reductionism that confirms suspicions regarding the use of the eye.[29] Yet, as the eye is narrowed, the capacity of the actor to respond is also delimited. Agency becomes the prime casualty of collective suspicions regarding the visual and the exercise of the gaze. The implication is that the actor can only see blindly, for false consciousness denies him access to redemptive sight. Yet, this would be to obliterate notions of agency in some blanket conceptual sweep of false consciousness where the actor is fated to myopia, but with no prospect of redemptive sight. If the actor does not like what he sees, then he commands the eye to seek to see something else.

Reflexivity suggests that he has the self-awareness to want to do so. As Synnott elegantly expresses it, 'the eye is the I in disposition'. The eye is symbolic of the self and what it inclines to see.[30] On the cultural field, as Bourdieu indicates, the eye has to *find* ways of seeing and as he suggests, one must learn to see in a manner of reading.[31]

The narrative of the biography is often a chronicle for what was seen. In seeing, one wants to be confirmed in what is seen. The act of seeing secures an identity, one based on having seen. As Urry suggests, tourists expect to have their gaze validated. What is seen is marked with ritual and ceremony.[32] The increased volume of objects in tourism stems from the fact that 'contemporary tourists are collectors of gazes and appear to be less interested in repeat visits to the same auratic site. The initial gaze is what counts'.[33] Yet, with something visually interesting a return visit is required, so that the self can mark off what was seen first, and assimilated, compared with what a second sight might reveal. The possibility of re-seeing lends a double-edged property to the gaze.

To see again might confirm there was nothing to see, but it might also be that something attracts that the viewer needs to see again to thread into his biography. Seeing again can be about the casting of a relationship with the seen. It can also be part of an endeavour to see past the seen. Thus, as Davey suggests,

> in hermeneutic thought, the notion of having something 'brought to mind' is connected with the idea of being able to see 'beyond' that which is immediately visible. We speak of 'seeing' what an artist 'is getting at' though the subject-matter need not be a visible object.[34]

Drawing from Gadamer, Davey draws out the unfolding revelatory nature of art, its capacity to bring a truth into actuality in ways that effect a fullness of being.[35] Earlier in his essay, he noted the way the central questions of theology emerge in hermeneutics of 'how does one breathe life back into an ancient text?'[36] A similar point applies to symbols and objects seen that need to be deciphered for the worlds of the unseen they expand and permit access to in the act of viewing. As with the text, the visual opens out in some mysterious manner aesthetic or emotional sensibilities for the viewer. The actor has to believe in what he sees, and if so religious images and icons can have mysterious powers of revelation.

Yet, in dealing with a hermeneutics of enlargement, one cannot assume some serendipitous revelation that enlarges sensibilities in the mere act of seeing. Sometimes those who look do not see, or like the eunuch in the chariot, have no grammar to read or to make sense of what is seen. In all this lies the paradoxical saying of Christ: 'for judgment I am come into this world, that they which see not might see, and that they which see might be made blind' (Jn 9:39). In sociological terms, how is the plight of the inly blind to be understood?

One obvious point is that those who yield to temptation, who follow false sights and desires, are likely to be locked in an inward blindness. If in sin, they see what they want. Thus of the wicked, it is noted, 'there is no fear of God before his eyes. For he flattereth himself in his own eyes, until his iniquity be found to be hateful' (Ps. 36:1–2). Seeing with an eye of indifference seems linked to a property of postmodernity, of living without boundaries. This is to forget what was warned about before: 'for brethren, ye have been called unto liberty; only use not liberty, for an occasion to the flesh...' (Gal. 5:13). If the visual has a necessary property of embodiment, what lies within? If dispositions matter in what is to be seen and there are cultural ways of perceiving that enable and disable then it might seem that something old-fashioned has entered issues of embodiment: inclinations and temptations.

III

Temptation is a facet of visual culture, where sights appear to satisfy all desires. But temptations also relate to what is yet to be seen, a case in point being those Christ suffered in moments of physical and spiritual weakness. Having spent forty days and nights in the desert and having eaten nothing, Jesus was hungry and the devil came to tempt Him. Taking Him up a high mountain, the devil showed Him all the kingdoms of the world in a moment of time. These were to be given to Christ if He would worship the devil. When he ended all his temptations the devil departed (Lk 4:1–13). Idolatry, greed, pride and covetousness are dramatically embodied in this temptation. In that other desert of consumerism, these nefarious traits operate in a more routine, but somewhat transmuted, form of temptation. At present it seems temptation is treated as a marketing device and not as an instrument of perdition.

Capitulation rather than resistance to temptation governs the lives of those who live by 'the consolations of consumerism'.[37] Yet, these images of consumerism perpetuate a sense of unsettlement, for the last thing sought by advertisers is something ultimately fulfilling. Advertising harnesses temptations in images that promise instant gratification and gain with no pain. A labour of acquisition is dismantled. The skill of advertising involves sleights of hand that confer properties of aura and magic on to mundane products in ways that transform their images. These images are consecrated by sponsorship and conserved through branding. The central concern of advertising is to manipulate appearance without being seen to do so. It is unworried by issues of superficiality. As Fowles observes, 'advertising's perfected style leads to an emphasis on surfaces at the expense of all else'.[38] In the relation between advertising and popular culture, a mixture is presented that is 'lavish, open, approachable. The symbolic material is treated by the viewer as a fruit orchard, some of its contents ripe for the taking'.[39]

Temptation does not have an image problem. Many pray to be led into temptation to rescue their lives from boredom. Temptation is exciting and bears its own logic, something denied to those who resist, who are designated as incomplete in some unarticulated way. To yield to temptation is to encounter a string of fascinating vices: lust, gluttony and sloth. Yielding to temptation is to validate the fallen self and to capitulate to its natural inclination: self-indulgence. Even the listing of vices gives pleasure.[40] Anyhow, temptation is not a sociological term. Even if it was, why should any resist it?

Yet, second thoughts are abroad that suggest that sociology might look darkly on those who fail to resist temptation. They might be treated as cultural drones deceived by the delights of the appearances temptation so recklessly presents. Three considerations arise. First, failure to regulate appetites generates many Durkheimian worries and a sociological sense that such yieldings subtract from the commonwealth. The fruit of failure to resist temptation is egoism. Secondly, some vices contradict established cultural conventions. Gluttony leads to fatness, and obesity suggests a fruit of the labours of eating that has become overripe. It violates notions of health and fitness. Efforts to sue fast-food chains reflect the disillusions of the plump who claim no blame for feeding on the allures of instant gratification. Likewise lust, initially treated as a term of allure for sexual practices, takes on a darker meaning when consent is denied and a right to violate women and children with impunity is declared. Thirdly, an incapacity to resist temptation points to a loss of control that might be self-destructive. Irresistible temptation suggests a fate of being a creature of carnal appetites that renders the actor asocial in activity and unproductive in realisation.

Temptation lies in the heart of the commodification of visual culture. Images are formed in ways where culpability is given a 'get out of jail free card'. Deficiencies of character that mark failures to resist temptation are increasingly treated as forms of compulsion, matters of medical interest not of theological concern. The price of such transference of disciplinary accountability effects a discounting of the choice to resist temptation.[41] A rehabilitation of choice appears in Giddens' treatment of addiction. It is treated as the negative index of the reflexive project of the self. His concerns are with sex as compulsive. What is addictive is placed against what is intimate, and here issues of character emerge with notions of an ethic of consent and mitigation of dominance. Although Giddens is not concerned with temptation, he is concerned with the issues of autonomy and forms of behaviour where the addictive qualifies these.[42] Although addiction might yield to the demands of a medical imperialism in the realm of vice, it does not reflect a theological notion that sin takes on its own logic of entrapment. Healing rather than curing is part of the expectation of recovery. Whether an addiction or a culpable failure to regulate, there is a sense of entrapment and a wanting to be free from the clutches of images that effected a decline and fall from expectations of character.

Few speak of temptation now, so its resurrection in the context of the vulnerability of the self in a search for an enduring intimacy is unexpected. Again, what appears as a defunct term of theological rhetoric seems to take on a logic when re-cast in the virtual religions of sociology and psychotherapy. The sting of sin might have been extracted from temptation, yet the anxieties and the guilt it generates remain. Far from resolving a sense of the incomplete, yielding to temptation seems to confirm the illusory basis of its allures.

Yielding to temptation carries necessary sensibilities of violation and trespass, a feeling of risk in entering an unknown territory. It is the sense of transgression into something ill-formulated that gives temptation a link with curiosity. The self is curious to know what it is like to yield to temptation. Some enlargement of pleasure, some growth of maturity is offered by temptation. Weakness of character and wanting to be part of an excitement are material for inquests on falls into temptation. Certain states leave the actor ripe for temptation, and boredom is one of these. It relates to inclinations to look – or not. To alleviate boredom, one ends up looking at anything and somehow seeing nothing. Rudderless in boredom, the self sometimes resolves by stirring the waters, but in so doing risks drowning in the waves so generated.

IV

In his essay, 'The Painter of Modern Life', Baudelaire treats the *flâneur* as the hero of urban life. He is heroic in terms of a capacity for curiosity. Endowed with the visual powers of the child to see everything new, the *flâneur* is 'a pure pictorial moralist', but he is so in a particular setting, that of the milieu of the crowd. He gazes in the midst of the fugitive and the infinite. But in this setting, away from home yet feeling so everywhere, the *flânuer* is able 'to see the world, to be at the centre of the world, and yet to remain hidden from the world'. Thus, for Baudelaire, 'the spectator is a *prince* who everywhere rejoices in his incognito'. There is a heroic task in seeing so much. Seeing so much is riven with the risk of a moral indifference in the face of a visual plenitude, so that compassion wilts. A state of blaséness is the occupational hazard of the stranger coping with the mental life of the metropolis. It is a condition linked with boredom. Such a state seemed inexplicable to Baudelaire who wrote that any man who becomes crushed in this capacity to see so much 'who can yet be *bored in the heart of the multitude*, is a block-head! A blockhead! and I despise him'.[43] Despite these hopes, it is in the multitude that the bored become blasé.[44]

The property of blaséness arises from the risk of seeing too much and of becoming blind, bored and fatigued in so gazing. In Simmel, this blaséness takes on a debilitating property that can lead to exhaustion, to a blunting of discrimination and to a state of indifference.[45] The outcome of this exhaustion is a cynicism, an attitude that has matured into being a defining trait of postmodernity. Bewes, who has explored this point, treats cynicism as a form of 'enlightened false consciousness', one that legitimises a disinclination to participate on the grounds of an endemic sense of the inauthentic. Besides the blasé city dweller, Bewes finds in Huysmans' hero Des Esseintes another archetypal character. He is the pioneer of decadence of the nineteenth-century *fin-de-siècle*.[46] He had a genius for the collection of fine objects and artefacts of religion whose private inspection offered the deepest of sensual pleasure. As an exemplary voyeur, Des Esseintes was sufficiently Catholic to discern how objects of sanctification could be re-appraised for the purposes of decadence. Yet, this collector found his gaze unfulfilled. Something still eluded him. Indeed,

> his boredom grew to infinite proportions. The pleasure he had felt in the possession of astonishing flowers was exhausted; their shapes and colours had already lost the power to excite him. Besides, in spite of all the care he lavished on them, most of his plants died; he had them removed from his rooms, but his irritability had reached such a pitch that was exasperated by their absence and his eye continually offended by the empty spaces they had left.[47]

The plight of the bored in relation to the visual is to see without relief and this has disturbing inward effects on the self. Far from offering relief, boredom marks a vexatious state. As Pascal observed,

> man finds nothing so intolerable as to be in a state of complete rest, without passions, without occupation, without diversion, without effort. Then he faces his nullity, loneliness, inadequacy, dependence, helplessness, emptiness. And at once there wells up from the depths of his soul boredom, gloom, depression, chagrin, resentment, despair.[48]

Boredom and a sense of blaséness signify sensibilities of lassitude and these have a spiritual counterpart in a related condition: acedia.

Oscar Wilde, pioneer of decadence, so influenced by Huysmans, strangely encountered this condition. In the *De Profundis*, Wilde reflected in his prison cell on his fall into humiliation, a fearful descent for 'a man who stood in symbolic relations to the art and culture' of the age.[49] Not yet in Catholicism, Wilde wondered how to be happy, remembering the lowly place of the wilfully sad in Dante's *Divine Comedy*, 'sullen in the sweet air which rejoiceth in the sunlight'. For them light was a burden of life, a curious echo of living under the eye in the tower. He went on to add 'I knew the church condemned *accidia*, but the whole idea seemed to me quite fantastic, just the sort of sin, I fancied, a priest who knew nothing about real life would invent'.[50] It cannot be said that many sociologists are aware of acedia.[51]

Acedia is the particular sin of those who confront the limits of self in monastic life. It is the occupational sin of liturgical workers who slave over

hot altars in the mid-day sun when things are most arid, when torpor penetrates and when the ritual round pleases no more. It is what emerges from
sins of human weakness. It is a condition linked to apathy thus linking
spiritual decay to a domain property of modernity: boredom. As Aquinas
has suggested, 'every vice breeds sadness and depression at the spiritual
good of virtuous acts'.[52] This sadness about spiritual good only becomes
sinful when reason converts the despond into a cloud of knowing that the
exercise of virtue is illusory. The adage that the devil gives time for idle
hands tells much about the nature of acedia. Indolence lowers the guard
and leaves the monk receptive to temptation and lulls him into not resisting
it. In this condition, the soul sleeps.[53] Acedia reflects a spiritual failure to see
distinctions between virtue and vice, and worse not to see their point. Acedia
also arises from a sense of pride, of wanting to possess holiness, but without
a spiritual endeavour to realise it. To that degree, acedia is a property of the
virtual religions discussed earlier. The sin of the spiritual voyeur, acedia is
the trait of the worldly wise who seek to see the unseen without humility, or
acceptance of demands of commitment, and who demand that their curiosity
be satisfied. This curiosity can relate to a passion to appropriate powers to
see the unseen in the seen, an ambition that forms part of Bernanos' novel
Under Satan's Sun. This underrated novel has had unexpected contemporary
resonances recently in France.[54]

In the novel, an old man of letters, author of the ironically titled *The Pascal
Candle*, had journeyed to see the elderly and dying parish priest of Lumbres.
Not finding him in his house, the old man went over to sit in the priest's
empty church. Sitting there, he felt an enormously powerful obsession to
open the door of the empty confessional to see if the priest was there. Earlier
he had mused, did not confession offer remorse, 'a rather rough and strange
remedy for the increasing insipidity of vice?'[55] Opening the door, he found
the odd, ill-formed, poverty-stricken elderly priest, standing in the box – dead.
This was enormously frustrating, for the priest was to be a subject of 'a game
only for the author of many books, a great provider of illusions. It would be
my last work, and I should write it for myself, the actor and the spectator in
turn'.[56] The purpose of the old man's journey was to inspect the basis of
powers to see the unseen. He had heard this elderly priest was gifted in this
way. Not only was the priest dead, but also his biography seemed one
highly unpropitious for the exercise of such powers. Yet, despite being a
simple, gangly, despair-ridden misfit, the priest had developed extraordinary
powers of discernment of souls, of seeing their inner states, a gift that
involved wrestling with good and evil in the manner of heroic virtue. The
concupiscence of the desire for knowledge led to a fatal state, for

> to know in order to destroy and in destroying to renew knowledge and
> desire – ah, Satan's Sun, the craving for nothingness sought out for its
> own sake, the abominable outpouring of the heart.[57]

The collector had come to the task of capturing the confessor for his book from a career of dealing with boredom and vice (the theme of the book).[58] Like Des Esseintes, he was fated to find that encapsulating the living was fatally elusive. In the end he was doomed to disappointment, for what he sought was not available through the eye of perception. Another form of visualisation was required.

In his weighty biography of Bernanos, von Balthasar draws out the notion of spiritual seeing. For him, 'the mystic has only one privilege: somehow to "see" what the ordinary Christian can "only" believe'.[59] The grace to see is a priestly power that relates to confession, and it is this power of looking into souls that gives the confessor a property of clairvoyance as against the voyeur who has the property of a vampire.[60]

There is something in modernity that causes it to kill the things it loves – a state of flourishing and endeavour. Somehow the pace of metropolitan life distracts from the need to nourish inward sensibilities. As Spacks observes,

> keeping an eye on small particularities has positive consequences but, inviting constant evaluation, also calls attention to the lack of emotional satisfaction in much ordinary experience. The inner life comes to be seen as consequential; therefore its inadequacies invite attention. The concept of boredom serves as an all-purpose register of inadequacy.[61]

It might be said that boredom and acedia overlap in Healy's elegant characterisation of the former as 'psychic anorexia'.[62] Although they are difficult to separate, boredom and acedia interconnect in terms of expressing a sense of lassitude, a psychic sense of inertia, and a malaise that entraps the self in some elusive way that is linked to social circumstance. Of course, boredom can be a delightful fantasy for those with busy lives, but when the state is attached to acedia, the spirit is incapable of supplying such dreams of escape. Raposa is right to draw attention to the ambiguities of states of boredom as lying between interest and despair. If boredom was just a malaise the self is locked into, then sociology would have little standing, but Raposa points to an important facet of this condition.

Its main facet is dispositional, for the crucial issue is what the actor elects to do about the state. The value of the concept is that it forces the actor to choose to resolve the problem and that means re-threading a story to link to a new narrative of escape.[63] Thus, what lurks in boredom is a deficiency of attention, a failure of agency.[64] This suggests that boredom is disconnected from the social and in a way is a product of an exaggerated individualism, one where the isolated self suffers an intolerable sense of inertia. Somehow, modernity has offered too much and as it matures, Spacks aptly suggests, 'boredom becomes a metaphor for the postmodern condition'. It marks the failure of rights to everything, to possess everything and to see everything.[65] In the saloons of liquid modernity, the individual sups alone.

Brooding forces the inspection of apathy, but closer scrutiny generates an uncomfortable feeling that the state is closer to something unfashionable than one might like to admit. Apathy comes near sloth, and efforts to differentiate both yield attention to the odd antinomial relationship between vice and virtue. Leisure is presumably virtuous, and vice belongs to inertia, sloth. How does one separate them and, anyhow, does it sociologically matter?

V

Virtues and vice are well cast antinomies.[66] With the advance of the politics of identity and recognition, there might be great sociological hesitations about the rehabilitation of vice. Yet, without reference to vice, it is hard to consider virtue in any meaningful terms. The loss of a sense of this antinomy carries a price, a decline of interest in hypocrisy. Although the public is diffident about the pleasures of temptation, it does like tales of fall from virtue, especially in matters of sexuality. It finds sexual inactivity dull and perplexing. Indeed, the virtue of virginity is now deemed the vice of the repressed. Despite its weird status, the issue of sexual inactivity became the unexpected concern of Foucault in his later dalliances with Patristics. His concern was to find a way out of sexual categorisation. Sexual liberty had become oppressive. In this context, he cited with perplexity an encounter with a young homosexual man with a compulsive sexual problem. It was not that he did not know how to stop; he did not understand why he should. Vernon suggests that Foucault was coming to wonder at the loss of asceticism where spirituality and friendship could be nurtured.[67] Foucault's interest in asceticism and the de-sexualisation it entails was related to a need to find forms of love and friendship that would transcend the categories and particularities of sexual politics. This interest in sexual restraint relates to capacities to see in spiritual terms. It points to a hard saying of Christ that '... whosoever looketh on a women to lust after her hath committed adultery with her already in his heart' (Matt. 5:28).[68] When John Paul II invoked this saying, he was subject to critical abuse.

Yet, for the adulterer the inward nurture of the eye enlarges the pleasures of seduction. For some, 'having eyes full of adultery' (2 Pet. 2:14) is a cultural ambition and a basis of identity, but for others it distorts views of the unseen. The link between spirituality and the senses is complex. St Augustine explored this link in the context of the notion that the pure in heart will see God.[69] Illumination marks the inner eye's perception and can complement that which is perceived outside. In the present culture, the inner eye seems to have gone blind and the outer eye has become bored. This returns to the issue of the liminal and the virtual, for as Raposa indicates 'boredom can serve as the midwife for the birth of religious knowledge; it is the pallid half-darkness that sometimes lingers just before the dawning of religious insight'. It is this twilight zone that fascinates this study, of being caught between what sociology can see and what can only be dimly discerned of what is of light and dark, the unseen. This leads to another point of Raposa, one that haunts the study. For him, boredom 'represents an epistemic blindness, not simply a refusal to pay attention but, rather, an inability to perceive the religious significance of things'.[70] Can this failure to so perceive be given a sociological location?

Vice might seem something of the antique, a horrible combination of Victorian repression and Taliban autocracy; and virtue might seem precious, presumptuous and pedestrian – neither deserving sociological attention. They do not belong to its traditions, but this is to forget that the issue of virtue was an instrument of modernisation and calculation for Weber. The regulation of virtue formed the basis of Weber's account of the elective affinity between Calvinism and capitalism. The type of virtue was very specific and it was aligned with a very definite theology.

Thrift, frugality and a denial of aesthetic pleasure were properties of this rationalisation of virtue that sought to alleviate salvation anxiety.[71] Sloth was the hidden enemy of this virtue, not least in wasting time. It is a vice with close links to acedia.[72] In his consideration of sloth, Pynchon suggested, '*acedia* is the vernacular of everyday moral life'.[73] It is ironical to find from Lyman's insights that the Protestant, for whom the world is his cloister, should have carried out from the monastery, one of its characterising vices: acedia.[74] As a term it is as corrosive as anomie or alienation. It points to a melancholic lack, a sickness, a disinclination to see. In this study, acedia comes to signify the eye of disregard, the disinclination to seek to see the unseen. The eye of disregard emerges from the spirit of acedia and the disinclination to look. Yet, boredom itself produces an insensibility of the social that is intolerable. It signifies a disconnection from the social rhythms of culture.[75] Most crucially, Brissett and Snow treat the emergence of boredom as the property of a culture where certainty and uncertainty seem eroded.[76] It is the indifference to both that worries, for boredom and acedia point to dangerous conditions in regard to the social fabric and its moral basis. There is something de-humanising about boredom in the end, and one area where this is expressed is in the indifference to suffering. In this regard, boredom becomes linked to the visual. Regard is replaced by disregard and rather than empathising, the gazer seeks a distance.

Public concerns about suffering have generated many highly publicised fund-raising events. Initially, these yielded extensive financial contributions and public concern, if not compassion. Yet, curiously the scale of the demand for public sympathy for all manner of good causes has become counterproductive. It has generated a famine fatigue. Tester has explored this paradox well when he observed that

> the media communicate harrowing representations of others, but the
> more the face of the other is communicated and reproduced in this way

the more it is denuded of any moral authority it might otherwise possess. Increased visibility to the gaze seems to go hand in hand with increasing invisibility from the point of view of the responsibility of moral solidarity. Media significance means moral insignificance.[77]

The spectator of mass suffering seems to have become bored, disengaged and morally irresponsible. Such indifference might seem to deserve condemnation. Yet, those who gaze at suffering on the screen do not have a co-presence with those who suffer. The voyeur is not seen to them either. Again, this is not something new. As Boltanski observes, the invention of the spectator in the eighteenth century points to a realisation of the power of the unseen who see and who are not part of the event described. The spectator who moves unaccountably, who sees and is not seen (or signified) is the original of the *flâneur*, the voyeur and the lurker.[78] In considering the responsibilities or otherwise of those who exercise pity in terms of a distance from the events of the suffering, Boltanski draws out well the contradictions of seeing felt by the unseen. They move between sentiment and sadism. Those who see unseen have their own orders of culpability. What they signify is that the eye refracts its own moral divisions and these antinomial dilemmas require the mind to choose what to see. Sight affects inner sensibilities in dangerous ways as Alypius found out.

Those bored and fatigued with the sophistications of modernity can unwittingly drift into experimentations with unseen forces whose dangers are often well disguised. Huysmans reflected that 'in the present disorganized state of letters there was but one tendency which seemed to promise better things. The unsatisfied need for the supernatural was driving people, in default of something loftier, to spiritism and the occult'. This comment emerged in the context of *La Bas*, Huysmans' account (written through his front Durtal) of his dabblings with Satanism.[79] This seemed a solution to the endemic fatigue of modernity that was so assiduously chronicled in the preceding book, *Against Nature*.

The project of *La Bas* was to construct a biography of the fifteenth-century sadist and child-murderer, Gilles de Rais. It is indicative of late medieval priorities in scrutinising acts of evil that his trial in a civil court took forty-eight hours whereas his ecclesiastical trial lasted five weeks. This illustrates the way evil was considered a theological rather than a secular problematic.[80] The basis of the nefarious activities of de Rais was alchemy. *La Bas* marked the journeying of an author from boredom into a fatal curiosity: a concern with chronicling evil, a sense of whose darkness is graphically conveyed in this book. Even the Internet and the visions of cyberspace do not quite prepare the reader for this journey into darkness. These dabblings with evil marked an underside of modernity. Properties of darkness can also be found in Baudelaire's fascination with evil. For both pioneers of modernity the one definite power that mattered and that satisfied all curiosity was evil.

It is not surprising that Huysmans so desperately sought a healing of the eyes that he sat in the back of Parisian churches and that he used art as a means of journeying back into the religion he had hitherto despised. Sitting there during the long services of Holy Week, 'his temptations to unbelief were gone' and he found a grace in 'the eloquent splendours of the liturgies' at St Sulpice.[81] The curiosity that effected his fall from grace was also the means of its recovery.

Boredom, acedia and distinctions between vice and virtue, all point to qualities or properties of looking. They signify questions of the quality of sight, the seeking of relief from vacuity and the worries of seeing blankly and without significance. They also point to the social expectations involved in looking, its relational basis and its implications for the viewer and the viewed. How somebody is seen is a matter as important as the right to see. Acts of looking, and the culpability they can entail, have become replete with implication.

VI

The question of the gaze and its object of sight have come into sociology from three tributaries. The first comes from Foucault's explorations of the gaze considered above. The second emerges from concerns with pornography and the images that it generates. This leads to the third tributary, the relationship between the gaze and gender. Before it withered into postmodern uncertainties, feminism treated the relational aspects of the gaze in terms of the power of subjection when exercised by males with impunity. The right of the male to look in a particular way was subject to critical scrutiny. Whatever his inclinations, the gaze was deemed to be possessive, to turn women into objects of desire and to tyrannise them in the categorisations made.

Despite the scale of the sex industry, few of its discerning customers leave tracts or testimonies regarding what they saw. As Plummer has noted, 'even though millions of people look at pornography every day, very few have been willing to talk about this experience. The pornography consumer is only starting to "come out".'[82] Yet, few tales exist of those who do. They still face a divided public where some abhor treating women as sexual objects whilst others regard these sex industry workers as having a right to trade.[83] Few women have explored the issue of the male gaze at pornography, save to write it off as corrupting and exploitative.[84] The issue of why they look is not as simple as it might seem. There seems something perverse about what Hardy's study reveals of men engaging with women in pornographic settings where the text of conversations marks a failure in relationships with the 'real thing'. It is not surprising that the use of pornography was a shameful secret for men in his sample.

The pernicious effects of endlessly exploring pornographic images in cyberspace have been well explored in an article by Aitkenhead. Amplifying Giddens' notion of sexual addiction, she argues that moral panics over child pornography have obscured the addictive and damaging nature of adult sex sites. Permutations of taste seem endless in matters of sexuality. She suggests that pornography forms 25 per cent of all Internet traffic. In the UK, more than a third of the 10 million users log on to pornography websites. The sheer availability of what can be found in cyberspace forms the basis of the quest for more and more. The effects on women whose images appear in cyberspace to fulfil sexual fantasies can be devastating. First, they lose control of their images which are endlessly reproduced on many screens; and secondly, their self-image is reduced to that of being sexual objects with no prospects of escape. Warnings over the dangers of pornography have long disappeared. Aitkenhead notes that Christians are the only visible group left fighting these trends. Speaking of the demise of feminist concerns with pornography, she writes that 'it is as if an entire generation of research into the emotional effects of porn has simply been forgotten, leaving us with porn galore and not the faintest idea what it does'. A reason for the amnesia surrounding the damage affected by pornography is that it has vanished into the private domain, seemingly having no social effects.[85] Acts of viewing increasingly become devoid of social constraints. Seeing is not a matter of shame but of the exercise of Internet arts.

Giddens has examined the way sexual desire can become a disorder, one that requires a medical diagnosis. Loss of self-esteem and of self-control are part of this compulsive behaviour that turns what might be a leisure activity into an addiction, one that generates its own anxieties. Addiction leads to sensibilities of shame and inadequacy and these can come to undermine the project of the self and its reflexivity. What seems a game becomes the search for a fix, as Giddens expresses it.[86] As was suggested above, curiously little attention has given to the virtues of sexual inactivity in the sociology of sexuality. Those who seek 'to decline from sin and incline to virtue', as in the anthem of Farrant/Hilton, 'Lord for thy tender mercy's sake' have a non-existent sociological profile, yet there are signs of change, as reflected in a growth of concern with the values of modesty as a post-feminist virtue.[87]

No image is fated to be permanent, particularly in the context of present visual culture. As Sturken and Cartwright suggest, 'reflexivity...takes the form in postmodern style of referencing context or framing in order to rethink the viewer's relationship to an image or narrative'.[88] A long-standing outlet for fantasising and re-casting images has been the cinema. Studies of film increasingly deal with issues of narrative, time, politics and performance in a sociologically recognisable manner.[89] While the cinema is clearly an important facet of visual culture, remarkably little attention has been devoted to the spectator, his identity and moral dispositions. This anonymity relates to another peculiarity of the cinema and studies surrounding its basis that religion is seldom dealt with directly in a sympathetic manner.[90] Perhaps, giving institutional religion a favourable image might pose a threat to the properties of virtual religion and to the aura that the cinema seeks to nurture.

Despite these absences, approaches to the cinema assume some form of spectator and also that what is seen contains something unapparent, something to be disclosed.

Cultural studies, psychoanalysis and feminist approaches have dominated approaches to the cinematic spectator. De-constructing the spectator's interest in the pleasure of seeing has been matched by the colonisation of the gaze to agendas of sexual politics, so that concerns are less with pleasure than the forms of desire that involve the re-setting of images to fulfil their expectations. Thus, the gaze and the image seen combine to realise a fulfilment, a merging that confirms and affirms.[91] In her much cited essay on 'Visual Pleasure and Narrative Cinema', Mulvey treated viewing in psychoanalytical terms so that the structuring of seeing in the unconscious could be used to unfold the plight of the woman cast to fulfil the needs and pleasures of patriarchal culture. There she is designated as an object for fantasy and obsession, a signifier for the male other and also captive to his sights.[92] Using a Freudian notion of scopophilia, a pleasure in seeing, Mulvey treats the woman as the silent object of desire ripe for male appropriation where the female is but an object of pleasure. In this setting, the male is active and the female passive. The female identity is stolen. Did Mulvey create a feminist fantasy both of the seer and of who is seen?

Stacey argues that the woman in the cinema audience is virtually absent from the accounts of much of feminist theories and approaches to spectatorship.[93] Little attention has been given to the contextual setting of the spectators and their expectations. What the woman spectator saw in the female on the screen, what was identified with and the functions of the image form the themes of her work. Her study marks a contrast between the expectations of film studies and those of cultural studies, where context, meaning and consumption of image matter.[94] What is drawn out from feminist interventions into the visual is the manner in which images are structured to be seen in a fixed, estranging and dominating way. Yet, what seems missing is the issue of agency, of what the spectator elects to see? Even more worrisome is not only the invisibility of the spectator, his moral status, but also the issue of his inclinations.

In an original study, Denzin explores how the gaze has been regulated by variables of gender, race and social class. Almost echoing the end of Huysman's *Against Nature*, Denzin treats the voyeur as the 'the iconic, post-modern self. Adrift in a sea of symbols, we find ourselves, voyeurs all, products of the cinematic gaze'.[95] For Denzin, the voyeur is a cinematic version of Foucault's gaze. Denzin's study is one of the obsessive desires to see where the gaze has investigative properties, of possible trespass into what is sacred and hidden. The critical ambition of this study is to unmask the voyeur who so demands to see the unseen with impunity. Unfortunately, as Denzin aptly suggests, the cinema creates the spectator in its own eye so that the gazer is empowered but in a way that validates what is presented to him.[96]

Seeing too much generates occupational hazards for those who live lives of surveillance of others. Thus, in the cinematic representations of the 'investigative voyeur', the professional gazer, the reporter and the private detective are portrayed as unhappy, neurotic and are often alcoholics. These illustrate the dangers of living by looking too closely.[97]

Denzin's vision of the plight of the voyeur is bleak. He inhabits 'a pornography of the visible' one that is all pervasive,[98] and like *Peeping Tom* in Powell's famous film, he has a murderous eye. This film forms the metaphor for his book, for Denzin argues that 'in the race to capture the visual field in its entirety, the cinematic society has insinuated an apparatus that kills what it seeks to understand'.[99] The moral responsibilities of the voyeur to be implicated in what is seen and to gaze with responsibility have become accentuated. As Denzin notes, 'postmodern culture is built upon a structure of visual mirrors: we see, but never feel or hear, the sounds of the other's mind'. In his consideration of the voyeur, Denzin raises two important queries? First, how is the cold gaze of Foucault to be replaced by something more compassionate, and more existential? Secondly, and more potently, he asks 'can a culture so heavily dependent on visual representations survive?'[100] These questions return back to the wider concerns of the study.

VII

Is the sin of Alypius in looking at gladiatorial sports that involved dismemberment of limbs for public amusement much different to present voyeurs who take pleasure in seeing the fate of the man who came as dinner? It is easy to be mesmerised by the miracles of the Internet and to engage in a moral panic about what it can portray. The sin of Alypius and the nerd who gains pleasure from seeing acts of cannibalism on the Internet is that both act as unfeeling spectators on the pain and death of others. Each is culpable. Alypius opened his eyes to become part of a ritual order that provided spectacles of cruelty to millions in the Coliseum. The computer nerd who seeks to see acts of cruelty on the Internet has at some stage to reconcile what is available on the Internet with what is unavailable in the practice of social life. Reference to the social does not resolve such issues. The spectacles that gave Alypius such pleasure had a decidedly ritual cast about them. What does emerge is what the social is harnessed, shaped and geared to do. Properties have to be stipulated and these lend a predictable and expected facet to operations with the social. It is but a means, a setting to see things better. Conventions for looking not only mark out values but also embody them in social transactions.

The sense of being seen seeing is the property missing in the voyeur. His viewing is anonymous. His disembodiment in seeing gives him a licence to be exempt from accusations of being caught in the act of seeing. His implication in the act of seeing becomes apparent only if he transfers the universe of his gaze from the virtual to the real. Preservation of a state of disembodiment is his best defence against being caught. But the more he stays removed from the social implications of seeing, the more he forgets protocols for seeing that would alert him to the dangers of his unfettered gaze. At some end point, the voyeur has to enter an arena of choice of how much more he wants to see and how free is his capacity to select. If he gets worried, he has to re-consider the issues of practices of seeing, unless he is to be but a mirror that refracts everything but nothing of his self.

Structuring the visual consciousness of the voyeur into a moral language of choice reverts to a highly significant notion of Goffman, one mentioned earlier: co-presence. It demands some etiquette, some form of looking appropriate to circumstances.[101] Manners for dealing with the visible bear on practices of seeing, but not being seen.

It is inconceivable that Goffman's *Stigma*, first published in 1963, could be issued now. First, it is a profoundly politically incorrect study, where the onus is on the stigmatised to act in ways that render life neat and easy for the 'normals'. Secondly, disability legislation makes redundant the apologetic grovelling of the stigmatised. Their pre-emptive manoeuvres that sought to avoid giving visual offence now seem offensive, but the price of their removal causes the basis of Goffman's analysis to disappear. Accession to the civil rights of the disabled has removed the need for such forms of etiquette of regard, for now the stigmatised are the beneficiaries of a politics of inclusion. Yet, the issues generated by the stigmatised anticipate many of the dilemmas of seeing or not that concern visual culture.

The stigmatised are those with blemishes either of appearance or life style. It is the former, those whose stigma is all too visible and discrediting, which are of most concern to Goffman. They face dilemmas over how to conceal and to reveal facets of the self in circumstances of evident social and visible discredit. In *Stigma*, Goffman is concerned with how the stigmatised inhabit a virtual social identity, one based on imputation by others who act on what they see. The dilemmas of the stigmatised relate to how they reconcile discrepancies between actual and virtual identities, the gap between how they should be seen and what the gaze of the others imputes. In considering how the stigmatised handle their dilemmas, Goffman points to their moral careers earlier mentioned, the personal adjustments that are made in response to the standpoint (the gaze) of the 'normal'. Goffman introduces an important concept of 'passing'. This points to a skill of the stigmatised, of 'passing' in ways that leave their marks of shame unsignified and so facilitates their acceptance by the 'normals'.[102] In this setting, the self takes on a capacity to partition itself in information strategies so that, even though seen, the stigmatised seek to control how they are seen or not.[103]

The subterfuges of the stigmatised are based on a need to minimise their social obtrusiveness. Their concern is with strategies of mitigation of marks of shame. These relate to Goffman's notion of covering, a property of restriction of display of failings.[104] For Goffman, passing and covering are about the arts of impression management. The skills of selective disclosure, of what is to be seen and what is not to be seen, led Goffman to claim that 'stigma management is a general feature of society'.[105] What emerges is the selectivity of what is seen in social acts of exchange that have moral dimensions. The need to cover, to regulate what is seen relates to the management of virtue and what is prudent to disclose.

The notion of shame in exposure and how to respond to it relates to another cultural practice: the veiling of Islamic women in public so that their faces are hidden. As nuns abandoned notions of appearing veiled in public in the mid-1960s, on the basis that this made their roles incredible, a decade later for different reasons Islamic women found the practice credible as a means of resistance to the allures of modernity.[106] It might seem such practices as the veiling of Islamic women are trivial, yet an enormous amount of symbolic and cultural dispute has centred on the implications of the practice. This has been especially so in France, where efforts to ban this practice of veiling in public divides the left. For some, it symbolises the repression of women, whereas for others it marks a right to a cultural and religious practice. For the French government, veiling violates the purity of the secularisation of public space, hence it is seeking to have the practice banned in schools, universities and other civic places.

These practices generated much perplexity in the West, where the female contribution to visual culture seems one of revealing all, and not concealing all. The act of concealing in veiling has a logic of its own. For Islamic women, veiling is about rights to view their face. The concealing is not about the masking of discredit, as in the case of the stigmatised, but about the preservation of credit, the virtues of modesty. The issue of veiling indicates how these women elect to be seen especially by non-Muslims.[107] The *burqa'*, a veil that covers the face of Islamic women, was a garment few knew about until the Afghan war. Leaving aside issues of fear about appearing unveiled with the face revealed, what does this practice indicate that is of sociological significance? In her account of veiling, Guindi draws attention to a number of important points. Veiling carries a woman's privacy into the public sphere and permits a regulation of who she sees, but also who is entitled to see her.[108] After the war, some women elected to keep wearing their *burqa'* in public. Those who abandoned the garment found that intrusive forms of public scrutiny replaced the civil inattention the *burqa'* facilitated. The women had to learn how to engage the face in public and to learn how its expressions might be read.[109]

Guindi's study reveals four important points. First, she links identity to virtue in terms of symbols and forms of resistance. She points to a re-invention of tradition in the circumstances of modernisation that enabled women to fulfil a religious sensibility felt after the Six Days War in 1967. Women started to re-invent a seventh-century custom for the circumstances of the gaze in the twentieth century. Secondly, she draws attention to the way the veil frees women from the risk of being seen as sexual objects. The veil enhances their sense of being and living as autonomous subjects. Oddly, this practice of veiling seems a radical response to feminist worries about women being treated as objects. Thirdly, she draws attention to the property of segregation, reflecting the harem and gate. This reflects a division between the public, where the woman is seen in de-sexualised terms, as covered, but in private, can reveal to certain eligible groups with a potential to deal with her in sexual terms.[110] Finally, she sees veiling as a form of empowerment of self-definition and autonomy. In concealing and revealing, the woman becomes an agent 'of self-identity, values and the virtues she aspires to embody.

Stigma and the notion of veiling draw attention to the sensitivities involved in the act of seeing and being seen. They express sensibilities of the visual, an awareness that the act of seeing or being seen has social implications. This elective conscious property to the visual underlines the potency of choice in decisions to see or to be seen. They provide in miniature in the detail of social interaction, a template for dealings with the seen and the unseen that form the basis of the study. Seeing and being seen bear on practices, protocols and rituals that sustain a social order, where the visual is treated as a vital ingredient. A particular facet of the visual, one that points to important properties of disclosure of sensibilities and understandings, is the observation of those who see. Their visual response speaks volumes.

This point was brought home in an exhibition of paintings in the National Gallery of Ireland that focused on late seventeenth- and eighteenth-century Dutch genre paintings dealing with responses to the receipt of letters. The domestic setting, the pose of the body, but above all the face caught reading matters of deep significance illustrated the intensity of the gaze and the rich variety of meanings captured in the act of seeing and being seen with a letter. Looking at these paintings, one realised that, as the preface to the catalogue suggested, a whole form of ritual had vanished with the advent of email communications.[111] It is unlikely that anyone would bother to paint a hapless recipient of emails. Rapidity of response hardly generates time or interest in summoning up some composure worthy of artistic attention. What has almost disappeared into memory is the ritualistic form of response to what is read and seen, a point Sutton makes well in his essay on the exhibition.[112]

The exhibition of paintings caught the act of looking as it dealt with reading between the lines of letters whose text could not be seen. One could only view the paintings in terms of inference, by concentrating not only on what is seen, but also on what is unseen. The novelty of a letter, its careful and stylistic composition and the hazards of delivery marked the significance of what was received. The occasion of seeing the letter and reading it encapsulated an image and suggested something singular, something noteworthy and something of the utmost significance. Something was received that was worthy of a gaze that caught the breadth of the human condition.

Lurking in the whole issue of the seen and the unseen is that some look and some do not and it is hard to think what sociology can say about a mere glance that might or might not be of biographical significance. This might be so, but there is a still a sociological issue about that which marks the voyeur's dilemma: does he elect to disappear from the social or to appear in it?

The voyeur who claims to see all without reference to the social is in denial over having anything to share in public. He is not going to manifest in public, in the realm of the social, a testimony to what he has seen. Such a sharing would undermine his autonomy as a faceless viewer, one with no identifiable sociological traits. Disembodiment offers a safe retreat, a place of anonymity amidst the multitudes of similarly unaccountable lurkers whose identity lies beyond sociological ken. As the technology for visual culture expands, the avenues for retreat into anonymity increase. As this occurs, the visual takes on a dangerous potency, for what one encounters is an attribute of a visual culture that increasingly lacks forms of sociological redress. When sociology looks to see who is mirrored in the viewing, it sees nobody in particular. To the sociological eye, the gazer has no qualities.

If the voyeur elects to resolve his dilemma, the isolation of disembodiment, and seeks embodiment, then a different agenda of aspiration emerges. He wishes to work back into social reality in a way that renders him liable to account for what he sees. He permits the act of looking to be seen and in so doing makes himself available for scrutiny perhaps sufficient for those who see him seeing to ask what he saw. His testimonies become instruments of self-recognition, as he turns what is refracted in the social back on to himself. Attention to embodiment in seeing marks the potential to take the act of seeing into the social realm, to re-cast the image so seen in a context where seeing can be claimed to be a form of believing. If acts of seeing were so trustworthy, he who so sees would have no scruples in telling tales that say so. Taking back to the social what is found in images on the Internet and in the mechanical reproduction of visual culture effect a fleshing out of the identity of the voyeur, an unmasking that yields a scrutiny of identity and what is identified. If pure in heart, the voyeur who comes out into the social should fear no scrutiny.

The voyeur's dilemma regarding the social leads to another point. One of the curiosities surrounding reports of cases of misuses of the Internet is that they refer to individuals who collect and store thousands of images. One shudders to think what they see in each, but what is clear is that these images generate no lasting satisfaction. Somehow temptation and boredom are the fate of those who so collect. Again, this is not to suggest that all on the Internet is open to such abuses. What is suggested is that technology applied to visual culture has masked an endemic problem in the mechanical reproduction of art – the loss of aura, but also the ritual surround that secured a distance from the image seen, one that served also to protect its vulnerability. The need to stand back has become less clear, so that acts of seeing have become fragile just at the point when a grammar for ways of seeing in the setting of the social runs the risk of being lost.

If ways of seeing are to be understood in a fullness of embodiment, they have to be located in sites of practice where the eye uses the cultural as a filter to form a basis of expectation and recognition. A capacity needs to be re-nurtured. This involves the cultivation of a gimlet eye, one fit for the making of fine distinctions, such as between the virtual and real and between the allures of temptation and the stability a life of virtue generates. Boredom and temptation pose demands of choice, imperatives to act, to attend to inner dispositions that have enabling powers for social realisation on some field. These dispositions reflect inclinations of ambition to wrest some ontology, some changed sense of self from what is seen.

It is not that the morality of seeing has in anyway been changed by the advent of the Internet. Nor has the issue of the seen and the unseen vaporised in a culture of postmodernity; if anything, the need to attend to it has increased, for increasingly the actor feels he is an outsider on what has gone before. Cultural memory suggests that those in the past saw from the inside in ways that did not require the invention of artificial forms of recollection of the visual talents of their predecessors. Those in the medieval past posted few forms in evidence that those who went before saw better than they could. In the present, there is an estrangement of the eyes, where the gazer is doomed to see from the margins, where all is packaged to be seen in expected ways. In the brilliance of the ordering of sights, like a mist, the unseen seems to have blown off the present ground of culture revealing lights that offer few comforts.

5
Piety and Visual Culture: Seeking to See the Unseen

The cold dark side of modernity that formed Weber's legacy to later sociologists seems to have left little scope or hope for little epiphanies. Yet, unexpectedly, these can still come. Sitting in the Lady Chapel of Ely Cathedral, some of the perplexities of the study came into visual and mental focus. One had gone over to Ely to escape the text and to sit and think about the way ahead. The enormous plain glass East window in the Lady Chapel was a fit object for gaze. The reredos that decorated this window was stripped bare. At the foot of the East window was a minor distraction, a most unsuitable modern statue of a woman in blue, who seemed to incarnate the Marian and the postmodern in some unfitting experiment that owed some debt to New Age sentiments. One gazed in awe at this very odd conglomeration of the visual where nothing seemed to add up. Something in the view was decidedly missing. The reverie was interrupted.

A guide came in with a tour party and they wandered around. He announced that only one of the many little figures recessed in the walls and the reredos retained a head. In 1539, a Protestant iconoclast on a horse had ridden around the Lady Chapel and had decapitated the lot. His sword marks were still visible on many of the headless statues. The medieval stained glass was also smashed at the same time. This dismantling of the links between visual culture and piety by those who confused the claims of religious beauty with those of idolatry caused an anonymous poet to protest about such practices elsewhere:

> Had you one spark of reason, you would finde
> Your selves like Idols to have eyes yet blind.
> 'Tis onely some base niggard Heresie
> To think Religion loves deformity,
> Glory did never yet make God the lesse,
> Neither can beauty defile holinesse.[1]

The tour guide left with his party and the art exhibition was closed. As the Lady Chapel became deserted, one sat in an enveloping silence for a quarter of an hour. The cathedral loomed large through the windows on the south side of the Chapel. Sitting there, one felt splendidly marooned from a culture of postmodernity and from artificial worlds of heritage and tourism. Indeed, this seemed a world safe from sociology – to misuse Goffman. Somehow the silence merged with a sense that there was a lot of light in the Chapel coming in from the plain glass windows. One sat and thought, peacefully enveloped in some sense of presence, one that elicited a need to attend to the seen and to look for the unseen, much of which seemed about. Somehow the light without irradiated within, perhaps in ways that Suger and St Bonaventure might have applauded.[2] Despite the Protestant on a horse who long ago had galloped off into history, a healing presence had settled down. Somehow, one saw what this study was about.

Then a verger and the precentor came in to prepare for the service. In some mysterious way the silence switched from something enveloping to something anticipating. Others came and sat down peacefully for evensong. Duly at 5.30 p.m., the choir of men and boys, in their red cassocks and long clean white surplices, swept in as if armed with a re-possession order to convert the Lady Chapel back to intended use. As the ritual unfolded, one felt something had been plucked back from the forces of secularisation. Canticles by Byrd and Parsons' plangent anthem *Ave Maria* were sung with due solemnity. At the end, duty done, in a matter of fact manner the choir, as captains and kings, marched out in orderly procession. The eye shifted again over the emptiness, but with a memory that the building had realised a designation. The way it was seen shifted in the light of the ritual event. It had left a stamp, an impress, unseen but there, that what was empty had been filled and that next Friday the Lady Chapel would be re-filled. What had been loosened in the memory was now re-chained in a steely manner. The seen had collided with the unseen but with some sociological ingredients. Halbwachs captured the issue well when he argued that

> religion transports us into another world, that its object is eternal and immutable, and that religious acts by which this idea is manifested – even though they occur in a specific place and at a specific date – imitate or at least symbolize this eternity and this fixity through their infinite repetition and their uniform aspects.[3]

Memories that resonate present a demand note for retrieval in some social manifestation, for as Halbwachs noted 'there is hence no memory without perception'.[4] But if memory needs to be re-made, it must not sustain a fiction that those in the past did not have struggles to see the unseen. After all, those who built the Lady Chapel sought also to see the unseen. They too had to realise an 'as if' property in the social to see the unseen. What is seen now in the remains of memory simply passes down the imperative to cope with the perplexity of how the unseen is to be seen. They too had to yield to something to see something. In past and present, the aspirations of the inner eye are given temporary visual relief in the outer forms of perception. It is, however, on the ground of the social, in particular practices, where theological truths are forged in their visual dimensions. Something is seen in the social that becomes indicative of the unseen. This is not just a sociologist's fantasy. This was well understood in the invention of Lourdes whose processions of the Eucharist were 'spectacle... for the poor, who would find solace in a revitalized nineteenth-century vision of medieval pageantry', as one observer at the time noted.[5] This emphasis on pious spectacle carried forward medieval traditions such as the Corpus Christi procession that served to link seeing to the affirmation of belief. What was of the unseen was displayed for those who believed they had eyes to so see.

Again, one keeps returning to a question that seems to haunt this study. Why do some see and others do not? Some might sit for months in the Lady Chapel and be blind to what others have seen. Clearly, these are matters of theological formulation, yet they have to be connected to the incarnational, for it is clear that in some mysterious way the social is a vital ingredient in the linking of the seen and the unseen. Ways of seeing, the edification secured and the basis of recognition and reception are all related back to the cultural. Its properties are not mechanical but rather facilitating. Somehow what is in social habiliment enables the unseen to be seen.

The sociology that characterises authentically this transformation finds a habitation in theology. Telling tales in its clumsy rhetoric and governed by an eye for detail that borders on scrupulosity, what can sociology speak of that theologians do not know? The tale sociology can utter is of what oddly seems to elude the theologians' gaze: the making of faith *on* the ground of culture and in this context, in relation to the visual.

The first section of the chapter settles on a sociological notion of religious capital that makes a vitally important contribution to theological understandings of how religiosity is constructed. The notion of capital with its resonance of exploitation and calculation might seem an odd concept to use for sociological understandings of the cultural basis of the reproduction of religiosity. Yet, far from signifying reductionist implications, the notion of religious capital supplies a focus to the stewardship of cultural and religious resources. The agnosticism inherent in the concept of religious capital facilitates understandings of how the actor on the field deals with the efforts to reconcile the seen with the unseen. Habitus supplies a crucial concept for reconciling activities on the field with the actor's perspective. The term habitus relates to capacities and dispositions. Happily it supplies the elective property to the visual that besets the study. This elective notion is completed when related to Bourdieu's notion of symbolic capital. The capacity to see and to act accordingly is given a sociological remit. The relational facets of the eye emerge signifying not only what it sees but also what it expects to see.

The second section comes to the issue of why some see and some do not. Incapacity to see relates to notions of blindness. In dealing with the seen and the unseen, sociology has to confront a paradox of sight, the notion that the blind see. But if seeing is possible, it needs some social path, some vision of how to move on the ground of culture but in ways that rise above it. This need relates to the third section of the chapter, a concern with pilgrimage. This notion of journeying links not only memory and tales, but also transformations in an endeavour that is undeniably social. Pilgrimage gives expression to a spiritual need, a questing that has a focal point to journeying. It is through the social that this is to be found. The journeying points to a need to forge links with the unseen, the other worldly, what is of the heavenly. This provides links into what *The City of God* opens out. These are matters of pilgrimage, of journeying to seek some end for the eyes to be restless no more.

Some image, some face, some end point lies at the end of the pilgrim journey, but in so travelling in a realm that is profoundly sociological, a theological conundrum is encountered that goes to the heart of the seen and the unseen. What assumptions and presumptions lie in the act of endeavouring to see the unseen? In facing these issues, in section four, sociology need not re-invent a theological wheel. This problem is long-standing in theology in the issues generated over iconography and the iconoclastic responses.

I

Seeing forms part of some collectivity, some consensus as to how symbols, icons, images and works of art are to be used. Geertz has suggested that culture and art have particular sensibilities that have a collective formation as wide as social existence.[6] Artistic products such as colourings or line representation signify social structures, relationships and rules of access. In this regard, the visual enables society to represent itself. Thus, flags not only give visual embodiment to national identity but also supply a focal point for the values of a culture to be represented. Those who pledge loyalty to the flag can give visual expression to their inner sentiments of patriotism. They know what to see when they look at *their* flag, for they know what the act of looking peculiarly effects for them. But what is presented for those with a capacity to see can generate acute sociological problems. The visual has a self-validating property where expectations of seeing often are confirmed in the act of looking. What is seen has a contingent character, a mirroring property that reflects social relationships. In Chapter 3, mention was made of Bourdieu's comment that the photograph was a statement of the group's social relationships. In his account, the camera is an instrument of social description. It supplies images through which a culture can see itself. But the social relationships so revealed also indicate stipulations and expectations as to how the visual *ought* to be seen. A brilliant work published in 1972, Baxandall's

Painting & Experience in Fifteenth Century Italy, anticipates many facets of Bourdieu's approach to the cultural context of the visual.

Baxandall suggested that 'a fifteenth-century painting is the deposit of a social relationship' between the painter and his client who provided exact specifications for what was to be painted.[7] These specifications related to matters of use, for the paintings were often religious in theme. In this context, as Baxandall elegantly expresses it, 'the painter was a professional visualizer of the holy stories'.[8] These stories were well known, hence the expected properties to the paintings and the images they portrayed. Likewise, a knowledge of the styles of particular painters enabled commissions to be relatively exact and the contracts were drawn to secure these expectations. In this context, Baxandall supplies an immensely valuable notion of the period eye, a term of Panofsky that is also used by Bourdieu.

The concept refers to the expectations of perception of the beholder, the skills of discrimination he possesses. The painting is set to capitalise on these skills and to be read in a particular way. Sharing habits of viewing and visual experience, both the painter and the beholder realise a mutuality where the expectations of both are confirmed in the image painted.[9] Working on the notion that things seen are more memorable than what is heard, these late medieval religious paintings gave directions as to what to venerate. If the painter realised his vocation, artistic and religious, 'he complements the beholder's interior vision'.[10] Giving external expression to these inner visual hopes, the painter becomes a crucial enabler of moving from the seen into the unseen. In this regard, he comes near to supplying that 'as if' to the visual. Baxandall points to the rituals that sought to link to the pictorial, so that both the social and the visual were directed to matters unseen and the realisation of a common sense of refraction, where the inner eye was satisfied by external forms of perception. Attached to religious imagery, the period eye pointed to realisations of believing through seeing that could be traced to a religious ambit.

Unfortunately, contingency fractures this self-confirming facet of the period eye. Now there are many eyes, with many sensibilities and skills of seeing and the expectations of use are rarely purely religious in terms of what Baxandall chronicled. Yet, in a curious way matters have come full circle. The societal property of the period eye has now been displaced by its individualised format. The security of the gaze that sought to reproduce the unseen in the seen came to an end at the close of the seventeenth century. Expectations of sight shifted from the heavenly to what the eye of reason could and should disclose on earth.[11]

Chronicling the unravelling of the link between the seen and the unseen in artistic representation is outside the scope and capacity of this study. War, plunder, venality, state intervention, the rise of civic expectations of art, and shifts in patronage have made their own contribution to the de-contextualisation of sacred art and the loss of its apparently monopolistic powers to link believing to seeing. The Reformation made its own contribution by seeking to disconnect the link between piety and visual representation. The structures and rituals that effected the link were demolished in English society and, as said before, were erased from memory. It might seem that secularisation, the outcome of these forces of disconnection, has won. If all this has occurred, why does the social process of seeing in Baxandall's period eye still have significance for sociological understandings of visual culture?

Curiously, it is cyberspace that has completed the circle. Access to the virtual means the beholder can make any image to exploit his skills and expectations of seeing. Technology now supplies what the painter hitherto supplied, images that affirm individual expectations of what should be seen. Almost any image can be made in virtual reality that confirms any expectation and indeed goes beyond it. The Internet is now the painter of anything for the new client, the voyeur. But in the endless array of images now available in this re-cast period eye, some end point, some capacity to discriminate, is required; for the eye that sees everything unselectively sees nothing. To see selectively presupposes a capacity to discern, select and see below the surface what is worth appreciating. It is true that instructions can be given on the screen as to how to discriminate between images, but this is to miss the point. Capacities for discernment relate to forms of negotiation and these presuppose cultural resources to do so. The eye has to know what it draws from within the field of culture to see and cyberspace tells only a partial tale of its borrowings.

As indicated earlier, Bourdieu constructs his sociology with an unexpected amount of reference to Catholicism and to metaphors and rhetoric derived from it. Transferring back his approach to culture to understand Catholicism and the visual seems a just form of restoration. His concepts of cultural and symbolic capital have been extended into notions of religious capital.

Bourdieu uses the notion of cultural capital to refer to resources of qualification and knowing that can be converted into instruments of power to maximise autonomy on a field of play, to ward off rivals, and to regulate entries and exits to it. Autonomy also refers to a capacity to keep secure the rules of play of that particular field. Expenditure of cultural capital aids in playing stakes to win. On the other hand, symbolic capital refers to a power of recognition exercised often metaphorically in religious language. Central to his sociology of culture, symbolic capital bears a property of ambiguity, for it points to powers of recognition and misrecognition. In his account, symbolic capital is an ideological instrument of misrepresentation, one that disguises interest and bases of power. It controls the contours of the field in misrepresentations whose basis sociology serves to unmask. Agency stands in a relationship to disclosure.

In a religious setting, symbolic capital might well yield unproductive notions of false consciousness, but it also points to realisations of what cannot be unmasked, what cannot be revealed, and in short what cannot be seen. In this regard, recognition and misrecognition are not a function of agency or of sociological powers of arbitration and revelation. Rather the issue of their revelation lies within a theology, a mystery of salvation, where the only discernments are based on a grace to see. Resolution of recognitions and misrecognitions take on different meanings when set in a religious field, for they point to capacities to discern but not to resolve. The habitus or disposition so nurtured is cultivated to cope with more provisional irresolvable ends, those that bear on the unseen.

In Bourdieu's characterisation of the field, mystification is a means of exclusion, and symbolic violence expresses the way those unfit to see collude in their own marginalisation. Those so unworthy affirm the profaning basis of their gaze and remove themselves from the field lest they be humiliated in a ranking and classification.[12] Because he does not deal with the actual content of the field, for example the notion of beauty in relation to aesthetics, Bourdieu is concerned with a process of enactment, its mapping and functions. His sociological interest lies in exposing marginality and the power to secure domination of those blind to see. By contextualising and by blending agency into structure through the notion of habitus, Bourdieu gets inside the game as played. At its minimum, his sociology is one of the places or situations to exercise the potential of the field. This has certain advantages for those who play with religion, not so much fiddling with it, but seeking to believe in it.

In a useful overview, Swartz draws attention to the almost neutralised approach to religion available in Bourdieu. Weber's approach to religion underlay Bourdieu's approach to culture. This related to issues of interest, where symbolic resources, goods and services were utilised to maximum effect. Bourdieu used the term religious capital to refer to the symbolic labour that constitutes the religious field. Now, at one level Bourdieu's approach is reductionist, for he follows Weber in seeing clerical power as a form of domination, of conversion of what reflects interest into disinterest. In this regard, Swartz reads Bourdieu well in regard to the outcomes of domination of symbolic labour.[13] But at another level, Bourdieu supplies a massively important means of opening sociology into theology. Contrary to those who see resources for faith, such as sacraments, icons and visual narratives, such as the Stations of the Cross, sacramentals and their aesthetics as in some way incredible and unfitting for a modern age, Bourdieu is arguing the reverse. For him, they are all too credible as resources of power, as forms of symbolic and cultural capital. Without these resources of capital, the domination he so criticises could not be effected. They *are* the instruments of power, and in this regard Catholicism has centre stage, given its immense reserves of richness of symbolic and cultural capital. What liberal theologians treat as incredible is in Bourdieu's usage all too credible as a resource of power. Leaving aside Bourdieu's mechanical approach to power (in terms of domination and revelation) what is taken for granted is that something highly significant is produced that is worth defending by the producers.

Working from a different route, Iannoccone provides a less reductionist and more enabling approach to religious capital, one more directed to understanding *how* belief is secured through enactment on a field. Locating capital in economics, the sociological concern is with the maximisation of resources in terms of skills and general education. Religious capital can be characterised in terms of a productive process, as an input into forms of realisation. Unlike in Bourdieu, the laity are treated as active parties in the realisation of this religious capital. In this regard, capital is a resource of investment, one that involves degrees of calculation of benefit, hence the way issues of conversion emerge in his approach. Capital refers to a familiarity 'with a religion's doctrines, rituals traditions and members'. This bears on properties of habit, a satisfaction in practice, but one whose production requires specialist skills.[14] The value of reference to religious capital is that it concentrates on how belief is reproduced. This gets around generalities that something in modernity precludes this possibility.

Stark and Finke use the term religious capital to refer to 'the degree of mastery of attachment to a particular religious culture'. The term is used in relation to conversion, affiliation and choice. Because converts need to justify their choice of movements, they seek to exploit religious capital as far as possible to re-constitute their re-cast biography and to root their newly found identity.[15] Religious capital compliments Weber's approach to office charisma in terms of illuminating the transmission of skills of clerical practice and its formation amongst novices and seminarians.[16] Habitus becomes linked to cultural and symbolic capital as a form of imitation and appropriation. By introducing a notion of calculation of difference in terms of investment, the use of religious capital, unexpectedly, causes sociology to criticise theology for failing to supply in cultural practice, specifications for the realisation of belief on the ground of culture. The notion of religious capital points to matters of stewardship of difference and detail wholly at odds with the generalised utterance and flabby pluralism of what came from Vatican II. Ironically, in use of religious capital sociology might seem to take on a fundamentalism, a literalism of belief that theologians might find perplexing. It is sociology that seeks to have made definite what theology likes to treat as indefinite. Following other critics, Stark and Finke suggest that the church itself, not modernity, effected the collapse in vocations that occurred after Vatican II. The notion that vocations to religious life, particularly for women, made no appreciable difference to heavenly prospects suggested that their sacrifices were in vain.[17] It was this notion of religious capital one wished to use for the proposed study of virtue and vocation that was abandoned, as mentioned in the Introduction.

The notion of religious capital treats what belongs to the visual as a resource for seeing the unseen. What is used is mobilised to point towards the unseen so that those so trained to see proceed 'as if' they do. Bourdieu is of particular value in drawing attention to the manner of expenditure of cultural capital, not so much in terms of some visual plausibility, but in relation to the demands made on the actor who so spends. For the game to be played, the actor has to have some interest in it. This draws attention to a concept of Bourdieu: *illusio*.

Every practice has a field of struggle with its own *illusio*. This term occurs in the context of interests in the struggle. For Bourdieu, the game cannot be played with disinterest or indifference. Interest forms a defence of autonomy of the field. *Illusio* is an expression and realisation of that notion of interest. It refers to the 'tacit recognition of the value of the stakes of the game and as practical mastery of its rules'. This bears on the practical sense of a socially constituted field and the games played on it.[18] To play, the players have to be taken in by the game. They have to make an act of faith to it and permit themselves to be seduced by it, otherwise they have no means of play. If they cannot invest, they cannot play. They collude together to play. Every game has its own trump card.[19] The notion of investment, of playing for stakes, provides a property of chance, of wager with what is of indeterminacy. It also bears on notions of hope and trust, for these are the virtues realised in the investment in the game. It is the harnessing of the religious capital to the liturgical game that enables its players to act 'as if' seeing into the unseen. They act 'as if' there is no gap between the earthly and the heavenly city, for their liturgical enactments represent a fusion of both. The actors let go of inhibition and doubt to permit that sense of walking under heavenly canopies that overshadow earthly ritual endeavours.

What is manifest in the social is an outcome of what the eye wishes to see and *illusio* expresses this disposition to participate within the ambit of what the image proclaims. Of course the actor could be charged with dealings in optical illusions, but then this is a wager his habitus cultivates him to make. It is the price *illusio* demands to play. The value of religious capital is that it draws attention to the property of collusion and expectation involved in seeing. A focus is supplied and a sense of not seeing alone is also delivered. The visual takes on a collective and affirming dimension. Yet, this is only part of the sociological question of the visual. What is seen has a property of the elusive; it belongs to matters of taste and aesthetics that elude sociological definition. If sociology is not to stand outside religious facets of the visual, it has to take into account paradoxes and contradictions of seeing or not that lie at the centre of the belief system: Catholicism. Again emerge the perplexing questions of why some see and some do not. What is seen cannot be 'proven' and indeed, re-seeing is often not possible. Sometimes it is about a magical moment of perception that might never come again, hence one's hesitation to return too soon to the Lady Chapel in Ely Cathedral. As one enters the theological terrain of the visual, sociology starts to face types of questions it is prone to resist. Here one enters a grey area of reflexivity, regarding not only how to choose but also how to act before what is visual that lies within theological remit.

II

The issue of why some see, and others do not, can be linked to two biblical texts. The first relates to the notion of seeing to believe and this concerns the plight of the Israelites who had been fatally bitten by serpents. In a reversal of the Garden of Eden, God told Moses to set a serpent on a pole so that any man who is bitten 'when he beheld the serpent of brass, he lived' (Num. 21:9). In his account of the symbolic and cultural basis of blindness, Barasch indicates the way the serpent, often symbolising the sun, could rejuvenate its eyes. It was also associated with restoration of sight to the blind.[20] This relates to another text where Christ prophesises his crucifixion: 'when ye have lifted up the Son of man, then shall ye know that I am he' (Jn 8:28). This was not only an expression of His claims to Divinity but also their recognition. Why are some who see so blind? They are unaffected by what they see, in contrast to others. This draws in the second biblical text.

When Jesus saw a man born blind, his disciples assumed the state was due to sin. Christ answered rather oddly: 'neither hath this man sinned, nor his parents; but that the works of God should be made manifest in him' (Jn 9:1–3). After curing the man, Christ announced that 'for judgement I am come into this world, that they which see not might see and that they which see might be made blind' (Jn 9:39). This tale of the cure of the blind man can be understood as referring to the symbol of baptismal re-birth, a regeneration, a conversion of the eyes to see the light of Christ.[21] Seeking God can become an ultimate goal, the consummation of all things. As Bernard of Clairvaux noted in a sermon, 'what virtue can be attributed to him who does not seek God? What limit is there for him who seeks him? "Always seek his face," it says' (Ps. 104:4).[22] Some elect not to see God. Some see what they want to see. Thus,

> The transgression of the wicked saith within my heart, that there is no fear of God before his eyes.
> For he flattereth himself in his own eyes, until his iniquity be found to be hateful (Ps. 36:1–2).

The iniquitous have no need to believe that 'the eyes of the Lord are upon the righteous' (Ps. 34:15). They do not believe that 'the Lord seeth not as man seeth; for man looketh on the outward appearance, but the Lord looketh on the heart' (1 Sam. 16:7).

In a work dealing with the seen and the unseen that is cast in a theological direction, it is simply impossible to ignore the central proposition of Christianity, the remaining lines of the Creed, that God was made man, was crucified, died and rose on the third day. In short the unseen God was seen in Christ Jesus. If the event of the Resurrection was confined to those present to see with their corporeal eyes, then it is unlikely Christianity could have evolved over time. The Resurrection is the cornerstone of the study, for it governs all its questions about the seen and the unseen. It is where the randomness of seeing or not emerges.

After the Resurrection, some saw and recognised the Christ, but others, who should have, did not. For instance, Mary Magdalene conversed with the Risen Christ, but mistook Him for the gardener (Jn 20:15). Then there is the famous account of the two disciples on the road to Emmaus, who conversed deeply about the rumours of the Resurrection. As they conversed, Christ joined them 'but their eyes were holden that they should not know him' (Lk 24:16). He sat down with them, blessed and broke bread at the meal 'and their eyes were opened, and they knew him, and he vanished out of their sight' (Lk 24:31). Even in these pivotal events, those who saw did not see. What of those after the Ascension, the orphans left? Have they no epiphanies?

The capacity to see the unseen has not vanished. Visions still come in the night and make an indelible mark on what is seen in the day. Those who see the unseen seek to do so with eyes of faith. They are the pure in heart, endowed with gifts of grace to discern. St Augustine posited three levels of vision: the corporeal, which is seen with the eyes of the body; 'spiritual vision', images in dreams and imagination; and 'intellectual visions', where truths of the Divine are discerned. The second form occurs repeatedly in the Old and New Testament.[23] Sociology should have no ambitions to resolve, what theologians cannot, about the link between spiritual and corporeal sight. The concern of sociology is with the cultural basis of understanding how to cope with the antinomial and ambiguous properties presented by the seen and the unseen. Those who see with the eye of perception may not see with the inner eye. What if the need to see with the inner eye becomes so great that the eye of perception is rendered blind? It does not follow that they will see better, but some might believe that they do and accordingly realise their discernments in ways denied to the sighted. This formed the basis of Flannery O'Connor's *Wise Blood*.

The novel was about the battle for followers in a marketplace of preachers all with tales to tell, but seemingly with no rules of recognition as to their veracity. This was a world of autonomy, where wanderers and strangers sought re-enchantment in the evangelical supermarket of South Georgia in the 1950s. In some ways it is a parable of what is later to be the ethos of a culture of postmodernity. This point is well expressed in Smith's appraisal of Bauman's approach to communitarian tendencies in a culture of postmodernity where ambivalence becomes so accentuated. It is a world 'full of missionaries each seeking converts for her or his own brand of "religion". The confused wanderer through the postmodern landscape is beckoned in several different directions all at once'.[24] Again, the matter of distinction between the virtual and the real arrives to be rubbed in the sociological face.

After service in the Korean War, Hazel Moses returned to the Evangelical Deep South to his city of birth, Eastrod, to find its streets cluttered with preachers, including one 'blind' preacher, with his daughter, who helped to trade his testimonies. Scoffing this babble, Moses set up a Holy Church of Christ without Christ to preach against these other prophets, including the 'blind' one who claimed to see best. In the end of the book, Moses realised he could not see where he was going. He was chased by an image he could not see. To see better, he blinded himself with quicklime, but using less water than the 'blind' prophet did. The blinded Moses seemed to his landlady to see something. Found in a ditch, and brought back to the lodgings to die, the landlady stared into his eyes

> and felt as if she had finally got to the beginning of something she couldn't begin, and she saw him moving farther and farther away, farther and farther into the darkness until he was the pin point of light.[25]

How can the blind seeing be understood? What happens when sight is restored?

Those born blind, or who become so when very young, inhabit a tactile world, one where sound and touch govern their contact with life outside the body. Denied an outward eye, they build up an inward culture of inference. Their incapacity to see arouses considerable curiosity as to the nature of their inner worlds. Famously, Diderot used the light of reason to explore these worlds unseen by the sighted, but discerned by the unsighted.[26] For the blind, Simmel suggests that in social interaction 'the other person is actually present only in the alternating periods of his utterance'. Yet, not seeing has consolations, for he goes on to add:

> the expression of the anxiety and unrest, the traces of all past events, exposed to view in the faces of men, escape the blind, and that may be the reason for the peaceful and calm disposition, and the unconcern toward their surroundings, which is so often observed in the blind.

The focal point of character is the face. It is the site of inference where truth or falsity is to be found. It is what one seeks to gaze at first, for the face can set the tenor of social exchange. As Simmel remarked, 'the face is the geometric chart of all these experiences. It is the symbol of all that which the individual has brought with him as the pre-condition of his life'.[27] Presenting a face discloses a story, a character that bears a language of inference that the blind are precluded from utilising.

Some conditions of blindness can be reversed with the advance of medical technology, for instance with the use of stem cells. Giving sight to the blind can have unexpected outcomes. The new 'sense' of sight is estranging and frightening. Suddenly, the brain is flooded with images and sights that have to be married to cultural values and categories. A visual literacy has to be acquired. Gestures and facial expressions have to be read for their tacit language.[28]

Those with sight restored encounter an oddity that they have to use the social to see properly. This is a new responsibility to be learnt anew. Inward seeing has to be connected to outward perception. The social has to be used to refract to see properly. Not only is there an issue of seeing, there is also the need to construct a social self. This bears on Cooley's looking-glass self. The newly sighted self has to learn to construct itself by interference from the responses of others. The problem that emerges for those with sight restored is that there is too much to see to assimilate. Again, in a curious way the issue of the visual comes back to the social. What about those who see but elect not to do so? They occupy a curious universe, like the veiled Islamic women who see but are not seen.

If a school nowadays were to have St Louis of Gonzaga as a pupil, his exercise of custody of the eyes might have led to an instant dispatch to the child psychologist. To preserve his virginity, he never raised his eyes in the streets or in society. Indeed, as James observes, when a young Jesuit, he refused to notice his surroundings, so that

> being ordered one day to bring a book from the rector's seat in the refectory, he had to ask where the rector sat, for in the three months he had eaten bread there, so carefully did he guard his eyes that he had not noticed the place.

A notion of what is *not* seen customarily relates to misrepresentations either in ideology or through symbolic violence. Wilfully not seeing seems perverse in a culture where the visual is in the ascendant as a dominant form of expression. It might seem more an act of cultural estrangement than engagement with its essence. Custody of the eyes relates to selectivity in looking, one that occurs in the pursuit of virtue and the maintenance of an inner sense of purity undisturbed by distractions without. It is a form of disciplining of what St Augustine termed ocular desire. Custody of the eyes was a Jesuit practice that marked the religious life of the English poet Gerald Manley Hopkins. James sees such concerns as reflecting a dropping of external relations to service a consciousness of spiritual things.[29] For Bernard of Clairvaux, failure of ocular discipline was amongst the elements that facilitated the first step of pride: curiosity.[30] Again, the heavenly prospects for the sociologist seem dubious.

Not seeing relates to many issues. Not only decisions and false consciousness, but also the absence of some cultural mechanism and some consensus as to what should be seen, affect the issues of discernment, of seeing or not. This returns to a point raised earlier that James had noted, but also one that attracted Bauman's attention. He wondered at the collective blindness of those who saw differences, but without categories of distinction before the invention of culture in the eighteenth century. All distinctions were subsumed under the universal providence of God, and all had a place in a 'natural' order. The eye of curiosity that sought powers to classify, to rank and to exclude on the basis of distinctions of the particular laid down boundaries whilst at the same time rejoicing in a universal humanity.[31] The problem is that one form of collective blindness attached to the pre-modern has been replaced by another form in modernity whose maturation into postmodernity has come to suggest that the eye of reason is myopic, if not dangerous. It is what the eye of reason cannot see that comes to concern Bauman as he confronts the issue of the massive evil of the Holocaust which modernity failed to see.

Speculatively, four forms of blindness emerge. The first form relates to the moral issues of etiquette in Goffman's *Stigma*. Routinely, the stigmatised hope for the charity of selective seeing. A degree of blindness to signifying distinctions is deemed the property of good manners, where one is seen *not* to look lest one amplifies that which is discrediting. The way one looks or not has profound implications for the basis of social exchange. Some exercise of custody of the eyes is required lest one looks too intently or with an unfitting disregard.

The second form of blindness, Hull has explored, relates to properties of ignorance and spiritual blindness that serves to exclude the disabled. Their plight becomes mixed up with the incapacity to see in spiritual terms. The blind might lack inner sight, but this is not necessarily a result of their disability. Blindness becomes a metaphor for the unsighted, both spiritual and perceptive.[32]

The third form of blindness arises from those who presume to see too much of the unseen and who are punished for their presumption. Buxton has provided a useful account of the Grecian myths surrounding blindness. He suggests that 'blindness is a powerful verbal and visual *metaphor* for the limits of humanity, limits of which the dramatist wants his audience to be aware'.[33] Buxton also draws attention to the link between blindness and prophecy, suggesting that the sightless might pay a price for their gift to see the unseen. The value of his account lies in drawing attention to the boundaries and transgressions surrounding sight and its presumption.[34] As these boundaries and transgressions surrounding sight fade into memory, other forms of blindness, of not quite seeing, emerge. These come to mark the myopia of a culture of postmodernity that cannot see the point of seeking to see the unseen. Being blinded to see better, noted in *Wise Blood*, is the fourth form of blindness. The blinding of Paul formed part of his conversion.

In his study of blindness, Barasch draws out its ambiguity, where deprivation of sight renders the blind closer to seeing the good. In his account, blindness marks a darkness but also a capacity for life with the light within. The blind, the prophet, the musician, the seer, the storyteller, all have a status of unsettling the social order. In lower forms of status, as beggars, they arouse pity, but others worry over what they can see that those with sight cannot. The credentials that lie behind their visual powers are unclear, even paradoxical, when as blind they see what the sighed cannot.

ion or loss of sight can aid inward contemplation and efforts to see
ɛcause they cannot see outside, the blind cultivate a sensibility of
ɔɛɛɪɪɡ within that gives them a self-contained property, a power of seeing
the unseen. Barasch draws out well the secularisation of blindness, its movement from an issue of fate and transgression, with its own tragic outcomes,
to a medical condition devoid of metaphysical and symbolic importance.
Blindness bears profound ambiguities and as Barasch well argues, like madness,
it is 'both a curse and a blessing, a punishment and a grace'.[35] This secularisation closes the polarities of the seen and the unseen and marks what is
available to physical sight as the only seeing that matters. At this point, one
arrives at a central dilemma of the study.

In confronting the issue of the seen and the unseen, sociology encounters
some dissatisfying points. Tales and narratives of seeing are likely to have a
property of subjective preference, emotional leanings that are as idiosyncratic
as they are individualised. What they claim to see of the unseen admits no
sociological proof, or verification, for the transformation of seeing involves
a conversion of the eyes that presents one vision amongst many that the
sociologist has to consider. All religions, mainstream, or cults and sects are
presented with dilemmas of authentication of claims to see the unseen. In this
regard, Weber's concentration on the forms of legitimacy sought for such
seeing is as understandable as is his concern with their routinisation.
His notion of the charismatic figure, as disclosing bases for recognition of
his powers, draws matters nearer to the concerns of this study with the seen
and the unseen. Something is made manifest that is seen in ways to be
believed and to be acted on. As sociology has no powers of arbitration, it
can only accept what seems credible. This opens out an elective dimension
to reflexivity, a consciousness of choice where the sociologist himself
proceeds on an 'as if' basis. What is too often ignored is that reflexivity has
properties of elective affinities and these emerge in the confused debate
Weber generated on the place of values in the discipline.

The refusal to mark any particular field as privileged precludes sociology from
excluding one particular site where ways of seeing the seen are nurtured, a
case in point being Catholicism. Secondly, there is an issue of agency, of choice
and of subjective preference that needs to be taken into account. This relates
to dispositions to see. An added complication is the issue of how the
individual wishes to be seen? As an object, passive and regarded, or as
a subject, autonomous and active, and acting on what is seen? This comes to
a problem of the gaze. Think of the adjectives associated with it: 'yearning',
'possessive', 'empty' and 'peaceful'. These adjectives represent states of
sensibility of enlargement, where the visual merges with the capacity to
visualise imaginatively. In the issue of the gaze is a property of prelude, of
anticipation of a need to act before what is incomplete. That is its domain
aspect. It is this need to act on 'as if' seen that returns the visual to sociology.
The actor has to find some social form to give expression to this imperfectly

seen vision, to give it a social shape so that it can be viewed for the purposes of action. An impress has to be made in the social to proceed through it and to act on the basis of what is visualised.

In that regard the social is the door of the study, the means of access into the unseen. What is decidedly social to the sociologist is incarnational to the theologian. It is scarcely surprising that reflecting a Durkheimian inheritance sociology tends to treat the social as having properties of the sacred. But the social is merely a means of manifestation, an imperfect looking glass for holy refractions of the unseen that give visual relief to yearnings that bubble up within. These can make the actor desperate to see more of the unseen. Any number of social outlets can be used to resolve the angsts of the visions within, so that strategies of resolution have an arbitrary cast. Pilgrimage fits the need not only to seek a vision but also to find it. Some journeying, some effort to seek an image in a particular place, gives a definite cast to the question of the seen and the unseen. But this quest needs a wider compass, a mobilising vision.

III

For some, the sociologist might seem to be the re-incarnation of Mr Worldly-Wiseman of the town of Carnal-Policy, who is doomed to give misleading directions out of the Slough of Despond.[36] Life in Vanity Fair seems to have come to a dubious fulfilment in liquid modernity, where everything is anything that can be sold for earthly pleasures. It is scarcely surprising that the few pilgrims who pass through should cry '*turn away mine eyes from beholding vanity*, and look upwards, signifying that their trade and traffic was in Heaven'.[37] This definite choice in favour of the other world might seem beyond sociological remit of understanding.

Going on pilgrimage involves efforts to reconnect memory to religious sites and places of worship. It is a process of retrieval peculiar in its scale to life in postmodernity. The need to reconnect to local forms of culture that bear religious memories, a process accentuated by globalisation, has become a motif of fundamentalism and the revival of traditional orthodox forms of religion.[38] This revival of interest in sacred sights draws attention to the pilgrimage, a notion rather neglected in sociology. The forces of modernity that gave rise to mass tourism also facilitated the growth of mass pilgrimage. Both were the beneficiaries of the collective organisation of sights to see, the development of transport links, and the invention of rituals and spectacles fit for the modern age. In both cases, though for contrasting reasons, the issue of the body became of critical importance.[39] All pilgrim journeys have an end: to see things differently. For the Christian, this involves seeking to see the heavenly hidden in what is of the earth. Few other theological works have given a better characterisation of this seeking to see than to be found in St Augustine in *The City of God*.

Two cities are presented in ways that embody the basis of choice for a direction of life. One is confined to this world, the earthly city, and is complete to itself but the other, the heavenly city, is about hope, ultimate destination and the model for aspiration for what might come for the virtuous. The cities of heaven and earth are allegories for 'two societies of human beings, one of which is predestined to reign with God for all eternity, the other doomed to undergo eternal punishment with the Devil'.[40] *The City of God* is also a tale of two journeys, one of a pilgrim, a stranger on earth, humble before what is yet unseen, and the other, of the worldly wise, blind to the notion that 'that our eyes may be the servants of our desires' reversing the use of the quotation made earlier.[41] With pride, the latter see what they wish, whereas the pilgrim travels with the light of the holy fellowship of the angels, seeking to spurn the darkness 'of the depraved minds of the evil angels who have rejected the light of righteousness'.[42] The two cities have values that are at odds with each other.

The earthly city is of mankind, whose standards form the basis of an ordering of life, whose vice is pride, and where self-love is to triumph. Unfortunately, this city 'is generally divided against itself by litigation'.[43] It represents the vain ambitions of those who live by the standards of man, but not of God. Spurning ambivalence and uncertainty, Beilharz felt that Bauman uncovered a plight that 'is a familiar one: uniformity breeds conformity; the enemy now lurks within the city walls, rather than outside as was originally the case'.[44]

The heavenly city, on the other hand, is where the highest glory is to be found. It realises the wisdom of rightful worship of God, a dependence on whom leads to ultimate happiness and the fulfilment of virtue.[45] Reflecting on the shadowy property of the heavenly city, Augustine noted the possibility of an image that pointed to rather than reproduced what was not yet to be seen. This image had the status of a servant, being lower than what it signified. This refers to the old and the new covenant, to the image of Sarah and her son, but in this context it has also a wider meaning. Thus, St Augustine suggested that

one part of the earthly city has been made into an image of the Heavenly City, by symbolizing something other than itself, namely that other City; and for that reason it is a servant. For it was established not for its own sake but in order to symbolize another City; and since it was signified by an antecedent symbol, the foreshadowing symbol was itself foreshadowed.[46]

St Augustine speaks for 'those who are strangers in this world and who fix their hope on a heavenly country'.[47] Their seeking of the heavenly involves denial of the earthly, and this generates misunderstandings. The virtuous will have to endure the obloquy of 'the lovers of this world'. But their reward will be to live in the City of God, which is eternal; no one is born there, because no one dies. There is the true felicity, which is no goddess, but the gift of God. From there we have received the pledge of our faith, in that we sigh for her beauty while on our pilgrimage.[48]

These two cities mark the distinction between the seen and the unseen, the visible and the invisible, belief and disbelief, and light and dark. Behind the study, there is no definite location, no privileged place where the heavenly city is to be found. Yet some sites come nearer than others. Thus, Martin refers to a 'sacred geography' that mutates through time and space, and that oscillates between centre and periphery and between Jerusalem, Rome and Athens, what he terms 'the cities of perpetual recollection'.[49] Memory and its revitalisation form part of not only the pilgrim's progress but also that of the tourist, and here one returns to Bauman's metaphors of the pilgrim and the tourist discussed earlier in Chapter 2.

In his understandings, the identity builders of modernity are like pilgrims, the inner directed actors of Weber, doomed to explore a desert, but one bereft of visual comforts. The tourist represents the weariness of wandering and the acceptance of living a life unfulfilled where fixedness and commitment are impossible dreams. The pilgrim metaphor moves in a Protestant direction away from the solaces of visual culture. No other comforts are offered, for the solidarity of the pilgrimage is denied. The journeying is within to the site of ethical integrity but the rules for establishing these have collapsed in the context of postmodernity.

Yet, there is a contradiction running through Bauman's metaphor of the pilgrim for modernity and the tourist for postmodernity. The ambition to be unfixed forms part of a more complex seeking of identity, one fated to be unsettled and incomplete. It is however a state of disenchantment that ill accords with the seeking of enchantment that marks postmodernity. There is still part of the pilgrim in the tourist.[50] In one sense, the Turners are right to suggest that one is a form of the other, 'a tourist is half a pilgrim, if a pilgrim is half a tourist'.[51] Indeed, understandings of mass tourism are understood in terms of virtual religion and the pilgrim metaphor is more attached than one might expect.[52] Far from being extinguished by forces of postmodernity, as Bauman's metaphor might indicate, pilgrimage has expanded to a remarkable degree of late. The elements that facilitate the rise of mass tourism bear some similarities to the development of mass pilgrimage. They share some characteristics that have important implications for visual culture. Both operate to confirm expectations of not only what is seen but also what should be.

Spectacle, the heritage industry, the re-ordering of city centres, all serve to confirm the gazes of tourists and the ways of seeing that advertising and image making strive to manipulate. In his *The Tourist Gaze*, Urry draws out well its expectations. Collectively formed and manufactured, the tourist gaze points to the regulation of the visual, of spectacle and image. The tourist is a consumer, and the contract with the company is that he will see what he has paid for. The visual becomes subject to an engineering to make sites safely predictable. These have established ceremonies for the ordering of the visual to service these contractual expectations.[53] Through niche marketing, the tourist industry manipulates expectations of seeing even more closely. The ambience of seeing is safely packaged to match with the common cultural capital of the clients of the tour. This means they all will see in a similarly self-conforming way. The tourist industry pedals anticipatory ways of seeing to arouse curiosity and expectation of pleasure.[54] Theme holidays also service expectations of what will be seen. In an echo back to Foucault, Urry suggests that

> contemporary societies are developing less on the basis of surveillance and the normalisation of individuals, and more on the basis of the democratisation of the tourist gaze and the spectacle-isation of place.[55]

In this opening out of the visual, the photograph confirms that the tourist has been there and has seen the sights to be consumed.[56] The photograph validates the basis of the journey and provides a memory of what was seen. The rise of the mass tourism and the heritage industry mark the way visual culture has become of inescapable sociological significance. It is not only the Internet that underlines the importance of visual culture. The ordering of mass tourism and the visual expectations that characterise its basis provide a foil for understanding pilgrimage. Clearly, its ordering and expectation are to markedly different ends, but what both mass tourism and pilgrimage have in common is the social organisation of the visual that is marked by a property of seeking.

The pilgrim travels in more petitionary and hesitant circumstances than does the tourist. Where the goal of the pilgrimage is a visual object, the pilgrim finds a validation, not in a photograph, but in the effects of being there and the sense of transformation this effects. In the pilgrimage, there is a strange democracy that all can travel and all might see. Healing, forgiveness, an identity crisis or something penitential, or the fulfilment of a vow, all form the basis of the pilgrim's progress. Seeking to see forms part of the pilgrim's purpose. Thus, being before an icon, as of the Virgin Mary at Cracow, Poland, after a long pilgrimage is deemed to have possible miraculous effects. The pilgrim travels in the hope of such a radical change in his spiritual life. As the Turners suggested,

> the innocence of the eye is the whole point here, the 'cleansing of the doors of perception'. Pilgrims have often written of the 'transformative' effect on them of approaching the final altar, or the holy grotto at the end of the way.[57]

Some pilgrimages involve little that is arduous, yet some forms in Catholicism still have an ascetic dimension. Thus, pilgrims on St Patrick's Purgatory, Lough Derg in Ireland, clamber around the stations in bare feet with little sleep or food for three days and three nights.[58] The Turners termed this an 'archaic pilgrimage'. Tradition, memory and continuity of practice merge in ways that mark lineages of culture, but above all the connections those on pilgrim journey seek.[59] The rise of the 'gap' year between school and university often has a property of pilgrimage for those who seek something deeper than the routine life has offered so far. Sociology has absurdly ignored the millions of young Catholics who now go on pilgrimage in the tracks of their predecessors. The pilgrimage is the exemplary site of the tale as Chaucer found. Present sociology is cursed with a barren imagination not to chronicle these tales of seeking and finding.

The Turners treat pilgrimage as a form of liminality for the laity. It is a form of release from the rhythms of the mundane to travel in between boundaries. Pilgrimage involves a 'movement from a mundane centre to a sacred periphery, which suddenly, transiently, becomes central for the individual'.[60] For each pilgrim, the journey is unique, for he travels to see what others saw before and in so seeking he too hopes to realise the promise of what they were given for making the pilgrimage. The imperative to be a pilgrim covers a multitude of subjective elements difficult to encapsulate in sociological terms. The need to go on pilgrimage relates to the recesses of biography and these influence the tales and testimonies to be told by the pilgrim not only on his journey but also on his return. As the Turners observed 'the mystery of choice resides in the individual, not in the group. What is secret in the Christian pilgrimage, then is the inward movement of the heart.'[61] Thus, the Turners treat the pilgrim 'as one who divests himself of the mundane concomitants of religion ... to confront, in a special "far" milieu, the basic elements and structures of his faith in their unshielded, virgin radiance'. In remarkable contrast to Weber's Protestant ethic, of the practice of virtues that bear on calculation in this world, the Turners mark the distance of the pilgrim from such concerns. The pilgrim's obligation is to the orbit of communitas, the solidarity that stands against structures. A theological judgement is made, one with acute sociological ramifications: 'to become more the Christian one must be less the successful citizen'.[62] The pilgrim travels to see in a new way the unseen and having so seen comes back transformed in relations to visual culture. He is the exemplar of dealings with liminoid virtualities, for in journeying virtuously between structure and anti-structure, his communitas gives him an urge to discern the seen and the unseen and in his life to seek to gaze from one into the other.

Perhaps only in the medieval world was the unseen so well imaged and stamped on stone and in pictorial art. The stress on linking visual culture to the truths of theology made faith a matter of recognition. It was with the eyes that one saw to believe. The visual grammar seemed available to all in the medieval world, for the cathedral or abbey stood as a testimony to the link between earth and heaven in ways that precluded the idea of any rival visions. As Mâle observed, the statues and windows of the church served to instruct the faithful in a vast array of truths. Thus,

> Churchmen understood perfectly well the power of art over minds still childish and unenlightened. For the vast masses of the unlettered, for the populace who possessed neither psalter nor missal, and who remembered only as much of Christianity as they could see with their own eyes, the idea had to be given substance, clothed in perceptible form.[63]

The medieval world had recourse to visual culture before the term was invented and this was something that its pilgrims well understood. Whatever the excesses, their journeying linked the seen to the unseen in indulgences, so that the pains of purgatory were mitigated in earthly travels towards what seemed fragments of the heavenly, images, relics and shrines.[64] These pilgrims suffered no anomie in their regard of the linkages between the seen and the unseen. For them, the well-trodden pilgrim roads to Rome and to Santiago involved not only arduous travelling but also the prospect of heavenly relief on arrival at their destination. In their world, all that was of the unseen could be placed in symbolic form. Everything had a place so that earthly mosaics were refractions of the heavenly. In their lives, as Huizinga elegantly expresses it, 'the world unfolds itself like a vast whole of symbols, like a cathedral of ideas. It is the most richly rhythmical conception of the world, a polyphonous expression of eternal harmony'.[65] It is a realisation of this that caught Huysmans' imagination and that formed the basis of his account of the cathedral.[66] He caught a glimpse of what modernity had lost. It is impossible that nowadays another Abbot Suger would come, who could construct another St-Denis in ways that would likewise combine vision and detail in a miraculous construction of visual culture so admirably fitted for the task of seeking the unseen in the seen.[67]

In emphasising the importance of visual culture for the stimulation of piety, it is important not to overlook risks of abuse, superstition, presumption and excess than can come from what Huizinga terms the crystallisation of religious thought in images.[68] Nevertheless the medieval world was wise in its use of visual culture so built for edifying purpose. It had its own truth of affairs and its own modernity in the realisation of the importance of visual culture.[69] Those who now seek to see the unseen are closer to those in medieval times than might be realised. In the medieval world they seemed to know what to look for to see the connections between the seen and the unseen. What did those who travelled seek to see?

IV

In so seeking as on the pilgrim journey, one acts in faith that something of the unseen will be seen. It is to hope for what Paul wished, that 'the eyes of your understanding being enlightened: that ye may know what is the hope of his calling, and what the riches of the glory of his inheritance in the saints' (Eph. 1:18). In seeking to see 'we have also a more sure word of prophecy, whereunto ye do well that ye take heed as unto a light that shineth in a dark place, until the day dawn, and the day star arise in your hearts' (2 Pet. 1:19). The capacity given to so see needs to be understood in a theological language of expectation. Nichols writes it well in this way:

> God empowers the 'eyes of our mind' with a new 'light' so that we can recognize in a visual medium an object which is God himself, communicated through the sacramental mystery of the form of the Word Incarnate. In this vision there is, further, a 'rapture' which carries us from the visible to the invisible reality made present in its sign, Jesus Christ.[70]

The eye, what it sees and what it constitutes, might seem a matter of optics and of psychology, where capacity is a property of scientific calibration devoid of sociological relevance. This would be to miss a strongly held notion in art, and in visual culture, that the 'innocent eye is blind', that seeing meaningfully is not just a matter of perception; it is also an act of interpretation. As Bourdieu has suggested, 'there is no perception which does not involve an unconscious code and it is essential to dismiss the myth of the "fresh eye", considered as a virtue attributed to naïveté and innocence'. Bourdieu makes another point regarding the illusion of 'the naked eye'. The illusion is an

> attribute of those who wear the spectacles of culture and who do not see that which enables them to see, any more than they see what they would not see if they were deprived of what enables them to see.[71]

This relates to a comment of Jenks that positivism has given birth to a myth of immaculate perception.[72] This myth disguises the degree to which what is seen needs to be culturally constituted to be seen. Thus, what is seen needs some property of recognition and this is supplied from the cultural, for as Bourdieu suggests, it is on the artistic field that levels of appreciation are marked and consecrations are made of what is to be deemed sacred in its aesthetic reach. Shifts in artistic fashion required a '*successful* symbolic revolution', a collective conversion, one where it 'was necessary to create a new world of which our *eye* itself is the product'.[73] To see bears a social construction, for the eye has to be trained to discern in the act of seeing. Perception has to be linked to a sense of vision and this embodies ideas. As Jenks suggests, it has long been understood in Western culture that there is a connection between the idea of vision and the idea as vision. Ideas illuminate, but they also serve to characterise what is to be seen. He also underlines the way the notion of 'idea' derives from the Greek verb 'to see'.[74] The idea of seeing links expectations that have cultural shapes. In the increase of sensibility this generates, approaches to visual culture change. As Jenks suggests, visual culture usually signifies painting, sculpture, design and architecture, but it now takes on a wider remit. Visual culture refers to 'those items of culture whose visual appearance is an important feature of their being or purpose'.[75]

If the innocent eye is a myth and seeing has a cultural shape, then this would suggest an elective property in regard to the visual. First, it suggests that the eye, innocent of appreciating the visual properties of religiosity, is either culpably blind, or is disinclined to do anything about its culturally disembodied state. Secondly, it implies that seeing in religious terms has a cultural dimension that deserves enhancement in ways that are specific to its field of activity. Thirdly, the ambience for seeing the unseen might have changed but not fatally, for lying in the issue of the eye and religiosity is a question of choice, the will, the disposition to decipher and to seek a transformative effect.

In looking at the ritual order, tiny matters count in Goffman's account of ritual interaction. In this, 'the fleeting facial move an individual can make in the game of expressing his alignment to what is happening' can push the limits of a social occasion.[76] Reflecting on Goffman's interest in embodiment, Jenkins observes that 'the face is the interactional presence of selfhood'.[77] Goffman himself argues that 'one's face, then, is a sacred thing, and the expressive order required to sustain it is therefore a ritual one'.[78] The regulation of the face points to an area of vulnerability for the actor, for it might disclose what is best left unsaid. As Lady Macbeth noted, whilst planning the murder, 'the false face must hide what the false heart doth know'.

The evolution of the face from a vehicle for the display of virtue to an instrument of self-enhancement not only marks the democratisation of beauty, but also denotes a process of secularisation where God is no longer the mirror sought. All is now in the eye of the beholder.[79] The application of the magical powers of cosmetics to the face increasingly denotes ideas of beauty as skin deep. Thus, as 'the mirroring body constitutes its objectives in its own self-reflection', the illusions of commodification become apparent. The body and the face come to mirror what they are told to expect and that is the price of being caught in the illusions which faith in commodification induces.[80] Being so stuck, no light shines forth from within and there is little seeking without.

For sociology and for theology, the face is a matter of common concern. As Ford suggests, 'each face is uniquely individual yet it is also a primary focus for relating to others and the world'.[81] Each face seeks another in the Other. In so seeking, the fundamental basis of ethics is realised, for as Bauman elegantly expresses it, 'responsibility conjures up the Face I face, but it also creates me as moral self'. He goes on to add that it is '*the act of looking there* which founds the moral self'.[82] What if what is seen is but a mirror of the self and that is all to be seen in the looking glass? Such self-reflection might cause the actor to seek for higher sights, for what Paul termed the liberty to be found in the Spirit of the Lord. This is where 'we all, with open face beholding as in a glass the glory of the Lord, are changed into the same image from glory to glory, even as by the Spirit of the Lord' (2 Cor. 3:18). In this understanding, *logos* 'is a kind of mirror in which God and man appear'.[83]

This mirroring has been well explored by Frank in her study: *The Memory of the Eyes*. Her pilgrims of Late Antiquity did not journey arduously to observe spiritual freaks, but to cast their eyes on those who gave living witness to having seen the unseen. Like the Wise Men, these pilgrims journeyed as strangers, hoping to see a light, one that might change them utterly. What they sought was what Frank termed their own 'eye of faith'. These holy men manifested a link between the visual and the virtue. On their faces shone evidence of having seen the unseen. Thus, Frank cites the account of 'a holy man who had lived as an anchorite in a small cell and had practised silence for thirty years . . . One could see him with the face of an angel giving joy to his visitors by his gaze and abounding with much grace'.[84]

These pilgrims travelled as spectators with holy purposes to find testimonies. As Frank suggested, for her pilgrims, 'action and ideal, perception and desire all merge in the travelogues, so that physical journey and spiritual progress are indistinguishable'.[85] The pilgrims found a radical and new way of seeing, one that had endless capacities for revitalisation. This facilitated renewed testimony for those with ears to hear. In her account, Frank treated pilgrimage in terms of visual practice. What was seen as the outcome of pilgrimage becomes the basis of memory, so 'recollection is understood as a visual process by which the mind's eye scans and retrieves specific visual images'.[86] To gaze at the face of somebody enveloped in prayer is to have a sense of not only trespass but also exploitation, for the person so praying has a property of absence as he or she looks within. In that blindness, God is seen – nearly – face to face. What Frank's pilgrims saw on the face had a tactile property, something that could be touched, for those with such holy visages seemed touched by God.[87]

In ways that echo Goffman, but expand on him in a theological direction, Frank devotes a chapter to the issue of how to read the face of the holy. This capacity to see beyond the body echoes some earlier themes that were raised in Bernanos and Huysmans. Spiritual discernment reflects the power to make distinctions between the virtuous and the prisoners of vice. Thus, Frank mentions a bishop 'who could detect sinners by their black, scorched faces and bloody eyes, and the righteous by their glowing white garments and shining faces'.[88] This capacity to see past surfaces into realms of the spiritual relates to the properties liturgical images are believed to incarnate. They represent capacities to link the seen to the activities of the unseen. In late medieval world, images of the liturgical labourers and angelic co-workers were mixed up so that one set was an imitation of the other.[89] A contemporary legacy of this power of image is the choirboy. In his long white surplice, his ruff and cassock, he mobilises a vast symbolic capital particularly at Christmas when he incarnates an angelic messenger who comes to tell again in song the tale of the birth of the Christ child. With his fellow symbolic labourers, he bears the burden of signifying solidarity with the angelic.[90] The choirboy points from the seen to the unseen.

In Frank's account the faces of the holy were avenues to the unseen. It was only those who longed to see who saw. She writes:

> underlying these efforts is the conviction that the biblical past would become visible only to those who were capable of both seeing and responding to the sacred presence they beheld. The 'eye of faith', as Christians referred to this interactive visuality was tactile as well as visual, not just in the sense of contact but even of engagement.[91]

Those with the 'eye of faith' had a gift of inversion so that what was seen on earth was virtual in its resemblance to the real order of the heavenly city. They exemplified notions of liminoid virtualities in getting so near the borderlines between the seen and the unseen, and finding a space where the virtual, what could be formed on earth, mirrored the real, what was of the heavenly. They could see 'as if' they felt what they saw in the unseen. Those who so saw had to be worthy to do so, for 'to "embrace" with the eyes signals not just the assumption that virtue is visible, but also the belief that seeing the holy provides an active, tactile encounter with it'.[92] They seemed to demonstrate some tangible grasp of what it was to have seen the unseen. They touched it and were touched by it. But how can sociology approach the issue of what they saw?

Frank supplies a basis to proceed when she attends to the issue of the regulation of the perception of those who so saw the unseen. There had to be some idea as to what the ascetic was to look like to embody the highest ideals of scripture.[93] What was the grammar of recognition and distinction so made? What was on the face or in the ordering of the body that suggested a testimony of contact with the unseen? Notwithstanding the intangibility of what is seen, some form of definiteness emerges that *is* tangible to those who see. Strangely, this was an issue Simmel raised in his approach to the distinctive properties of religiosity considered in the final chapter. Focusing on the seen and the unseen forces sociology back into the clutches of theological choice, of assumption and presumption in discerning, of entitlement to look or one denied.

In some mysterious manner, religious images participate in what they reveal. Because God is unseen, seeing what is revealed can be treated as an act of presumption, something idolatrous, something that belongs to a false god. To see God face to face is so presumptuous that Islam and Judaism share a common prohibition on making images of what is forbidden to reveal in visual form.[94] These prohibitions bring out more starkly Catholic and Orthodox entitlements to make images of the unseen God, given that Christ is the revelation in flesh of that unseen God. Given the scandal of particularity of this Incarnation, a presumption that marks off Christianity from Islam and Judaism, protocols emerge for dealing with a seen God that beg questions about the status of such images. Protestant rebellions against Catholicism focused on the presumption of making images of Divine and also the idolatrous risks such visual representations of the unseen generated. Further, theological worries related to scruples that such images would be confused with their prototype or original. The deepest of sins is to confuse the virtual with the real. It is only in limited theological and sociological circumstances that these can be interwoven in ways that facilitate edification not confusion.

Those who use sociological instruments to read theology better suffer deep scruples over the usurping powers of sociology to take on virtual powers that convert it into an imitation of Catholicism, where God is expelled. These worries face a crux in the link between piety and visual culture. The more the link between the two is expanded to enhance sociological understandings, the more comfort is given to adherents of the discipline operating under the mantle of a virtual religion. The images so made take on anthropomorphic properties that endorse both Feuerbach's notion that religion is a mere human projection, and Durkheim's idea that the sacred is but a mirror of collective values expressed in ultimate form. In efforts to mirror a Divinity in some image, the subversive notion hovers that the image so cast is nothing but a reflection of man himself caught in the mirror. To escape this doleful prospect of canonising the man with no qualities, the pious sociologist needs to fall back on the long-standing theological stipulation that the unseen God is not bound to an image. If He were, this would give powers of confinement and manipulation of a deity to those who see. In all this, the actor is caught in an antinomy that peculiarly arises from sociological ventures into visual culture and religion. Taking Foucault's route, one is left with the eye in the tower, where man acts as if seen but by something not there. The other route, the more inductive one on the ground of culture, is the folly of projection. Each operates in a pincher-like movement to entrap the hapless sociologist seeking to understand how the unseen is to be seen. Older theological debates clarify these dilemmas regarding seeing the unseen. Did images of the unseen enable or disable faith? Enabling notions centred on icons, images of the invisible God. Adherents of the disabling effects of such images on faith were the iconoclasts who sought to destroy such material refractions of the unseen. The Protestant on the horse in the Lady Chapel of Ely Cathedral did his bit for this school of theology.

Referring to the formulae of the Second Council of Nicea (AD 787), Illich summarises their use well. The Council concluded that

> an icon...is a form of revelation: the light of Christ's resurrected body showing itself. The icon is like a threshold beyond which the devout eye reaches into the realm of the invisible. For the believer, it provides color to the truth that he has accepted and come to know through his act of faith in the Word of God.[95]

Debates on secularisation, that religion has withered before the corrosive acids of modernity, mask the degree to which it facilitated a massive expansion of the visual culture of piety in the late nineteenth and early twentieth centuries. Icons were examples of this flourishing of religiosity in visual culture. Thus, Besançon notes the way the introduction of modern Western art into Russian society drew attention to the value of the icon. Its restoration served to signify the power of the visual and its link to spirituality for Russian identity. The light of the icon was Russia's witness to Western culture.[96] A similar process of recovery and re-invention operated in terms of the link between visual piety and Protestantism in mass culture that Morgan has explored. The place of the devotional in relation to mass production of images points to a return of aura, not as a category of emphasis, but one of popular retrieval. In the conclusion of his study, Morgan notes that 'the aura that radiated from prints and halftones of religious masterpieces promised to reanimate a world bereft of spiritual presence'.[97] In a peculiar way Benjamin was wrong in his frets over the mechanical reproduction of art. He seemed to believe that through some mechanical power, the redemptive properties of aura were fatally lost. For a Christian, aura is a function of grace not of some reverential distancing which is a prelude to being acted on by what is seen.

The promise of reanimation needs to be counter-balanced by a sense of loss and exile, one traceable back to the Fall. As Besançon elegantly writes: 'even after it has fallen into the sensible world, the human soul is homesick for the heavenly world'.[98] Lying in the issue of the icon is a property of restoration, a dim recollection when the seen and the unseen were not in such stark antinomial forms as in the present, where no interconnection seems either possible or desirable.

Not having seen the prototype, the believer has to struggle with a likeness. Besançon captures the dilemma posed by images for iconodules (advocates of visual piety) that the Word made flesh permits making something visible for carnal eyes, whereas the iconoclasts felt that in so doing the 'inaccessible divinity of Christ' was compromised.[99] For the latter, there was a disjunction between the spirit so represented and 'the baseness of its means of representation', tolerable in profane art and intolerable in sacred art.[100] The reason for the concern with the status of the icon and its forms of representation is that the dilemmas these represent also occur in social manifestations of the unseen, not so much of the Divinity, but of what surrounds it. It is this surround that forms an enabling device, the frame of the door on the unseen. The instructions for opening the door need to be read carefully.

Besançon brings out well the authority of the icon as a form of writing or text to be deciphered. But as a visual text, it is part of a history, of liturgy and 'it is in prayer that the deifying contact with the prototype comes about through the image'.[101] Citing Bonaventura's point that 'what we see elicits our feelings more than what we hear', Besançon asserts that 'faith comes through the ears, fervor comes through the eyes'.[102] The prayer to give light to the eyes involves a seeking of a gift of spiritual perception. Again, it might seem as if the question of the seen and the unseen has drifted out of the clutches of sociology and has drifted back into a theological realm where the resolution of such issues properly belong.

In the commonwealth of liquid modernity and the slight bonds of citizenship it now effects, it might seem that the prospects for seeing the unseen have become decidedly dim. In England, church attendance figures dip further, and the need to attend to the unseen seems more and more archaic. There is too much of the light of day to see that makes such a search seem the task of bygone days. Increasingly, those who stroll around cathedrals and churches do so as outsiders. They gaze at the names on the plaques on the walls of these buildings and wonder at times, when those of flesh and blood sought to see the unseen. Now gone to dust, they leave no legacy that would revitalise the gaze. For them, judging by the rhetoric on their memorials, faith was a living hope. The need for that hope seems to have vanished. Somehow, the present time seem so definite, so filled with activity and replete with so many images that the notion of the past and the future seems unreal. The only reality is of the moment. But this places a premium on the gaze, for everything seems to have become intensified in the act of looking, seeing and being seen.

This premium on the gaze places sociology in a quandary. Why should the sociologist need to look closely at the seen and the unseen, of all the conundrums? The discipline might fret over charges that it has soaked up too much of the fatigue and boredom of modernity to bother looking. Yet, boredom leads to emptiness and this leads to an indifference to the social that would cause Weber's ghost to rotate in its grave. There is another dry rot abroad that bears sociological scrutiny: acedia. A dangerous state, it hovers around the issue of *why* the sociologist should look at the seen and the unseen. There is no point in saying that this issue of discernment is not a sociological matter. Weber and Simmel both made theological marks on the discipline that force out matters of choice over dealings with the seen and the unseen. The Edomite watchman left sociology with conundrums about night and day. It is not difficult to treat these as matters of dark and light.

6
Dark into Light: A Sociological Navigation

As a ritual expression of the passage of light into the dark, the vigil mass of Holy Saturday is difficult to equal. In the best of Catholic cathedrals, a fire is lit outside. It is blessed by the bishop with the words 'make this fire + holy, and inflame us with new hope'. Marking the Alpha and Omega, five studs are screwed into the Pascal Candle. It is lit from the new fire. The bishop then says aloud 'may the light of Christ, rising in glory, dispel the darkness of our hearts and minds'. Then the deacon carries the lit Pascal Candle into the darkened cathedral followed by the bishop, the priests, the servers, the choir and the congregation stretching back in long procession. As it proceeds into the darkened cathedral, the small light of the Candle casts shadows thus conveying a spectral property, a sense of a flickering light being brought into a tomb to find something. What is sought is the light of Christ, but that light does not exist for itself but only as something to be passed on and this is symbolised at the second stop made in the procession, when six boys, clad in white albs, as if angels, light their tapers from the Candle and take these back to those behind. Their little lights bob back into the darkened procession, and gradually as each lights the candles of the congregation, a sense of illumination spreads. All the little lights make up a mosaic in the dark, a testimony of those who have come not only to see, but also to affirm what is unseen but is believed in with the eyes of faith that Christ is Risen.

This ritual gives visual expression to the promise of the new covenant, of 'a light that shined in a dark place, until the day dawn, and the day star arise in your hearts' (2 Pet. 1:19). The hope of this covenant is expressed in the prayer for the dead: 'lighten our darkness we *beseech* you O Lord and let perpetual shine upon them. May they rest in peace'. The light only comes to those who seek to see it, for it is written that 'light is come into the world, and men loved darkness rather than light, because their deeds were evil' (Jn 3:19).

Discerning a light in the dark might seem a hopeless task for the sociological gaze. Riddled with neo-Platonic overtones, what seems a question of just looking is amplified into all manner of philosophical and theological complications that threaten to engulf sociological ventures into these territories. Light and dark have some mysterious associations with discernments of good and evil. What is of the light is revealed as virtuous and what is of the dark belongs to vice, to what one hesitates to reveal. Seeking the light forms part of what is known as visual piety. Morgan refers to this 'as the set of practices, attitudes, and ideas invested in images that structure the experience of the sacred'. He goes on to suggest that visual piety 'cancels the dualistic separation of mind and matter, thought and behavior, that plagues a great deal of work on art and religion'.[1] The trouble with notions of light in relation to theology is that it has one set of meanings at the level of perception, where what is seen expresses in symbolic form the notion of illumination, as in the case of the Pascal Candle. But another set of meanings relates to inner illumination, to a conversion of disposition and view. It also bears on religious emotions, conversions and sensibilities of identity, one where the self is changed radically in its habitus. The actor becomes disposed to link what is seen at the level of perception to this sense of inner illumination. Such linkages are not mechanical, but can be treated as gifts of grace. The capacities given by grace require not only nurture but also the pursuit of their expression in the social, where the injunction to give witness to the eyes of faith is realised and fulfilled. The importance of nurturing links between the seen and the unseen for the social to flourish was well stated by St Augustine. In a sermon 'on faith in things unseen', he noted that

> when we do not believe what we cannot see, concord will perish, and human society itself will not stand firm. How much more, then, ought faith to be placed in divine things, even if they are not seen. If this faith is not applied, it is not the friendship of some men which is violated, but the very essence of religion itself, so that the very depth of misery results.[2]

This comment bears on the effort of James to characterise the life of religion in its broadest terms possible. He suggested that religion 'consists of the belief that there is an unseen order, and that our supreme good lies in harmoniously adjusting ourselves thereby'.[3] If it is not continually to fail eye tests for gazing at an unseen order, sociology needs to make radical adjustments in its ways of seeing. It needs to take on board an observation of Oliver that '"religion" does not consist of a set of given "facts" waiting – passively as it were – to be observed; what counts as religion is mediated through the theoretical spectacles one wears'.[4] These spectacles have theological frames. If used, what *can* they see?

Reflexivity and habitus are terms whose implications for the visual are not well considered in sociology. They bear on dispositions and capacities to see. What is seen can reflect biographical change, but this change is seldom cast in ways that face the visual. As one looks into issues of light and dark, broad-brushed terms that belong to theology and philosophy, they do have sociological resonances. They relate not only to moral properties, but also to styles of discernment, of hope or gloom, of blindness or an ability to see. Weber and Simmel had decidedly definite sociological approaches to these issues in their treatment of religion. Their attitudes to theology have profound sociological implications.

In the first two sections of this chapter, it is argued that Weber and Simmel incorporated far more theology into their sociological standpoints than might be realised. Facets of the unseen are littered through not only Weber's approach to religion but also the image and basis of the sociology he sought to construct. The issue of grace is of central importance to his writings on notions of legitimacy of oracles, prophets and virtuosi as their ocular charismatic gifts are recognised and routinised, but it is in Weber's Protestantism that questions of the seen and the unseen are of central significance. The suspicion regarding the visual, noted earlier in relation to the influence of Levinas, is endemic in the theology Weber invokes to provide a sociological solution to the issue of rational calculation, the property so characteristic of modernity whose legacy of disenchantment laid a mantle of gloom on the discipline. The visual only appears momentarily in Weber's brief appraisals of aesthetics. In this setting, it is treated in terms of a virtual religion, one that replaces theological options capriciously deemed unfit for life in modernity. What he concedes to virtual religion, he denies to the theology that governs his sociology. His sociological approach to religion incorporates a theological stance that denies solace from the visual. The images of the next world are cast into sociological darkness. Weber's gaze has only one direction: inward, where the ethic of duty is forged without ameliorating visual distractions. Thus, his sociology is cast to mark a distance from the concerns of visual culture and the social elements it embodies. His theological stance dooms his sociology to live heroically in the noble circumstances of darkness.

By contrast, Simmel's approach to religion is directed to its social manifestations in ways that direct attention towards refractions of the unseen. These are expressed in terms of the colour, the vivid property of light of religion, properties that bind form into a theological content. Unusually for a major sociologist, Simmel is concerned with what it is to be *in* religious belief and how the actor copes with the demands to manifest this in some social form that is characteristically in tension with an elusive content. Simmel enjoins the sociologist to seek to see the colour of religion, its light, if his notion of religiosity is to be understood. Yet, here one encounters an odd paradox. There is a sense that darkness is more fascinating for sociological study than the issue of light. As suggested earlier, the virtuous are deemed unworthy of sociological attention. Its ambitions are more often directed to matters of vice, and the dispersal of judgemental properties in the agendas of identity politics. Oddly, Simmel's approach to the sociology of religion makes little reference to evil. Predominantly, as they might say in other quarters, his approach is 'sunny side up'. His sociology is directed to understandings of passages into light, where the dark lurks hidden but unsignified. Even in its most exalted mode, sociology would not seek to deny the antinomy of light and dark. Its problem is how to characterise it and Simmel offers a solution, or rather scope for one, for it is much the case that darkness and evil cast long shadows on the sociological gaze. The term hope often emerges as solace, but in this setting its use is amplified into the unseen. It is the utter devastation of modernity, its gloom, the boredom it invokes that cause one to attend to the acedia that hovers within, for solutions to the dark can only move into a theological direction of light. There is no other passage available for the sociological gaze to discern. In dealing with modernity, one wonders why sociology permits the devil to have the best tricks. This issue of evil emerges in the third strand of the chapter.

There are three reasons that justify attending to the dark side of modernity and the unconfronted evil that lies in its genesis and effects. The first links Huysmans and Baudelaire to a common fascination with evil. Boredom and curiosity led Huysmans to move from decadence in modernity to a concern with Satanism as a solution to the vacuity of these states. Such was the darkness encountered that Huysmans was desperate for a religious light to shine to rescue him.[5] The second strand emerges from the unresolved and gratuitous inhumanity that marks the unfolding of modernity. There is a realisation that moral indifference leads to a tolerance of what can be termed evil. One book, of singular importance, which has commanded sociology to attend to the issue of evil is Bauman's *Modernity and the Holocaust*. It reflects on the dark side of modernity, the capacity to produce and to calculate that marked civilisation, but one that facilitated the industrialisation of death in ways where the scale of the murder was unrecognised. A god had been created in the machine that produced an unrecognised evil. The eye of this god saw no evil and, with God absent, nobody protested. Thirdly, fantasies about evil where Satanism has a recreational status, in films and the mass media, have generated unsettlements where rumours thrive about malevolent presences in the moral panics society habitually encounters. This sense of being watched generates interest in a notion of an evil eye. This is a notion that very much belongs to anthropology, but not to either sociology or visual culture.

Writing the remaining part of the study turned out to be difficult, for the antidote to the evil eye should be the good eye. But the latter refers to a quality of sight, not one of morality. In any event, to offset the evil eye with the good eye would be to reduce the latter to a magical response set at the same level as the former. This would generate an untenable theological position of inventing a god that was subject to manipulation and whose powers could be known by its opposite to evil. Sociological reasons for exploring issues of evil, discussed in the third section of the chapter, are remarkably different to the sensibilities of the unseen the gaze might catch, that form the concluding sections of the study.

To understand visual piety in its fullest dimensions, one has to refer to the notion of sacramentals. These refer to the grace effected by the actions of the believer, and reflect a spiritual endorsement of his sociological efforts to engage with the unseen. If acts of visual piety are to be fully understood in sociological terms, they require a theological setting that permits their greatest use. In this regard, Protestantism cannot supply sociology with this legitimisation; it can only come from Catholicism. Some sense of being acted on, some sensibility of the unseen responding, needs to be given a focus. Numerous examples could be given of facets of visual piety that denote subjective preferences. Here, one returns to the issue of the icon and the face as they realise sensibilities of the unseen. The way images come to haunt points to the sensibilities of the unseen that profoundly affect those who see. Something of a world unseen is revealed, claims are realised and transformations are effected in ways that are difficult to articulate in tales. As only so much can be put into one study, the concluding sections are to be treated as illustrative of how sociology might proceed into understandings of visual piety and its dealings with the seen and the unseen. The tale of the study that marks its conclusion is, what if the visual was re-set in the context of religiosity? The property of 'as if' runs through the study and its conclusion and to that degree it has been a tale of pious re-imaginings.

I

The illusion that sociology in its prime thinks outside theological categories breaks down in the face of the fine-tunings of Weber's *The Protestant Ethic*. Although concerned with the link between interests, ideals and the formation of capitalism and therefore belonging to economic history, the study has a theological ambit sociologists often neglect to consider.[6] This exemplary sociological tale has theological lineages, for as Carroll reminds us there is a need to retell stories in more familiar images, thus 'Weber retold seventeenth-century Puritan theology, which had retold Calvin, who had retold Augustine, who had retold Paul and so on'.[7] Weber's study of the Protestant Ethic is about the shaping of a personality in the world, where subject to a calling, an ethic of duty of stewardship is found. This need to render to account becomes all the more necessary in an unfolding modernity, where routinisation and calculation loom ever larger and evermore irresistibly so. In Weber's thesis, the ascetic underpinnings of Calvinism unleashed productive forces that facilitated the emergence of capitalism. As Goldman observes, what Weber caught was the new type of self or character forged in the Reformation.[8] This issue of character has come to be seen as the key to understandings of Weber.[9] Central to the study is the relation between psychological sanctions that stem from religious belief and the methodical control of conduct.[10] Interests and ideas converge in an elective affinity.[11]

Weber made a theological choice for sociology that only Protestantism was fit for life in modernity. This had decided repercussions for understandings of culture. If, as Eagleton argues correctly, culture is the way society imagines itself and it has become a sort of displaced religion, then 'postmodernity is really a belated form of Protestantism'. Its hallmarks are privacy of judgement and the cultivation of a heroic individualism. The outcome is what Eagleton has characterised as a world that is 'a dark, fearful, inhospitable place where we can never feel at home'.[12] This sense of estrangement offers no visual solace and finds no grace of redemptive sight. His points seem to echo Arnold, for whom the advance of utilitarianism, and a spirit of manufacture that Protestantism so facilitated, led to his interest in sweetness and light to ameliorate the darkness of culture that was becoming so evident in the Victorian era. Matters have got worse since as the spiritual authority of higher culture is being eroded.[13]

What should be of the universal has been ground into the particular. In all, this is a loss of vision that religion can only supply in culture and for which there is no adequate substitute. Thus, Eagleton argues that what the West ideally requires

is some version of culture, which would win the life-and-death allegiance of the people, and the traditional name for this allegiance is, precisely, religion. No other form of culture has proved more potent in linking transcendent values with popular practices, the spirituality of the elite with the devotion of the masses. Religion is not effective because it is otherworldly, but because it incarnates this otherworldliness in a practice form of life.[14]

The practice of life Eagleton advocates, which incarnates the otherworldly, reflects a Catholic option that is at odds with the implicitly prescriptive position Weber adapts in his concerns with the Protestant Ethic where salvation anxiety was to be resolved in *this* world. This prescriptive position flows into his vision of sociology but in ways that affirmed the marginalisation of Catholicism in the discipline. If Protestantism was the implicit religion of sociology, then the price of this choice becomes evident when the discipline tries to make sense of the rise of visual culture. The theology that might have supplied sociology with the means of coping with visual culture had been unhitched. Seeing sociology as a rival, a virtual religion, Catholicism was happy to collude in the symbolic violence placed against it and acted to affirm its marginalisation. The outcome was that Catholicism came to be seen as a profoundly unsociological belief system. The mutual disdain between Catholicism and sociology was tragic. Catholicism abdicated access to the analytical instruments of sociology that would have accounted for the shifting basis of its place in a culture of postmodernity that has now liquefied. On the other hand, sociology was denied access to a theology that would have given it a vision of the spirituality of culture and that would have undermined its disciplinary disdain of the visual.

In *The Protestant Ethic*, Catholicism was what belonged to the monastic, to the late medieval world of magic and superstition. It might seem that monasticism appealed to the non-rational, its stewardship directed to the other world, that of the unseen, and not to the necessary demands of accountability for this world.[15] For the Puritan, however, his cloister was the world. There, grace was to be found in circumstances of his own making in the pursuit of a calling sanctified by an ascetic stewardship of resources of character and capital. Calculation was in reference to this world, not to the other, to the seen but not to the unseen. The Calvinist need to prove his faith in worldly activity meant that sanctification was to be found in the mundane, not in the imaginative. Thus, in the case of Calvinism,

> by founding its ethic in the doctrine of predestination, it substituted for the spiritualised aristocracy of monks outside of and above the world the spiritual aristocracy of the predestined saints of God within the world.[16]

The issue of grace greatly complicates the intersections between sociology and theology. As a form of favour, capacity or recognition, grace is given as a Divine gift. How it is channelled, on what authority and in what form are not only matters of theological deliberation, but also matters of sociological concern as Weber has stipulated. His concerns centred on not only the validity of forms of conferral of grace, but also its routinisation in types of charisma.[17] Bourdieu secularised and widened this notion of conferral to include powers of consecration in fields of culture. But Weber used theological notions of grace to highlight and to resolve a sociological problem, of accounting for the rise of capitalism. Distinctions between Protestant and Catholic theologies were fundamental for his arguments and, in turn, these related to worries over relationships with the seen and the unseen, what is of this world and of the next.

Proof of salvation for Protestants, in this case Puritans, was individual and inner.[18] For Catholics, salvation involved the use of communal instruments (sacramentals and some sacraments) that gave solace to the individual. These supplied a vision that would ameliorate the lonely struggle to secure salvation. Comforts of sacramental grace gave to the seeker of salvation a stake in the social where outward signs were marked and stipulated. Unlike the Calvinist, the Catholic knows where he stands on the field of culture, as he seeks to scrutinise the heavens for reflections of the unseen.[19] In Catholicism, grace is also a mysterious gift, one that involves participation in the life of God, channelled through the sacraments. These embody visible signs of conferral of grace, and to that degree are the templates of the action of the unseen on the seen.[20]

Weber's Calvinist was the gravedigger of his own religiosity, opening out forces his theology was ill-fitted to resist in the long term, hence sowing the seeds of its demise. Unintentionally, the interest of Protestantism in modernisation amplified a secularisation, a spirit of indifference, as capitalism dispensed with the theological values that facilitated its expansion. The Calvinist, as the prototype of the thesis, has long passed from theological view.[21] He lost the capacity to resist the world whose spirit his theology had done so much to formulate and to legitimise. In concentrating on the inner self, Weber left the actor ill-disposed to seek amelioration for his plight in the visual, in images of the other world so redolent of Catholicism. His notion of office charisma does mark an exception to this point. It involves the depersonalisation of office, as in the priesthood and a movement from a concern with magic to powers of interpretation of symbols.[22] Such symbols point to forms of regulation of relationships between the seen and the unseen. But the most important point to note is that fundamental to Weber's thesis on the Protestant ethic is the detachment of piety from the visual, a disconnection whose price few sociologists have scrutinised.

Weber's Calvinists followed an individualised, private calling, devoid of any ameliorating ritual comforts. Thus, Weber argued that

> the genuine Puritan even rejected all signs of religious ceremony at the grave, and buried his nearest and dearest without song or ritual in order that no superstition, no trust in the effects of magical and sacramental forces on salvation, should creep in.

For Weber, the Calvinist break with Catholicism was decisive. Puritanism displayed an entirely negative attitude 'to all the sensuous and emotional elements in culture and in religion, because they are of no use toward salvation and promote sentimental illusions and idolatrous superstitions'.[23] In summary, Weber suggested that

> this worldly Protestant asceticism... acted powerfully against the spontaneous enjoyment of possessions; it restricted consumption, especially of luxuries.[24]

Thrift, not expenditure on the aesthetic, meant that implicit in his thesis was the exercise of a custody of the eyes, a selectivity in looking, which was to guard against distracting visual pleasures. But this custody of the eyes went much further. It prohibited the use of visual expressions of the unseen, and more particularly images of the Divine.

There is a sense in Weber's *The Protestant Ethic* that what belongs to the visual, as it relates to the aesthetic and to piety, operates as a form of theological false consciousness; it undermines the need to attend to the preservation of an ethical duty of stewardship in the world. But the suspicion regarding the visual goes further. There is a theological assumption in the concentration on Calvin that images of the heavenly are idolatrous distractions.[25] This rupture between the visual and piety is fundamental to Weber's thesis. The vocation of the Puritan is to live inwardly without outdoor relief from a theology that offered sacramental comforts, tokens and images of the unseen presented in ritual wrappings and visual representations. The Puritan is to live in this world in a calling devoid of visual relief. His calling is not to seek to see visual expressions of the unseen, for these distract from his ethical duty to struggle in this world. His vision is inward and there he finds the proof of his salvation. Carroll has argued that this sense of calling is linked to fate, but more importantly to a certain blindness in the face of an ambivalence before God. What is of the other world belongs to God, and man has to live to find what he cannot see to resolve.[26] By playing the Puritan card Weber has locked the actor in an iron cage, and has thrown away the theological key – Catholicism – that would supply a means of escape. The theology that impregnates much of his sociology denies this option.

Although, as Swatos and Kivisto indicate, *The Protestant Ethic* had no polar Catholic opposite, as Lutheranism was the target of the study, they do indicate earlier in their essay that the Webers were fascinated with Catholicism.[27] Weber had intended to expand the Catholic facets of his study. Nevertheless, despite these interests, Weber had an equivocal attitude to Catholicism. At one level, it represented a possibility of escaping the full implications of fulfilling a call to duty *in* the world. Catholicism diluted the need for a lonely struggle in the world for the Calvinist by supplying not only communal solidarity but also relief from salvation anxiety through the sacrament of confession. Affiliation to Catholicism seemed to Weber to attract a price. Thus *The Protestant Ethic* commences with a concern with the under-representation of Catholics in schools and occupations. Weber attributes this under-representation in Germany to a greater other-worldliness and an indifference towards the good things of the world[28] although, as in Ireland in the nineteenth century, matters may have been more complex.[29]

At another level, Ekstrand indicates that Weber repeatedly suggested that 'religious faith in modern society requires a *sacrificium intellectus*' and what was in mind was a falling back to the older Churches and by implication to the visual and sacramental comforts of Catholicism.[30] For both these reasons, Catholicism has been placed at a remove from sociology but in ways that suggest it might be a threat to its disciplinary integrity. To a limited degree, Bourdieu managed to rectify this estranging property by assimilating aspects of Catholicism into the sociological fold. But this simply rehabilitated a noble French tradition of recognising the sociological potency of Catholicism, where its religion was accepted but its God is not. In this approach a religion was affirmed to the degree to which a theology was denied.

If Weber's concerns with theological niceties had just been confined to his thesis of the Protestant ethic, its ramifications for sociology might well have been limited. As sociology inspects its origins, its Protestant heritage, particularly in America, comes to the fore as Vidich and Lyman have well illustrated.[31] In his appraisal of the study, Kivisto notes the way that 'for the most part major figures in American sociology have sought, implicitly or explicitly, to construct their discipline as a surrogate for Protestant theology'.[32] Yet there is a sense of ambivalence in American sociology that the Protestantism that facilitated its rise bore a price of an endemic loss of nerve in matters of morality and secularisation.[33] There is also a feeling that sociology is unable to rectify the deficiencies of this inheritance. In much of sociology, there is a wish to get out of religion altogether, not because it represents an illusion of the vacuous but because it represents issues the discipline cannot handle. If Protestantism is sociology's blocked memory syndrome, Catholicism represents its worst nightmares.

Earlier, in Chapter 2, Bauman's references to Weber were mentioned, where *The Protestant Ethic* was treated by some as sociology's exemplary text. Beilharz has drawn attention to the Bauman's estimation of the Protestant ethic itself as a sociological myth. The Calvinist is presented as heroic in his endurance, a theological image set for and by sociologists.[34] The Puritan also became part of the myth of modernity, equivocal in his relationship to capitalism, but undeniably attractive in the inner-directed pursuit of perfection that his virtues exemplified.[35] The power of calculation and accountability derived from a theology was secularised and appropriated for sociological purpose. Amongst the virtues of Protestantism, diligence, endurance and hard work were marked as the exemplary traits to be cultivated by novices to sociology, if they are to be placed amongst the elect of the discipline.[36]

Calvinism is not the whole tale of Protestant relationships to the visual. Links can be found between aesthetics, symbols and Protestantism, for instance in the writings of Tillich.[37] Also, as Morgan's recent study well shows, visual culture was part of American Protestantism, but in ways directed to domestic consumption rather than to rituals or public displays for acts of veneration.[38] Facets of visual culture might now be admitted to Protestant eyes, yet its traditions veer towards worries about idolatry. Visual piety as a theological option for many Protestants belongs to the kingdom of the blind. Justification of the exclusion of visual piety serves to endorse the comment of James that 'Protestantism will always show to Catholic eyes the almshouse physiognomy'.[39] Although treated as superstitious and magical in its operations, Catholic liturgical practices and their relation to visual culture aroused envy in the Protestant mind.[40] English Protestant visitors to Catholic countries particularly in the seventeenth century were awestruck at the public displays of religious rituals and spectacles forbidden and unseen at home.[41]

In dealing with Weber, a number of contradictions emerge. Theology is decidedly on the sociological map but in an unsatisfactory manner for this study. In so far as it exemplifies his values, Sennett points to an oddity of *The Protestant Ethic* – it facilitates a retreat from the social, a property of narcissism, where the self gets locked into a privacy, one that denies solutions in the external world.[42] Likewise, the aesthetic seemed excluded as a matter of sociological concern. Weber did refer to the link between religion and art but only very briefly. For Weber, art was a successor to religion, but one that faced similar forces of disenchantment.[43] O'Toole has commented on these brief references of Weber to art and religion. He concludes that for Weber, art had redemptive claims as a surrogate for religion, one that offered a means of escape from forces of rationalisation.[44] In treating art as a virtual religion he gave to it powers of relief seemingly denied to Catholicism. What is depressing about Weber is the legacy of retreat, individualism and isolation from the social he leaves to sociology. From the perspective of this study, a blindness is implanted in sociology not only in regard to visual culture, but also in relation to efforts to seek to see the unseen. Locked in an unpropitious theology, sociology is impoverished in its capacities to deal with visual culture. Debts to Judaism force it to treat the visual with suspicion; obligations to the Calvinism mark the venture as in someway unnatural to sociology.

Parking sociology in a theological cul-de-sac might leave most sociologists happy to have been so parked as so many are refugees from institutional religions. Being so exiled, few are disposed to inspect the theological credentials underpinning their disciplinary stances. In matters of theology, sociology has its own index. Inspect any introductory text in sociology and it would be extraordinary to find in the index any reference to theology, whether Protestant or Catholics. By default of any inspection, Protestantism became the natural religion of sociology to the degree to which Catholicism became its unnatural version. Yet in another setting, choices were made regarding theological preferences – in Durkheim's case, Catholicism over Protestantism. The individualism of the latter seemed to subtract from his notion of the sacred as being manifested in the social, in rituals and in a moral order, an approach that reflected Catholic values. In her section on Isambert, Hervieu-Léger draws attention to his assertion that Durkheim's notion of the sacred reflects an 'implicit sociology of Catholicism', something noted earlier in relation to Comte. She observes that Isambert felt that Durkheim's distinction between the sacred and the profane was a theological distinction, one between the spiritual and the temporal, or in this case the unseen and the seen.[45]

Matters regarding sociology's relationship to distinctions between Protestantism and Catholicism might have remained inconclusive, peripheral and unpersuasive but for the recent translation of Simmel's essays on sociology of religion. As suggested in the introduction, Simmel opened out a sociological route into theology that few seemed to have followed. In these essays, Simmel supplies an antidote to Weber's retreat from the social and visual. Accepting faith as a form of yearning, Simmel offers theology a sociological means of understanding what it seeks to make manifest, the radiance of religiosity.

Unlike Weber's, Simmel's route into theology is specifically through social forms. To that degree, his approach is purely sociological. But Simmel goes further by adding in a notion of content to religion that has definite visual and aesthetic dimensions. Apart from Bourdieu, few other sociologists have ventured into the realms of aesthetics. Likewise, few theologians deal with a theology of aesthetics, a notable example being the late great Swiss theologian, von Balthasar. Beauty is something that has been marginalised in a culture of postmodernity.[46] As the progenitor of postmodernity, Simmel's concerns with religious aesthetics supply sociology with a door for looking into the unseen in ways that would merit theological approval.

II

In his introduction to this collection of essays, Hammond notes that before 1907 many German Catholic intellectuals approved of Simmel's writings. This approval is unsurprising, given the amount of Catholic theology that flows into his writings on religion. Born a Jew, he became a baptised Christian but ended his days as an agnostic.[47] Now it is not argued that Simmel had a coherent theology that was implicitly Catholic. What is argued is that many facets of his essays facilitate the use of sociology in the direction of Catholic theology.

Erickson opens out a number of important considerations regarding Simmel on religion. First, he is concerned with narratives of the soul, its tales of a search for God. In this context, faith becomes an issue of sociological interest. Secondly, she points to his persistent concern with the soul, its spiritual state in the setting of modernity, where a crisis of form suggests that relief is not to be found in the institutional churches. Thirdly, in a most curious and creative turn, she speaks of a sociology of the theology of limbo. This returns to the notion of liminoid virtualities of Shields. It is this sense of a space between that throws back a choice, but one where in the setting of postmodernity there is no means of exercise. There is no handle to the door. Thus, Erickson suggests that Simmel caught the fate of an era. Even though she suggests he could not name it, what he provided was 'a sociology of limbo which might well be the sociology of postmodernity'.[48] Here again, one encounters a most perplexing situation. Repeatedly, one finds sociology reaching for metaphors that are drawn from theology, but which it has jettisoned on the expedient grounds that the originals are incredible in modern culture, hence are downplayed. Somehow, sociology still needs these notions which sections of theology treat as antique.

Vatican II was a tragic case of misreading the cultural times. It affirmed a belief in modernity when two decades later it was marked as incredible, hence the invention of postmodernity. It marked ritual and symbol as entities characterised by a noble simplicity and transparency when a decade later, anthropology stressed their complexity and ambiguous basis. The attachment of a notion of limbo to sociology as the basis for dealing with a culture of postmodernity is, however, more embarrassing. Limbo is a term that has been dropped in recent Catholicism – it does not appear in the Catechism of 1994. The reason for its disappearance is because limbo endorses the notion that there is no salvation for the unbaptised, a stance incompatible with efforts of Catholicism to open out a dialogue with non-Christians. Casting limbo into a theological liminality forms part of a downplaying of images of the unseen, of life in heaven and hell, which have been considerably softened compared to their starker medieval representations. Taking the fear out of the afterlife has fuelled an indifference to institutional religion, one often confused with the effects of secularisation. Rational choice theory applied to religion involves a concern with calculation and the after-life. Efforts to make more definite links with the unseen generate discomfort for liberal theologians for whom a strategy of fudge better fits the spirit of the times. Fundamentalist responses of sociologists to such strategies seem illiberal, unscientific and idiosyncratic. But this is to overlook the sociologist's dilemma.

As a discipline, sociology might claim to read the ground of culture better than theologians. Not being a theology, but in it in this study, sociology, avoiding charges of founding a virtual religion, posts back issues found on the ground of culture to theology for arbitration. Sometimes, the replies disappoint. There is a strange sense that in its dalliances with theology, sociology always ends up with conservative formulations and stresses oddly incompatible with the modernity theologians strive to convert. Both disciplines differ in their strategies towards the world. Put simply, sociologists increasingly endorse forms of resistance to modernity and its successors, whereas theologians seem to capitulate to these. These differences of approach greatly complicate this study. If hell is treated as a rest home for the existentially challenged, and heaven as an inclusive multi-faith paradise, why on earth bother to seek to see the unseen? Liberal theological concessions can cut the ground from under sociological efforts to understand the seen and the unseen. What is clear is that sociology draws culture in more vivid colours of light and dark in ways that point to a more demanding theology than many theologians would expect. A sense of this emerges in Simmel's sociological response to religion. Something more definite is sought from the indefinite state of affairs he uncovers.

It has become difficult to under-estimate the importance of Simmel. A prophet of a culture of postmodernity, Simmel is treated as the fourth man of sociology, one whose reputation can only ascend. Very much the sociologists' sociologist, his influence has been profound. Weber, Goffman, Bourdieu and Bauman and the Chicago School, to name a few, have all been indebted to his work. Given that Simmel had written on ethics, aesthetics, philosophy, on fashion, tourism, cosmopolitan culture and money, and was a unique polymath, his ventures into religion might not seem that surprising. What is surprising, however, is the way these essays formed a chronology in his intellectual life and display a continual interest in the sociology of religion.

Simmel's sociological interest in religion explores how the self seeks to realise faith through social manifestations. The social is the door to the spiritual. His notion of religion supposes theological fixtures of God, doctrine, faith and ritual. Far from locking sociology into some reductionist exercise, Simmel's concern is with edification, the building up of faith that takes on a property of inner certainty. Religious belief in its intimate sense is to be found not so much in intellectual sensibilities but as an *actuality*, where the seeker finds emotional fusion with God, one experienced as a 'real event'. Echoing Paul, Simmel argues that 'the attempt to form a mental image of God is only a looking-glass reflection of these events'.[49]

Whereas Simmel's notion of the tragedy of culture was based on the disjunction between form, ever expanding, and content never quite assimilated into the social, his approach to religion centres on efforts to reconcile the subjective impulses to belief with their necessarily objective forms of manifestation. It is God, not sociology, which is the focal point of efforts to reconcile what is often irreconcilable, a point Simmel derives from Nicholas of Cusa.[50] The contradictions of religious practice arise from distance and proximity, need and fulfilment, and the relationships between desire and its ultimate provider. In all these points, religious language is used in its real sense, and not in some metaphorical misappropriation so habitual in sociology. Almost uniquely, as a sociologist, Simmel writes of Christian approaches to the concept of salvation in terms of the universally valid that embraces the unique and the particular.

Simmel's distinctive contribution to understanding the link between visual culture and piety lies in his emphasis on how the unseen acts on the seen through the means of the artistic imagination. Religiosity is treated in terms of discernible properties in art. For Simmel, Fran Angelico and Rembrandt have in common a concern with painting religious persons. In looking at the figures portrayed in Rembrandt's religious painting, Simmel observes that

> religiousness is a quality of these figures – an inner attribute, just like their wisdom or stupidity, their energy or their indolence. They may believe or act as they wish: piety is a determining factor of their subjective being as such, a quality that shines out all the more clearly as a distinctive coloring of their own personality because it manifests itself in the earthliness of their behavior.[51]

This comment draws attention to a crucial distinction Simmel makes between money and religion. Because money is colourless, it derives its power from its incapacity to reflect cultural values, but religion is characterised by a colouring that endows it with a capacity to express properties of the spirit.

Whereas money is a creature of calculation, religion in the image of Rembrandt elicits a gaze at what is beyond calculation and legislation. For Simmel, Rembrandt is the painter of the soul. His figures are not about doctrines, but about something that gives sociology its theological opportunity – an aura that is a 'process of life itself, a function that can be fulfilled only within the individual'.[52] Rembrandt's

> particular light emanates neither from the sun nor from some artificial source but from his artistic imagination, and yet it is of a totally spiritual and sensory character. Its stature and its otherworldliness are thoroughly earthly features that one might describe as deriving from artistic experience.[53]

For Simmel, religion is a capacity, an ability, a disposition for belonging, not founded on illusion and projection but on faith and here he makes an unexpectedly orthodox theological point, one that links to prayer. It refers to a belief, a trust based on a conviction of relationship. Faith is expressed in the simple statement, 'I believe in God'. Simmel goes on to add that

> the *quality* of the religious soul expressed in this statement is the fountain of youth from which theoretical belief in the existence of God draws its perpetual energy despite all evidence and probabilities to the contrary.[54]

The religious impulse is always there as the miracle of sociological manifestation. In summary, Simmel argues that

> religious life creates the world anew; it represents the whole of existence in a particular key, so that in its pure form it *cannot* come into conflict with those world constructs created according to other categories – even though an individual's life may pass through all these.[55]

Yearning is a necessary imperative for the pursuit of a faith seeking understanding. From Simmel's account, one can amalgamate the purely sociological and the theological in characterisations of virtuous activities of religiosity, notably those of prayer. One has to bear in mind that religion rises above the tentative and experimental cast of endeavours of the social to unify. The social becomes the viaduct for channelling a particular religious mood or circumstance. Thus, in Simmel the religious and the social provide a means of spiritual refraction, a resolution of harmony and the need for unity. It is in his social relations that man finds an idea of God.

Simmel treats these strivings, impulses and desires of the soul in relation to the need to use the social in some subservient manner to realise their basis. This involves a spiritual career in seeking salvation. Thus, Simmel's concerns are not with mere religion, as some sort of mechanism of reproduction geared to the de-spiritualising gaze of sociology, but as serving ambitions theology cannot but endorse. No orthodox theologian could reject Simmel's reflection on the nature of the individualistic form of the seeking of salvation of the soul. It is something realised in the here and now, and denotes 'the fulfilment of the soul's ultimate desires, the achievement of absolute spiritual perfection, possible only as an agreement between itself and its God'. He goes on to add 'that what we *ought* to be permeates the imperfect reality of our actual self as a latent ideal'.[56]

Starting from within the soul, Simmel works from its attitudes to God out into a manifestation of their social form, the means through which these can be realised and expressed. Religiosity is 'a quality of spiritual being, *the religious life process*'.[57] It is not something that springs from the social and falls on the believer, but rather is something that comes from faith, from a disposition and a capacity that is distinctly spiritual and theological. It arises from a sense of dependence on God, a trust and a yearning. The object of faith is a being 'which the intellect and the imagination cannot encompass with their qualitative and quantitative definitions'. Religious content (as against form, the objectifying facilitating social shape) relates to a definition of God, the doctrines of salvation and imperatives of conduct.[58] In this regard, the concern of this study is the content of faith, the unseen as it pertains to salvation and the forms of the seen that refract and mirror its basis.

The issue of faith expresses both an ambition of journeying and its site of fulfilment. The former emerges in the notion of salvation. This involves the exercise of virtue and discipline, the release from selfishness and what militates against the advance of the soul. Salvation signifies this ambition. It might seem that Simmel is writing a theology rather than sociology. It is better to suggest that he is using what belongs to theology to formulate a sociology, one that is set to deal with dilemmas they both have in common. This emerges in relation to the antinomies that complicate the religious endeavour as it proceeds through social means to find God. Examples lie in notions of destitution and abundance of life, of having and not having, of proximity and distance, of need and fulfilment, of the social and spiritual, the imperative to render objective what is felt in the subjective and the relationships of the individual to the community or the group. What is distinctive in his approach is his recourse to theology to resolve these sociological antinomies.

In Simmel's major works on culture is a concern with its tragedy, the way forms, because they can be rendered definite, malleable, commodified and subject to calculation, risk engulfing a more elusive, intangible content. The majesty of form and the opportunities it presents enervates more ephemeral notions of content, properties of the spirit to be handled with no easy grace. In his essay on religion and contradictions of life, Simmel presents a notion of God that transcends these contradictions. Mysticism is the means of transcending these manifold contradictions. It is the condition that redeems the fate of the tragedy of culture, a plight that has expanded endlessly in the condition of postmodernity. It is about the seeking of possession, of coming to dependence in the act of love of God, where the will is engulfed but freed, a phenomenon James also often notices. For Simmel, this is not a demeaning illusory state of compensation for short-comings, but 'expresses life's supreme bliss, man's excess, a step he takes beyond himself, where he is not too small for himself, but too great'.[59] It embodies a yearning to be possessed, an ultimate longing that involves a process of seeking perfection as a moral endeavour, hence the notion of sanctification. This notion of yearning and yielding links both Simmel and James. Yielding as self-surrender appears in the context of his approach to conversion.[60] Faith lies in issues of trust, of belief in another, and to that degree it is a fundamental ingredient of the social bond, but it is also a matter of theological obligation and duty. Simmel observed that the social role of this faith (this belief in somebody) has never been adequately investigated. He goes on to add that 'without it, society would disintegrate'.[61] For Simmel, 'practical faith is a fundamental quality of the soul that in essence is sociological, that is, it becomes concretized as a relationship with some being external to the self'.[62]

Spiritual capacities are not a function of agency, but of a request for grace, and this is well illustrated in his approach to prayer, which is linked to the notion of faith. Prayer is not a capacity derived through agency but through a gift given, one to be requested. It requires a bracketing of inhibition if the yearning to communicate is to be realised. As Simmel observes, 'to be able to pray, one must dismiss both doubt that God exists and doubt that God is in a position to answer prayers'.[63] Prayer is the means of realisation of faith.

In his treatment of the form of the religious life and that of art, the issue of proximity and distance emerges and this is treated in relation to the wholeness and symbolic unity of the body. Simmel suggests that 'the particular significance of the visual form as an expression of a spiritual condition lies in strict formal concentration which is pervaded by powerful inner emotion'. In some way, the body finds an image, as in prayer that supplies a testimony, a witness caught in the act.[64] This harmony and integration of body and spirit suggest the need for appropriation and emulation by those who see. It is this sense that alerts the self to exercise a disposition to integrate what is of the unseen, however elusively seen, with what the eye of perception sees too definitely. In his essay on Christianity and Art, Simmel concludes with a comment that 'art empowers the soul to supplement one world with the other and thereby to experience itself at the point of union...'.[65] Supplementation carries well the property of seeking to complete what is missing, to unify what is disconnected in the seen and the unseen, as the inner eye seeks to dance with its ocular partner whose gaze is without.

In all this, the social is a means of manifesting an attitude of the soul. Religion heals the rifts of otherwise debilitating disharmonies between the subjective and the objective, the spirit of life and its social means of manifestation and the disjunctions of the self and the spiritual. In this setting, prayer is an instrument of salvation and sanctification, a strategy of self-envelopment in the Divine. This capacity to pray is given gratuitously. Religiousness is a capacity for discernment, recognition and appropriation. It is about running between desire and provision, something to be found not on the plain of the social but in the realm of the spiritual and it is this capacity to move from one to the other that denotes what Simmel means by a religious person. For Simmel, 'his very *being* is religious; he functions in a religious way, so to speak, just as the human body functions organically'. In short, he embodies what he believes. He adopts the specifically detailed, of piety, the qualities of the soul: 'the feelings of dependence and hopefulness, humility and yearning, indifference to mortality and the constraints of life'.[66] It is these properties that formed what those in Frank's *The Memory of the Eyes* sought. Even the young who act as symbolic labourers in liturgy have an eye for those who pray and those who do not. They look because they want to avoid feeling deluded in what they do, and in seeing habitually they discern those who pray and those who are only empty vessels. The eye can be trained to distinguish and to know the *actuality* of others whose prayerful activities betray the flourishing qualities of the soul. Desire and provision, need and fulfilment are all dilemmas religious petition seeks to have harmonised.

The colour of faith is an expression of the unseen; belief is realised through the social; and the antinomies sociology uncovers are given over to theology to seek to understand the mystery of their transcendence. Understanding the making of religion on the ground, Simmel deals in edification, imitation and its colluding properties that work through the social. If good can be found on the ground of the social, so can evil.

III

Those dedicated to evil fascinate in ways those devoted to the pursuit of the good do not. The children of the light have an image problem. They are deemed boring, escapist, presumptuous, insipid, and the young and virtuous who come out as virgins are often savaged by their peers. On the other hand, the children of the dark seem much more interesting. Bizarrely, they seem closer to humanity than the children of light. The fallen state seems nearer to 'real life' for the worldly weary. Exotic, pioneering and fascinatingly transgressive, those who are evil seem to play with impunity on the edge of life. They exhibit a nobility of experimentation at the limits of the human condition. Their descent is far more interesting than the ascent of the virtuous.

These images of life, of good and evil, bear on notions of final judgement in the other world where heaven and hell reflect divisions of allocation in the unseen. Reflecting Simmel's interest in salvation, these divisions are reflected back to cultural images made for this world. For some, matters of the other world are matters of cynicism if not indifference. Given their boring status on earth, the prospects of everlasting life with the virtuous in heaven seem less than tempting. As the term 'wicked' has become one of endearment, so worries over Divine retribution have vanished. Hell has become a term for distaste rather than a state of fret about eternal happiness denied. In short, in a culture of postmodernity, hell is not a burning issue.

Disembodied from judgemental outcomes in a culture, with the eye of God firmly shut, evil, it seems, has unexpectedly prospered. The dalliances of the pioneers of modernity with evil have left it as something recreational in the climate of postmodernity. Images of evil, of horror, such as in the film *The Omen*, are things to be gazed at for pleasure, and are to be seen without sensibilities of fear or danger. Indifference to its theological authentication has meant that evil thrives on forms of misrecognition where technological capacities to mix the real and the virtual have greatly amplified its enticements and disguises. Evil derives its capacities from an *under-estimation* of its powers. Presenting an image of glamour, evil fascinates. It speaks to the human condition and marks an enduring interest in its basis – regardless of cultural sentiment. At one level, evil might seem innocuous, but at an other level it leaves traces in the humdrum that cause the eye to look again and to worry over what has been misrecognised. Perhaps unexpectedly, interest in evil has greatly increased within a culture of postmodernity.

In the decade before the millennium and shortly after, there has been considerable public interest in the cinema adaptations of *The Lord of the Rings* and the films and books on Harry Potter. These point to a mass public interest in the heroic facets of good struggling with evil that is far too extensive to discount. It is in events that inescapably darker facets of evil emerge. These catch the public by surprise, for few expect something so evil to disturb the tenor of civilised and routine life. Events in England, such as the murder of Jamie Bulger, a child, by two boys generated a near moral panic. Recourse to notions of evil brought back theological issues a post-secular society thought had been forgotten. The need to consider forgiveness but above all the unreasonableness of evil unsettled many observers. Evil has no reason bar a dangerous destructive power suddenly unleashed in a society whose sense of order suggested that such events belonged to a savage, uncivilised past. More perplexing and unsettling is the realisation that modernity, civilisation and technology have generated capacities for slaughter that cannot but generate worries about evil and invisible forces.[67] These worries cannot be reduced to claims of moral panics from fundamentalists. Somehow, evil has flourished on a more massive scale than almost at any time before.

Genocide and ethnic cleansing are terms particular to the twentieth century. Each leaves traces on human sensibility of something deeply evil. Every human life is of value, so ranking the evilness of forms of mass extinction seems an unworthy exercise. Was the systematic butchery of Rwanda, a supposedly Catholic country, worse than the cold clinical mass murders in

Auschwitz? In both cases, evil had the upper hand. Each presents a dilemma. Was Rwanda worse because it pointed to the evil in all, the base animal instinct exercised in a brutal, individual de-humanising fashion? Or was Auschwitz worse for the way such baseness was disguised through a brilliant use of technology and bureaucracy crassly dedicated to the slaughter of the innocent. In both settings, God seemed peculiarly absent, but this generates its own problems as Neiman has well indicated. She argues that

> modern conceptions were developed in the attempt to stop blaming God for the state of the world, and to take responsibility for it on our own. The more responsibility for evil was left to the human, the less worthy the species seemed to take it on. We are left without direction. Returning to intellectual tutelage isn't an option for many, but hopes for growing up now seem void.[68]

Certain types of evils that seem barbaric and unfit for public display have vanished. If present, even Hannibal Lector might have averted his eyes at the spectacle of the public dismemberment of a regicide in 1757, a graphic account of which infamously opens Foucault's *Discipline and Punish*. Following this account appears a listing of the timetable at a French prison some eighty years later. The ecclesiastical comforters on the ritual of dismemberment vanish, to be replaced by guards in the new regime of discipline and order.[69] The shift from body to soul, from embodiment to disembodiment, from what is best not seen to what is not seen at all, marks a movement from rituals of barbarity and superstition to institutions structured to instilling civility through the light of reason. So displaced, the evil of punishment seems to have vanished from sight of the public eye. The removal of spectacles of bodily dismemberment from the public gaze might seem to confirm the advance of civilisation, but it also marks a re-distribution of evil. More pernicious evils emerge in Foucault's account, which kill the spirit and destroy the social bond in an all pervasive structuring of punishment in a diffusion of power. Ironically, it seems as if modernity has enhanced the powers of dissimulation of evil. In a vision of the world that denies heaven and hell, issues of authorship become peculiarly problematic and unsettling.

Evil rarely appears as a term in sociological texts. As a term it betokens magic, myth and superstition. Evil is deemed proper to anthropology but improper to sociology. It belongs to the pre-modern but not to the modern. Bauman's sociological study, *Modernity and the Holocaust*, led to second thoughts about the place of evil in modernity. Something emerged that sociology had neglected to recognise. An uncomfortable realisation dawned that civilisation had not expelled evil but had peculiarly disguised its basis. Sociology faced a quandary: was this evil something metaphorical or did it exist?

Surveying Auschwitz, the usual question to ask is, where was God? Bauman opens out a more relevant question: where is sociology in the account?

Sociology cannot just characterise Auschwitz as some sort of bureaucratic experiment and neglect to consider the morality of its ends: the industrialisation of death. The tragedy of the Holocaust, in his account, is that the Jews were the pioneers of the very modernity and civilisation that incorporated powers to effect the destruction that engulfed so many of them. Implicit in Bauman's work is a realisation that the forces that gave rise to civilisation and modernisation facilitated the expansion of an evil so enormous that it could not be characterised in any other language than one that referred to a theodicy. In the expansion of calculation and the unfettered interest in curiosity, a bond of human mutuality weakened and resistance in some manner became enfeebled. The powers man took to himself seemed to have facilitated the misrecognition of evil.

Looking at Milgram's experiments, Bauman encountered a link between authority and cruelty. When a form of authority was based on a value-free pursuit of ends, as Weber so advanced, the effects in terms of the organisation of the Holocaust were frightening. What so deeply worried Bauman was the ease with which people can slip into a moral blindness, when legitimated by reference to rational ends. The lulling powers of the bureaucratic order and the trust it inspired in its gifts of calculation gave to this technological order of slaughter a certain logic. Evil was incorporated into a bureaucratic regime that undermined capacities for both recognition and resistance. Civilisation had taken to itself mythical powers for the expulsion of evil and in so doing undermined the need to cultivate virtues of resistance. These seemed no longer required. The evil in the Holocaust was its absolute power of disregard, of uprooting or destroying with impunity. Adherence to a bureaucratic ordering permitted an enormous cruelty to be exercised in the industrialisation of death. In the powers of abstraction and depersonalisation untold numbers died as numbers. Distance suggested no face to see and no eye to engage in mutual glance. By making everything seem reasonable, all is possible, and as Bauman observes:

> *in a system where rationality and ethics point in opposite directions, humanity is the main loser.* Evil can do its dirty work, hoping that most people most of the time will refrain from doing rash, reckless things – and resisting evil is rash and reckless.[70]

The unchecked individualism that also so worried Durkheim points to an unfettering of social bonds, a loss of trust and commitment, but above all a concern with self-preservation, perhaps the facet of evil that most worried Bauman.

An earlier and neglected effort to formulate a sociology of evil was made by Lyman in 1978. Like Bauman, Lyman sought to place the issue of evil in sociological deliberations as a response to the inhumanity of the times. His concerns arose from the Vietnam War and the cruel racism of many facets of American life. Contrary to its allure, Lyman, like Bauman, sees evil as a form of estrangement; a property that emerges from a loosening of mutual obligation. It is this isolation and disregard of the effects of acts that lead to an atomisation of society in ways that force sociology to attend. The evil of pride and greed are all too self-evidently socially damaging. Again, following Bauman and also Pascal, Lyman places the morality of the act as something emergent from the social. Thus, he suggests that 'modern dramas of evil occur on stages where the originating actions are all too routine'.[71] Somehow, in the ordering of the social and the surface it presents, matters of the unseen and the seen are seldom inspected and so entrap the unwary. Although evil seems self-evident, it is a term riven with definitional difficulties. Certainly, evil has banal and destructive properties, so that in some ways its traits are easy to mark, but to say what it actually is and where it comes from turns out to be unexpectedly difficult.

One wishes to follow St Augustine and treat evil as the absence of good.[72] In arguing later that evil is the privation of good, St Augustine writes 'there is a scale of value stretching from earthly to heavenly realities, from the visible to the invisible; and the inequality between these goods makes possible the existence of them all'.[73] The issue relates to a theological question of how a good God permits evil but also how it emerges in the divisions of the human condition.[74] Because evil is derived from sin in Catholic theology, the notion of culpability emerges. Despite its almost tangible properties, a considerable degree of mystery surrounds evil, not least in the realm of its recognition. Evil thrives on the false, not least conveying a notion of absence when it is present. Spiritual resources are required to recognise what is hidden in appearance and what is being misrepresented. Thus, writing on Bernanos, von Balthasar noted the imperative for Christians to see and recognise evil. In so doing, he suggested that the actor should not approach the issue of recognition 'with his own eyes, but must attempt to come to see evil with the eyes of God, which is to say, in prayer'.[75] Evil can represent a state of social affairs, but fundamentally its roots are interior and spiritual. As is noted of vices that include the use of the evil eye, 'all these evil things come from within, and defile the man' (Mk 7:21–3).

Neiman has chronicled well the way evil has been an unrecognised but important part of modern thought. Her concern is with the way evil is disengaged from God and becomes a matter of human agency and choice. The issue of evil evolves from a concern with its representation in nature, in disasters, to questions of moral choice and accountability. Efforts to remove evil from Christianity seem to end in its imitation in the writings of Nietzsche where endurance and suffering are the traits of the heroic. In a shrewd appraisal of the implications of Auschwitz, Neiman draws attention to the way functionaries in these camps seemed normal, even when their activities were profoundly abnormal. Arguing that they simply fulfilled a task, some charged with mass murder claimed that evil was not among their intentions. All this is highly perplexing for sociology. It faces a term whose genealogy has become obscured with the triumph of secularisation. Even worse, its use in relation to Auschwitz generates peculiar social conundrums. Usually, evil is associated with the primitive, the superstitious, and with a social disorder that is deemed pre-civilised. Auschwitz, on the other hand, presented a manifestation of evil that emerged from a fetish with order where a technological and bureaucratic excellence was employed – to highly nefarious ends. The scale of the murder and its soulless and dehumanising properties point to a manifestation of evil devoid of its usual romanticism, its excitement and is fascination. What is so unexpected is how evil could so thrive in such boring and predictable social circumstances.

At the end, evil *is* the only word left for anybody to characterise what happened in Auschwitz, but as Neiman well indicates, it reveals a conceptual crisis in twentieth-century thought about how to use the term without reference to a theodicy. More importantly, she indicates that 'Auschwitz was conceptually devastating because it revealed a possibility in human nature that we hoped not to see'.[76] Even worse, it came from something profoundly inhuman. With God dead, who was there to blame? Humanity somehow could not measure up to the charge of evil – only a deity could bear that burden. Thus, great disasters reveal operations of fate and tragedy, whose memory enlarges human sensibility of the heroic responding to exceptional circumstances. In the case of those slight figures behind the Holocaust, this was not the case. With reference to Eichmann, she notes that he 'caused tragedy; he wasn't fit to be a subject of it'.[77] Two final telling points from Neiman's study deserve sociological attention. The first is her warning that 'true evil aims at destroying moral distinctions themselves' and second is that

> those who care about resisting evils must be able to recognize them however they appear. Surrendering the word *evil* to those who perceive only its simplest forms leaves us fewer resources with which to approach the complex ones.[78]

Evil relates to moral panics, unsettlements and anxieties that spread like a contagion. Allegations over child abuse are often linked with rumours about links with Satanism. These were investigated by La Fontaine and shown to be unwarranted. Her study showed that few Satanists existed in the UK. The issue of tales was central to her analysis. The value of her account lay in showing the vested interests involved in the construction of evil, even as a rumour. Accusations stemmed from those who felt on the margins of society. More unexpectedly, it appeared that tales of evil of the victims or soul survivors were facilitated not by clergy but by therapists and those with an interest in moral scapegoating. Feminists and Evangelical Christians formed an unlikely alliance of interest in maintaining notions of evil.[79] If anything, the secularisation of evil has increased the scope for misrecognition.

The issue of the truth or falsity of evil is beside the point, for few other notions better exhibit the sociological dictum of W.I. Thomas, beliefs are real in their consequences, a point that emerges in his notion of the definition of the situation.[80] This notion emerges in relation to visual culture and the gaze in Foucault and in Big Brother. The issue of the existence of the gazer is irrelevant: it is the belief that one *is* being watched that matters. It is this belief that effects a re-ordering of the social and the relationship of the self to it and therein lies the central sociological facet of visual culture. Paranoia causes the gazer to discern patterns of implication that have no basis in fact. This sense of being watched by malevolent forces emerges in a long-standing anthropological interest in the evil eye, 'one of the most widespread symbols in all religious representation'.[81]

Anthropological accounts of the evil eye point to a very wide diversity of settings, use and antidote. The evil eye relates to powers of witchcraft, and the casting of spells that produce illness and misfortune. It points to the aggressive nature of seeing and being seen. Jealousy and envy give the idea of the evil its own rationale and logic, one of the instrumental uses of the spirits for reasons of malevolence.[82] The use of the eye invokes powers that can be dangerous. Everyday phrases such as 'casting an eye', 'giving somebody an eye' or 'guarding the eye', point to its powers and capacities. Its misuse poses enormous dangers. The capacity to see all in malevolent ways generates worries over the existence of the evil eye. Those believed to have an evil eye might not know they possess these powers of malevolence. It is a visual presence marked by an 'incompleteness, irresolution and regeneration – like the clothing infected with the evil eye, left at the crossroads for another to find and bring into the community'.[83] This points to the property of contagion in the visual as it affects the social. It also highlights the sense of irresolution the visual generates for the social and the need to attend to what is or was seen. Because the evil eye is related to incompleteness, worries emerge over its completion in violence and misfortune. Lurking unseen in the culture, the evil eye has a symbolic power arising from the belief that its use or presence accounts for misfortune.[84]

The evil eye draws attentions to sensibilities of the unseen, forces that require regulation. Possession, dispossession, misfortune and theft of the spirit mark not only the dangers of the evil eye, but also the need to develop symbolic and cultural resources of resistance. These antidotes to the evil eye range from almuts, to facial markings, to the veiling of the face and to talismans. These have been given wide cultural currency, not least in the West in terms of the influences of New Age religions and concerns with superstition. These antidotes to the evil eye can be decorative, but they also can signify definite capacities for warding off forces of evil. The evil eye draws attention to the powers of looking that can be invoked for reasons that bear on issues of virtue and vice. Thus, envy forms a common facet of accounting for those who invoke the powers of the evil eye on others.[85]

If evil can be so well found sown into the social often in invisible stitches, what about witnesses to the good? Do they have a place in the social? In many respects the social is more malleable than one might think. It is a resource whose ordering can be turned to good or evil, to what enables or disables. In whichever form, the social provides an indispensable basis of refraction whose use as much relates to agency and collective perception as to its possible uses, for good or evil. Here one returns to a point Raposa finds in Pascal.

Habit and routine are often treated as boring, unreflexive and enemies of religious flourishing. But Pascal observed that habit 'plays the most decisive role in religious conversion'. He advised those seeking to believe to behave 'just as if they did believe, taking holy water, having masses said, and so on'. Thus, he suggested that 'anyone who grows accustomed to faith believes it'.[86] Again, this 'as if' property returns. Raposa suggests that it is in the routines, in the rhythms and in the redundancies of ritual orders, areas where boredom is likely to arise, where paradoxically ultimate meanings are to be found.[87] What is seen as apparently boring is the response to the surface of a transaction. Moving below the surface, to the hidden depths of a ritual order, forms the means of yielding to the surplus meanings of the event. The ritual presents a misleading façade that invites interrogation by those with a capacity, a disposition to look more deeply. It is from that effort to decipher that a property of 'as if' emerges. Suspicion is bracketed, and the gazer proceeds to seek to see more of the unseen.

IV

'As if' haunts the study. It sidles into second place with the conundrum of who sees and who does not see the unseen. A spectrum of symbols of the sacred is available for scrutiny. So seeing, a sense of the good, what flourishes, what harmonises, is available to the eye and in that regard all that is seen has potential for conversion and transformation. In no sense can sociology supply a prescriptive notion of what to see and in what detail that will shift the eye of perception to engage with the inner view. Yet, there has to be some belief that *that* symbol and *that* event are carriers of greater meanings, ones that permit a passage of understanding through perception into a sense of inner view. Something seen bears a stipulation, an authority for the exercise of 'as if'. What is seen has to be able to bear transformations into something beyond mere perception. Those who see need the capacity to read what is seen into the unseen. All this is of grace, individual sensibility, and all one can write is of what *might* be seen that so transports.

Liturgies serve to remind of the hope of life beyond the grave. They mark movements of the earthly citizens towards their heavenly homeland. They are performed as social manifestations of what presently lies unseen. Thus, one can catch in the monastery a procession of monks in their black cowls stepping eastwards behind the choirboys in their ruffs, cassocks and long white surplices. These might seem more washed in Surf than in the Blood of the Lamb, and although their cotton polyester surplices might not be the finest linen of the righteous, these choirboys innocently proclaim a manifestation, a sense of vision of what is to come, of what is promised in Revelations, when white robes that never need washing are distributed to the new arrivals (Rev. 3:4–5 and 7:13–14). To follow Simmel, in the ritual form the social is painted with the colour of religion, and those who spot the difference, act 'as if' on that gift. Liminoid virtualities signify these transformations of visual culture for those with eyes to see to believe.

In the redundancy of the ritual action, its routine habit disguises not only the symbolic baggage borne, but also the theological ambition it seeks to realise of forging the seen into the unseen. As Ratzinger observed regarding the figures of the angels in Romanesque art:

> they show that we are joining with the cherubim and seraphim, with all the heavenly powers, in praise of the Lamb. In the liturgy the curtain between heaven and earth is torn open, and we are taken into a liturgy that spans the whole cosmos.[88]

Reflecting on the angels gathered on the altar-piece of Fra Angelico in the choir chapel of San Marco, Saward notes that they transmit an aura, a luminosity. But these images are not for the idle gaze. They designate a sense of purpose that goes beyond mere appreciation. The images serve to sow seeds of hope of emulation, for he writes that

> the holy angels plant good thoughts in our minds by clothing them in images of virtue, while the fallen angels entice us towards evil through images of vice. The saint artist is one who lets his imagination be purified and enriched by the icons given him by the angels.[89]

Simmel saw something similar in Fra Angelico. Noting his 'childlike simplicity', Simmel observed that he 'carries over the attitude of his real life into his artistic work'.[90]

As suggested earlier, in the fourteenth century there occurred an artistic colonisation of the angels so that the unseen was married to the seen in representations in liturgical transactions. The angels were given symbolic clothing to complement their earthly co-workers. Both those in the unseen and those in the seen were given common habiliments, long white surplices, albs and amices. Thus, the angels and the deacons and the acolytes and the choirboys all appeared alike in an indivisible manner.[91] The social poured into the ritual order served to refract the unseen, and the angelic host mirrored their heavenly activities back to the field on earth, so all were one in the pilgrim march to the City of God.

In his study of religious paintings, Latour draws attention to the angels that often appear. This leads him to indicate that 'if we are in society it is because we live among these delegates, very few of which look like fellow humans. If sociology is the study of society it has to take full account of these crowds of non-humans mingled with humans'.[92] Latour reminds that for any Flemish viewer in the seventeenth century, a religious painting was designated for prayer. But in seeing, the viewer formed part of a lineage of others who had also seen to pious effect. Thus, Latour suggests that 'in a religious painting, the pre-fix "re" of re-presentation means *again and anew*'. This leads to a highly important point that a religious painting 'never offers direct access to the sacred. It is a renewed commemoration of what other people – usually apostles or saints – said and saw'.[93] What is sought is the hope of seeing 'as if' for the first time the original actions the painting portrays. Oddly, Latour reflects a theme of *Sociology and Liturgy*, the inexhaustible basis of re-presentation. For him, absence should not be confused with a forgetfulness of God. Whereas that study dealt with ritual, Latour's concerns are with paintings. In these, the amnesia of absence is redeemed. Thus, he argues that 'what the religious painting does for the iconophiles is to cancel out this forgetting by repeating and renewing for the viewer the presence of God'.[94] His interest is not in the visual characteristics of the painting 'but the regime of re-presentation of which the visual implementation is but a consequence'.[95] His worries are that the literal has invaded the spiritual, thus reaching for the sky instead of heaven. Techniques of representation have won out and so have crowded the angels out and so clouding over the unseen.

It is not in the sociologist's gift to effect through analysis a re-population of the fields of culture with the heavenly horde. As von Balthasar argued 'if we can speak of a *theological* aesthetics it is only because it is *on his own initiative* and independently of man's particular anthropological structure that God takes form and allows himself to be seen, heard and touched'.[96] This self-disclosure of God seems to resolve the issue of the completeness of the gaze. It is God acting on the act that completes what cannot be done through sociology. All it can do is to chronicle endeavours with liminoid virtualities of the virtuous who seek in hope to gaze in ways that marry the seen to the unseen. As Saward suggests, 'the holiness of beauty is ordered to the beauty of holiness. Sacred art is intended to encourage saintly life'.[97] It is this property of emulation through seeing that lies in the heart of theological *and* sociological understandings of religiosity. The Divine permits an image of itself to be made, in icon and in ritual symbols, and there lies the miracle of the seen *seeming* to connect to the unseen. It is the kiss of grace that melts the seen into a tangible inner sense of the unseen in a sensibility that sets the self to glow with the colour of religion. As the unseen sets on the face, those who gaze do so with a strange diffidence. Where is this movement of reflection, this sensibility to be found?

One facet of this study that starts to emerge is that there is more of free will abroad in the decipherments of the seen and the unseen than one would expect. This emerges around the issue of prayer. Earlier, Simmel's notion that prayer and faith were interconnected was noted. In theological terms, prayer is of consummate importance. As Taylor observed, 'our prayer is a mirror of our life'.[98] At this point, one reaches a divide between sociology as a virtual religion and as providing a form of analysis that leads into theology.

For religion's cultural despisers such as Nietzsche, prayer is a deluding activity 'devised for such men as have never any thoughts of their own, and to whom an elevation of the soul is unknown, or passes unnoticed...'. As an activity it involves a 'long, mechanical labour of the lips, united with an effort of the memory, and with a uniform, prescribed attitude of hands and feet – *and* eyes'.[99] It is a deceptive and emptying transaction. Yet curiously in Comte's effort to form a virtual religion for sociology, prayer was marked out as being an act of specific importance. In his Positivist Catechism, Comte treated prayer as an issue of central significance in his 'sociolatry'. In his fantasy of relations between priest and woman, Comte noted that the omission of this 'great institution of prayer' would be 'extremely serious, if it were real'. The priest observed that

> the regular practice of prayer, private or public, is the capital condition of any worship whatever. Far from failing therein, Positivism satisfies it better than Catholicism; for it purifies this institution at the same time that it develops it.[100]

Although the efficacy of prayer as social activity might be given a sociological endorsement, its confinement to the social empties it of spiritual significance as an act of communication with God and not with the god of society. Prayer is good for the soul, and those who pray understand this well. Seeing somebody praying is not the same as understanding what he or she does, for there is something interior about the activity. A fulfilment is found and for those who pray it is not just a social activity; it is one filled with implication. But how is sociology to understand their claims?

This relates to a point of Winch that the issue of whether somebody is praying or not can only be clarified for a sociologist of religion by reference to the beliefs embodied. As a religious activity, prayer has to be contextualised. Yet, something more is required, for as Winch notes 'if the judgements of identity – and hence the generalizations – of the sociologist of religion rest on criteria taken from religion, then his relation to the performers of religious activity cannot be just that of the observer to the observed'. In short, the sociologist must have 'some religious feeling if he is to make sense of the religious movement' under study and what governs the lives of its participants.[101] This point echoes a stipulation of Anselm that 'whoever does not believe will experience nothing and whoever has not experienced anything will also perceive nothing'.[102] It is only in the experience of seeing the unseen that one can understand what the actor displays when acted on. Some refraction, some mirroring occurs on the social. It can be seen and needs to be looked for. In this area is the issue of testimony, one of seeing distinctions whose understandings reflect the ambitions of the study.

V

Scrutinising the posture of the body and its expression of piety was a means of authenticating the visions of Bernadette Soubirous. In particular, those who observed her having visions remembered the beauty of her face.[103] The need to scrutinise at the level of the social relates to two important points. First, religious sensibility and its basis of imitation spreads like a contagion so that what is seen is imitated within. If what is false is displayed, then a fruitless and deceiving imitation occurs. Secondly, transparency is a vital facet of edification. It represents a calling to be authentic in witness. It is the power of the visual to transform but also to offer some sort of fulfilment of the promise of belief that concerns the final part of the study where what is seen of religion that is good links the seen to the unseen. Within manifestations of the social can be found glimpses of the Divine, refractions on the face that suggest a contact well made. As Pachomius wrote: 'when you see a man who is pure and humble, that is a vision great enough. For what is greater than such a vision, to see the invisible God in a visible man, his temple?'[104] Those who are to give witness to the unseen have duties conferred on them, when in rites of passage it is marked out how they are to act to become. Through what they manifest in their appearances, they give testimonies to seeing the unseen in an indivisible light.

This expectation is well expressed in a recent sermon, titled 'Heaven Bound', on the occasion of a young Carthusian Cloister monk receiving his white habit. The preacher for the occasion observed: 'your taking of the habit today symbolises a deep commitment to orientate all your forces and desire towards the kingdom of heaven'. In so wearing his habit, the young man is told 'you must become what you are called'.[105] His habit comes to signify to him the particularity of his life as a means of pursuing the sights of the unseen in the seen.

This vocation is a calling to transparency so what is seen refracts the good of the unseen. This bears on an injunction in Thomas Á Kempis that

> the life of a good Religious should shine with all the virtues, that he may be inwardly as he appears outwardly to men. Indeed, there should rightly be far more inward goodness than appears outwardly.[106]

This relates to a need for exemplary behaviour so that the truth of virtue acts as a light, a basis of edification for others.[107] To gaze at those who pray deeply is to encounter a wonder similar to that felt by the Council who looked at Stephen and found that they 'saw his face as it had been the face of an angel' (Acts 6:15). He displayed a realisation of what Moses asked to be given to Aaron and his sons, the blessing that 'the Lord make his face shine upon thee, and be gracious unto thee' (Num. 6:25).[108] Faces so blessed seem mysteriously to refract the unseen in ways that are seen. A nun teaching the young to pray wrote that 'the faces of children at prayer dazzle me like icons' and this led her to wonder 'whence comes this wonderful light?'.[109] In the listings of the corporal effects characterising supernatural mystical ecstasy, one characteristic is the 'luminous expression on the face of the ecstatic, reflecting the vision'.[110] Such effects are extremely rare. In the face, prayer as a petition can be read and it can be of a response to an invitation 'not only to look at a map of the spiritual country, but to possess it and walk in it without fear of losing your way'.[111] Strangely, those into religion, avid to retrieve their light from under a bushel are often oblivious of what they project. The visual effects of dealing with the unseen are not for them. This reflects a comment of Goffman that

> in general, then, through demeanor the individual creates an image of himself, but properly speaking this is not an image that is meant for his own eyes.[112]

Why should the virtuous not be the beneficiary of what they project? The reason is that what is transparent as a testimony in acts of seeing can become an instrument of self-regard, a navel watching that hinders acts of edification. In the case of the prayerful, the face gives it away, for the eyes are closed and sight is directed to within to see the better. It might seem that such a disjunction has no place in sociological deliberations, yet again, this to forget the words of its founder. These appear in the instructions of the Positivist priest to a woman on the topic of private worship. There it is recorded: 'for the Positivist shuts his eyes during his private prayers, the better to see the internal image; the believer in theology opened them to see without him an object which was an illusion'.[113] Unexpectedly, what is seen within facilitates a better seeing without. What they cannot see, others do. This asymmetry of sight protects the virtuous from pride and vanity in appearance lest it is the self that is worshipped and not God.[114] This need to be seen but not to be self-regarding bears on the notion of virtuous dissimulation explored in *Sociology and Liturgy*.

Seeing properties of the spiritual is to discern something luminous, distinctions few now would bother to make. Consider an excerpt from a letter of Huysmans, written at the time of *En Route*, the account of his return to Catholicism in 1896. He was no mean art critic, given his role in the acceptance of the French Impressionists. He knew well what to look for. Reflecting on his past, on how easily he had gazed on forms of sensuality,

Huysmans pondered on a remarkable contrast in seeing the state of the chaste and wrote

> chastity seems to have an undeniable grandeur, and to be the only decent thing that exists. I know young men with souls of perfect whiteness, as their bodies; these children have an aura, have something exquisite about them that those who 'know' a woman or a man will never have. One really needs to have lived in these opposing worlds to have any notion that such people belong to the same race. Clothing can be misleading. Yet their bodies are the same, but that is where the soul, so much denigrated, emerges. It completely transforms everything.[115]

Journeying to see the unseen requires reference to many sites, for nothing is precluded as a means of the grace to see. Some focal points fit best to the needs of the study and, again, one returns to the icon. To see the face of God in an icon is not to see face to face, but rather something visible that effects a journeying into the invisible. The New Covenant permits the making of images of God that offer doors to the spiritual and the invisible. An inscription on an icon in San Marco that Kessler recorded states clearly that physical seeing was only intended to elicit spiritual contemplation. The inscription read: 'the image teaches of God but is not itself God. You revere the image, but worship with your mind Him whom you recognize in it'.[116]

Thus, in the icon, Ratzinger finds a means of opening up the inner senses to see above the sensible. This releases man from a closure of the senses. Evdokimov indicates that icon painters 'must learn how to fast with their eyes and prepare themselves by a long path of prayerful asceticism. This is what marks the transition from art to sacred art'.[117] Evdokimov formed the basis of Keenan's demand for a 'more affirmative way of seeing the created order of things' that would form the basis of a spiritualised sociology.[118] It has to deal with sites of edification and one can only mourn their destruction. The Reformation marked a systematic effort to uncouple piety from the visual.[119] It followed in another format the disputes of the eighth and ninth centuries that centred on iconoclasm where efforts were made to destroy visual representations of the Divine.

As visual culture comes to the centre of sociological deliberations, where all can be seemingly seen, and where the curiosity of the gaze is open to endless satisfaction in ways that have no precedent, surely Jervis is right to suggest

> other issues come to the fore: how 'truth' is produced as an *effect* of surfaces and appearances, how content and context are constituted through the image and its transformation, how 'multiple realities' are constructed, reproduced – and contested.[120]

So the visual presents many dilemmas. It arouses emotions, facilitates identity, mirrors hopes and sensibilities, but above all it presents no mere refraction, for the idle gaze risks disturbance in its passing glance. Deconstruction and suspicion serve to keep the gaze at bay, to preserve it in disembodiment and cynicism, the exemption clause of the bored. But as the gaze wanders, the roving eye risks seeing something that fixes it irretrievably. This occurred in the case of two who dallied in modernity and nihilism.

Huysmans and Dostoyevsky have one thing in common: a fascination with paintings of the crucified figure of Christ. For Huysmans, his painting was the *Crucifixion* by Matthaeus Grünewald. All extremities of suffering and mysticism were in that painting.[121] In Dostoyevsky's case, it was Holbein's painting of Christ taken down from the cross that grabbed his attention and that percolated into *The Idiot*. Both paintings portrayed brutal images of Christ crucified, battered and only recently dead. Little romanticism, little hope was to be seen in either painting, for they expressed the darkest point of Christianity, before the light of the Resurrection was to come. Yet, somehow, the paintings caught the eye of each in their plight in modernity, where all was gloom and horror. More than any other writer, Dostoyevsky caught the plight of life in nihilism, of the vulnerability of the innocent before the worlds of experience, evil and crime.

In *The Idiot*, Myshkin, a prince but also an innocent unfit for the world, saw a copy of the Holbein painting. Initially, he gave it but a cursory glance. His companion Rogozhin, who drew it to his attention, commented at this first look: 'why some people may lose their faith by looking at that picture!'[122] That painting of Rogozhin comes to haunt in the setting of Ippolit's curious manuscript. He also looks and sees a face, smashed, battered and damaged and 'the eyes open and squinting; the large, open whites of the eyes have a sort of dead and glass glint'. There was no resurrection in this painting, only terror of what was to be seen by those attending on the tragedy. No nostalgia, no romanticism, no easy hope, but terror and despair over what was seen.[123] Myshkin and Rogozhin are as light and dark in the novel and both embody the polarities of the human condition in ways where one is watching the other. In her three letters to Aglaya that Myshkin sees, Nastasya predicts her own murder by Rogozhin. She also wants a portrait of Christ, but one of Him with a little child, gazing into the horizon with a great thought dwelling in his eyes.[124] What emerges in *The Idiot* is a point made earlier by St Augustine that the face of God is the meaning of His revelation. Gazing at the face in a picture is to confront a dilemma of seeing with the eye of perception but also seeing with the 'eye of the heart'. It is this conundrum that he could not resolve. A dualism of the visual is presented for which there is not even a theological resolution, let alone one from sociology. How is sociology to characterise the connection between the seen and the unseen on the ground of culture, given that St Augustine treated such viewing as fundamentally inward?[125]

It is in an essay on the seen and the unseen in relation to Hindu distinctions that one finds a phrase that expresses the ambitions of this study. In his account of cultural reasoning and binary distinctions, Khare notes a recurrent sociological issue of 'how to' conjoin 'worldly life with the otherworldly reality'. This bears on the notion of the way the seen is knitted into the unseen.[126] It is this knitting as an act but also as a means of following a pattern made that suggests how the movement from the seen to the unseen might be understood. Acts of seeing and being seen make social patterns that lead into a realisation of the unseen. These present something newly made that requires attention, hence the property of the liminoid in the act. This bears on Turner's comment that the liminoid points not only to transitions that require ritualisation, but also an effort to pass through and beyond them. In this regard one can discern a movement from the seen, the activity of ritual and its movement towards the unseen.[127] It bears on the notion that the liminal is fundamentally about communication and in its dealings with the sacra it exhibits, in actions that involve and implicate. But more importantly, it instructs by displaying the manifestation of invisible faculties.[128] The metaphor of knitting carries the notion of weaving what is of the social, the manifest, into what is of the invisible, what is unseen.

Acts of perception, those that have a social construction, have a duality that foxes sociology. These acts relate to capacities, ways of seeing that enable those who gaze to distinguish between the hidden and apparent. This is to say little new, for the whole basis of the interpretation of symbols depends on this point. What is new, however, is the realisation that capacities to see, which enhance sensibilities of the visual and its social implications, have transformative effects that percolate into other communicative abilities. Thus, both of the writers above, who faced the image of Christ, ended up being haunted in ways that shaped and changed their literary imaginations. How does this apply back to sociology itself?

VI

Lurking in the issue of the seen and the unseen is a question of disposition, of inclination, but one dependent on what is available for the gaze and the field it surveys. As the secularisation of visual piety proceeds, with outlets for relief in cyberspace, the layout of the religious field has become constricted, incredible and empty, for it is deemed to have no cultural significance. This compounds disinclinations to exercise a visual piety. In the politics of representation, of what was marked to memorialise 2000 years, the Millennium Dome involved a displacement of other claims of temporal lineage that commemorated another belief system: Christianity. The Dome made a statement, setting in visual form an inclusivity that marked a triumph over the more exclusive and archaic claims of Christianity.

Between February and May 2000, an important exhibition of images of Christ was held in the National Gallery in London. In his foreword to the catalogue for the exhibition, the Director of the Gallery indicated that roughly a third of its collection was of Christian subjects. Indeed, one could go further and indicate that the vast majority of these were likely to be of Catholic origin and commission. The exhibition had a property of restoration, of presenting a fusion of the human and divine in a way that signified a theological triumph.[129] What was seen was represented in ways that amplified the artificial line between the real – of theology – and the virtual, the quasi-religious cast of the art gallery where aesthetics is given a secular ambit. The problem of the exhibition, *Seeing Salvation*, was that it drew out the contradictions of sites of seeing in terms of the rituals of response that governed these.

Duncan has characterised the art museum in terms of the ritual of viewing enacted by the viewer. In her appraisal of these rituals she comes near to recognising the real and the virtual when she concludes that

> a ritual experience is thought to have a purpose, an end. It is seen as transformative: it confers or renews identity or purifies or restores order in the self or to the world through sacrifice, ordeal, or enlightenment. The beneficial outcome that museum rituals are supposed to produce can sound very like claims made for traditional, religious rituals.[130]

Seeing Salvation had a cultural impact far outside what is usually associated with an exhibition in an art gallery. In her assessment of its impact, and also the letters that came to the National Gallery during and after the exhibition, Davie notes that over 350,000 visitors came to see it. In 2000, the catalogue was reprinted three times. What struck Davie in studying the letters of response was the way many congratulated the Director of the Gallery for his courage in putting on a display that seemed to have evolved as a counterattraction to the Millennium Dome. She was also struck by the notable absence of a Protestant response to what was a markedly Catholic exhibition whose theological basis so galvanised a national imagination.[131] This assembly of paintings, like the collection in the National Gallery of Ireland on Dutch letter writing, points to the way those arranging such exhibitions set out a tale, a narrative to what is seen. Guidance is placed as to the way of seeing to be followed in what is represented. The collection of images to be seen is not randomly cast; it is set to a purpose for the visual to reveal a tale. This sets an expectation that is made available for the eye of the connoisseur. All this leads back to a facet of reflexivity seldom examined, but one that the issue of the visual presents. This relates to the inward sensibilities of the sociologist who sees. A need, a want, a circumstance of life, causes the eye to seek to see, to re-cast its visual expectations. This need to look can arise when the virtual religion of sociology no longer suffices. Earlier, Zimmer's prayer to the gods of sociology was noted. There was a slightly ironic, if not sceptical, cast to this prayer that was more of a query than a petition. When death enters considerations, however, the inadequacy of sociology's masquerades as a virtual religion become all too apparent.

This query arose for Ian Craib, a British sociologist who looked to the sociology of death and dying to ally his own fears of these when he had been diagnosed with a brain tumour that was cancerous. Few sociologists in this field spoke to his fears or indeed offered understandings of his state. In Durkheim, he did find his intellectual understanding turning into an emotional understanding. Yet in the end, it was the absence of attention to the emotional dynamics of death, its inward sensibilities, which so worried him about what sociology had so far to offer. Just concentrating on the social scripts revealed the poverty of what could be said about a heroic death or the good death. The complexity of the human condition was masked.[132] In a response to this essay, Seale fell back on the Weberian edict of austerity as the necessary path for coping with such pain and fear. Reading the spirit of the times was *the* sociological duty and that was the only consolation available – even for the dying.[133]

Seldom have the limits of sociology in regard to the seen been so coldly exposed, for with Craib and Seale there is no ameliorating vision and no sense of the unseen that would enlarge the sense of a life after death. The sociologist's prayer, made in the spirit of his virtual religion, seems to reflect an apparatus of analysis, one with nugatory degrees of visual relief attached compared to those that emerge from outside the discipline. Sociology might mark the absence of solace; it seldom supplies it. If one wants ultimate solace, one turns to the real thing, to the theology that ultimately speaks to the complexities of the human condition.

The adage 'never judge a book by its cover' does not apply to this tome. Its cover betrays its tale. Every author longs for an image for his book something that would give visual expression to the nascent vision that underwrote the text. Wandering around the National Gallery of Ireland, an oak panel marked as 'Scenes from the life of St Augustine' caught this sociologist's eye. The panel was one of a triptych. Designated as anonymous and attributed to a master who worked in Bruges around 1490–1500, the painting seemed to offer in visual form what the study sought to encapsulate in the crippled language of sociological insight into theological matters.

In the panel, at the top on the left, was a scholar, seen through the frame of a door (the overtones in relation to Simmel were obvious). It was only when the manuscript of the present study was nearly finished that one found what the image on the jacket cover was about. The image was of St Augustine sitting at a desk, interrupted by a vision. What the vision was about lay as an unresolved puzzle in the writing of the text. One could not work out what he had seen. It seemed especially unfortunate to have an image on the jacket cover of a sociological study of the unseen that was so incomplete. By chance, when the manuscript was nearly completed, in late December 2003, one discovered a commentary on the painting that indicated what St Augustine had seen.

He had been writing a letter to St Jerome and was greatly surprised to be interrupted by a vision of him. There was something slightly ironical about the vision. A master of the biblical word, St Jerome had appeared to St Augustine to provide some consoling idea of what the unseen looked like. He had come back from the heavenly city to speak of the unseen.[134] Both men had worked together on many things.[135] Somehow, it seemed that the primacy of visual culture over the Word had its origins earlier than this sociological imagination realised. Whether the vision came or not, some consolation was given to the writer of this study that St Augustine also needed to see something of the unseen.

There was never one mobilising vision, one image that could be set as the trump card for this sociological study: that was not only its strength but also its weakness. All one has done is to provide a tale of the seen and the unseen, its complex cultural circumstances and the way the sociological eye might see the interchange of both in terms of realising a visual dimension to reflexivity. The gods invoked in secularisation have worked so hard to unravel the knitting of the seen and the unseen so that no pattern can be discerned in culture. If the book has an ambition, it is to supply a testimony for the need to re-knit these patterns that weave the seen into unseen so that a sense of the eye of God will return. It is not that the eye of God has gone dead; it is that the culture of postmodernity has gone on the blink and cannot focus to look. Sociology might help this culture to look better. As God's glass polisher on culture, sociology is peculiarly able to wipe away the muck so that those who wish to see the unseen better will and more than 'as if'. In his poem 'The author to his book', Thomas Heywood, an English seventeenth-century poet, supplied lines for the conclusion of this study. He wrote:

> If then the world a Theater present,
> As by the roundnesse it appears most fit,
> Built with starre-galleries of hye ascent,
> In which *Jehove* doth as spectator sit,
> And chiefe determiner to applaud the best,[136]

Notes and References

Introduction

1. Information on this church is taken from its entry in Simon Jenkins, *England's Thousand Best Churches* (Harmondsworth: Penguin, 1999), pp. 581–2. In his ranking, the church received four stars (the maximum was five).
2. Callum G. Brown, *The Death of Christian Britain* (London: Routledge, 2001). As one writes in November 2003, there is an increased sociological acceptance that English society is post-Christian. See for example, Chapter 14 of Stephen J. Hunt, *Alternative Religions: A Sociological Introduction* (Aldershot: Ashgate, 2003), especially pp. 232–7. See also David Voas, 'Is Britain a Christian Country?' in Paul Avis (ed.), *Public Faith? The State of Religious Belief and Practice in Britain* (London: SPCK, 2003), pp. 92–105.
3. Alex Wright, *Why Bother with Theology?* (London: Darton, Longman & Todd, 2002), see especially pp. ix–xv. In speaking of the decline of theology, Wright particularly assails its impenetrability but also its lack of engagement with a culture of postmodernity. See pp. 53–5. Wright writes as a former editor of theology for a number of well-known English publishers. In the study he seems mainly concerned to sketch out a secular theology.
4. See the splendid polemic by Nigel Holmes, *Losing Faith in the BBC* (Carlisle: Paternoster Press, 2000).
5. Phillip Jenkins, *The New Anti-Catholicism: The Last Acceptable Prejudice* (New York: Oxford University Press, 2003).
6. Transcript of a talk between Joan Bakewell and James Macmillan, *Belief*, BBC Radio 3, 2 January 2001.
7. Steve Bruce, *God is Dead: Secularization in the West* (Oxford: Blackwell, 2002).
8. See Rodney Stark, 'Secularization, R.I.P.', in William H. Swatos, Jr and Daniel V.A. Olson (eds), *The Secularization Debate* (Lanham: Rowman & Littlefield Publisher, Inc., 2000), pp. 41–66. Some sociologists, notably David Martin, have had great doubts about the viability of the term. See his essay 'Towards Eliminating the Concept of Secularisation', in J. Gould (ed.), *Penguin Survey of the Social Sciences* (Harmondsworth: Penguin, 1965), pp. 169–82.
9. For useful comment on this discrepancy, see the foreword by Nigel McCulloch, Anglican Bishop of Manchester, to Peter Brierley (ed.), *U.K. Christian Handbook. Religious Trends 4* (London: Christian Research, 2003), pp. 3–4. See also, Leslie J. Francis, 'Religion and Social Capital: The Flaw in the 2001 Census in England and Wales', in Avis (ed.), *Public Faith?* pp. 45–64.
10. For a useful assessment of their contribution in the USA, see Thomas C. Reeves, *The Empty Church: The Suicide of Liberal Christianity* (New York: The Free Press, 1996).
11. Kieran Flanagan, *Sociology and Liturgy: Re-presentations of Sociology* (Basingstoke: Macmillan, 1991).
12. Roy A. Rappaport, 'Veracity, Verity and *Verum* in Liturgy', *Studia Liturgica*, vol. 23, 1993, pp. 35–50. See also his important work completed just before his death: *Ritual and Religion in the Making of Humanity* (Cambridge: Cambridge University Press, 1999).

13. Kieran Flanagan, *The Enchantment of Sociology: A Study of Theology and Culture* (Basingstoke: Macmillan, 1996).
14. Robert K. Merton, *Sociological Ambivalence and Other Essays* (New York: The Free Press, 1976). The title essay of this collection was first published in 1963.
15. See Kieran Flanagan, 'The Return of Theology: Sociology's Distant Relative', in Richard K. Fenn (ed.), *The Blackwell Companion to Sociology of Religion* (Oxford: Blackwell, 2001), pp. 432–44. Some of the themes of this study started to emerge in that essay. For other notable excursions into the terrain of sociology and theology, see David Martin, John Orme Mills and W.S.F. Pickering (eds), *Sociology and Theology: Alliance and Conflict* (Brighton: Harvester Press, 1980). See also John Orme Mills, 'Introduction: Of Two Minds' to a re-issue of this collection (Leiden: Brill, 2004), pp. 1–12. Also see David Martin, *Reflections on Sociology and Theology* (Oxford: Clarendon Press, 1997); Pål Repstad, 'Between Idealism and Reductionism: Some Sociological Perspectives on Making Theology', in Pål Repstad (ed.), *Religion and Modernity: Modes of Co-existence* (Oslo: Scandinavian University Press, 1996), pp. 91–117; and 'Theology and Sociology – Discourses in Conflict or Reconciliation under Postmodernism?' in E. Helander (ed.), *Religion and Social Transitions* (Helsinki: Helsinki University Press, 1999), pp. 141–55.
16. Charles Suaud, *La Vocation: Conversion et reconversoin des prêtres ruraux* (Paris: Les Éditions de Minuit, 1978). For a useful essay review of sociological studies in this area, see Jacques Sutter, 'Vocations Sacerdotales et Séminaries: Le Dépérissement du Modèle Clérical', *Archives des Sciences Sociales des Religions*, vol. 59, no. 2, 1985, pp. 177–96. These studies illustrate the changing context of vocation and the importance of developing a sacerdotal habitus early in liturgical life. Both the choirboy and the altar server (male) are the secret apprentices on the priest. As they grow older, they feel they can do better in the performance than the priest. The failure to attend to this link between the boy, as server or choirboy, and a possible vocation to the priesthood has had devastating effects. In his liturgical part, the boy is pursuing a career of anticipatory socialisation into a vocation. A theology of gesture to matters of gender has meant that with the introduction of girls into choirs, the boys have fled. Many facets of the decline in Church attendance are self-inflicted. Until notions of internal secularisation and Weber's notion of office charisma and routinisation are better understood in terms of recruitment, matters can only get much worse.
17. Pascal Dibie, *La Tribu Sacrée: Ethnologie des prêtres* (Paris: Bernard Grasset, 1993).
18. *Directives on Formation of Religious Institutes* (London: Catholic Truth Society, 1990).
19. Georg Simmel, *Essays on Religion*, ed. and trans. Horst Jürgen Helle with Ludwig Nieder (New Haven: Yale University Press, 1997).
20. I am grateful to my former colleague, Dr Willie Watts Miller for drawing my attention to this translation later published. See Marcel Mauss, *On Prayer: Text and Commentary*, trans. Susan Leslie (Oxford: Berghahn Books, 2003).
21. Mark Jordan (ed.), *The Church's Confession of Faith*, trans. Stephen Wentworth Arndt (San Francisco: Ignatius Press, 1987), p. 90.
22. Some of these themes are well discussed in Anthony N.S. Lane (ed.), *The Unseen World: Christian Reflections on Angels, Demons and the Heavenly Realm* (Grand Rapids, Michigan: Paternoster Press, 1999).
23. Alain Besançon, *The Forbidden Image: An Intellectual History of Iconoclasm*, trans. Jane Marie Todd (Chicago: The University of Chicago Press, 2000), p. 101.

24. St Augustine, *Concerning the City of God against the Pagans*, trans. Henry Bettenson (Harmondsworth: Penguin, 1972), p. 5. For a useful essay on the relevance of the City of God, see Robert L. Wilken, 'Augustine's City of God Today', in Carl E. Braaten and Robert W. Jenson (eds), *The Two Cities of God: The Church's Responsibility for the Earthly City* (Grand Rapids, Michigan: William B. Eerdmans, 1997), pp. 28–41. See also John Neville Figgis, *The Political Aspects of S. Augustine's 'City of God'* (Gloucester, Mass: Peter Smith, 1963).

25. Tom Beaudoin, *Virtual Faith: The Irreverent Spiritual Quest of Generation X* (San Francisco: Jossey-Bass, 1998), p. 13.

26. Ibid., p. 115.

27. Ibid., p. 52.

28. Joseph Ratzinger, *The Spirit of Liturgy*, trans. John Saward (San Francisco: Ignatius Press, 2000), p.135.

29. Gianni Vattimo, 'The Trace of the Trace', in Jacques Derrida and Gianni Vattimo (eds), *Religion*, trans. Samuel Weber (Cambridge: Polity Press, 1998), p. 87.

30. For an innovative effort to award the virtual its sociological significance, see Ben Agger, *The Virtual Self: A Contemporary Sociology* (Oxford: Blackwell, 2004).

31. Erving Goffman, *Encounters* (Harmondsworth: Penguin, 1972), p. 134.

32. Murray S. Davis, 'Georg Simmel and Erving Goffman: Legitimators of the Sociological Investigation of Human Experience', *Qualitative Sociology*, vol. 20, no. 3, 1997, p. 385.

33. Cited in Ralph M. Leck, *Georg Simmel and Avant-Garde Sociology: The Birth of Modernity, 1880–1920* (New York: Humanity Books, 2000), p. 280.

34. Charles Baudelaire, *The Painter of Modern Life and Other Essays* (London: Phaidon, 1995), p. 12.

35. Zygmunt Bauman, *Liquid Love* (Cambridge: Polity Press, 2003), pp. vii–viii.

36. Max Weber, 'Science as a Vocation', in H.H. Gerth and C. Wright Mills (eds), *From Max Weber: Essays in Sociology* (New York: Oxford University Press, 1958), pp. 153–5.

1   Sociology and virtual religion: issues of memory and identity

1. Anthony Giddens, *The Consequences of Modernity* (Cambridge: Polity Press, 1991), p. 43.

2. *The Times*, 5 June 1998.

3. *Evening Standard*, 18 June 1998.

4. Andrew Wernick, *Auguste Comte and the Religion of Humanity: The Post-Theistic Program of French Social Theory* (Cambridge: Cambridge University Press, 2001), p. 114.

5. See Pierre Nora, 'The Era of Commemoration', in Pierre Nora (ed.), *Realms of Memory*, vol. III, Symbols, trans. Arthur Goldhammer (New York: Columbia University Press, 1998), pp. 609–37.

6. Pierre Nora, preface, 'From *Lieux de mémoire* to Realms of Memory', in Pierre Nora (ed.), *Realms of Memory*, vol. I, Conflicts and Divisions, trans. Arthur Goldhammer (New York: Columbia University Press, 1996), pp. 6–7.

7. Ibid., pp. 12–13.

8. W. Watts Miller, 'Secularism and the Sacred: Is There Really Something Called "Secular Religion"?' in Thomas A. Idinopulos and Brian C. Wilson (eds), *Reappraising Durkheim for the Study and Teaching of Religion Today* (Leiden: Brill, 2002), pp. 36–8. The quotation cited above comes from p. 38.

9. This was the central theme of *Sociology and Liturgy*.
10. Maurice Halbwachs, *On Collective Memory*, trans. Lewis Coser (Chicago: The University of Chicago Press, 1992), pp. 178–9.
11. Kieran Flanagan, 'Sociology and Religious Difference: Limits of Understanding Anti-Catholicism in Northern Ireland', *Studies*, vol. 89, no. 355, Autumn 2000, pp. 234–42.
12. Danièle Hervieu-Léger, *Religion as a Chain of Memory*, trans. Simon Lee (Cambridge: Polity Press, 2000), pp. 132–3.
13. Practically every parish church in England has a record of memory, a history. What is rare is to find one cast in a frame of sociological expectation. See Timothy Jenkins, *Religion in English Everyday Life: An Ethnographic Approach* (Oxford: Berghahn, 1999), Chapter 2, on the country church of Comberton, pp. 41–73.
14. Eamon Duffy, *The Voices of Morebath: Reformation & Rebellion in an English Village* (New Haven: Yale University Press, 2001), see especially Chapter 4.
15. See Peter C. Jupp, 'Virtue Ethics and Death: The Final Arrangements', in Kieran Flanagan and Peter C. Jupp (eds), *Virtue Ethics and Sociology: Issues of Modernity and Religion* (Basingstoke: Palgrave, 2001), pp. 217–35.
16. Duffy, *Morebath*, Chapter 6 contains a most painful account of acts of barbarism against the visual piety of an inoffensive people.
17. André Vauchez, 'The Cathedral', in Pierre Nora (ed.), *Realms of Memory*, vol. II, Traditions, trans. Arthur Goldhammer (New York: Columbia University Press, 1997), pp. 43–4. Appraisals of the cathedral by sociologists are extremely rare. For a singular example of one, see Robert A. Scott, *The Gothic Enterprise: A Guide to Understanding the Medieval Cathedral* (Berkeley: University of California Press, 2003). Although he does not consider the cathedral directly, some useful issues that relate to time and the sacred can be found in William Watts Miller, 'Durkheimian Time', *Time & Society*, vol. 9, no. 1, 2000, pp. 5–20.
18. Hans Urs von Balthasar, *Prayer*, trans. A.V. Littledale (London: Geoffrey Chapman, 1961), p. 226.
19. See J.-K. Huysmans, *The Cathedral*, trans. Clara Bell (Sawtry, Cams.: Dedalus, 1998). Huysmans' account of Chartres, in a symbolic appraisal that could be linked to the needs of modernity, is of enormous importance in terms of re-centring the cathedral into the domain of present culture.
20. Erwin Panofsky, *Gothic Architecture and Scholasticism* (New York: Penguin, 1976).
21. David Frisby and Mike Featherstone (eds), *Simmel on Culture* (London: Sage, 1997), pp. 173–4.
22. J.-K. Huysmans, *En Route*, trans. W. Fleming (Sawtry, Cambs.: Dedalus, 1989), pp. 108–9.
23. See for example, Margaret M. Poloma, 'Toward a Christian Sociological Perspective: Religious Values, Theory and Methodology', *Sociological Analysis*, vol. 41, no. 2, 1982, pp. 95–108; and Ronald J. Burwell, 'Sleeping with an Elephant: The Uneasy Alliance Between Christian Faith and Sociology', *Christian Scholar's Review*, 1981, pp. 195–203. Although written two decades ago, these two articles have remarkable contemporary resonances.
24. For a discussion of this shift in understanding, see Russell T. McCutcheon (ed.), *The Insider/Outsider Problem in the Study of Religion* (London: Cassell, 1999). See also Elisabeth Arweck and Martin D. Stringer (eds), *Theorizing Faith: The Insider/Outsider Problem in the Study of Ritual* (Birmingham: The University of Birmingham Press, 2002).

25. Rodney Stark and Roger Finke, *Acts of Faith: Explaining the Human Side of Religion* (Berkeley: University of California Press, 2000), p. 21.
26. Roy A. Rappaport, 'Concluding Comments on Ritual and Reflexivity', *Semiotica*, vol. 30, no. 1/2, 1980, p. 187.
27. Ibid., p. 192.
28. Cited in Gerth and Mills, (eds), *From Max Weber*, p. 156.
29. See William H. Swatos, Jr and Peter Kivisto, 'Weber as "Christian Sociologist"', *Journal of the Scientific Study of Religion*, vol. 30, no. 4, December 1991, pp. 347–62.
30. Wolfgang Schluchter, 'The Battle of the Gods: From the Critique to the Sociology of Religion', *National Taiwan University Journal of Sociology*, no. 19, May 1988, pp. 176–7.
31. For a useful summary of this study, see Don Martindale, *The Nature and Types of Sociological Theory* (Boston: Houghton Mifflin Company, 1960), pp. 515–8.
32. Alison Lurie, *Imaginary Friends* (London: Vintage, 1999), p. 11. The book was originally published in 1967.
33. Ibid., p. 34.
34. Ibid., pp. 275–6.
35. Fred D'Agostino, 'The Necessity of Theology and the Scientific Study of Religious Beliefs', *Sophia*, vol. 32, no. 1, 1993, p. 27.
36. Gad Yair *et al.*, '*Ex Cathedra*: The Representation of American Society in ASA Presidential Addresses, 1906–98', *Sociology*, vol. 35, no. 2, May 2001, pp. 492–5.
37. Annie Petit, 'Du Catholicisme au Positivisme', *Revue Internationale de Philosophie*, vol. 1, no. 203, March 1998, p. 155.
38. Susan Stedman Jones, *Durkheim Reconsidered* (Cambridge: Polity Press, 2001), p. 203.
39. Ibid., p. 201.
40. See for example, Michael P. Hornsby-Smith, 'Researching Religion: The Vocation of the Sociologist of Religion', *Social Research Methodology*, vol. 5, no. 2, 2002, see especially p. 137. While identifying with these movements of affiliation, Hornsby-Smith finds no contradiction between his scientific and religious vocation. See also William H. Swatos, 'The Comparative Method and the Special Vocation of the Sociology of Religion', *Sociological Analysis*, vol. 38, no. 2, 1977, pp. 106–14, especially pp. 112–13.
41. See for example, Alan Wolfe, 'Sociology as a Vocation', *The American Sociologist*, vol. 21, no. 2, 1990, pp. 136–49; and Gordon Clanton, 'Sociology as a Vocation in the California State University', *California Sociologist*, vol. 16, nos 1–2, 1993, pp. 31–51. For an argument within the context of Weber's notion of vocation that science and religion cannot be reconciled, see Keith Tester, 'Disenchantment and Virtue: An Essay on Max Weber', in Flanagan and Jupp (eds), *Virtue Ethics and Sociology*, pp. 35–50.
42. John Carroll, *Puritan, Paranoid, Remissive: A Sociology of Modern Culture* (London: Routledge & Kegan Paul, 1977), p. 134.
43. Niklas Luhmann, *Observations on Modernity*, trans. William Whobrey (Stanford: California: Stanford University Press, 1998), p. ix.
44. For a useful inquest on the death of God, see Simon Blackburn, *Being Good: A Short Introduction to Ethics* (Oxford: Oxford University Press, 2001), pp. 10–19.
45. Katherine Bergeron, 'The Virtual Sacred', *The New Republic*, 27 February 1995, p. 34.
46. For more on these themes, see Katherine Bergeron, *Decadent Enchantments: The Revival of Gregorian Chant at Solesmes* (Berkeley: University of California Press, 1998).

47. Beaudoin, *Virtual Faith*. See pp. 37–41 for a wider discussion. The quotation is taken from p. 41.
48. Richard W. Flory and Donald E. Miller (eds), *GenX Religion* (New York: Routledge, 2000), p. 246.
49. These issues are well discussed in Brenda E. Brasher, *Give me that Online Religion* (San Francisco: Jossey-Bass, 2001).
50. See for example, Julia Winden Fey, 'Spirituality Bites: Xers and the Gothic Cult/ure', in Flory and Miller (eds), *GenX Religion*, pp. 31–53. See also David Keyworth, 'The Socio-Religious Beliefs and Nature of the Contemporary Vampire Subculture', *Journal of Contemporary Religion*, vol. 17, no. 3, October 2002, pp. 355–70.
51. Marita Sturken and Lisa Cartwright, *Practices of Looking: An Introduction to Visual Culture* (Oxford: Oxford University Press, 2001), pp. 144–9.
52. St Augustine, *The City of God*, pp. 229–30. St Augustine's comment on the productivity of Varro, might also be applied to the Swiss theologian, Hans Urs von Balthasar, whose works have so influenced the three studies of this writer. St Augustine was puzzled over the achievements of Varro, 'a man who read so much that we marvel that he had any time for writing; who wrote so much that we find it hard to believe that anyone could have read it all'. Ibid., p. 230.
53. Ivan Oliver, 'Current Revivals of Interest in Religion: Some Sociological Observations', *Archives des Sciences Sociales des Religions*, vol. 58, no. 2, 1984, p. 163.
54. See Chris Shilling and Phillip A. Mellor, *The Sociological Ambition* (London: Sage, 2001), Chapter 3, 'Sacred Sociology', pp. 40–56.
55. Pierre Bourdieu, *Pascalian Meditations*, trans. Richard Nice (Cambridge: Polity Press, 2000), p. 245.
56. See G.K. Peatling, 'Who Fears to Speak of Politics? John Kells Ingram and Hypothetical Nationalism', *Irish Historical Studies*, vol. 31, no. 122, November 1998, p. 207.
57. Ibid., p. 210.
58. This need to go beyond the purely secular in its language of persuasion has been well explored by Fred D'Agostino in his essay 'The Sacralization of Social Scientific Discourse', *Philosophy of Social Science*, vol. 18, 1988, pp. 21–39.
59. Pierre Bourdieu, *In Other Words: Essays Towards a Reflexive Sociology*, trans. Matthew Adamson (Cambridge: Polity Press, 1990), p. 15.
60. Ibid., p. 196.
61. Ian Duncan, 'Bourdieu on Bourdieu: Learning the Lesson of the *Leçon*', in Richard Harker, Cheleen Mahar and Chris Wilkes (eds), *An Introduction to the Work of Pierre Bourdieu: The Practice of Theory* (Basingstoke: Macmillan, 1990), pp. 186–7. The enormous public and political response to the death of Bourdieu in January 2002 illustrates the degree to which he had a prophetic status, an almost sacerdotal accord as an intellectual, very rarely awarded to a sociologist. See Anne Friederike Müller, 'Sociology as a Combat Sport', *Anthropology Today*, vol. 18, no. 2, April 2002, pp. 5–9.
62. For a rare treatment of this issue, see Arnaldo Nesti, *La religione implicita. Sociologi e teologi a confronto* (Bologna: Edizioni Dehoniane, 1994). For an interview on this book before its publication, see Severiono Dianich and Arnaldo Nesti, dialoghi/documenti, *Religion e Societa*, vol. 8, no. 2, May–August 1993, pp. 48–57.
63. See David Macey, *The Lives of Michel Foucault* (London: Vintage, 1994).
64. Jeremy R. Carrette (ed.), *Religion and Culture by Michel Foucault* (Manchester: Manchester University, 1999), pp. 175–8. His essay on 'The battle for chastity' is particularly concerned with Cassian's approach to sexuality. See pp. 188–97.

65. Michel Maffesoli, *The Time of the Tribes: The Decline of Individualism in Mass Society*, trans. Don Smith (London: Sage, 1996), pp. 38–45.
66. Ibid., pp. 86–90. See also p. 94. The strategy of analysis, of approaching from the side, is derived from apophatic theology, the knowing of God indirectly, and in this case, mass society. See p. 5.
67. Ibid., pp. 20–2.
68. Ibid., p. 100.
69. Dennis Smith, *Zygmunt Bauman: Prophet of Postmodernity* (Cambridge: Polity Press, 1999), p. 89.
70. Cited in Clinton Bennett, *In Search of the Sacred: Anthropology and the Study of Religion* (London: Cassell, 1996), pp. 13–14.
71. Richard J. Martin, 'Cultic Aspects of Sociology: A Speculative Essay', *The British Journal of Sociology*, vol. 25, no. 1, March 1974, pp. 24–5.
72. Ibid., pp. 20–3.
73. See for example, Bernice A. Pescosolido, 'The Sociology of the Professions and the Profession of Sociology: Professional Responsibility, Teaching, and Graduate Training', *Teaching Sociology*, vol. 19, no. 3, July 1991, pp. 351–61. The need to provide some anticipatory socialisation for what is to come appears in Gary T. Marx, 'Of Methods and Manners for Aspiring Sociologists: 37 Moral Imperatives', *The American Sociologist*, vol. 28, no. 1, Spring 1997, pp. 102–25.
74. Jean E. Jackson, ' "Deja Entendu": The Liminal Qualities of Anthropological Field-notes', *Journal of Contemporary Ethnography*, vol. 19, no. 1, April 1990, pp. 8–43.
75. Frances Chaput Waksler, 'Erving Goffman's Sociology: An Introductory Essay', *Human Studies*, vol. 12, nos 1–2, June 1989, p. 8.
76. Benedict Anderson, *Imagined Communities: Reflections on the Origin and Spread of Nationalism* (London: Verso, 1983), p. 15.
77. Pierre Bourdieu, *Homo Academicus*, trans. Peter Collier (Cambridge: Polity Press, 1988).
78. Robert N. Bellah, *Beyond Belief: Essays on Religion in a Post-Traditionalist World* (Berkeley: University of California Press, 1991), p. 175. Bellah sought to ally charges that he was supporting a notion of civil religion as an idolatrous worship of the nation in a response to his critics in Donald R. Culter (ed.), *The Religious Situation: 1968* (Boston: Beacon Press, 1968), pp. 388–93. See also ibid., for his original essay, pp. 331–56, and comments by his critics, pp. 356–88. For more recent criticisms of the term, see Richard K. Fenn, *Beyond Idols: The Shape of a Secular Society* (Oxford: University Press, 2001), especially Chapter 5.
79. Robert Wuthnow, *Producing the Sacred: An Essay on Public Religion* (Chicago: University of Illinois Press, 1994), p. 130. See also Robert Wuthnow, *Christianity and Civil Society: The Contemporary Debate* (Valley Forge, Penn.: Trinity Press, 1996).
80. Despite such constitutional prohibitions, the National Episcopalian Cathedral in Washington has come to serve as the focal point for needs of commemoration and to that degree, as in England, so fulfilling some of the functions of a civil religion.
81. For a characteristically and beautifully written account of the sacredness of place, see David Martin, *Christian Language and its Mutations: Essays in Sociological Understanding* (Aldershot: Ashgate, 2002), Chapters 7–8.
82. St Augustine, *The City of God*, pp. 229–53.
83. Ibid., p. 250.
84. Ibid., p. 260.
85. Ibid., p. 235.

86. Emile Durkheim, *The Elementary Forms of Religious Life*, trans. Joseph Ward Swain (London: George Allen & Unwin, 1915), p. 419.
87. Stedman Jones, *Durkheim Reconsidered*, p. 204.
88. St Augustine, *The City of God*, p. 92.
89. Ibid., p. 289.
90. Stedman Jones, *Durkheim Reconsidered*, p. 217.
91. Watts Miller, 'Secularism and the Sacred', p. 36.
92. Ibid., p. 44.
93. Grace Davie uses the term vicarious to characterise the stewardship of religious memory exercised by the minority for the majority. See *Religion in Modern Europe: A Memory Mutates* (Oxford: Oxford University Press, 2000), pp. 177–80.
94. Erving Goffman, *Interaction Ritual* (Harmondsworth: Penguin, 1972), p. 95.
95. Jane Alexander, *Rituals for Sacred Living* (London: HarperCollins, 1999).
96. These comments on Jean Séguy are based on Danièle Hervieu-Léger's exposition of his work in *Religion as a Chain of Memory*, pp. 66–75. For a useful appraisal of Séguy's contribution to the sociology of religion in France, see Roberto Cipriani, *Sociology of Religion: An Historical Introduction* (New York: Aldine de Gruyter, 2000), pp. 212–15.
97. Fenn, *Beyond Idols*, see especially pp. 113–15.
98. See Robert N. Bellah, 'Public Philosophy and Public Theology in America Today', in Leroy S. Rouner (ed.), *Civil Religion and Political Theology* (Notre Dame, Indiana: University of Notre Dame Press, 1986), pp. 79–97.

2 Who sees there? Tales of character, virtue and trust

1. For a comprehensive account of these themes, see David Freedberg, *The Power of Images: Studies in the History and Theory of Response* (Chicago: University of Chicago Press, 1991).
2. See Peter McMylor, 'Classical Thinking for a Postmodern World: Alasdair MacIntyre and the Moral Critique of the Present', in Flanagan and Jupp (eds), *Virtue Ethics and Sociology*, pp. 28–9. For reasons that deserve further exploration, McMylor is correct to suggest that MacIntyre's notion of tradition is unavailable to Bauman.
3. Zygmunt Bauman and Keith Tester, *Conversations with Zygmunt Bauman* (Cambridge: Polity Press, 2001), pp. 96–8.
4. Zygmunt Bauman, *Modernity and Ambivalence* (Cambridge: Polity Press, 1991), pp. 26–39.
5. Zygmunt Bauman, *Intimations of Postmodernity* (London: Routledge, 1992), p. xxii.
6. Ibid., p. 216.
7. Zygmunt Bauman, *Liquid Modernity* (Cambridge: Polity Press, 2000), p. 216.
8. Bauman, *Intimations of Postmodernity*, p. 209.
9. Zygmunt Bauman, *Morality, Immortality & Other Life Strategies* (Stanford: Stanford University Press, 1992).
10. See Kieran Flanagan, 'Religion and Modern Personal Identity', in Anton van Harskamp and Albert W. Musschenga (eds), *The Many Faces of Individualism* (Leuven: Peeters, 2001), pp. 239–66.
11. Zygmunt Bauman, 'Postmodern Religion?' in Paul Heelas (ed.), *Religion, Modernity and Postmodernity* (Oxford: Blackwell, 1998), pp. 55–78.
12. Smith, *Zygmunt Bauman*, pp. 134–5.
13. Ibid., p. 123.
14. Bauman and Tester, *Conversations with Zygmunt Bauman*, p. 132.

15. Ibid., p. 135.
16. Peter Beilharz, *Zygmunt Bauman: Dialectic of Modernity* (London: Sage, 2000), p. 123.
17. Zygmunt Bauman, *Modernity and the Holocaust* (Cambridge: Polity Press, 1991), pp. 166–8. The notion of the evil is discussed in the context of the Milgram experiment on authority and the implementation of pain.
18. Beilharz, *Dialectic of Modernity*, pp. 105–6.
19. Zygmunt Bauman, *The Individualized Society* (Cambridge: Polity Press, 2001), p. 3.
20. Bauman and Tester, *Conversations with Zygmunt Bauman*, p. 88.
21. Ibid., pp. 133–6.
22. Seán Hand, (ed.), *The Levinas Reader* (Oxford: Blackwell, 1989), pp. 82–4.
23. The tale of Gillian Rose's movement into Christianity has still not been given the biography it deserves. For the moment, one has to make use of 'The Final Notebooks of Gillian Rose', *Women: A Cultural Review*, vol. 9, no. 1, Spring 1998, pp. 6–18. Simone Weil seems to have been the angelus bell of her movements into Christianity, although she too never quite made it into Catholicism. See pp. 9–10.
24. Zygmunt Bauman, *Life in Fragments: Essays in Postmodern Morality* (Oxford: Blackwell, 1995). The discussion of the broken middle appears on pp. 72–5 and the quality of life and identity on pp. 77–82.
25. Ibid., pp. 82–91.
26. Beilharz, *Zygmunt Bauman: Dialectic of Modernity*, pp. 172–3.
27. Bauman, *Life in Fragments*, pp. 92–104.
28. Zygmunt Bauman, *Community: Seeking Safety in an Insecure World* (Cambridge: Polity Press, 2001), pp. 15–18.
29. Bauman and Tester, *Conversations with Zygmunt Bauman*, p. 69.
30. Bauman, *The Individualised Society*, pp. 248–9.
31. Kelvin Knight (ed.), *The MacIntyre Reader* (Cambridge: Polity Press, 1998), pp. 276–94. For comments on theology, see p. 287. For a useful debate on the significance of his work, see John Horton and Susan Mendus (eds), *After MacIntyre: Critical Perspectives on the Work of Alasdair MacIntyre* (Cambridge: Polity Press, 1994). See also Peter McMylor, *Alasdair MacIntyre: Critic of Modernity* (London: Routledge, 1994).
32. For his comments on Weber, see pp. 25–7 and on Goffman see p. 32 and pp. 115–17 in Alasdair MacIntyre (ed.), *After Virtue: A Study in Moral Virtue*, second edition (London: Duckworth, 1985).
33. Bauman, *Modernity and the Holocaust*, pp. 9–11.
34. For a useful defence of Weber against charges of emotivism, see Keith Tester, 'Weber's Alleged Emotivism', *The British Journal of Sociology*, vol. 50, no. 4, December 1999, pp. 563–73.
35. McMylor, 'Classical Thinking for a Postmodern World', pp. 23–7.
36. G.E.M. Anscombe, 'Modern Moral Philosophy', in Roger Crisp and Michael Slote (eds), *Virtue Ethics* (Oxford: Oxford University Press, 1997), p. 31.
37. Ibid., p. 38.
38. Ibid., pp. 43–4.
39. Iris Murdoch, 'The Sovereignty of Good over Other Concepts', in Crisp and Slote (eds), *Virtue Ethics*, p. 101.
40. MacIntyre, *After Virtue*, p. 191.
41. Ibid., p. 187.
42. Ibid., p. 122.
43. Ibid., p. 219.
44. Ibid., p. 149.

45. Ibid., p. 144.
46. John Alt, 'Sport and Cultural Reification: From Ritual to Mass Consumption', *Theory, Culture & Society*, vol. 1, no. 3, 1983, pp. 93–107.
47. See Sidonie Smith and Julia Watson (eds), *Getting a Life: Everyday Uses of Autobiography* (Minneapolis: University of Minnesota Press, 1996).
48. See especially, Robert K. Merton, 'Some Thoughts on the Concept of Sociological Autobiography', in Matilda White Riley (ed.), *Sociological Lives* (Newbury Park, California: Sage, 1988), pp. 17–21.
49. David Frisby, *George Simmel* (London: Tavistock, 1984). See especially, Chapter 2, 'Life and Context', pp. 21–44.
50. I am grateful to my colleague, Dr Willie Watts Miller for this information.
51. See the splendid essay by Hans Rollmann, '"Meet Me in St. Louis": Troeltsch and Weber in America', in Hartmut Lehmann and Guenther Roth (eds), *Weber's Protestant Ethic: Origins, Evidence, Contexts* (Cambridge: Cambridge University Press, 1995), pp. 379–80.
52. Pierre Bourdieu and Loïc J.D. Wacquant, *An Invitation to Reflexive Sociology* (Cambridge Polity Press, 1992), p. 41.
53. Ibid., p. 46.
54. Pierre Bourdieu *et al.*, *The Weight of the World: Social Suffering in Contemporary Society*, trans. Priscilla Parkhurst Ferguson *et al.* (Cambridge: Polity Press, 1999), p. 614.
55. Bauman and Tester, *Conversations with Zygmunt Bauman*, pp. 1–6.
56. Julia A. Ericksen, *Kiss and Tell: Surveying Sex in the Twentieth Century* (Cambridge, Mass.: Harvard University Press, 1999).
57. C. Wright Mills, *The Sociological Imagination* (New York: Grove, 1961).
58. Charlotte Aull Davies, *Reflexive Ethnography: A Guide to Researching Selves and Others* (London: Routledge, 1999).
59. Piotr Sztompka, *Trust: A Sociological Theory* (Cambridge: Cambridge University Press, 1999), pp. 4–5.
60. See Howard S. Becker and Michal M. McCall (eds), *Symbolic Interaction and Cultural Studies* (Chicago: The University of Chicago Press, 1990).
61. Ken Plummer, *Documents of Life 2: An Invitation to a Critical Humanism* (London: Sage, 2001), pp. 12–14.
62. Pertti Alasuutari, *Researching Culture: Qualitative Method and Cultural Studies* (London: Sage, 1995), pp. 50–3.
63. Anthony Giddens, *Modernity and Self-Identity: Self and Society in the Late Modern Age* (Cambridge: Polity Press, 1991).
64. James A. Holstein and Jaber F. Gubrium, *The Self We Live By* (New York: Oxford University Press, 2000), pp. 219–20.
65. David R. Maines, 'Narrative's Moment and Sociology's Phenomena: Toward a Narrative Sociology', *The Sociological Quarterly*, vol. 34, no. 1, 1993, pp. 17–38.
66. See Alasdair MacIntyre, *Three Rival Versions of Moral Enquiry* (London: Duckworth, 1990), Chapter 9, 'Tradition against Genealogy: Who Speaks to Whom?' pp. 196–215.
67. See Lester H. Hunt, *Character and Culture* (Lanham: Rowman & Littlefield, 1997), especially Chapter 6, 'Character and the Social World', pp. 149–64.
68. For a useful overview of some of these trends, see Paul Atkinson, 'Voiced and Unvoiced', *Sociology*, vol. 33, no. 1, February 1999, pp. 191–7.
69. See Helen Rose Fuchs Ebaugh, *Becoming an Ex: The Process of Role Exit* (Chicago: The University of Chicago Press, 1988). For a rather acid appraisal of this work,

see Loïc J.D. Wacquant, 'Exiting Roles or Exiting Role Theory? Critical Notes on Ebaugh's *Becoming an Ex*', *Acta Sociologica*, vol. 33, no. 4, 1990, pp. 397–404.

70. For an excellent account of the way postmodernism forces out issues of identity and the self, see Madan Sarup, *Identity, Culture and the Postmodern World* (Edinburgh: Edinburgh University Press, 1996).

71. Ken Plummer, *Telling Sexual Stories: Power, Change and Social Worlds* (London: Routledge, 1995), pp. 170–5.

72. Erving Goffman, *Asylums* (Harmondsworth: Penguin, 1968), p. 119.

73. Erving Goffman, *Stigma* (Harmondsworth: Penguin, 1968), p. 45.

74. Ibid., p. 52.

75. Cited in Mary Louise Buley-Meissner, Mary McCaslin Thompson and Elizabeth Bachrach Tan (eds), *The Academy and the Possibility of Belief: Essays on Intellectual and Spiritual Life* (Cresskill, New Jersey: Hampton Press, 2000), p. 11.

76. For what is claimed to be the first investigation of the teaching and practice of religion in the USA, see Conrad Cherry, Betty A. DeBerg and Amanda Porterfield, *Religion on Campus* (Chapel Hill, North Carolina: The University of North Carolina Press, 2001).

77. Kieran Flanagan, 'Reflexivity, Ethics and the Teaching of the Sociology of Religion', *Sociology*, vol. 35, no. 1, February 2001, pp. 1–19.

78. See Plummer, *Documents of Life 2*, especially Chapters 10–11, pp. 204–54.

79. Ibid., p. 247.

80. William James, 'On a Certain Blindness in Human Beings', in *Pragmatism and Other Writings* (Harmondsworth: Penguin, 2000), pp. 282–4.

81. Clifford Geertz, *Works and Lives: The Anthropologist as Author* (Cambridge: Polity Press, 1989), pp. 4–5.

82. Christine Hine, *Virtual Ethnography* (London: Sage, 2000), pp. 46–7.

83. Ibid., p. 56.

84. Sissela Bok, *Lying: Moral Choice in Public and Private Life* (London: Quartet Books, 1980), pp. 18–20.

85. Guido Möllering, 'The Nature of Trust: From Georg Simmel to a Theory of Expectation, Interpretation and Suspension', *Sociology*, vol. 35, no. 2, May 2001, pp. 403–20.

86. Zygmunt Bauman, *Postmodern Ethics* (Oxford: Blackwell, 1993), pp. 115–16.

87. The distinctions between dyads and triads was one of fundamental importance in Simmel's work. See Georg Simmel, *The Sociology of Georg Simmel*, ed. and trans. Kurt H. Wolff (New York: The Free Press, 1964), pp. 118–69.

88. Bauman and Tester, *Conversations with Zygmunt Bauman*, pp.140–3.

89. Bauman, *Community*, pp. 2–5.

90. Onora O'Neill, *A Question of Trust* (Cambridge: Cambridge University Press, 2002), p. 68.

91. Ibid., p. 7.

92. Ibid., pp. 18–19.

93. Sztompka, *Trust: A Sociological Theory*, see especially Chapter 4, pp. 69–101.

94. Giddens, *The Consequences of Modernity*, pp. 29–36.

95. See Phillip Manning, *Erving Goffman and Modern Sociology* (Cambridge: Polity Press, 1992), pp. 85–87.

96. Giddens, *The Consequences of Modernity*, pp. 80–3.

97. Ibid., p. 109. The above discussion is taken from Chapter 3. For later discussions by Giddens of trust, see *Modernity and Self-Identity* (Cambridge: Polity Press, 1991), particularly in relation to what he terms 'tribulations of the self', pp. 181–208; and Ulrich Beck, Anthony Giddens and Scott Lash, *Reflexive Modernization:*

Politics, Tradition and Aesthetics in the Modern Social Order (Cambridge: Polity Press, 1994), especially pp. 184–97.

98. St Augustine, *The City of God*, p. 1069.
99. Michel Foucault, *The Birth of the Clinic*, trans. A.M. Sheridan (London: Routledge, 1989), see Chapter 9, 'The Visible Invisible', especially pp. 166–8 where the above quotation appears. See also Thomas Osborne, 'Medicine and Epistemology: Michel Foucault and the Liberality of Clinical Reason', *History of the Human Sciences*, vol. 5, no. 2, 1992, especially pp. 79–80.
100. Michel Foucault, *Discipline and Punish: The Birth of the Prison*, trans. Alan Sheridan (London: Penguin, 1977), p. 228.
101. Ibid., p. 214.
102. Michel Foucault, *Power/Knowledge: Selected Interviews and Other Writings 1972–1977*, ed. Colin Gordon (Brighton: The Harvester Press, 1980), p. 147.
103. Foucault, *Discipline and Punish*, pp. 216–17.
104. Goffman, *Asylums*, p. 68.
105. Goffman, *Interaction Ritual*, p.10.
106. Foucault, *Power/Knowledge*, p.157.
107. John O'Neill, 'Foucault's Optics: The (in)vision of Mortality and Modernity', in Chris Jenks (ed.), *Visual Culture* (London: Routledge, 1995), p. 192.
108. George Orwell, *Nineteen Eighty-Four* (London: Penguin, 1989), p. 302.
109. Jean Ritchie, *Inside Big Brother: Getting In & Staying In* (London: Channel 4 Books, 2002), p. 210.
110. Ibid., p. 246.

3 Visual culture and the virtual: the Internet and religious displays

1. Adapted excerpt from Georg Simmel, *Sociologie*, in Robert E. Park and Ernest W. Burgess (eds), *Introduction to the Science of Sociology*, third edition revised (Chicago: The University of Chicago Press, 1969), p. 361.
2. Simon Cooper, 'Plenitude and Alienation: The Subject of Virtual Reality', in David Holmes (ed.), *Virtual Politics: Identity and Community in Cyberspace* (London: Sage, 1997), pp. 100 and p. 105.
3. David Holmes, 'Introduction', in ibid., p. 17.
4. W.J.T. Mitchell, 'Interdisciplinarity and Visual Culture', *Art Bulletin*, vol. 77, no. 4, December 1995, p. 540.
5. W.J.T. Mitchell, 'What is Visual Culture?' in Irving Lavin (ed.), *Meaning in the Visual Arts: Views from the Outside; A Centennial Commemoration of Erwin Panofsky (1892–1968)* (Princeton: Institute for Advanced Study, 1995), pp. 210–11.
6. John A. Walker and Sarah Chaplain, *Visual Culture: An Introduction* (Manchester: Manchester University Press, 1997), p. 3.
7. Nicholas Mirzoeff, *An Introduction to Visual Culture* (London: Routledge, 1999), p. 5.
8. Ibid., p. 13.
9. Mitchell, 'Interdisciplinarity and Visual Culture', p. 544.
10. Ibid, p. 541.
11. For a useful account of the battles between sociology and cultural studies, see Gregor McLennan, 'Sociology and Cultural Studies: Rhetorics of Disciplinary Identity', *History of the Human Sciences*, vol. 11, no. 3, 1998, pp. 1–17.
12. Collections often indicate a consensus, a selection of topics that can be deemed exemplary. See for example, Nicholas Mirzoeff (ed.), *Visual Culture Reader* (London:

Routledge, 1999). It deals with the genealogy of visual culture, from art to culture; visual culture and everyday life; virtuality, bodies and space; race and identity; gender and sexuality; and pornography. There is one reference to religious objects in the index, and no contribution dealing with religion and visual culture.

13. Mirzoeff, *An Introduction to Visual Culture*, pp. 22–6.
14. Terry Eagleton, *The Idea of Culture* (Oxford: Blackwell, 2000), p. 25.
15. Ibid., p. 72.
16. Ibid., p. 83.
17. Martin Jay, *Downcast Eyes: The Denigration of Vision in Twentieth-Century French Thought* (Berkeley: University of California Press, 1994).
18. John Berger, *Ways of Seeing* (London: Penguin, 1972), pp. 10–11.
19. Ibid., pp. 20–1.
20. Issues of the place of altar pieces as having devotional or liturgical use illustrate the complexity of applying notions of memory to image. What is required is to work out the end for which the image was produced in its original context and this is very difficult to trace. The issues relate not only to public and private forms of use, but also to entitlements to see. For example, see Beth Williamson, 'Liturgical Image or Devotional Image? The London *Madonna of the Firescreen*', in Colum Hourihane (ed.), *Objects, Images and the Word: Art in the Service of the Liturgy* (Princeton: Princeton University Press, 2003), pp. 298–318.
21. Mitchell, 'What is Visual Culture?' p. 211.
22. Walter Benjamin, 'The Work of Art in the Age of Mechanical Reproduction', in Hannah Arendt (ed.), *Illuminations*, trans. Harry Zohn (London: Jonathan Cape, 1970), pp. 225–6.
23. Ibid., pp. 242–3. See also David Chaney, '"Ways of Seeing" Reconsidered: Representation and Construction in Mass Culture', *History of the Human Sciences*, vol. 9, no. 2, 1996, pp. 39–51.
24. See the essay review on books on visual culture, by David C. Chaney, 'Contemporary Socioscapes', *Theory, Culture & Society*, vol. 16, no. 6, 2000, p. 113.
25. Baudelaire, *The Painter of Modern Life*, pp. 4–5.
26. Ibid., pp. 16–17.
27. Susan Sontag, *On Photography* (London: Penguin, 1977), p. 55.
28. Roland Barthes, *Camera Lucida: Reflections on Photography*, trans. Richard Howard (London: Vintage, 1993), p. 4.
29. Benjamin, 'The Work of Art in the Age of Mechanical Reproduction', p. 222.
30. Don Slater, 'Photography and Modern Vision: The Spectacle of "Natural Magic"', in Chris Jenks (ed.), *Visual Culture* (London: Routledge, 1995), pp. 218–37.
31. See John Jervis, *Exploring the Modern: Patterns of Western Culture and Civilization* (Oxford: Blackwell, 1998), Chapter 11, 'The Image, the Spectral and the Spectacle: Technologies of the Visual', pp. 280–309.
32. Sontag, *On Photography*, p.14.
33. Ibid., p. 163.
34. Ibid., p. 123.
35. Ibid., p. 153.
36. Foucault, *The Birth of the Clinic*, p. 172. The above comments come from pp. 164–72. See also Martin Jay, 'In the Empire of the Gaze: Foucault and the Denigration of Vision in Twentieth-century French Thought', in David Hoy (ed.), *Foucault: A Critical Reader* (Oxford: Basil Blackwell, 1986), pp. 175–204; and Maurice Merleau-Ponty, *The Visible and the Invisible*, trans. Alphonso Lingis (Evanston: Northwestern University Press, 1968).

37. Pierre Bourdieu, *Photography: A Middle-brow Art*, trans. Shaun Whiteside (Cambridge: Polity Press, 1990), p. 26.
38. Ibid., p. 94.
39. Sontag, *On Photography*, pp. 23–4.
40. Ibid., p. 159.
41. Ibid., p. 119.
42. Jervis, *Exploring the Modern*, pp. 280–1.
43. Ibid., pp. 289–93.
44. Bauman, *The Individualized Society*, p. 179.
45. John Tiffin and Nobuyoshi Terashima (eds), *Hypereality: Paradigm for the Third Millennium* (London: Routledge, 2001), especially Chapters 1 and 2.
46. Howard Rheingold, *Virtual Reality* (New York: Simon & Schuster, 1992), p. 19.
47. Michael Cranford, 'The Social Trajectory of Virtual Reality: Substantive Ethics in a World without Constraints', *Technology in Society*, vol. 18, no. 1, 1996, first quotation appears on p. 83 and the second on p. 81.
48. Hine, *Virtual Ethnography*, pp. 30–4.
49. G. Coates, 'Disembodied Cyber Co-presence: The Art of Being There While Somewhere Else', in Nick Watson and Sarah Cunningham-Burley (eds), *Reframing the Body* (Basingstoke: Palgrave, 2001), pp. 213–18. See also Mary Chayko, 'What is Real in the Age of Virtual Reality? "Reframing" Frame Analysis for a Technological World', *Symbolic Interaction*, vol. 16, no. 2, 1993, pp. 171–81.
50. See Michele Wilson, 'Community in the Abstract: A Political and Ethical Dilemma?' in Holmes (ed.), *Virtual Politics*, pp. 145–62.
51. Coates, 'Disembodied Cyber Co-presence', p. 222. See also Christine Hine, *Virtual Ethnography*, pp. 43–50.
52. Jodi Dean, 'Virtually Citizens', *Constellations*, vol. 4, no. 2, 1997, p. 264.
53. See the highly useful chronology of the Internet and virtual reality technologies in Rob Shields, *The Virtual* (London: Routledge, 2003), pp. 56–7.
54. David Holmes, 'Introduction', *Virtual Politics*, p. 6.
55. Cranford, 'The Social Trajectory of Virtual Reality', p. 88.
56. Hine, *Virtual Ethnography*, pp. 24–5.
57. Coates, 'Disembodied Cyber Co-presence', p. 211.
58. Hine, *Virtual Ethnography*, p. 64.
59. Ibid., pp. 149–50.
60. Ibid., p. 62.
61. Brasher, *Give me that Online Religion*, p. 6.
62. See www.cnn.com/US/9803/25/heavens.gate/. For a brief account of the movement, see Alan Aldridge, *Religion in the Contemporary World* (Cambridge: Polity Press, 2000), pp. 178–9.
63. Maria Luisa Maniscalco, 'A New Global Risk: the Rise of the Killer Sects', *International Review of Sociology*, vol. 7, no. 3, November 1997, pp. 485–97.
64. Wendy Gale Robinson, 'Heaven's Gate: The End?' *JCMC*, vol. 3, no. 3, December 1997, p. 12. *JCMC* is an online journal.
65. Ibid., p. 2.
66. According to Robinson, a survivor indicated that only one recruit was recruited to the cult through the Internet. See ibid., footnote 16, p. 33. Further scepticism on the impact of the Internet on recruitment to new religions is well expressed in Lorne L. Dawson and Jenna Hennebry, 'New Religions and the Internet: Recruiting in a New Public Space', *Journal of Contemporary Religion*, vol. 14, no. 1, 1999, pp. 17–39.
67. Brasher, *Give me that Online Religion*, p. 170.

68. Robinson, 'Heaven's Gate: The End?' pp. 25–6.
69. Maniscalco, 'A New Global Risk: The Rise of the Killer Sects', pp. 487–8. Reference to the propensity to sexual abuse is on p. 492.
70. See for example, Jean-François Mayer, 'Religious Movements and the Internet: The New Frontier of Cult Controversies'; and Massimo Introvigne, '"So Many Evil Things": Anti-Cult Terrorism via the Internet', in Jeffrey K. Hadden and Douglas E. Cowan (eds), *Religion on the Internet: Research Prospects and Promises* (New York: Elsevier Science, 2000), pp. 249–306.
71. Christopher Helland, 'Online-Religion/Religion-Online and Virtual Communitas', in ibid., pp. 205–23.
72. Ralph Schroeder, Noel Heather and Raymond M. Lee, 'The Sacred and the Virtual: Religion in Multi-User Virtual Reality', *JCMC*, vol. 4, no. 2, December 1998, p. 6. For a useful discussion of 'going to cyberchurch', see David Lyon, *Jesus in Disneyland: Religion in Postmodern Times* (Cambridge: Polity Press, 2000), pp. 66–72.
73. This practice of 'on-line confessions' has been banned by the Vatican. See report in *The Times*, 10 January 2003.
74. Pontifical Council for Social Communication, *Ethics, Internet and Communications* (London: Catholic Truth Society, 2002), p. 52.
75. Ibid., pp. 48–9.
76. See Fey, 'Spirituality Bites: Xers and the Gothic Cult/ure', pp. 37–9.
77. See Lyon, *Jesus in Disneyland*, especially Chapters 4 and 6, pp. 55–72 and pp. 97–119.
78. Ibid., p. 104.
79. Kirin Narayan, 'Refractions of the Field at Home: American Representations of Hindu Holy Men in the 19th and 20th Centuries', *Cultural Anthropology*, vol. 8, no. 4, 1993, p. 500.
80. William James, *The Varieties of Religious Experience* (London: Longmans, Green, and Co., 1920), p. 489.
81. Brasher, *Give me that Online Religion*, pp. 25–6.
82. John Dagenais, 'A Medieval Pilgrimage to Santiago de Compostela on the Information Highway', in Maryjane Dunn and Linda Kay Davidson (eds), *The Pilgrimage to Compostela in the Middle Ages* (New York: Routledge, 2000), pp. 143–51.
83. Lorne L. Dawson, 'Researching Religion in Cyberspace: Issues and Strategies', in Hadden and Cowan (eds), *Religion on the Internet*, p. 46.
84. Ibid., p. 35.
85. Ibid., p. 43.
86. Brasher, *Give me that Online Religion*, pp. 78–85. A notable number of entries in a recent guide to European Monasteries and Convents contain websites giving information on how to visit and stay as a guest. See Kevin J. Wright, *Europe's Monastery and Convent Guesthouses* (Missouri: Liguori, 2000).
87. *The Times*, 18 January 2003, p. 42.
88. Goffman, *Stigma*, pp. 12–13.
89. Shields, *The Virtual*, pp. 2–6.
90. Shusaku Endo, *Silence*, trans. William Johnston (London: Quartet Books, 1978).
91. Pontifical Council for Social Communication, *Ethics, Internet and Communications*, pp. 13–14. Brasher notes that off-line churches have rarely sought to 'redress online moral lacunae'. She makes this comment in the context of a chapter on cyber-virtue and cyber vice. See Brasher, *Give me that Online Religion*, Chapter 8, pp. 94–119. The comment cited above appears on p. 94. This makes the Vatican document that came out after the publication of her book all the more interesting for its rarity.

92. Shields, *The Virtual*, pp. 3–4 and 11–15.
93. Victor Turner, *From Ritual to Theatre: The Human Seriousness of Play* (New York: Performing Arts Journal Publications, 1982), pp. 52–5.

4 To see or not to see: the plight of the voyeur

1. David Rowan, 'Spies Like Us', *The Times Magazine*, 13 December 2003, pp. 45–8.
2. Meaghen Morris cited in Jay, *Downcast Eyes*, p. 544 and his comment on p. 545.
3. St Augustine, *The Confessions*, trans. Maria Boulding (London: Hodder & Stoughton, 1996), pp. 144–7.
4. Ibid., pp. 273–5.
5. Jay, *Downcast Eyes*, pp. 545–6 and p. 583. It is noteworthy that the chapter in which this discussion appears is entitled 'The Ethics of Blindness and the Post-modern Sublime'.
6. Ivan Illich, 'Guarding the Eye in the Age of Show', *RES*, vol. 28, Autumn 1995, p. 49.
7. Daniel Albright (ed.), *W.B. Yeats: The Poems* (London: J.M. Dent, 1990), p. 376. I am very grateful to my colleague, Professor Tim Webb, for finding the above for me.
8. Everett C. Hughes, *The Sociological Eye: Selected Papers* (Chicago: Aldine Atherton, 1971). See especially the two essays, 'The Improper Study of Man' and 'The Dual Mandate of Social Science: Remarks on the Academic Division of Labour', pp. 431–42 and 443–54.
9. Marx, 'Of Methods and Manners for Aspiring Sociologists', p. 103
10. For a critique of reliance on the visual, see Anthony Woodiwiss, *The Visual in Social Theory* (London: The Athlone Press, 2001).
11. See Elizabeth Chaplin, *Sociology and Visual Representation* (London: Routledge, 1994), pp. 218–23, for her comments on visual sociology.
12. See Anna Grimshaw, *The Ethnographer's Eye: Ways of Seeing Modern Anthropology* (Cambridge: Cambridge University Press, 2001).
13. Hal Foster (ed.), *Vision and Visuality* (Seattle: Bay Press, 1986), pp. ix–x.
14. Georgia Frank, *The Memory of the Eyes: Pilgrims to Living Saints in Christian Antiquity* (Berkeley: University of California Press, 2000), p. 103.
15. Amanda Coffey, *The Ethnographic Self: Fieldwork and the Representation of Identity* (London: Sage, 1999).
16. Alvin W. Gouldner, *The Coming Crisis of Western Sociology* (London: Heinemann, 1970), pp. 484–6.
17. Ibid., p. 490.
18. Ibid., pp. 509–10.
19. Malcolm Barnard, *Approaches to Understanding Visual Culture* (Basingstoke: Palgrave, 2001), pp. 1–2.
20. Berger, *Ways of Seeing*, pp. 146–9.
21. Simmel, *Sociologie*, pp. 358–9.
22. See Norman Bryson, *Visions and Painting: The Logic of the Gaze* (Basingstoke: Macmillan, 1983), pp. 87–131.
23. Peter Brown, *The Body and Society: Men, Women and Sexual Renunciation in Early Christianity* (London: Faber & Faber, 1988), p. 331.
24. Hans Urs von Balthasar, *Bernanos: An Existential Existence*, trans. Erasmo Leiva-Merikakis (San Francisco: Ignatius Press, 1996), p. 143.
25. Guy Debord, *The Society of the Spectacle*, trans. Donald Nicholson-Smith (New York: Zone Books, 1995), p. 12.

26. Ibid., p. 30.
27. Ibid., p. 20.
28. This collection of essays follows cinematic themes. See Fredric Jameson, *Signatures of the Visible* (New York: Routledge, 1992), p. 1.
29. This closing down of sight to a matter of suspicion formed the central theme of Jay, *Downcast Eyes*.
30. Anthony Synnott, 'The Eye and I: A Sociology of Sight', *International Journal of Politics, Culture and Society*, vol. 5, no. 4, 1992, p. 630.
31. This notion of seeing as reading appears in the context of a set of essays on the pure gaze and art. See Pierre Bourdieu, *The Field of Cultural Production*, trans. Randal Johnson (Cambridge: Polity Press, 1993), p. 245. See also John Codd, 'Making Distinctions: The Eye of the Beholder', in Harker, Mahar and Wilkes (eds), *An Introduction to the Work of Pierre Bourdieu*, pp. 132–59.
32. John Urry, *The Tourist Gaze* (London: Sage, 1990), p. 129.
33. Ibid., p. 46.
34. Nicholas Davey, 'The Hermeneutics of Seeing', in Ian Heywood and Barry Sandywell (eds), *Interpreting Visual Culture: Explorations in the Hermeneutics of the Visual* (London: Routledge, 1999), p. 11.
35. Ibid., p. 22.
36. Ibid., p. 4.
37. This is the title of Chapter 4 of Jervis, *Exploring the Modern*, Chapter 4, pp. 91–116.
38. Jib Fowles, *Advertising and Popular Culture* (Thousand Oaks, California: Sage: 1996), p. 14.
39. Ibid., p. 25.
40. Robert C. Solomon, *Wicked Pleasures: Meditations on the Seven "Deadly" Sins* (Lanham: Rowman & Littlefield, 1999), pp. 1–10.
41. Jackson Toby, 'Medicalizing Temptation', *The Public Interest*, no. 130, Winter 1998, pp. 64–78.
42. Anthony Giddens, *The Transformation of Intimacy: Sexuality, Love & Eroticism in Modern Societies* (Cambridge: Polity Press, 1993), pp. 74–81 and pp. 92–6.
43. Baudelaire, *The Painter of Modern Life*, pp. 9–10.
44. See Keith Tester, '"Bored and Blasé" Television, the Emotions and Georg Simmel', in Gillian Bendelow and Simon J. Williams (eds), *Emotions in Social Life: Critical Themes and Contemporary Issues* (London: Routledge, 1998), pp. 83–96. See also his *Moral Culture* (London: Sage, 1997), especially Introduction and Chapter 1 on indifference.
45. Simmel, *The Sociology of Georg Simmel*, pp. 414–15.
46. Timothy Bewes, *Cynicism and Postmodernity* (London: Verso, 1997), pp. 32–7.
47. J.-K. Huysmans, *Against Nature*, trans. Robert Baldick (Harmondsworth: Penguin, 1959), p. 108.
48. Blaise Pascal, *Pensées*, trans. A.J. Krailsheimer (Harmondsworth: Penguin, 1966), p. 235.
49. Oscar Wilde, *De Profundis in The Works of Oscar Wilde* (London: Galley Press, 1987), p. 857.
50. Ibid., p. 862.
51. A singular exception is Lyman who boldly explored the whole issue of vice, and related sloth to acedia. See Stanford M. Lyman, *The Seven Deadly Sins: Society and Evil*, second edition (New York: General Hall Inc., 1989), pp. 5–52. In a highly imaginative point, Lyman sees a property of acedia in Chekhov's *The Three Sisters*. For him, the drama is about the impact of acedia, 'the conversion of the world

into a meaningless void, full of sound and silence, smoldering feeling and affectless neutrality, meaningless actions and uncertain outcomes. One can neither wait nor hope, move on or give up. Life becomes pure existence', p. 42.

52. Timothy McDermott (ed.), *St. Thomas Aquinas, Summa Theologiae: A Concise Translation* (London: Methuen 1991), p. 365.

53. For an extended treatment of the monastic struggles with acedia, see *John Cassian: The Institutes*, trans. Boniface Ramsey (New York: The Newman Press, 2000), pp. 217–38. See also Columba Stewart, *Cassian the Monk* (Oxford: Oxford University Press, 1998).

54. By one of those odd coincidences, at the time of writing the above, it was announced that Gerard Depardieu, the French film star, had returned to Catholicism. The occasion of this announcement was that he had insisted on reading from St Augustine's *Confessions* at the funeral of the director who had cast him in the role of the priest in *Under Satan's Sun*. See *The Observer*, 9 February 2003.

55. Georges Bernanos, *Under Satan's Sun*, trans. J.C. Whitehouse (Lincoln: University of Nebraska Press, 2001), p. 250.

56. Ibid.

57. Ibid., p. 179. A useful set of essays on Georges Bernanos appears in a special issue of *New Blackfriars*, vol. 79, no. 933, November 1998. See especially the essay by Mark Edney, 'The Time of the Saints Always Comes', pp. 483–92.

58. J.C. Whitehouse, *The Vertical Man* (London: The St Austin Press, 1999), pp. 128–33.

59. Hans Urs von Balthasar, *Bernanos*, p. 283.

60. Ibid., pp. 419–29 and especially pp. 420–1.

61. Patricia Meyer Spacks, *Boredom: The Literary History of a State of Mind* (Chicago: The University of Chicago Press, 1996), p. 23.

62. Cited in ibid., p. 14.

63. Michael L. Raposa, *Boredom and the Religious Imagination* (Charolottesville: University Press of Virginia, 1999), pp. 34–40.

64. Spacks, *Boredom*, p. 140.

65. Cited in ibid., p. 260.

66. Kieran Flanagan, 'Vice and Virtue or Vice Versa: A Sociology of Being Good', in Flanagan and Jupp (eds), *Virtue Ethics and Sociology*, pp. 104–24. The issue of vice and virtue was the theme of seven leading article reflections on Christmas in *The Times* starting on the 22 December 2003.

67. Mark Vernon, '"I Am Not What I Am" – Foucault, Christian Asceticism and a "Way Out" of Sexuality', in Carrette (ed.), *Religion and Culture by Michel Foucault*, pp. 199–201 and 207–8. See also J. Joyce Shuld, *Foucault and Augustine: Reconsidering Power and Love* (South Bend, Indiana: University of Notre Dame Press, 2003).

68. Commenting on this verse, Cassian notes that the issue was not one of the eye, but of the guarding of a purity of heart within. See John Cassian, *The Monastic Institutes*, trans. Jerome Bertram (London: The Saint Austin Press, 1999), pp. 100–1.

69. See the entry on the relationship between the senses and the spiritual by Carol Harrison, in Allan D. Fitzgerald (ed.), *Augustine Through the Ages: An Encyclopaedia* (Grand Rapids, Michigan: William B. Eerdmans, 1999), pp. 767–8.

70. Raposa, *Boredom and the Religious Imagination*, pp. 2–3.

71. Max Weber, *The Protestant Ethic and the Spirit of Capitalism*, trans. Talcott Parsons (London: Unwin, 1930).

72. For an excellent characterisation of the interconnection between acedia and sloth, see Raposa, *Boredom and the Religious Imagination*, pp. 11–40.

73. Thomas Pynchon, 'Sloth', in Solomon (ed.), *Wicked Pleasures*, p. 84.

74. Lyman, *The Seven Deadly Sins*, pp. 21–5.
75. Dennis Brissett and Robert P. Snow, 'Boredom: Where the Future Isn't', *Symbolic Interaction*, vol. 16, no. 3, 1993, pp. 243–5.
76. Ibid., pp. 250–2.
77. Keith Tester, *Media, Culture and Morality* (London: Routledge, 1994), p. 130. See also his later study, *Compassion, Morality and the Media* (Buckingham: Open University Press, 2001).
78. Luc Boltanski, *Distant Suffering: Morality, Media and Politics*, trans. Graham Burchell (Cambridge: Cambridge University Press, 1999), pp. 24–30.
79. J.-K. Huysmans, *La Bas* (London: Dedalus, 1986), p. 11. A tragic confirmation of this point appeared in *The Times*, 28 August 2001, in an account of worries of authorities in Germany at the rise of interest in devil worship amongst teenagers that led to a rash of suicides.
80. Ibid., p. 210.
81. J.-K. Huysmans, *En Route*, pp. 22–3.
82. Plummer, *Telling Sexual Stories*, p. 115.
83. Simon Hardy, *The Reader, the Author, His Woman and Her Lover: Soft-Core Pornography and Heterosexual Men* (London: Cassell, 1998), especially pp. 5–26.
84. Ibid., pp. 100–1.
85. Decca Aitkenhead, 'Net Porn', *The Observer*, review section, 30 March 2003, pp. 1–2.
86. The above discussion is taken from Chapter 5 of Giddens, *The Transformation of Intimacy*, pp. 65–86.
87. See for example, Wendy Shalit, *A Return to Modesty: Discovering the Lost Virtue* (New York: Simon & Schuster, 2000).
88. Sturken and Cartwright, *Practices of Looking*, p. 258.
89. See for example, Richard Maltby, *Hollywood Cinema* (Oxford: Blackwell, 1995).
90. For a rare, if not idiosyncratic treatment of religion and the cinema from a perspective of cultural studies, see Margaret R. Miles, *Seeing and Believing: Religion and Values in the Movies* (Boston: Beacon Press, 1996).
91. See for example, Pam Cook and Mieke Bernink (eds), *The Cinema Book*, second edition (London: British Film Institute, 1999), Part 7, 'Theoretical Foundations', pp. 319–73. Structuralism, psychoanalysis, feminism are its main areas, with the issue of spectatorship set between brief considerations of cultural studies and audience research.
92. Laura Mulvey, 'Visual Pleasure and Narrative Cinema', in John Caughie and Annette Kuhn (eds), *The Sexual Subject: A Screen Reader in Sexuality* (London: Routledge, 1992), p. 23.
93. Jackie Stacey, *Star Gazing: Hollywood Cinema and Female Spectatorship* (London: Routledge, 1994), p. 36. One suspects that matters might have moved on since 1988, when concerns were raised about the absence of material on how women look at men. Again the same issues of anonymity would arise of who the women are who view male pornography. See Suzanne Moore, 'Here's Looking at You, Kid' and Avis Lewallen, '*Lace*: Pornography for Women', in Lorraine Gamman and Margaret Marshment (eds), *The Female Gaze: Women as Viewers of Popular Culture* (London: The Women's Press, 1988), pp. 44–59 and 86–101. See especially p. 45 in the former and p. 98 in the latter.
94. Moore, 'Here's Looking at You Kid', pp. 22–4.
95. Norman K. Denzin, *The Cinematic Society: The Voyeur's Gaze* (London: Sage, 1995), p. 1.
96. Ibid., pp. 28 and 36.

97. Ibid., p. 49–57.
98. Ibid., p. 191.
99. Ibid., p. 194.
100. Ibid., p. 211.
101. Laura Bovone, 'Ethics as Etiquette: The Emblematic Contribution of Erving Goffman', *Theory, Culture & Society*, vol. 10, no. 4, November 1993, pp. 25–39. For a consideration of the intellectual origins of the link between etiquette and ceremony, see Gary D. Jaworski, 'Park, Doyle and Hughes: Neglected Antecedents of Goffman's Theory of Ceremony', *Sociological Inquiry*, vol. 66, no. 2, May 1996, pp. 160–74.
102. Goffman, *Stigma*, pp. 58–68.
103. Ibid., p. 104.
104. Ibid., p. 125–8.
105. Ibid., p. 155.
106. Susan O. Michelman, 'Changing Old Habits: Dress of Women Religious and Its Relationship to Personal and Social Identity', *Sociological Inquiry*, vol. 67, no. 3, August 1997, pp. 350–63.
107. See M. Catherine Daly, 'The *Paarda* Expression of *Hejaaab* among Afghan Women in a Non-Muslim Community', in Linda B. Arthur (ed.), *Religion, Dress and the Body* (Oxford: Berg, 1999), pp. 147–61.
108. Fadwa El Guindi, *Veil: Modesty, Privacy and Resistance* (Oxford: Berg, 1999).
109. Erving Goffman, *Behaviour in Public Places: Notes on the Social Organization of Gatherings* (New York: The Free Press, 1963), Chapter 6, 'Face Engagements', pp. 83–111.
110. El Guindi, *Veil*, p. 137.
111. See the preface by Raymond Keaveney and Peter C. Sutton in Peter C. Sutton, Lisa Vergara and Ann Jensen Adams, *Love Letters: Dutch Genre Paintings in the Age of Vermeer* (Bruce Museum of Arts and Science, Greenwich, Connecticut and National Gallery of Ireland, Dublin, 2003), pp. 9–10.
112. Peter C. Sutton, 'Love Letters: Dutch Genre Paintings in the Age of Vermeer', ibid., p. 15.

5 Piety and visual culture: seeking to see the unseen

1. Anon, 'From a Poem, in defence of the decent Ornaments of Christ-Church, Oxon, occasioned by a Banbury brother, who called them Idolatries', in H.J.C. Grierson and G. Bullough (eds), *The Oxford Book of Seventeenth Century Verse* (Oxford: Clarendon Press, 1934), p. 804.
2. See Umberto Eco, *Art and Beauty in the Middle Ages*, trans. Hugh Bredin (New Haven: Yale University Press, 1986), Chapter IV on the 'The Aesthetics of Light', pp. 43–51.
3. Halbwachs, *On Collective Memory*, p. 92.
4. Ibid., p. 169.
5. Ruth Harris, *Lourdes: Body and Spirit in the Secular Age* (Harmondsworth: The Penguin Press, 1999), p. 280.
6. Clifford Geertz, 'Art as a Cultural System', *Modern Language Notes*, vol. 91, 1976, p. 1478.
7. Michael Baxandall, *Painting & Experience in Fifteenth Century Italy: A Primer in the Social History of Pictorial Style*, second edition (Oxford: Oxford University Press, 1988), p. 1.

8. Ibid., p. 45.
9. Ibid., p. 40.
10. Ibid., p. 47.
11. See Marcel Gauchet, *The Disenchantment of the World: A Political History of Religion*, trans. Oscar Burge (Princeton: Princeton University Press, 1997).
12. See Pierre Bourdieu, *Distinction: A Social Critique of the Judgement of Taste*, trans. Richard Nice (London: Routledge, 1986).
13. David Swartz, 'Bridging the Study of Culture and Religion: Pierre Bourdieu's Political Economy of Symbolic Power', *Sociology of Religion*, vol. 57, no. 1, 1996, pp. 75–7.
14. Laurence R. Iannaccone, 'Religious Practice: A Human Capital Approach', *Journal for the Scientific Study of Religion*, vol. 29, no. 3, 1990, p. 289. See also pp. 300–1.
15. Stark and Finke, *Acts of Faith*, p. 120.
16. Roger Finke and Kevin D. Dougherty, 'The Effects of Professional Training: The Social and Religious Capital Acquired in Seminaries', *Journal for the Scientific Study of Religion*, vol. 41, no. 1, 2002, pp. 103–20.
17. Stark and Finke, 'Catholic Religious Vocations: Decline and Revival', *Review of Religious Research*, vol. 42, no. 2, December 2000, especially p. 143.
18. Bourdieu and Wacquant, *An Invitation to Reflexive Sociology*, pp. 117–22. The quotation above is from p. 117.
19. Ibid., p. 98.
20. Moshe Barasch, *Blindness: The History of a Mental Image in Western Through* (New York: Routledge, 2001), p. 49.
21. For an excellent meditation on John 9:1–38, see A Carthusian, *From Advent to Pentecost: Carthusian Novice Conferences*, trans. Carmel Brett (London: Darton, Longman & Todd, 1999), Chapter 13, 'The Man Born Blind', pp. 85–8.
22. *Bernard of Clairvaux: Selected Works*, trans. G.R. Evans (New York: Paulist Press, 1987), p. 274.
23. Cynthia Hahn, '*Visio Dei*: Changes in Medieval Visuality', in Robert S. Nelson (ed.), *Visuality Before and Beyond the Renaissance* (Cambridge: Cambridge University Press, 2000), pp. 171–4.
24. Smith, *Zygmunt Bauman*, p. 148.
25. Flannery O'Connor, *Wise Blood* (London: Faber & Faber, 1980), p. 226.
26. For a useful assessment of Diderot's *Lettre sur les aveugles*, see Barasch, *Blindness*, pp. 147–57.
27. Simmel's *Sociologie*, pp. 358–60.
28. See the excellent article by Helen Echlin on Mike May's return to sight in *The Sunday Telegraph*, 22 September 2002. This formed the background to a television documentary *The Man who Learned to See*.
29. See James, *The Varieties of Religious Experience*, pp. 350–3. The quotation appears on p. 352.
30. Bernard of Clairvaux, 'On the Steps of Humility and Pride', in *Bernard of Clairvaux: Selected Works*, pp. 123–5.
31. Zygmunt Bauman, *Legislators and Interpreters* (Cambridge: Polity Press, 1987), pp. 82–4.
32. John M. Hull, '"Sight to the Inly Blind"? Attitudes to Blindness in the Hymn-books', *Theology*, vol. 150, no. 827, September/October 2002, pp. 333–41.
33. R.G.A. Buxton, 'Blindness and Limits: Sophokles and the Logic of Myth', *The Journal of Hellenic Studies*, vol. C, 1980, p. 25.
34. Ibid., pp. 30–5.

35. Barasch, *Blindness*, p. 36.
36. John Bunyan, *The Pilgrim's Progress* (Harmondsworth, Middlesex: Penguin, 1987), pp. 18–19.
37. Ibid., p. 80.
38. See for example, Stephen Sharot, 'Traditional, Modern or Postmodern? Recent Religious Developments among Jews in Israel', in Kieran Flanagan and Peter C. Jupp (eds), *Postmodernity, Sociology and Religion* (Basingstoke: Macmillan, 1996), especially pp. 119–20.
39. These issues form themes of Harris, *Lourdes*.
40. St Augustine, *The City of God*, p. 595.
41. Ibid., p. 1069.
42. Ibid., pp. 450–1.
43. Ibid., p. 599.
44. Beilharz, *Zygmunt Bauman*, p. 157.
45. St Augustine, *The City of God*, pp. 593–4.
46. Ibid., p. 597. This quotation appears under the section marked 'the children of the flesh and the children of the promise'.
47. Ibid., p. 16.
48. Ibid., p. 205.
49. David Martin, *Christian Language and its Mutations: Essays in Sociological Understanding* (Aldershot: Ashgate, 2002), p. 116.
50. Eeva Jokinen and Soile Veïjola, 'The Disoriented Tourist: The Figuration of the Tourist in Contemporary Cultural Critique', in Chris Rojek and John Urry (eds), *Touring Cultures: Transformations of Travel and Theory* (London: Routledge, 1997), pp. 38–42.
51. Victor Turner and Edith Turner, *Image and Pilgrimage in Christian Culture* (New York: Columbia University Press, 1978), p. 20.
52. Urry, *The Tourist Gaze*, pp. 8–10.
53. Ibid., p. 129.
54. Ibid., p. 3.
55. Ibid., p. 156.
56. Carol Crawshaw and John Urry, 'Tourism and the Photographic Eye', in Rojek and Urry (eds), *Touring Cultures*, p. 179.
57. Turner and Turner, *Image and Pilgrimage in Christian Culture*, p. 11.
58. Deidre Purcell, *Lough Derg* (Dublin: Veritas, 1988).
59. Lough Derg clearly had an impact on the Turners who devoted a whole chapter and an appendix to St Patrick's Purgatory. See *Image and Pilgrimage in Christian Culture*, Chapter 3, and Appendix B which gives a chronology of its basis, pp. 256–9.
60. Ibid., p. 34.
61. Ibid., p. 8.
62. Ibid., p. 15. This notion of communitas as characterising the pilgrimage has been subject to much criticism. See John Eade and Michael J. Sallnow (eds), *Contesting the Sacred: The Anthropology of Christian Pilgrimage* (London: Routledge, 1991), pp. 4–5.
63. Emile Mâle, *Religious Art from the Twelfth to the Eighteenth Century* (Princeton: Princeton University Press, 1982), p. 95.
64. Diana Webb, *Pilgrimage in Medieval England* (London: Hambledon and London, 2000).
65. J. Huizinga, *The Waning of the Middle Ages*, trans. F. Hopman (Harmondsworth: Penguin, 1955), pp. 194–5.

66. Huysmans, *The Cathedral*.
67. Erwin Panofsky, ed. and trans., *Abbot Suger on the Abbey Church of St-Denis and its Art Treasures*, second edition (Princeton: Princeton University Press, 1979).
68. See Chapter 12 of Huizinga, *The Waning of the Middle Ages*, especially pp. 159–63.
69. See Olivier Boulnois, 'The Modernity of the Middle Ages', *Communio*, vol. 30, Summer 2003, pp. 234–59.
70. Aidan Nichols, *The Art of God Incarnate: Theology and Image in Christian Tradition* (London: Darton, Longman & Todd, 1980), p. 137.
71. Bourdieu, *The Field of Cultural Production*, p. 217.
72. Jenks, 'Introduction', *Visual Culture*, pp. 5–11.
73. Bourdieu, *The Field of Cultural Production*, p. 239.
74. Jenks, *Visual Culture*, p. 1.
75. Ibid., p.16.
76. Goffman, *Interaction Ritual*, p. 1.
77. Richard Jenkins, *Social Identity* (London: Routledge, 1996), p. 69.
78. Goffman, *Interaction Ritual*, p. 19.
79. Synnott provides an exceptionally useful account of the evolution of the face, which he characterises as a movement from being a mirror of the soul to a mask of the self, a setting in which the ideology of beauty has become a battlefield in feminist writings. These hinge on the degree to which ideas of beauty are male impositions on the female, confining her to a language of the surface. See Anthony Synnott, 'Truth and Goodness, Mirrors and Masks: a Sociology of Beauty and the Face', Parts 1 and 2, *The British Journal of Sociology*, vol. 40, no. 4, 1989 and vol. 41, no. 1, 1989 and 1990, pp. 607–36 and 55–76.
80. Mike Featherstone, Mike Hepworth and Bryan S. Turner (eds), *The Body: Social Process and Cultural Theory* (London: Sage, 1991), pp. 61–8.
81. David F. Ford, *Self and Salvation: Being Transformed* (Cambridge: Cambridge University Press, 1999), p. 19.
82. Bauman, *Postmodern Ethics*, pp. 75–6.
83. Samuel IJsseling, *Mimesis: On Appearing and Being*, trans. Hester IJsseling and Jeffrey Bloechl (Kampen, Netherlands: Kok Pharos, 1997), p. 56.
84. Cited in Georgia Frank, *The Memory of the Eyes*, p. 51.
85. Ibid., p. 100.
86. Ibid., p. 126.
87. Ibid., pp. 13–29 and 124.
88. Ibid., p. 154.
89. See Maurice B. McNamee, *Vested Angels: Eucharistic Allusions in Early Netherlandish Paintings* (Leuven: Peeters, 1998).
90. See David Keck, *Angels and Angelology in the Middle Ages* (Cambridge: Cambridge University Press, 1998), pp. 178–9.
91. Frank, *The Memory of the Eyes*, p. 173.
92. Ibid., p. 14.
93. Ibid., pp. 76–7.
94. For a useful discussion of these themes, see Besancon, *The Forbidden Image*, Chapter 2, on biblical prohibitions.
95. Illich, 'Guarding the Eye in the Age of Show', p. 56.
96. Besançon, *The Forbidden Image*, pp. 133–7.
97. David Morgan, *Protestants and Pictures: Religion, Visual Culture and the Age of American Mass Production* (New York: Oxford University Press, 1999), p. 348.
98. Besançon, *The Forbidden Image*, p. 29.

99. Ibid., p. 115.
100. Ibid., p. 125.
101. Ibid., p. 140.
102. Ibid., p. 165.

6   Dark into light: a sociological navigation

1. David Morgan, *Visual Piety: A History and Theory of Popular Religious Images* (Berkeley: The University of California Press, 1999), pp. 2–3.
2. St Augustine, 'On Faith in Things Unseen', trans. Roy Joseph Deferrari and Mary Francis McDonald, in *The Fathers of the Church*, vol. 4 (Washington D.C.: The Catholic University of America Press, 1947), pp. 455–6.
3. See James, *Varieties of Religious Experience*, especially Chapter 3, 'The Reality of the Unseen'. The quotation comes from p. 53.
4. Oliver, 'Current Revivals of Interest in Religion: Some Sociological Observations', p. 159.
5. Kieran Flanagan, 'J.-K. Huysmans: The First Postmodernist Saint?' *New Blackfriars*, vol. 71, no. 813, May 1990, pp. 217–29. Huysmans was a very important influence on *The Enchantment of Sociology*.
6. For a useful exception, see Keith Tester, 'Between Sociology and Theology: The Spirit of Capitalism Debate', *The Sociological Review*, vol. 48, no. 1, February 2000, pp. 43–57. The essays that Weber intended to develop further in 1920 have been subject to numerous studies. See for example, Gordon Marshall, *In Search of the Spirit of Capitalism: An Essay on Max Weber's Protestant Ethic thesis* (London: Hutchinson, 1982).
7. John Carroll, *Puritan, Paranoid, Remissive*, p. 132.
8. Harvey Goldman, *Max Weber and Thomas Mann: Calling and the Shaping of the Self* (Berkeley: University of California Press, 1991), pp. 18–21.
9. Wilhelm Hennis, *Max Weber: Essays in Reconstruction*, trans. Keith Tribe (London: Allen & Unwin, 1988).
10. Ibid., pp. 97–8.
11. J.J.R. Thomas, 'Ideology and Elective Affinity', *Sociology*, vol. 19, no. 1, February 1985, pp. 39–54. For a thorough examination of the use of the term, see Richard Herbert Howe, 'Max Weber's Elective Affinities: Sociology within the Bounds of Pure Reason', *The American Journal of Sociology*, vol. 84, no. 2, 1978, pp. 366–85.
12. Eagleton, *The Idea of Culture*, p. 84.
13. Ibid., pp. 70–1.
14. Ibid., p. 69.
15. The issue of calculation and accummulation of capital in relation to monasticism is a complex issue. See Ilana Friedrich Silber, 'Monasticism and the "Protestant Ethic": Asceticism, Rationality and Wealth in the Medieval West', *The British Journal of Sociology*, vol. 44, no. 1, March 1993, pp. 103–23. See also her study, *Virtuosity, Charisma and Social Order: A Comparative Sociological Study of Monasticism in Theravada Buddhism and Medieval Catholicism* (Cambridge: Cambridge University Press, 1995).
16. Weber, *The Protestant Ethic*, p. 121.
17. See for example, his discussion of institutional grace in Max Weber, *Economy and Society*, trans. Guenther Roth and Claus Wittich, vol. 1 (Berkeley: University of California Press, 1978), pp. 557–63.

18. See Adam Seligman, 'Inner-Worldly Individualism and the Institutionalization of Puritanism in late Seventeenth-Century New England', *The British Journal of Sociology*, vol. 41, no. 4, December 1990, pp. 537–57. For a famous account of saving grace that is decidedly Protestant, see Jonathan Edwards, *Treatise on Grace* (Cambridge: James Clarke, 1971).

19. Wolfgang Schluchter, *Paradoxes of Modernity: Culture and Conduct in the Theory of Max Weber*, trans. Neil Solomon (Stanford: Stanford University Press, 1996), pp. 235–9.

20. *Catechism of the Catholic Church* (London: Geoffrey Chapman, 1994), sec. 1996–2004, pp. 434–6.

21. This was a point that particularly worried Bauman as he sought to formulate the onset of postmodernity, where the principle actor of sociology, the Puritan, had 'disappeared'. See *Legislators and Interpreters*, pp. 192–3.

22. Weber, *Economy and Society*, vol. 2, pp. 1139–45.

23. Weber, *The Protestant Ethic*, p. 105. One might wonder if Weber's glorification of English Protestantism and its Puritan heritage might have been sullied by worries over the exercise of iconoclasticism in places such as the Lady Chapel at Ely Cathedral. See Guenther Roth, 'Weber the Would-Be-Englishman: Anglophilia and Family History', in Lehmann and Roth (eds), *Weber's Protestant Ethic*, pp. 83–121.

24. Weber, *The Protestant Ethic*, pp. 170–1.

25. Besançon, *The Forbidden Image*, pp. 185–90.

26. For a brilliant discussion of this point, see Carroll, *Puritan, Paranoid, Permissive*, pp. 125–31. Few others besides Carroll have looked at the link between Calvinism and the thesis. For an exception, see Gianfranco Poggi, *Calvinism and the Capitalist Spirit: Max Weber's Protestant Ethic* (London: Macmillan, 1983).

27. On the absence of a polar opposite, see Swatos and Kivisto, 'Max Weber as "Christian Sociologist"', pp. 357–8 and on his interest in Catholicism, see p. 352.

28. Weber, *The Protestant Ethic*, pp. 35–43. See in particular p. 40 and notes on the issue on pp. 188–9.

29. Thomas Nipperdey, 'Max Weber, Protestantism and the Context of Debate around 1900', in Lehmann and Roth (eds), *Weber's Protestant Ethic*, pp. 73–81.

30. Thomas Ekstrand, *Max Weber in a Theological Perspective* (Leuven: Peeters, 2000), pp. 93–6. The quotation comes from p. 93.

31. Arthur Vidich and Stanford Lyman, *American Sociology: Worldly Rejections of Religion and Their Directions* (New Haven: Yale University Press, 1985).

32. Peter Kivisto, 'Sociology as a Vocation: A Weberian Analysis of the Origins and Subsequent Development of American Sociology', *The British Journal of Sociology*, vol. 38, no. 1, 1987, p. 114.

33. See Lyman, *The Seven Deadly Sins*, where in his effort to find a sociology of sin he feels let down by the legitimation crisis of the secular Protestant American moral hierarchy. See pp. 290–5.

34. Beilharz, *Zygmunt Bauman*, p. 82.

35. Bauman, *Legislators and Interpreters*, pp. 149–54.

36. For an imaginative account of the postgraduate in sociology becoming part of the elect, see Eric Plutzer, 'The Protestant Ethic and the Spirit of Academia: An Essay on Graduate Education', *Teaching Sociology*, vol. 19, no. 3, 1991, pp. 302–7.

37. See for example, Paul Tillich, *Theology of Culture* (Oxford: Oxford University Press, 1959), pp. 53–60 for a discussion of the theological efficacy of symbols.

38. Morgan, *Protestants and Pictures*.

39. James, *The Varieties of Religious Experience*, p. 461.

40. See for example, John Davis, 'Catholic Envy: The Visual Culture of Protestant Desire', in David Morgan and Sally M. Promey (eds), *The Visual Culture of American Religions* (Berkeley: University of California Press, 2001), pp. 105–28.
41. See John Lough, *France Observed in the Seventeenth Century by British Travellers* (Stockfield: Oriel Press, 1984), pp. 213–29.
42. Richard Sennett, *The Fall of Public Man* (Cambridge: Cambridge University Press, 1977), pp. 333–5.
43. Max Weber, *The Sociology of Religion*, trans. Ephraim Fischoff (London: Methuen, 1965), pp. 242–5, especially p. 244.
44. Roger O'Toole, 'Salvation, Redemption and Community: Reflections on the Aesthetic Cosmos', *Sociology of Religion*, vol. 57, no. 2, 1996, pp. 127–48.
45. See section on François-André Isambert in Hervieu-Léger, *Religion as a Chain of Memory*, pp. 48–51, but especially p. 50.
46. Edward Farley, *Faith and Beauty: A Theological Aesthetic* (Aldershot: Ashgate, 2001), pp. 2–6.
47. Simmel, *Essays on Religion*, p. xvi.
48. See Victoria Lee Erickson, 'Georg Simmel: American Sociology Chooses the Stone the Builders Refused', in Fenn (ed.), *The Blackwell Companion to Sociology of Religion*, p. 117. Simmel's range of interests and the interweaving of religion into his considerations of culture have left a legacy of thought, a plight, which contemporary sociology has neither confronted nor endeavoured to think past. His range of interests in relation to matters of soul and spirit bear many complex readings. Leck draws attention to the difficulties of supplying a biography of Simmel, given the loss of his papers in the Second World War. Until these are recovered, it is likely that his stance in relation to theology will be a matter of conjecture. See Leck, *Georg Simmel*, pp. 28–9.
49. Simmel, *Essays on Religion*, pp. 129–30.
50. Ibid., pp. 36–7.
51. Ibid., p. 82.
52. Ibid., p. 84.
53. Ibid., p. 92.
54. Ibid., p. 166.
55. Ibid., p. 141.
56. Ibid., p. 194.
57. Ibid., p. 209.
58. Ibid., p. 46.
59. Ibid., p. 42.
60. See James, *The Varieties of Religious Experience*, lecture 9, 'Conversion', especially pp. 208–16.
61. Simmel, *Essays on Religion*, p. 109.
62. Ibid., p. 169.
63. Ibid., p. 131.
64. Ibid., pp. 68–9.
65. Ibid., p. 77
66. Ibid., p. 10.
67. Gordon Graham, *Evil & Christian Ethics* (Cambridge: Cambridge University Press, 2001).
68. Susan Neiman, *Evil in Modern Thought: An Alternative History of Philosophy* (Princeton: Princeton University Press, 2002), p. 4.
69. Foucault, *Discipline and Punish*, pp. 3–7.

70. The above discussion is based on Bauman, *Modernity and the Holocaust*. The quotation cited comes from p. 206.
71. Lyman, *The Seven Deadly Sins*, p. 274.
72. St Augustine, *The City of God*, p. 440. See also the summary of the views of Aquinas on evil in Timothy McDermott (ed.), *Summa Theologiae*, pp. 91–4.
73. St Augustine, *The City of God*, p. 454.
74. See G.R. Evans, entry on evil in Allan D. Fitzgerald (ed.), *Augustine Through the Ages*, pp. 340–4.
75. Hans Urs von Balthasar, *Bernanos*, p. 171.
76. Neiman, *Evil in Modern Thought*, p. 254.
77. Ibid., p. 273.
78. Ibid., pp. 286–7.
79. J.S. La Fontaine, *Speak of the Devil: Tales of Satanic Abuse in Contemporary England* (Cambridge: Cambridge University Press, 1998).
80. William I. Thomas, 'The Definition of the Situation', in Jerome G. Manis and Bernard N. Meltzer (eds), *Symbolic Interaction: A Reader in Social Pyschology* (Boston: Allyn and Bacon, 1967), pp. 315–21.
81. Michel Meslin, entry on the eye, in Mircea Eliade (ed.), *The Encyclopaedia of Religion* (New York: Macmillan, 1987), p. 236.
82. Fiona Bowie, *The Anthropology of Religion* (Oxford: Blackwell, 2000), pp. 235–44. It is noteworthy that Aquinas considered the evil eye and its capacity to invoke spirits of sufficient importance to refute its basis. See McDermott, *Summa Theologiae*, p. 162.
83. Tobin Siebers, *The Mirror of Medusa* (Berkeley: University of California Press, 1983), p. 47.
84. Frode F. Jacobsen, 'Interpretations of Sickness and Misfortune among Beja Pastoralists', *Anthropology & Medicine*, vol. 5, no. 2, 1998, pp. 145–67.
85. Vivian Garrison and Conrad M. Arensberg, 'The Evil Eye: Envy or Risk of Seizure? Paranoia or Patronal Dependency?' in Clarence Maloney (ed.), *The Evil Eye* (New York: Columbia University Press, 1976), especially pp. 297–302 for an overview of the ecology and beliefs surrounding the evil eye. For a useful effort to write a sociology of envy, see Lyman, *The Seven Deadly Sins*, especially Chapter 5, pp. 184–211.
86. Raposa, *Boredom and the Religious Imagination*, p. 120.
87. Ibid., pp. 105–20.
88. Ratzinger, *The Spirit of the Liturgy*, p. 125.
89. John Saward, *The Beauty of Holiness and the Holiness of Beauty: Art, Sanctity & the Truth of Catholicism* (San Francisco: Ignatius Press, 1997), p. 33.
90. Simmel, *Essays on Religion*, p. 90.
91. Information on this theme is derived from McNamee, *Vested Angels*.
92. Bruno Latour, 'Visualisation and Social Reproduction: Opening One Eye While Closing the Other . . . a Note on Some Religious Paintings', in Gordon Fyfe and John Law (eds), *Picturing Power: Visual Depiction and Social Relations* (London: Routledge, 1988), p. 16.
93. Ibid., pp. 20–1.
94. Ibid., p. 24.
95. Ibid., p. 26.
96. Hans Urs von Balthasar, *The Glory of the Lord: A Theological Aesthetics*, trans. Erasomo Leiva-Merikakis, vol. 1 (Edinburgh: T. & T. Clark, 1982), p. 311.
97. Saward, *The Beauty of Holiness*, p. 84.

98. Brian C. Taylor, *Spirituality for Everyday Living: An Adaptation of the Rule of St. Benedict* (Collegeville, Minnesota: The Liturgical Press, 1989), p. 34.
99. Friedrich Nietzsche, *The Joyful Wisdom*, trans. Thomas Common (London: George Allen & Unwin, 1910), p. 171.
100. Auguste Comte, *The Catechism of Positive Religion*, trans. Richard Congreve, third edition (London: Kegan Paul, Trench, Trübner, 1891), p. 74.
101. Peter Winch, *The Idea of a Social Science and its Relation to Philosophy* (London: Routledge & Kegan Paul, 1963), pp. 87–8.
102. Hans Urs von Balthasar, *The Glory of the Lord*, vol. 1, p. 286.
103. Harris, *Lourdes*, pp. 94–5.
104. Cited in Frank, *The Memory of the Eyes*, p. 85.
105. Sermon, 15 August 1991, reproduced in anon, *The Spirit of Place: Carthusian Reflections* (London: Darton, Longman & Todd, 1998), pp. 15–16.
106. Thomas À Kempis, *The Imitation of Christ*, trans. Leo Sherley-Price (Harmondsworth: Penguin, 1952), p. 48.
107. John Stratton Hawley (ed.), *Saints and Virtues* (Berkeley: University of California Press, 1987).
108. This notion of God's face shining on his followers reflects a belief in His favour. See for example, Psalm 67:1. Only Moses had been permitted to see God face to face.
109. Hélène Caumeil, 'Small Children's Prayer: Interrogation of Adults; The Experience of a Prayer-School', in Casiano Floristán and Christian Duquoc (eds), *Learning to Pray* (Edinburgh: T. & T. Clark, 1982), p. 49.
110. A Carthusian, *Interior Prayer, Carthusian Novice Conferences*, trans. Maureen Scrine (London: Darton, Longman & Todd, 1996), p. 163.
111. Jean-Pierre de Caussade, *The Sacrament of the Present Moment*, trans. Kitty Muggeridge (London: Fount, 1996), p. 94.
112. Goffman, *Interaction Ritual*, p. 78.
113. Comte, *The Catechism of Positive Religion*, pp. 65–6.
114. See John Woodforde, *The History of Vanity* (Stroud: Alan Sutton, 1992).
115. J.-K. Huysmans, *The Road from Decadence: Letters of J.K. Huysmans*, ed. and trans. Barbara Beaumont (London: The Athlone Press, 1989), p. 157.
116. Herbert L. Kessler, *Spiritual Seeing: Picturing God's Invisibility in Medieval Art* (Philadelphia: University of Pennsylvania Press, 2000), p. 18.
117. Cited in Ratzinger, *The Spirit of the Liturgy*, p. 121.
118. William J.F. Keenan, 'Rediscovering the Theological in Sociology: Foundation and Possibilities', *Theory, Culture & Society*, vol. 20, no. 1, February 2003, pp. 28–9.
119. For a graphic account of the tragedy of these acts of destruction and their aftermath, see Eamon Duffy, *The Stripping of the Altars: Traditional Religion in England 1400–1580* (London: Yale University Press, 1992).
120. Jervis, *Exploring the Modern*, p. 304.
121. Robert Baldick, *The Life of J.-K. Huysmans* (Oxford: The Clarendon Press, 1955), pp. 123–4.
122. Fyodor Dostoyevsky, *The Idiot*, trans. David Magarshack (London: Penguin, 1955), p. 210.
123. Ibid., pp. 390–2. See also George A. Panichas, *The Burden of Vision: Dostoyevsky's Spiritual Art* (Chicago: Gateway, 1985), especially Chapter 2 on terror that deals with *The Idiot*.
124. Dostoyevsky, *The Idiot*, pp. 436–7.

125. For St Augustine, the issue of the ability to see the immaterial is treated in terms of the 'eye of the heart', the inward sense. The exercise of this capacity is set in the context of seeing God face to face. See St Augustine, *The City of God*, pp. 1083–7.
126. R.S. Khare, 'The Seen and the Unseen: Hindu Distinctions, Experiences and Cultural Reasoning', *Contributions to Indian Sociology* (n.s.) vol. 27, no. 2, July–December 1993, p. 209.
127. Victor Turner (ed.), *Celebration: Studies in Festivity and Ritual* (Washington, D.C.: Smithsonian Institution Press, 1982), p. 26.
128. Ibid., p. 204.
129. Neil MacGregor, 'Introduction', in Gabriele Finaldi (ed.), *The Image of Christ* (London: National Gallery, 2000), p. 6.
130. Carol Duncan, *Civilizing Rituals: Inside Public Art Museums* (London: Routledge, 1995), p. 13.
131. Grace Davie, 'Seeing Salvation: The Use of Text as Data in the Sociology of Religion', in Paul Avis (ed.), *Public Faith? The State of Religious Belief and Practice in Britain* (London: SPCK, 2003), pp. 28 and 37.
132. Ian Craib, 'Fear, Death and Sociology', *Mortality*, vol. 8, no. 3, August 2003, pp. 285–95. I am very grateful to the Revd Dr Peter C. Jupp for drawing this to my attention.
133. Clive Seale, 'Fear, Death and Sociology: A Response to Ian Craib', *Mortality*, vol. 8, no. 4, December 2003, pp. 388–91.
134. Christiaan Vogelaar, *Netherlandish Fifteenth and Sixteenth Century Paintings in the National Gallery of Ireland: A Complete Catalogue* (Dublin: The National Gallery of Ireland, 1987), pp. 46–9.
135. See the entry on Mark Vessey on the relationships between St Augustine and St Jerome in Allan D. Fitzgerald (ed.), *Augustine through the Ages*, pp. 460–2.
136. Thomas Heywood, 'The Author in His Booke', in Grierson and Bullough (eds), *The Oxford Book of Seventeenth Century Verse* (Oxford: Clarendon Press, 1934), p. 183.

Bibliography

Agger, Ben, *The Virtual Self: A Contemporary Sociology* (Oxford: Blackwell, 2004).

Aitkenhead, Decca, 'Net Porn', *The Observer,* review section, 30 March 2003, pp. 1–2.

Alasuutari, Pertti, *Researching Culture: Qualitative Method and Cultural Studies* (London: Sage, 1995).

Albright, Daniel (ed.), *W. B. Yeats: The Poems* (London: J.M. Dent, 1990).

Aldridge, Alan, *Religion in the Contemporary World* (Cambridge: Polity Press, 2000).

Alexander, Jane, *Rituals for Sacred Living* (London: HarperCollins, 1999).

Alt, John, 'Sport and Cultural Reification: From Ritual to Mass Consumption', *Theory, Culture & Society*, vol. 1, no. 3, 1983, pp. 93–107.

Anderson, Benedict, *Imagined Communities: Reflections on the Origin and Spread of Nationalism* (London: Verso, 1983).

Anon., 'From a Poem, in Defence of the Decent Ornaments of Christ-Church, Oxon, Occasioned by a Banbury Brother, Who Called them Idolatries', in H.J.C. Grierson and G. Bullough (eds), *The Oxford Book of Seventeenth Century Verse* (Oxford: Clarendon Press, 1934), pp. 803–5.

Anon., Carthusian, *Interior Prayer, Carthusian Novice Conferences*, trans. Maureen Scrine (London: Darton, Longman Todd, 1996).

——, *From Advent to Pentecost. Carthusian Novice Conferences*, trans. Carmel Brett (London: Darton, Longman Todd, 1999).

Anscombe, G.E.M., 'Modern Moral Philosophy', in Roger Crisp and Michael Slote (eds), *Virtue Ethics* (Oxford: Oxford University Press, 1997), pp. 26–44.

Arweck, Elisabeth and Martin D. Stringer (eds), *Theorizing Faith: The Insider/Outsider Problem in the Study of Ritual* (Birmingham: The University of Birmingham Press, 2002).

Atkinson, Paul, 'Voiced and Unvoiced', *Sociology*, vol. 33, no. 1, February 1999, pp. 191–7.

Bakewell, Joan and James Macmillan, *Belief,* BBC Radio 3, 2 January 2001.

Baldick, Robert, *The Life of J.-K. Huysmans* (Oxford: The Clarendon Press, 1955).

Balthasar, Hans Urs von, *Prayer*, trans. A.V. Littledale (London: Geoffrey Chapman, 1961).

——, *The Glory of the Lord: A Theological Aesthetics*, trans. Erasomo Leiva-Merikakis, vol. 1 (Edinburgh: T. & T. Clark, 1982).

——, *Bernanos: An Existential Existence*, trans. Erasmo Leiva-Merikakis (San Francisco: Ignatius Press, 1996).

Barasch, Moshe, *Blindness: The History of a Mental Image in Western Through* (New York: Routledge, 2001).

Barnard, Malcolm, *Approaches to Understanding Visual Culture* (Basingstoke: Palgrave, 2001).

Barthes, Roland, *Camera Lucida: Reflections on Photography*, trans. Richard Howard (London: Vintage, 1993).

Baudelaire, Charles, *The Painter of Modern Life and Other Essays*, trans. Jonathan Mayne (London: Phadon, 1995).

Bauman, Zygmunt, *Legislators and Interpreters* (Cambridge: Polity Press, 1987).

——, *Modernity and Ambivalence* (Cambridge: Polity Press, 1991).

——, *Modernity and the Holocaust* (Cambridge: Polity Press, 1991).

——, *Intimations of Postmodernity* (London: Routledge, 1992).

——, *Morality, Immortality & Other Life Strategies* (Stanford: Stanford University Press, 1992).

——, *Postmodern Ethics* (Oxford: Blackwell, 1993).

——, *Life in Fragments: Essays in Postmodern Morality* (Oxford: Blackwell, 1995).

——, 'Postmodern Religion?' in Paul Heelas (ed.), *Religion, Modernity and Postmodernity* (Oxford: Blackwell, 1998), pp. 55–78.

——, *Liquid Modernity* (Cambridge: Polity Press, 2000).

——, *Community: Seeking Safety in an Insecure World* (Cambridge: Polity Press, 2001).

——, *The Individualized Society* (Cambridge: Polity Press, 2001).

——, *Liquid Love* (Cambridge: Polity Press, 2003).

Bauman, Zygmunt and Keith Tester, *Conversations with Zygmunt Bauman* (Cambridge: Polity Press, 2001).

Baxandall, Michael, *Painting & Experience in Fifteenth Century Italy: A Primer in the Social History of Pictorial Style*, second edition (Oxford: Oxford University Press, 1988).

Beaudoin, Tom, *Virtual Faith: The Irreverent Spiritual Quest of Generation X* (San Francisco: Jossey-Bass, 1998).

Beck, Ulrich, Anthony Giddens and Scott Lash, *Reflexive Modernization: Politics, Tradition and Aesthetics in the Modern Social Order* (Cambridge: Polity Press, 1994).

Becker, Howard S. and Michal M. McCall (eds), *Symbolic Interaction and Cultural Studies* (Chicago: The University of Chicago Press, 1990).

Beilharz, Peter, *Zygmunt Bauman: Dialectic of Modernity* (London: Sage, 2000).

Bellah, Robert, 'Civil Religion in America', in Donald R. Culter (ed.), *The Religious Situation: 1968* (Boston: Beacon Press, 1968), pp. 331–56.

——, 'Public Philosophy and Public Theology in America Today', in Leroy S. Rouner (ed.), *Civil Religion and Political Theology* (Notre Dame, Indiana: University of Notre Dame Press, 1986), pp. 79–97.

——, *Beyond Belief: Essays on Religion in a Post-Traditionalist World* (Berkeley: University of California Press, 1991).

Benjamin, Walter, 'The Work of Art in the Age of Mechanical Reproduction', in Hannah Arendt (ed.), *Illuminations*, trans. Harry Zohn (London: Jonathan Cape, 1970), pp. 219–53.

Bennett, Clinton, *In Search of the Sacred: Anthropology and the Study of Religion* (London: Cassell, 1996).

Berger, John, *Ways of Seeing* (London: Penguin, 1972).

Bergeron, Katherine, 'The Virtual Sacred', *The New Republic*, 27 February 1995, pp. 29–34.

——, *Decadent Enchantments: The Revival of Gregorian Chant at Solesmes* (Berkeley: University of California Press, 1998).

Bernanos, Georges, *Under Satan's Sun*, trans. J.C. Whitehouse (Lincoln: University of Nebraska Press, 2001).

Bernard of Clairvaux: Selected Works, trans. G.R. Evans (New York: Paulist Press, 1987).

Besançon, Alain, *The Forbidden Image: An Intellectual History of Iconoclasm*, trans. Jane Marie Todd (Chicago: The University of Chicago Press, 2000).

Bewes, Timothy, *Cynicism and Postmodernity* (London: Verso, 1997).

Blackburn, Simon, *Being Good: A Short Introduction to Ethics* (Oxford: Oxford University Press, 2001).

Bok, Sissela, *Lying: Moral Choice in Public and Private Life* (London: Quartet Books, 1980).

Boltanski, Luc, *Distant Suffering: Morality, Media and Politics*, trans. Graham Burchell (Cambridge: Cambridge University Press, 1999).

Boulnois, Olivier, 'The Modernity of the Middle Ages', *Communio*, vol. 30, Summer 2003, pp. 234–59.

Bourdieu, Pierre, *Distinction: A Social Critique of the Judgement of Taste*, trans. Richard Nice (London: Routledge, 1986).

——, *Homo Academicus*, trans. Peter Collier (Cambridge: Polity Press, 1988).

——, *In Other Words: Essays Towards a Reflexive Sociology*, trans. Matthew Adamson (Cambridge: Polity Press, 1990).

——, *Photography: A Middle-brow Art*, trans. Shaun Whiteside (Cambridge: Polity Press, 1990).

——, *The Field of Cultural Production*, trans. Randal Johnson (Cambridge: Polity Press, 1993).

——, *Pascalian Meditations*, trans. Richard Nice (Cambridge: Polity Press, 2000).

Bourdieu, Pierre *et al.*, *The Weight of the World: Social Suffering in Contemporary Society*, trans. Priscilla Parkhurst Ferguson *et al.* (Cambridge: Polity Press, 1999).

Bourdieu, Pierre and Loïc J.D. Wacquant, *An Invitation to Reflexive Sociology* (Cambridge Polity Press, 1992).

Bovone, Laura, 'Ethics as Etiquette: The Emblematic Contribution of Erving Goffman', *Theory, Culture & Society*, vol. 10, no. 4, November 1993, pp. 25–39.

Bowie, Fiona, *The Anthropology of Religion* (Oxford: Blackwell, 2000).

Brasher, Brenda E., *Give me that Online Religion* (San Francisco: Jossey-Bass, 2001).

Brissett, Dennis and Robert P. Snow, 'Boredom: Where the Future Isn't', *Symbolic Interaction*, vol. 16, no. 3, 1993, pp. 237–56.

Brown, Callum G., *The Death of Christian Britain* (London: Routledge, 2001).

Brown, Peter, *The Body and Society: Men, Women and Sexual Renunciation in Early Christianity* (London: Faber Faber, 1988).

Bruce, Steve, *God is Dead: Secularization in the West* (Oxford: Blackwell, 2002).

Bryson, Norman, *Visions and Painting: The Logic of the Gaze* (Basingstoke: Macmillan, 1983).

Buley-Meissner, Mary Louise, Mary McCaslin Thompson and Elizabeth Bachrach Tan (eds), *The Academy and the Possibility of Belief: Essays on Intellectual and Spiritual Life* (Cresskill, New Jersey: Hampton Press, 2000).

Bunyan, John, *The Pilgrim's Progress* (Harmondsworth, Middlesex: Penguin, 1987).

Burwell, Ronald J., 'Sleeping with an Elephant: The Uneasy Alliance between Christian Faith and Sociology', *Christian Scholar's Review*, 1981, pp. 195–203.

Buxton, R.G.A., 'Blindness and Limits: Sophokles and the Logic of Myth', *The Journal of Hellenic Studies*, vol. C, 1980, pp. 22–37.

Carrette, Jeremy R. (ed.), *Religion and Culture by Michel Foucault* (Manchester: Manchester University, 1999).

Carroll, John, *Puritan, Paranoid, Remissive: A Sociology of Modern Culture* (London: Routledge & Kegan Paul, 1977).

Cassian, John, *The Monastic Institutes*, trans. Jerome Bertram (London: The Saint Austin Press, 1999).

——, *The Institutes*, trans. Boniface Ramsey (New York: The Newman Press, 2000).

Catechism of the Catholic Church (London: Geoffrey Chapman, 1994).

Caumeil, Hélène, 'Small Children's Prayer: Interrogation of Adults; The Experience of a Prayer-School', in Casiano Floristán and Christian Duquoc (eds), *Learning to Pray* (Edinburgh: T. & T. Clark, 1982), pp. 49–54.

Chaney, David, '"Ways of Seeing" Reconsidered: Representation and Construction in Mass Culture', *History of the Human Sciences*, vol. 9, no. 2, 1996, pp. 39–51.

226   *Bibliography*

——, 'Contemporary Socioscapes', *Theory, Culture & Society*, vol. 16, no. 6, 2000, pp. 111–24.

Chaplin, Elizabeth, *Sociology and Visual Representation* (London: Routledge, 1994).

Chayko, Mary, 'What is Real in the Age of Virtual Reality? "Reframing" Frame Analysis for a Technological World', *Symbolic Interaction*, vol. 16, no. 2, 1993, pp. 171–81.

Cherry, Conrad, Betty A. DeBerg and Amanda Porterfield, *Religion on Campus* (Chapel Hill, North Carolina: The University of North Carolina Press, 2001).

Cipriani, Roberto, *Sociology of Religion: An Historical Introduction* (New York: Aldine de Gruyter, 2000).

Clairvaux, Bernard of, Treatise 'On the steps of Humility and Pride', in *Bernard of Clairvaux. Selected Works*, trans. G.R. Evans (New York: Paulist Press, 1987), pp. 99–143.

Clanton, Gordon, 'Sociology as a Vocation in the California State University', *California Sociologist*, vol. 16, nos 1–2, 1993, pp. 31–51.

Coates, G., 'Disembodied Cyber Co-presence: The Art of Being There While Somewhere Else', in Nick Watson and Sarah Cunningham-Burley (eds), *Reframing the Body* (Basingstoke: Palgrave, 2001), pp. 209–27.

Codd, John, 'Making Distinctions: The Eye of the Beholder', in Richard Harker, Cheleen Mahar and Chris Wilkes (eds), *An Introduction to the Work of Pierre Bourdieu: The Practice of Theory* (Basingstoke: Macmillan, 1990), pp. 132–59.

Coffey, Amanda, *The Ethnographic Self: Fieldwork and the Representation of Identity* (London: Sage, 1999).

Comte, Auguste, *The Catechism of Positive Religion*, trans. Richard Congreve, third edition (London: Kegan Paul, Trench, Trübner, 1891).

Cook, Pam and Mieke Bernink (eds), *The Cinema Book*, second edition (London: British Film Institute, 1999).

Cooper, Simon, 'Plenitude and Alienation: The Subject of Virtual Reality', in David Holmes (ed.), *Virtual Politics: Identity and Community in Cyberspace* (London: Sage, 1997), pp. 93–106.

Craib, Ian, 'Fear, Death and Sociology', *Mortality*, vol. 8, no. 3, August 2003, pp. 285–95.

Cranford, Michael, 'The Social Trajectory of Virtual Reality: Substantive Ethics in a World without Constraints', *Technology in Society*, vol. 18, no. 1, 1996, pp. 79–92.

Crawshaw, Carol and John Urry, 'Tourism and the Photographic Eye', in Chris Rojek and John Urry (eds), *Touring Cultures: Transformations of Travel and Theory* (London: Routledge, 1997), pp. 176–95.

D'Agostino, Fred, 'The Sacralization of Social Scientific Discourse', *Philosophy of Social Science*, vol. 18, 1988, pp. 21–39.

——, 'The Necessity of Theology and the Scientific Study of Religious Beliefs', *Sophia*, vol. 32, no. 1, 1993, pp. 12–30.

Dagenais, John, 'A Medieval Pilgrimage to Santiago de Compostela on the Information Highway', in Maryjane Dunn and Linda Kay Davidson (eds), *The Pilgrimage to Compostela in the Middle Ages* (New York: Routledge, 2000), pp. 143–51.

Daly, M. Catherine, 'The *Paarda* Expression of *Hejaaab* Among Afghan Women in a Non-Muslim Community', in Linda B. Arthur (ed.), *Religion, Dress and the Body* (Oxford: Berg, 1999), pp. 147–61.

Davey, Nicholas, 'The Hermeneutics of Seeing', in Ian Heywood and Barry Sandywell (eds), *Interpreting Visual Culture: Explorations in the Hermeneutics of the Visual* (London: Routledge, 1999), pp. 3–29.

Davie, Grace, *Religion in Modern Europe: A Memory Mutates* (Oxford: Oxford University Press, 2000).

——, 'Seeing Salvation: The Use of Text as Data in the Sociology of Religion', in Paul Avis (ed.), *Public Faith? The State of Religious Belief and Practice in Britain* (London: SPCK, 2003), pp. 28–44.

Davies, Charlotte Aull, *Reflexive Ethnography: A Guide to Researching Selves and Others* (London: Routledge, 1999).

Davis, John, 'Catholic Envy: The Visual Culture of Protestant Desire', in David Morgan and Sally M. Promey (eds), *The Visual Culture of American Religions* (Berkeley: University of California Press, 2001), pp. 105–28.

Davis, Murray S., 'Georg Simmel and Erving Goffman: Legitimators of the Sociological Investigation of Human Experience', *Qualitative Sociology*, vol. 20, no. 3, 1997, pp. 369–88.

Dawson, Lorne L., 'Researching Religion in Cyberspace: Issues and Strategies', in Jeffrey K. Hadden and Douglas E. Cowan (eds), *Religion on the Internet: Research Prospects and Promises* (New York: Elsevier Science, 2000), pp. 25–54.

Dawson, Lorne L. and Jenna Hennebry, 'New Religions and the Internet: Recruiting in a New Public Space', *Journal of Contemporary Religion*, vol. 14, no. 1, 1999, pp. 17–39.

Dean, Jodi, 'Virtually Citizens', *Constellations*, vol. 4, no. 2, 1997, pp. 264–82.

Debord, Guy, *The Society of the Spectacle*, trans. Donald Nicholson-Smith (New York: Zone Books, 1995).

de Caussade, Jean-Pierre, *The Sacrament of the Present Moment*, trans. Kitty Muggeridge (London: Fount, 1996).

Denzin, Norman K., *The Cinematic Society: The Voyeur's Gaze* (London: Sage, 1995).

Dianich, Severiono and Arnaldo Nesti, dialoghi/documenti, *Religion e Societa*, vol. 8, no. 2, May–August 1993, pp. 48–57.

Dibie, Pascal, *La Tribu Sacrée: Ethnologie des prêtres* (Paris: Bernard Grasset, 1993).

Directives on Formation of Religious Institutes (London: Catholic Truth Society, 1990).

Dostoyevsky, Fyodor, *The Idiot*, trans. David Magarschack (London: Penguin, 1955).

Duffy, Eamon, *The Stripping of the Altars: Traditional Religion in England 1400–1580* (London: Yale University Press, 1992).

——, *The Voices of Morebath: Reformation & Rebellion in an English Village* (New Haven: Yale University Press, 2001).

Duncan, Carol, *Civilizing rituals: Inside Public Art Museums* (London: Routledge, 1995).

Duncan, Ian, 'Bourdieu on Bourdieu: Learning the Lesson of the *Leçon*', in Richard Harker, Cheleen Mahar and Chris Wilkes (eds), *An Introduction to the Work of Pierre Bourdieu: The Practice of Theory* (Basingstoke: Macmillan, 1990), pp. 180–94.

Durkheim, Emile, *The Elementary Forms of Religious Life*, trans. Joseph Ward Swain (London: George Allen & Unwin, 1915).

Eade, John and Michael J. Sallnow (eds), *Contesting the Sacred: The Anthropology of Christian Pilgrimage* (London: Routledge, 1991).

Eagleton, Terry, *The Idea of Culture* (Oxford: Blackwell, 2000).

Ebaugh, Helen Rose Fuchs, *Becoming an Ex: The Process of Role Exit* (Chicago: The University of Chicago Press, 1988).

Echlin, Helen, on Mike May's return to sight, *The Sunday Telegraph*, 22 September 2002.

Eco, Umberto, *Art and Beauty in the Middle Ages*, trans. Hugh Bredin (New Haven: Yale University Press, 1986).

Edney, Mark, 'The Time of the Saints Always Comes', *New Blackfriars*, vol. 79, no. 933, November 1998, pp. 483–92.

Edwards, Jonathan, *Treatise on Grace* (Cambridge: James Clarke, 1971).

Ekstrand, Thomas, *Max Weber in a Theological Perspective* (Leuven: Peeters, 2000).

El Guindi, Fadwa, *Veil: Modesty, Privacy and Resistance* (Oxford: Berg, 1999).

Endo, Shusaku, *Silence*, trans. William Johnston (London: Quartet Books, 1978).

Ericksen, Julia A., *Kiss and Tell: Surveying Sex in the Twentieth Century* (Cambridge, Mass.: Harvard University Press, 1999).

Erickson, Victoria Lee, 'Georg Simmel: American Sociology Chooses the Stone the Builders Refused', in Richard Fenn (ed.), *The Blackwell Companion to Sociology of Religion* (Oxford: Blackwell, 2001), pp. 105–19.

Evans, G.R., entry on evil in Allan D. Fitzgerald (ed.), *Augustine Through the Ages: An Encyclopaedia* (Grand Rapids, Michigan: William B. Eerdmans, 1999), pp. 340–4.

Evening Standard, 18 June 1998.

Farley, Edward, *Faith and Beauty: A Theological Aesthetic* (Aldershot: Ashgate, 2001).

Featherstone, Mike, Mike Hepworth and Bryan S. Turner (eds), *The Body: Social Process and Cultural Theory* (London: Sage, 1991).

Fenn, Richard K., *Beyond Idols: The Shape of a Secular Society* (Oxford: University Press, 2001).

Figgis, John Neville, *The Political Aspects of S. Augustine's 'City of God'* (Gloucester, Mass: Peter Smith, 1963).

Finke, Roger and Kevin D. Dougherty, 'The Effects of Professional Training: The Social and Religious Capital Acquired in Seminaries', *Journal for the Scientific Study of Religion*, vol. 41, no. 1, 2002, pp. 103–20.

Flanagan, Kieran, 'J.-K. Huysmans: The First Postmodernist Saint?' *New Blackfriars*, vol. 71, no. 813, May 1990, pp. 217–29.

——, *Sociology and Liturgy: Re-presentations of Sociology* (Basingstoke: Macmillan, 1991).

——, *The Enchantment of Sociology: A Study of Theology and Culture* (Basingstoke: Macmillan, 1996).

——, 'Sociology and Religious Difference: Limits of Understanding Anti-Catholicism in Northern Ireland', *Studies*, vol. 89, no. 355, Autumn 2000, pp. 234–42.

——, 'Reflexivity, Ethics and the Teaching of the Sociology of Religion', *Sociology*, vol. 35, no. 1, February 2001, pp. 1–19.

——, 'Religion and Modern Personal Identity', in Anton van Harskamp and Albert W. Musschenga (eds), *The Many Faces of Individualism* (Leuven: Peeters, 2001), pp. 239–66.

——, 'The Return of Theology: Sociology's Distant Relative', in Richard K. Fenn (ed.), *The Blackwell Companion to Sociology of Religion* (Oxford: Blackwell, 2001), pp. 432–44.

——, 'Vice and Virtue or Vice Versa: A Sociology of Being Good', in Kieran Flanagan and Peter C. Jupp (eds), *Virtue Ethics and Sociology: Issues of Modernity and Religion* (Basingstoke: Palgrave, 2001), pp. 104–24.

Flory, Richard W. and Donald E. Miller (eds), *GenX Religion* (New York: Routledge, 2000).

Fontaine, J.S. La, *Speak of the Devil: Tales of Satanic Abuse in Contemporary England* (Cambridge: Cambridge University Press, 1998).

Ford, David F., *Self and Salvation: Being Transformed* (Cambridge: Cambridge University Press, 1999).

Foster, Hal (ed.), *Vision and Visuality* (Seattle: Bay Press, 1986).

Foucault, Michel, *Discipline and Punish: The Birth of the Prison*, trans. Alan Sheridan (London: Penguin, 1977).

——, *Power/Knowledge: Selected Interviews and Other Writings 1972–1977*, ed. Colin Gordon (Brighton: The Harvester Press, 1980).

——, *The Birth of the Clinic*, trans. A.M. Sheridan (London: Routledge, 1989).

Fowles, Jib, *Advertising and Popular Culture* (Thousand Oaks, California: Sage, 1996).

Francis, Leslie J., 'Religion and Social Capital: The Flaw in the 2001 Census in England and Wales', in Paul Avis (ed.), *Public Faith? The State of Religious Belief and Practice in Britain* (London: SPCK, 2003), pp. 45–64.

Frank, Georgia, *The Memory of the Eyes: Pilgrims to Living Saints in Christian Antiquity* (Berkeley: University of California Press, 2000).

Freedberg, David, *The Power of Images: Studies in the History and Theory of Response* (Chicago: University of Chicago Press, 1991).

Friederike Müller, Anne, 'Sociology as a Combat Sport', *Anthropology Today*, vol. 18, no. 2, April 2002, pp. 5–9.

Frisby, David, *George Simmel* (London: Tavistock, 1984).

Frisby, David and Mike Featherstone (eds), *Simmel on Culture* (London: Sage, 1997).

Garrison, Vivian and Conrad M. Arensberg, 'The Evil Eye: Envy or Risk of Seizure? Paranoia or Patronal Dependency?' in Clarence Maloney (ed.), *The Evil Eye* (New York: Columbia University Press, 1976), pp. 286–328.

Gauchet, Marcel, *The Disenchantment of the World: A Political History of Religion*, trans. Oscar Burge (Princeton: Princeton University Press, 1997).

Geertz, Clifford, 'Art as a Cultural System', *Modern Language Notes*, vol. 91, 1976, pp. 1473–99.

——, *Works and Lives: The Anthropologist as Author* (Cambridge: Polity Press, 1989).

Giddens, Anthony, *Modernity and Self-Identity: Self and Society in the Late Modern Age* (Cambridge: Polity Press, 1991).

——, *The Consequences of Modernity* (Cambridge: Polity Press, 1991).

——, *The Transformation of Intimacy: Sexuality, Love & Eroticism in Modern Societies* (Cambridge: Polity Press, 1993).

Goffman, Erving, *Behaviour in Public Places: Notes on the Social Organization of Gatherings* (New York: The Free Press, 1963).

——, *Asylums* (Harmondsworth: Penguin, 1968).

——, *Stigma* (Harmondsworth: Penguin, 1968).

——, *Encounters* (Harmondsworth: Penguin, 1972).

——, *Interaction Ritual* (Harmondsworth: Penguin, 1972).

Goldman, Harvey, *Max Weber and Thomas Mann: Calling and the Shaping of the Self* (Berkeley: University of California Press, 1991).

Gouldner, Alvin W., *The Coming Crisis of Western Sociology* (London: Heinemann, 1970).

Graham, Gordon, *Evil & Christian Ethics* (Cambridge: Cambridge University Press, 2001).

Grimshaw, Anna, *The Ethnographer's Eye: Ways of Seeing Modern Anthropology* (Cambridge: Cambridge University Press, 2001).

Hahn, Cynthia, '*Visio Dei*: Changes in Medieval Visuality', in Robert S. Nelson (ed.), *Visuality Before and Beyond the Renaissance* (Cambridge: Cambridge University Press, 2000), pp. 169–96.

Halbwachs, Maurice, *On Collective Memory*, trans. Lewis Coser (Chicago: The University of Chicago Press, 1992).

Hand, Seán (ed.), *The Levinas Reader* (Oxford: Blackwell, 1989).

Hardy, Simon, *The Reader, the Author, His Woman and Her Lover: Soft-Core Pornography and Heterosexual Men* (London: Cassell, 1998).

Harris, Ruth, *Lourdes: Body and Spirit in the Secular Age* (Harmondsworth: The Penguin Press, 1999).

Harrison, Carol, entry on senses and spirituality in Allan D. Fitzgerald (ed.), *Augustine Through the Ages: An Encyclopaedia* (Grand Rapids, Michigan: William B. Eerdmans, 1999), pp. 767–8.

Helland, Christopher, 'Online-Religion/Religion-Online and Virtual Communitas', in Jeffrey K. Hadden and Douglas E. Cowan (eds), *Religion on the Internet: Research Prospects and Promises* (New York: Elsevier Science, 2000), pp. 205–23.

Hennis, Wilhelm, *Max Weber: Essays in Reconstruction*, trans. Keith Tribe (London: Allen & Unwin, 1988).

Hervieu-Léger, Danièle, *Religion as a Chain of Memory*, trans. Simon Lee (Cambridge: Polity Press, 2000).

Heywood, Thomas, 'The Author in His Booke', in H.J.C. Grierson and G. Bullough (eds) *The Oxford Book of Seventeenth Century Verse* (Oxford: Clarendon Press, 1934), pp. 182–3.

Hine, Christine, *Virtual Ethnography* (London: Sage, 2000).

Holmes, David, 'Introduction', in David Holmes (ed.), *Virtual Politics: Identity and Community in Cyberspace* (London: Sage, 1997), pp. 1–25.

Holmes, Nigel, *Losing Faith in the BBC* (Carlisle: Paternoster Press, 2000).

Holstein, James A. and Jaber F. Gubrium, *The Self We Live By* (New York: Oxford University Press, 2000).

Hornsby-Smith, Michael P., 'Researching Religion: The Vocation of the Sociologist of Religion', *Social Research Methodology*, vol. 5, no. 2, 2002, pp. 133–46.

Horton, John and Susan Mendus (eds), *After MacIntyre: Critical Perspectives on the Work of Alasdair MacIntyre* (Cambridge: Polity Press, 1994).

Howe, Richard Herbert, 'Max Weber's Elective Affinities: Sociology within the Bounds of Pure Reason', *The American Journal of Sociology*, vol. 84, no. 2, 1978, pp. 366–85.

Hughes, Everett C., *The Sociological Eye: Selected Papers* (Chicago: Aldine Atherton, 1971).

Huizinga, J., *The Waning of the Middle Ages*, trans. F. Hopman (Harmondsworth: Penguin, 1955).

Hull, John M., '"Sight to the Inly Blind"? Attitudes to Blindness in the Hymnbooks', *Theology*, vol. 150, no. 827, September/October 2002, pp. 333–41.

Hunt, Lester H., *Character and Culture* (Lanham: Rowman & Littlefield, 1997).

Hunt, Stephen, *Alternative Religions: A Sociological Introduction* (Aldershot: Ashgate, 2003).

Huysmans, J.-K., *Against Nature*, trans. Robert Baldick (Harmondsworth: Penguin, 1959).

——, *La Bas* (London: Dedalus, 1986).

——, *En Route*, trans. W. Fleming (Sawtry, Cambs.: Dedalus, 1989).

——, *The Road from Decadence: Letters of J.K. Huysmans*, ed. and trans. Barbara Beaumont (London: The Athlone Press, 1989).

——, *The Cathedral*, trans. Clara Bell (Sawtry, Cams.: Dedalus, 1998).

Iannaccone, Laurence R., 'Religious Practice: A Human Capital Approach', *Journal for the Scientific Study of Religion*, vol. 29, no. 3, 1990, pp. 297–314.

IJsseling, Samuel, *Mimesis: On Appearing and Being*, trans. Hester IJsseling and Jeffrey Bloechl (Kampen, Netherlands: Kok Pharos, 1997).

Illich, Ivan, 'Guarding the Eye in the Age of Show', *RES*, vol. 28, Autumn 1995, pp. 47–61.

Introvigne, Massimo, '"So Many Evil Things": Anti-Cult Terrorism via the Internet', in Jeffrey K. Hadden and Douglas E. Cowan (eds), *Religion on the Internet: Research Prospects and Promises* (New York: Elsevier Science, 2000), pp. 277–306.

Jackson, Jean E., '"Deja Entendu": The Liminal Qualities of Anthropological Fieldnotes', *Journal of Contemporary Ethnography*, vol. 19, no. 1, April 1990, pp. 8–43.

Jacobsen, Frode F., 'Interpretations of Sickness and Misfortune among Beja Pastoralists', *Anthropology & Medicine*, vol. 5, no. 2, 1998, pp. 145–67.

James, William, *The Varieties of Religious Experience* (London: Longmans, Green, and Co., 1920).

——, 'On a Certain Blindness in Human Beings', in *Pragmatism and Other Writings* (Harmondsworth: Penguin, 2000), pp. 267–85.

Jameson, Fredric, *Signatures of the Visible* (New York: Routledge, 1992).

Jaworski, Gary D., 'Park, Doyle and Hughes: Neglected Antecedents of Goffman's Theory of Ceremony', *Sociological Inquiry*, vol. 66, no. 2, May 1996, pp. 160–74.

Jay, Martin, 'In the Empire of the Gaze: Foucault and the Denigration of Vision in Twentieth-century French Thought', in David Hoy (ed.), *Foucault: A Critical Reader* (Oxford: Basil Blackwell, 1986), pp. 175–204.

——, *Downcast Eyes: The Denigration of Vision in Twentieth-Century French Thought* (Berkeley: University of California Press, 1994).

Jenkins, Phillip, *The New Anti-Catholicism: The Last Acceptable Prejudice* (New York: Oxford: University Press, 2003).

Jenkins, Richard, *Social Identity* (London: Routledge, 1996).

Jenkins, Simon, *England's Thousand Best Churches* (Harmondsworth: Penguin, 1999).

Jenkins, Timothy, *Religion in English Everyday Life: An Ethnographic Approach* (Oxford: Berghahn, 1999).

Jenks, Chris, 'The Centrality of the Eye in Western Culture: An Introduction', in Chris Jenks (ed.), *Visual Culture* (London: Routledge, 1995), pp. 1–25.

Jervis, John, *Exploring the Modern: Patterns of Western Culture and Civilization* (Oxford: Blackwell, 1998).

Jokinen, Eeva and Soile Veïjola, 'The Disoriented Tourist: The Figuration of the Tourist in Contemporary Cultural Critique', in Chris Rojek and John Urry (eds), *Touring Cultures: Transformations of Travel and Theory* (London: Routledge, 1997), pp. 23–51.

Jordan, Mark (ed.), *The Church's Confession of Faith*, trans. Stephen Wentworth Arndt (San Francisco: Ignatius Press, 1987).

Jupp, Peter C., 'Virtue Ethics and Death: The Final Arrangements', in Kieran Flanagan and Peter C. Jupp (eds), *Virtue Ethics and Sociology: Issues of Modernity and Religion* (Basingstoke: Palgrave, 2001), pp. 217–35.

Keaveny, Raymond and Peter C. Sutton, preface, in Peter C. Sutton, Lisa Vergara and Ann Jensen Adams (eds), *Love Letters: Dutch Genre Paintings in the Age of Vermeer* (Bruce Museum of Arts and Science, Greenwich, Connecticut and the National Gallery of Ireland, Dublin, 2003), pp. 8–9.

Keck, David, *Angels and Angelology in the Middle Ages* (Cambridge: Cambridge University Press, 1998).

Keenan, William J.F., 'Rediscovering the Theological in Sociology: Foundation and Possibilities', *Theory, Culture & Society*, vol. 20, no. 1, February 2003, pp. 19–42.

Kempis, Thomas, À, *The Imitation of Christ*, trans. Leo Sherley-Price (Harmondsworth: Penguin, 1952).

Kessler, Herbert L., *Spiritual Seeing: Picturing God's Invisibility in Medieval Art* (Philadelphia: University of Pennsylvania Press, 2000).

Keyworth, David, 'The Socio-Religious Beliefs and Nature of the Contemporary Vampire Subculture', *Journal of Contemporary Religion*, vol. 17, no. 3, October 2002, pp. 355–70.

Khare, R.S., 'The Seen and the Unseen: Hindu Distinctions, Experiences and Cultural Reasoning', *Contributions to Indian Sociology* (n.s.), vol. 27, no. 2, July–December 1993, pp. 191–212.

Kivisto, Peter, 'Sociology as a Vocation: A Weberian Analysis of the Origins and Subsequent Development of American Sociology', *The British Journal of Sociology*, vol. 38, no. 1, 1987, pp. 112–20.

Knight, Kelvin (ed.), *The MacIntyre Reader* (Cambridge: Polity Press, 1998).

Lane, Anthony N.S. (ed.), *The Unseen World: Christian Reflections on Angels, Demons and the Heavenly Realm* (Grand Rapids, Michigan: Paternoster Press, 1999).

Latour, Bruno, 'Visualisation and Social Reproduction: Opening one Eye While Closing the Other . . . a note on some Religious Paintings', in Gordon Fyfe and John Law (eds), *Picturing Power: Visual Depiction and Social Relations* (London: Routledge, 1988), pp. 15–38.

Leck, Ralph M., *Georg Simmel and Avant-Garde Sociology: The Birth of Modernity, 1880–1920* (New York: Humanity Books, 2000).

Lewallen, Avis, '*Lace*: Pornography for Women', in Lorraine Gamman and Margaret Marshment (eds), *The Female Gaze: Women as Viewers of Popular Culture* (London: The Women's Press, 1988), pp. 86–101.

Lough, John, *France Observed in the Seventeenth Century by British Travellers* (Stockfield: Oriel Press, 1984).

Luhmann, Niklas, *Observations on Modernity*, trans. William Whobrey (Stanford: California: Stanford University Press, 1998).

Lurie, Alison, *Imaginary Friends* (London: Vintage, 1999).

Lyman, Stanford M., *The Seven Deadly Sins: Society and Evil*, second edition (New York: General Hall Inc., 1989).

Lyon, David, *Jesus in Disneyland: Religion in Postmodern Times* (Cambridge: Polity Press, 2000).

Macey, David, *The Lives of Michel Foucault* (London: Vintage, 1994).

MacGregor, Neil, 'Introduction', in Gabriele Finaldi (ed.), *The Image of Christ* (London: National Gallery, 2000), pp. 6–7.

MacIntyre, Alasdair, *After Virtue: A Study in Moral Theory*, second edition (London: Duckworth, 1985).

——, *Three Rival Versions of Moral Enquiry* (London: Duckworth, 1990).

Maffesoli, Michel, *The Time of the Tribes: The Decline of Individualism in Mass Society*, trans. Don Smith (London: Sage, 1996).

Maines, David R., 'Narrative's Moment and Sociology's Phenomena: Toward a Narrative Sociology', *The Sociological Quarterly*, vol. 34, no. 1, 1993, pp. 17–38.

Mâle, Emile, *Religious Art from the Twelfth to the Eighteenth Century* (Princeton: Princeton University Press, 1982).

Maltby, Richard, *Hollywood Cinema* (Oxford: Blackwell, 1995).

Maniscalco, Maria Luisa, 'A New Global Risk: The Rise of the Killer Sects', *International Review of Sociology*, vol. 7, no. 3, November 1997, pp. 485–97.

Manning, Phillip, *Erving Goffman and Modern Sociology* (Cambridge: Polity Press, 1992).

Marshall, Gordon, *In Search of the Spirit of Capitalism: An Essay on Max Weber's Protestant Ethic Thesis* (London: Hutchinson, 1982).

Martin, David, 'Towards Eliminating the Concept of Secularisation', in J. Gould (ed.), *Penguin Survey of the Social Sciences* (Harmondworth: Penguin, 1965), pp. 169–82.

——, *Reflections on Sociology and Theology* (Oxford: Clarendon Press, 1997).

——, *Christian Language and its Mutations: Essays in Sociological Understanding* (Aldershot: Ashgate, 2002).

Martin, David, John Orme Mills and W.S.F. Pickering (eds), *Sociology and Theology: Alliance and Conflict* (Brighton: Harvester Press, 1980).

Martin, Richard J., 'Cultic Aspects of Sociology: A Speculative Essay', *The British Journal of Sociology*, vol. 25, no. 1, March 1974, pp. 15–31.

Martindale, Don, *The Nature and Types of Sociological Theory* (Boston: Houghton Mifflin Company, 1960).

Marx, Gary T., 'Of Methods and Manners for Aspiring Sociologists: 37 Moral Imperatives', *The American Sociologist*, vol. 28, no. 1, Spring 1997, pp. 102–25.

Mauss, Marcel, *On Prayer: Text and Commentary*, trans. Susan Leslie (Oxford: Berghahn Books, 2003).

Mayer, Jean-François, 'Religious Movements and the Internet: The New Frontier of Cult Controversies', in Jeffrey K. Hadden and Douglas E. Cowan (eds), *Religion on the Internet: Research Prospects and Promises* (New York: Elsevier Science, 2000), pp. 249–76.

McCulloch, Nigel, foreword, in Peter Brierley (ed.), *U.K. Christian Handbook. Religious Trends 4* (London: Christian Research, 2003), pp. 3–4.

McCutcheon, Russell T. (ed.), *The Insider/Outsider Problem in the Study of Religion* (London: Cassell, 1999).

McDermott, Timothy (ed.), *St. Thomas Aquinas, Summa Theologiae: A Concise Translation* (London: Methuen, 1991).

McLennan, Gregor, 'Sociology and Cultural Studies: Rhetorics of Disciplinary Identity', *History of the Human Sciences*, vol. 11, no. 3, 1998, pp. 1–17.

McMylor, Peter, *Alasdair MacIntyre: Critic of Modernity* (London: Routledge, 1994).

——, 'Classical Thinking for a Postmodern World: Alasdair MacIntyre and the Moral Critique of the Present', in Kieran Flanagan and Peter C. Jupp (eds), *Virtue Ethics and Sociology: Issues of Modernity and Religion* (Basingstoke: Palgrave, 2001), pp. 21–34.

McNamee, Maurice B., *Vested Angels: Eucharistic Allusions in Early Netherlandish Paintings* (Leuven: Peeters, 1998).

Merleau-Ponty, Maurice, *The Visible and the Invisible*, trans. Alphonso Lingis (Evanston: Northwestern University Press, 1968).

Merton, Robert K., *Sociological Ambivalence and Other Essays* (New York: The Free Press), 1976.

——, 'Some Thoughts on the Concept of Sociological Autobiography', in Matilda White Riley (ed.), *Sociological Lives* (Newbury Park, California: Sage, 1988), pp. 17–21.

Meslin, Michel, entry on the eye in Mircea Eliade (ed.), *The Encyclopaedia of Religion* (New York: Macmillan, 1987), pp. 236–9.

Michelman, Susan O., 'Changing Old Habits: Dress of Women Religious and Its Relationship to Personal and Social Identity', *Sociological Inquiry*, vol. 67, no. 3, August 1997, pp. 350–63.

Miles, Margaret R., *Seeing and Believing: Religion and Values in the Movies* (Boston: Beacon Press, 1996).

Miller, William Watts, 'Durkheimian Time', *Time & Society*, vol. 9, no. 1, 2000, pp. 5–20.

——, 'Secularism and the Sacred: Is there really something called "secular religion"?' in Thomas A. Idinopulos and Brian C. Wilson (eds), *Reappraising Durkheim for the Study and Teaching of Religion Today* (Leiden: Brill, 2002), pp. 27–44.

Mills, C. Wright, *The Sociological Imagination* (New York: Grove, 1961).

Mills, John Orme, 'Introduction: Of Two Minds', in David Martin, John Orme Mills and W.S.F. Pickering (eds), *Sociology and Theology: Alliance and Conflict* (Leiden: Brill, 2004), pp. 1–12.

Mirzoeff, Nicholas, *An Introduction to Visual Culture* (London: Routledge, 1999).

——, (ed.), *Visual Culture Reader* (London: Routledge, 1999).

Mitchell, W.J.T., 'Interdisciplinarity and Visual Culture', *Art Bulletin*, vol. 77, no. 4, December 1995, pp. 540–4.

——, 'What is Visual Culture?' in Irving Lavin (ed.), *Meaning in the Visual Arts: Views from the Outside; A Centennial Commemoration of Erwin Panofsky (1892–1968)* (Princeton: Institute for Advanced Study, 1995), pp. 206–17.

Möllering, Guido, 'The Nature of Trust: From Georg Simmel to a Theory of Expectation, Interpretation and Suspension', *Sociology*, vol. 35, no. 2, May 2001, pp. 403–20.

Moore, Suzanne, 'Here's Looking at You, Kid', in Lorraine Gamman and Margaret Marshment (eds), *The Female Gaze: Women as Viewers of Popular Culture* (London: The Women's Press, 1988), pp. 44–59.

Morgan, David, *Protestants and Pictures: Religion, Visual Culture and the Age of American Mass Production* (New York: Oxford University Press, 1999).

——, *Visual Piety: A History and Theory of Popular Religious Images* (Berkeley: The University of California Press, 1999).

Mulvey, Laura, 'Visual Pleasure and Narrative Cinema', in John Caughie and Annette Kuhn (eds), *The Sexual Subject: A Screen Reader in Sexuality* (London: Routledge, 1992), pp. 22–33.

Murdoch, Iris, 'The Sovereignty of Good over Other Concepts', in Roger Crisp and Michael Slote (eds), *Virtue Ethics* (Oxford: Oxford University Press, 1997), pp. 99–117.

Narayan, Kirin, 'Refractions of the Field at Home: American Representations of Hindu Holy Men in the 19th and 20th Centuries', *Cultural Anthropology*, vol. 8, no. 4, 1993, pp. 476–509.

Neiman, Susan, *Evil in Modern Thought: An Alternative History of Philosophy* (Princeton: Princeton University Press, 2002).

Nesti, Arnaldo, *La religione implicita. Sociologi e teologia a confronto* (Bologna: Edizioni Dehoniane, 1994).

Nichols, Aidan, *The Art of God Incarnate: Theology and Image in Christian Tradition* (London: Darton, Longman Todd, 1980).

Nietzsche, Friedrich, *The Joyful Wisdom*, trans. Thomas Common (London: George Allen & Unwin, 1910).

Nipperdey, Thomas, 'Max Weber, Protestantism and the Context of Debate around 1900', in Hartmut Lehmann and Guenther Roth (eds), *Weber's Protestant Ethic: Origins, Evidence, Contexts* (Cambridge: Cambridge University Press, 1995), pp. 73–81.

Nora, Pierre, preface, 'From *Lieux de mémoire* to Realms of Memory', in Pierre Nora (ed.), *Realms of Memory*, vol. I, Conflicts and Divisions, trans. Arthur Goldhammer (New York: Columbia University Press, 1996), pp. xv–xxiv.

——, 'The Era of Commemoration', in Pierre Nora (ed.), *Realms of Memory*, vol. III, Symbols, trans. Arthur Goldhammer (New York: Columbia University Press, 1998), pp. 609–37.

O'Connor, Flannery, *Wise Blood* (London: Faber Faber, 1980).

O'Neill, John, 'Foucault's Optics: The (in)vision of Mortality and Modernity', in Chris Jenks (ed.), *Visual Culture* (London: Routledge, 1995), pp. 190–201.

O'Neill, Onora, *A Question of Trust* (Cambridge: Cambridge University Press, 2002).

O'Toole, Roger, 'Salvation, Redemption and Community: Reflections on the Aesthetic Cosmos', *Sociology of Religion*, vol. 57, no. 2, 1996, pp. 127–48.

Oliver, Ivan, 'Current Revivals of Interest in Religion: Some Sociological Observations', *Archives des Sciences Sociales des Religions*, vol. 58, no. 2, 1984, pp. 159–74.

Orwell, George, *Nineteen Eighty-Four* (London: Penguin, 1989).

Osborne, Thomas, 'Medicine and Epistemology: Michel Foucault and the Liberality of Clinical Reason', *History of the Human Sciences*, vol. 5, no. 2, 1992, pp. 63–93.

Panichas, George A., *The Burden of Vision: Dostoyevsky's Spiritual Art* (Chicago: Gateway, 1985).

Panofsky, Erwin, *Gothic Architecture and Scholasticism* (New York: Penguin, 1976).

——, ed. and trans., *Abbot Suger on the Abbey Church of St.-Denis and its Art Treasures*, second edition (Princeton: Princeton University Press, 1979).

Pascal, Blaise, *Pensées*, trans. A.J. Krailsheimer (Harmondsworth: Penguin, 1966).

Peatling, G.K., 'Who Fears to Speak of Politics? John Kells Ingram and Hypothetical Nationalism', *Irish Historical Studies*, vol. 31, no. 122, November 1998, pp. 202–21.

Pescosolido, Bernice A., 'The Sociology of the Professions and the Profession of Sociology: Professional Responsibility, Teaching, and Graduate Training', *Teaching Sociology*, vol. 19, no. 3, July 1991, pp. 351–61.

Petit, Annie, 'Du Catholicisme au Positivisme', *Revue Internationale de Philosophie*, vol. 1, no. 203, March 1998, pp. 127–55.

Plummer, Ken, *Telling Sexual Stories: Power, Change and Social Worlds* (London: Routledge, 1995).

——, *Documents of Life 2: An Invitation to a Critical Humanism* (London: Sage, 2001).

Plutzer, Eric, 'The Protestant Ethic and the Spirit of Academia: An Essay on Graduate Education', *Teaching Sociology*, vol. 19, no. 3, 1991, pp. 302–7.

Poggi, Gianfranco, *Calvinism and the Capitalist Spirit. Max Weber's Protestant Ethic* (London: Macmillan, 1983).

Poloma, Margaret M., 'Toward a Christian Sociological Perspective: Religious Values, Theory and Methodology', *Sociological Analysis*, vol. 41, no. 2, 1982, pp. 95–108.

Pontifical Council for Social Communication, *Ethics, Internet and Communications* (London: Catholic Truth Society, 2002).

Purcell, Deidre, *Lough Derg* (Dublin: Veritas, 1988).

Raposa, Michael L., *Boredom and the Religious Imagination* (Charolottesville: University Press of Virginia, 1999).

Rappaport, Roy A., 'Concluding Comments on Ritual and Reflexivity', *Semiotica*, vol. 30, no. 1/2, 1980, pp. 181–93.

——, 'Veracity, Verity and *Verum* in Liturgy', *Studia Liturgica*, vol. 23, 1993, pp. 35–50.

——, *Ritual and Religion in the Making of Humanity* (Cambridge: Cambridge University Press, 1999).

Ratzinger, Joseph, *The Spirit of Liturgy*, trans. John Saward (San Francisco: Ignatius Press, 2000).

Reeves, Thomas C., *The Empty Church: The Suicide of Liberal Christianity* (New York: The Free Press, 1996).

Repstad, Pål, 'Between Idealism and Reductionism: Some Sociological Perspectives on Making Theology', in Pål Repstad (ed.), *Religion and Modernity: Modes of Co-existence* (Oslo: Scandinavian University Press, 1996), pp. 91–117.

——, 'Theology and Sociology – Discourses in Conflict or Reconciliation under Postmodernism?' in E. Helander (ed.), *Religion and Social Transitions* (Helsinki: Helsinki University Press, 1999), pp. 141–55.

Rheingold, Howard, *Virtual Reality* (New York: Simon & Schuster, 1992).

Ritchie, Jean, *Inside Big Brother: Getting In & Staying Out* (London: Channel 4 Books, 2002).

Robinson, Wendy Gale, 'Heaven's Gate: The End?' *JCMC*, vol. 3, no. 3, December 1997, pp. 1–47.

Rollmann, Hans, '"Meet Me in St. Louis": Troeltsch and Weber in America', in Hartmut Lehmann and Guenther Roth (eds), *Weber's Protestant Ethic: Origins, Evidence, Contexts* (Cambridge: Cambridge University Press, 1995), pp. 357–83.

Rose, Gillian, 'The Final Notebooks of Gillian Rose', *Women: A Cultural Review*, vol. 9, no. 1, Spring 1998, pp. 6–18.

Roth, Guenther, 'Weber the Would-Be-Englishman: Anglophilia and Family History', in Hartmut Lehmann and Guenther Roth (eds), *Weber's Protestant Ethic: Origins, Evidence, Contexts* (Cambridge: Cambridge University Press, 1995), pp. 83–121.

Rowan, David, 'Spies Like Us', *The Times Magazine*, 13 December 2003, pp. 45–8.

Sarup, Madan, *Identity, Culture and the Postmodern World* (Edinburgh: Edinburgh University Press, 1996).

Saward, John, *The Beauty of Holiness and the Holiness of Beauty: Art, Sanctity & The Truth of Catholicism* (San Francisco: Ignatius Press, 1997).

Schluchter, Wolfgang, 'The Battle of the Gods: From the Critique to the Sociology of Religion', *National Taiwan University Journal of Sociology*, no. 19, May 1988, pp. 165–78.

——, *Paradoxes of Modernity: Culture and Conduct in the Theory of Max Weber*, trans. Neil Solomon (Stanford: Stanford University Press, 1996).

Schroeder, Ralph, Noel Heather and Raymond M. Lee, 'The Sacred and the Virtual: Religion in Multi-User Virtual Reality', *JCMC*, vol. 4, no. 2, December 1998, pp. 1–14.

Scott, Robert A., *The Gothic Enterprise: A Guide to Understanding the Medieval Cathedral* (Berkeley: University of California Press, 2003).

Seale, Clive, 'Fear, Death and Sociology: A Response to Ian Craib', *Mortality*, vol. 8, no. 4, December 2003, pp. 388–91.

Seligman, Adam, 'Inner-worldly Individualism and the Institutionalization of Puritanism in Late Seventeenth-Century New England', *The British Journal of Sociology*, vol. 41, no. 4, December 1990, pp. 537–57.

Sennett, Richard, *The Fall of Public Man* (Cambridge: Cambridge University Press, 1977).

Sermon, 15 August 1991, reproduced in anon. *The Spirit of Place: Carthusian Reflections* (London: Darton, Longman & Todd, 1998), pp. 15–16.

Shalit, Wendy, *A Return to Modesty: Discovering the Lost Virtue* (New York: Simon & Schuster, 2000).

Sharot, Stephen, 'Traditional, Modern or Postmodern? Recent Religious Developments among Jews in Israel', in Kieran Flanagan and Peter C. Jupp (eds), *Postmodernity, Sociology and Religion* (Basingstoke: Macmillan, 1996), pp. 118–33.

Shields, Rob, *The Virtual* (London: Routledge, 2003).

Shilling, Chris and Phillip A. Mellor, *The Sociological Ambition* (London: Sage, 2001).

Shuld, Joyce, *Foucault and Augustine: Reconsidering Power and Love* (South Bend, Indiana: University of Notre Dame Press, 2003).

Siebers, Tobin, *The Mirror of Medusa* (Berkeley: University of California Press, 1983).

Silber, Ilana Friedrich, 'Monasticism and the "Protestant Ethic": Asceticism, Rationality and Wealth in the Medieval West', *The British Journal of Sociology*, vol. 44, no. 1, March 1993, pp. 103–23.

——, *Virtuosity, Charisma and Social Order: A Comparative Sociological Study of Monasticism in Theravada Buddhism and Medieval Catholicism* (Cambridge: Cambridge University Press, 1995).

Simmel, Georg, *The Sociology of Georg Simmel*, ed. and trans. Kurt H. Wolff (New York: The Free Press, 1964).

——, *Sociologie*, in Robert E. Park and Ernest W. Burgess (eds), *Introduction to the Science of Sociology*, third edition revised (Chicago: The University of Chicago Press, 1969), pp. 356–61.

——, *Essays on Religion*, ed. and trans. Horst Jürgen Helle with Ludwig Nieder (New Haven: Yale University Press, 1997).

Slater, Don, 'Photography and Modern Vision: The Spectacle of "Natural Magic"', in Chris Jenks (ed.), *Visual Culture* (London: Routledge, 1995), pp. 218–37.

Smith, Dennis, *Zygmunt Bauman: Prophet of Postmodernity* (Cambridge: Polity Press, 1999).

Smith, Sidonie and Julia Watson (eds), *Getting a Life. Everyday Uses of Autobiography* (Minneapolis: University of Minnesota Press, 1996).

Solomon, Robert C., *Wicked Pleasures: Meditations on the Seven "Deadly" Sins* (Lanham: Rowman & Littlefield, 1999).

Sontag, Susan, *On Photography* (London: Penguin, 1977).

Spacks, Patricia Meyer, *Boredom: The Literary History of a State of Mind* (Chicago: The University of Chicago Press, 1996).

Stacey, Jackie, *Star Gazing: Hollywood Cinema and Female Spectatorship* (London: Routledge, 1994).

Stark, Rodney, 'Secularization, R.I.P.', in William H. Swatos, Jr and Daniel V.A. Olson (eds), *The Secularization Debate* (Lanham: Rowman & Littlefield Publisher, Inc., 2000), pp. 41–66.

Stark, Rodney and Roger Finke, 'Catholic Religious Vocations: Decline and Revival', *Review of Religious Research*, vol. 42, no. 2, December 2000, pp. 125–45.

——, *Acts of Faith: Explaining the Human Side of Religion* (Berkeley; University of California, 2000).

St Augustine, 'On Faith in Things Unseen', trans. Roy Joseph Deferrari and Mary Francis McDonald, in *The Fathers of the Church*, vol. 4 (Washington D.C.: The Catholic University of America Press, 1947), pp. 451–69.

——, *Concerning the City of God against the Pagans*, trans. Henry Bettenson (Harmondsworth: Penguin, 1972).

——, *The Confessions*, trans. Maria Boulding (London: Hodder & Stoughton, 1996).

Stedman Jones, Susan, *Durkheim Reconsidered* (Cambridge: Polity Press, 2001).

Stewart, Columba, *Cassian the Monk* (Oxford: Oxford University Press, 1998).

Sturken, Marita and Lisa Cartwright, *Practices of Looking: An Introduction to Visual Culture* (Oxford: Oxford University Press, 2001).

Suaud, Charles, *La Vocation: Conversion et reconversoin des prêtres ruraux* (Paris: Les Éditions de Minuit, 1978).

Sutter, Jacques, 'Vocations Sacerdotales et Séminaries: Le Déspérissement du Modèle Clérical', *Archives des Sciences Sociales des Religions*, vol. 59, no. 2, 1985, pp. 177–96.

Sutton, Peter C., 'Love Letters: Dutch Genre Paintings in the Age of Vermeer', in Peter C. Sutton, Lisa Vergara and Ann Jensen Adams (eds), *Love Letters: Dutch Genre Paintings in the Age of Vermeer* (Bruce Museum of Arts and Science, Greenwich, Connecticut and the National Gallery of Ireland, Dublin, 2003), pp. 14–49.

Swartz, David, 'Bridging the Study of Culture and Religion: Pierre Bourdieu's Political Economy of Symbolic Power', *Sociology of Religion*, vol. 57, no. 1, 1996, pp. 71–85.

Swatos, William H., 'The Comparative Method and the Special Vocation of the Sociology of Religion', *Sociological Analysis*, vol. 38, no. 2, 1977, pp. 106–14.

Swatos, William H, Jr and Peter Kivisto, 'Weber as "Christian Sociologist"', *Journal of the Scientific Study of Religion*, vol. 30, no. 4, December 1991, pp. 347–62.

Synnott, Anthony, 'Truth and Goodness, Mirrors and Masks: A Sociology of Beauty and the Face', Part 1, *The British Journal of Sociology*, vol. 40, no. 4, 1989, pp. 607–36.

——, 'Truth and Goodness, Mirrors and Masks: A Sociology of Beauty and the Face', Part 2, *The British Journal of Sociology*, vol. 41, no. 1, 1990, pp. 55–76.

——, 'The Eye and I: A Sociology of Sight', *International Journal of Politics, Culture and Society*, vol. 5, no. 4, 1992, pp. 617–36.

Sztompka, Piotr, *Trust: A Sociological Theory* (Cambridge: Cambridge University Press, 1999).

Taylor, Brian C., *Spirituality for Everyday Living: An Adaptation of the Rule of St. Benedict* (Collegeville, Minnesota: The Liturgical Press, 1989).

Tester, Keith, *Media, Culture and Morality* (London: Routledge, 1994).

——, *Moral Culture* (London: Sage, 1997).

——, '"Bored and blasé" Television, the Emotions and Georg Simmel', in Gillian Bendelow and Simon J. Williams (eds), *Emotions in Social Life: Critical Themes and Contemporary Issues* (London: Routledge, 1998), pp. 83–96.

——, 'Weber's Alleged Emotivism', *The British Journal of Sociology*, vol. 50, no. 4, December 1999, pp. 563–73.

——, 'Between Sociology and Theology: The Spirit of Capitalism Debate', *The Sociological Review*, vol. 48, no. 1, February 2000, pp. 43–57.

——, 'Disenchantment and Virtue: An Essay on Max Weber', in Kieran Flanagan and Peter C. Jupp (eds), *Virtue Ethics and Sociology: Issues of Modernity and Religion* (Basingstoke: Palgrave, 2001), pp. 35–50.

——, *Compassion, Morality and the Media* (Buckingham: Open University Press, 2001).

The Observer, 9 February 2003.

The Times, 5 June 1998.

The Times, 28 August 2001.

The Times, 10 January 2003.

The Times, 18 January 2003.

The Times, 22 December 2003.

Thomas, J.J.R., 'Ideology and Elective Affinity', *Sociology*, vol. 19, no. 1, February 1985, pp. 39–54.

Thomas, William I., 'The Definition of the Situation', in Jerome G. Manis and Bernard N. Meltzer (eds), *Symbolic Interaction: A Reader in Social Pyschology* (Boston: Allyn and Bacon, 1967), pp. 315–21.

Tiffin, John and Nobuyoshi Terashima (eds), *Hypereality: Paradigm for the Third Millennium* (London: Routledge, 2001).

Tillich, Paul, *Theology of Culture* (Oxford: Oxford University Press, 1959).

Toby, Jackson, 'Medicalizing Temptation', *The Public Interest*, no. 130, Winter 1998, pp. 64–78.

Turner, Victor (ed.), *Celebration: Studies in Festivity and Ritual* (Washington: Smithsonian Institution Press, 1982).

——, *From Ritual to Theatre: The Human Seriousness of Play* (New York: Performing Arts Journal Publications, 1982).

Turner, Victor and Edith Turner, *Image and Pilgrimage in Christian Culture* (New York: Columbia University Press, 1978).

Urry, John, *The Tourist Gaze* (London: Sage, 1990).

Vattimo, Gianni, 'The Trace of the Trace', in Jacques Derrida and Gianni Vattimo (eds), *Religion*, trans. Samuel Weber (Cambridge: Polity Press, 1998), pp. 79–94.

Vauchez, André, 'The Cathedral', in Pierre Nora (ed.), *Realms of Memory*, vol. II, Traditions, trans. Arthur Goldhammer (New York: Columbia University Press, 1997), pp. 37–68.

Vernon, Mark, ' "I Am Not What I Am" – Foucault, Christian Asceticism and a "way Out" of sexuality', in Jeremy R. Carrette (ed.), *Religion and culture by Michel Foucault* (Manchester: Manchester University Press, 1999), pp. 199–209.

Vessey, Mark, entry on the relationships between St. Augustine and St. Jerome, in Allan D. Fitzgerald (ed.), *Augustine Through the Ages: An Encyclopaedia* (Grand Rapids, Michigan: William B. Eerdmans, 1999), pp. 460–2.

Vidich, Arthur and Stanford Lyman, *American Sociology: Worldly Rejections of Religion and Their Directions* (New Haven: Yale University Press, 1985).

Voas, David, 'Is Britain a Christian Country?' in Paul Avis (ed.), *Public Faith? The State of Religious Belief and Practice in Britain* (London: SPCK, 2003), pp. 92–105.

Vogelaar, Christiaan, *Netherlandish Fifteenth and Sixteenth Century Paintings in the National Gallery of Ireland: A Complete Catalogue* (Dublin: The National Gallery of Ireland, 1987).

Wacquant, Loïc J.D., 'Exiting Roles or Exiting Role Theory? Critical Notes on Ebaugh's *Becoming an Ex*', *Acta Sociologica*, 1990, vol. 33, no. 4, pp. 397–404.

Waksler, Frances Chaput, 'Erving Goffman's Sociology: An Introductory Essay', *Human Studies*, vol. 12, nos 1–2, June 1989, pp. 1–18.

Walker, John A. and Sarah Chaplain, *Visual culture: An Introduction* (Manchester: Manchester University Press, 1997).

Webb, Diana, *Pilgrimage in Medieval England* (London: Hambledon and London, 2000).

Weber, Max, *The Protestant Ethic and the Spirit of Capitalism*, trans. Talcott Parsons (London: Unwin, 1930).

——, 'Science as a Vocation', in H.H. Gerth and C. Wright Mills (eds), *From Max Weber: Essays in Sociology* (New York: Oxford University Press, 1958), pp. 129–56.

——, *The Sociology of Religion*, trans. Ephraim Fischoff (London: Methuen, 1965).

——, *Economy and Society*, trans. Guenther Roth and Claus Wittich, vol. 1 (Berkeley: University of California Press, 1978).

Wernick, Andrew, *Auguste Comte and the Religion of Humanity: The Post-Theistic Program of French Social Theory* (Cambridge: Cambridge University Press, 2001).

Whitehouse, J.C., *The Vertical Man* (London: The St Austin Press, 1999).

Wilde, Oscar, *De Profundis* in *The Works of Oscar Wilde* (London: Galley Press, 1987), pp. 853–88.

Wilken, Robert L., 'Augustine's City of God Today', in Carl E. Braaten and Robert W. Jenson (eds), *The Two Cities of God: The Church's Responsibility for the Earthly City* (Grand Rapids, Michigan: William B. Eerdmans, 1997), pp. 28–41.

Williamson, Beth, 'Liturgical Image or Devotional Image? The London *Madonna of the Firescreen*', in Colum Hourihane (ed.), *Objects, Images and the Word: Art in the Service of the Liturgy* (Princeton: Princeton University Press, 2003), pp. 298–318.

Wilson, Michele, 'Community in the Abstract: A Political and Ethical Dilemma?' in David Holmes (ed.), *Virtual Politics: Identity & Community in Cyberspace* (London: Sage, 1997), pp. 145–62.

Winch, Peter, *The Idea of a Social Science and its Relation to Philosophy* (London: Routledge & Kegan Paul, 1963).

Winden, Julia Fey, 'Spirituality Bites: Xers and the Gothic Cult/ure', in Richard W. Flory and Donald E. Miller (eds), *GenX Religion* (New York: Routledge, 2000), pp. 31–53.

Wolfe, Alan, 'Sociology as a Vocation', *The American Sociologist*, vol. 21, no. 2, 1990, pp. 136–49.

Woodforde, John, *The History of Vanity* (Stroud: Alan Sutton, 1992).

Woodiwiss, Anthony, *The Visual in Social Theory* (London: The Athlone Press, 2001).

Wright, Alex, *Why Bother with Theology?* (London: Darton, Longman & Todd, 2002).

Wright, Kevin J., *Europe's Monastery and Convent Guesthouses* (Missouri: Liguori, 2000).

Wuthnow, Robert, *Producing the Sacred: An Essay on Public Religion* (Chicago: University of Illinois Press, 1994).

——, *Christianity and Civil Society: The Contemporary Debate* (Valley Forge, Penn.: Trinity Press, 1996).

www.arras.com/br/igrposit/foto2html.

www.clarissen.eindhoven@inter.nl.net.

www.cnn.com/US/9803/25/heavens.gate/.

Yair, Gad *et al.*, '*Ex Cathedra*: The Representation of American Society in ASA Presidential Addresses, 1906–98', *Sociology*, vol. 35, no. 2, May 2001, pp. 477–500.

Index

acedia
  and Aquinas, 116
  and boredom, 117, 119
  as eye of disregard, 119
  and Lyman, 119
  and sloth, 119, 210–11n51,
    211n72
  and sociology, 157
  and virtual religion, 116
  virtue and vice, 116
  and Wilde, 115
Aitkenhead, Decca
  on pornography, 121–2
allegory, 87–8
Alt, John
  sport as virtuous, 55
Alypius
  and gladiators, 103–4
  and the voyeur, 124
angels
  and art, 183
  and choirboys, 154
  and Latour, 184
  and St Stephen, 187
Anscombe, Elisabeth
  and goodness, 53
Anselm, St
  on experience and belief, 185–6
Aquinas, St Thomas
  on acedia, 116
'as if'
  and Bentham's Panopticon, 67
  at the end, 192
  and *illusio*, 138
  and Latour, 184
  and liminoid virtualities, 183
  and memory, 131–2
  and the painter, 134
  and paintings, 184
  and the prudent, 71
  and reflexivity, 144–5
  and religious capital, 137–8
  and ritual orders, 182–3
  and sociology, 77, 144–5

  and trust, 63
  and the virtual, 77
  and virtual reality, 89
  Waksler on Goffman, 36
Augustine, St
  on Alypius, 103–4
  Besançon's appraisal, 10
  in a door, 192–3
  on evil, 179
  on the eye, 104, 189, 222n125
  faith in the unseen, 159
  seeing St Jerome, 192–3
  on seeing the unseen, 118, 140,
    159, 179
  on Varro's productivity, 199n52
  on Varro's theological distinctions, 38
  see also The City of God

Balthasar, Hans Urs von
  on Bernanos, 110, 117, 179
  on the cathedral, 22
  on recognition of evil, 179
  on restoration of religious sight, 10
  on seeing the unseen, 117
  on theological aesthetics, 184
Barasch, Moshe
  secularisation of blindness, 144
  social forms of blindness, 143–4
Barnard, Malcolm
  on forms of visual culture, 109
Barthes, Roland
  on the photograph, 83
Baudelaire, Charles
  on the bored, 114
  and evil, 120
  and the *flâneur*'s gaze, 83
  and modernity, 12
Bauman, Zygmunt
  and ambiguity, 46
  and biography, 43–4, 47–8
  and blindness, 142–3
  and cathedrals, 51–2
  and *The City of God*, 50
  and the death of God, 47–50

Bauman, Zygmunt – *continued*
    and ethics, 46, 48, 63
    and evil, 177–9
    on the exemplary actor of
        modernity, 12
    and the Holocaust, 48,
        161, 177–9
    and John Paul II, 48
    and Judaism, 47–8
    and liquid modernity, 4, 10, 45, 51,
        66, 89
    on love, 51
    and MacIntyre, 43–4, 201n2
    and a Pauline metaphor, 33–4
    on pilgrims and tourists, 51, 147
    postmodernity and ethics, 46, 48, 63
    on the *Protestant Ethic*, 51, 167
    and Protestantism, 50–1
    and religion, 47–8
    his sociological journey, 4
    and trust, 63
    and Weber, 48, 50–1, 167, 178
Baxandall, Michael
    and the period eye, 133–4
Beaudoin, Tom
    Generation X and spirituality, 10, 28
    and virtual religion, 28
Bellah, Robert
    civil religion and Christianity, 37
    criticisms of civil religion, 200n78
Benjamin, Walter
    on reception and appreciation, 82
    significance in visual culture, 81–2
Berger, John
    on images, 81
Bergeron, Katherine
    (second form) virtual liturgies, 27–8
Bernanos, Georges
    and von Balthasar, 110, 117
    The Pascal Candle, 116–17
Besançon, Alain
    icon as a visual text, 157
    prototypes and icons, 156–7
    on the significance of
        St Augustine, 10
Bewes, Timothy
    cynicism, 114–15
Big Brother
    Orwell's vision, 69–70
    television series, 70–1

blaséness
    Baudelaire and Simmel, 114
    and cynicism, 114–15
blindness
    and Barasch, 143–4
    and Bauman, 142–3
    and boredom, 119
    and Buxton, 143
    and Christ, 139–40
    as a form of power, 143
    four forms, 143–4
    and healing, 139–42
    the inly blind, 111–12
    and seeing, 140–1
    and seeing the unseen, 139–41,143–5
    and Simmel, 141
    and tales, 61
    and temptation, 112
    and Weber, 166
    in *Wise Blood*, 140–1, 143
Bok, Sissela
    lies and trust, 62
boredom
    and acedia, 117, 119
    as ambiguous, 117
    and Baudelaire, 114
    and Des Esseintes, 115
    as epistemic blindness, 119
    and evil, 120, 161
    as failure of agency, 117
    as liminal, 118–19
    and Pascal, 115
    and ritual, 182
    as social disconnection, 119
    and Spacks, 117
    and temptation, 113
Bourdieu, Pierre
    'as if' and *illusio*, 138
    Catholic borrowings, 30–2, 56
    and cultural capital, 135–8
    and the eye, 111, 210n31
    and the 'fresh eye', 151
    on photography, 86–7
    and reflexivity, 56, 60
    and religious capital, 135–8
    reputation, 199n61
    and symbolic capital, 135–6
Brasher, Brenda
    Internet and memory, 96–7
    religion and the Internet, 92, 208n91

Bunyan, John
vanity fair, 145
Buxton, Richard
blindness and prophecy, 143

candles
The Pascal Candle, 116–17
the Pascal Candle, 158–9
cannibalism
and the Internet, 102–3
Carroll, John
on the *Protestant Ethic*, 162, 166
Cassian, St John
and Foucault, 32–3
and purity of heart, 211n68
cathedrals
von Balthasar, 22
and Bauman, 51–2
doors, 22
Episcopalian Cathedral, Washington, 200n80
and Huysmans, 197n19
and Maffesoli, 33
and sociology, 22, 197n17
as testimony of the unseen, 150
and Vauchez, 21–2
see also Ely cathedral
Catholicism
and Bourdieu, 30–2, 56
and Comte, 30–1
and Durkheim, 168
and Eagleton, 163
and English memory, 20–1
and English society, 2
and grace, 164
and the Internet, 95, 97–8, 208n91
and Irish Positivists, 31
and Protestant envy, 167
and Protestantism, 162–8
and the *Protestant Ethic*, 163–8
as real religion, 18, 27
and Simmel, 169
and sociological borrowings, 18, 27, 30–2, 163–4
Vatican II, 137, 169–70
and virtual communities, 98
and virtue ethics, 53
and visual piety, 162
and Weber, 166

choirboy
pointer to the unseen, 154, 183
study of vocation, 6, 195n16
Church of England
and Evangelicals, 16
memory and the Reformation, 20–1
ocular dysfunctions, 2
City of God, The
and Bauman, 50
and Comte, 26
the heavenly and the earthly cities, 10, 146–7
see also Augustine, St; Varro, Marcus
civil religion
as architectural manifestation, 38
and Protestantism, 37–8, 40
as virtual religion, 37
Wuthnow's definition, 38
Coates, G.
co-presence and cyberspace, 90–1
cyberspace and isolation, 91
colour of religion
and Durkheim, 23
as expression of the unseen, 175
and Simmel, 110, 171–2, 175
Comte, Auguste
his church of humanity, 19, 30–1
on the practice of prayer, 185, 187
and St Augustine, 26
see also positivist religion
Cooper, Simon
on virtual reality, 73–4
co-presence
and culpability, 95
and the Internet, 90–1
cultural memory
and Catholicism, 20–1
and the virtual, 16
see also Halbwachs, Maurice; Hervieu-Léger, Danièle; memory; Nora, Pierre
cultural studies
and sociology, 80
and visual culture, 80
custody of the eyes
and holiness, 142
and St Augustine, 104
and St Louis, 142

cyberspace
  and co-presence, 90–1
  and Dawson, 98
  and the face, 91
  and isolation, 93
  and memory, 96–7
  and pornography, 121–2
  the seen and the unseen, 72
  and the virtual, 75–6, 135
  see also Internet

Davey, Nicholas
  on the hermeneutics
    of seeing, 111
Davie, Grace
  and *Seeing Salvation*, 191
  and vicarious religion, 39, 201n93
Davis, Murray S.
  Goffman and Simmel
    compared, 12
Dawson, Lorne L.
  religion in cyberspace, 98
death
  and the sociologist, 192
death of God
  and Bauman, 47–50
  and Foucault, 68
  as a sociological inconvenience, 27, 31
'death of man'
  and god, 69, 205n107
Debord, Guy
  on spectacle, 110
Denzin, Norman
  and the cinematic gaze, 123–4
disembodiment
  and embodiment, 128–9
  and viewing, 104–5
  and the voyeur, 104, 124–5
doors
  and cathedrals, 22
  and Huysmans, 23
  and icons, 157
  and St Augustine, 192–3
  and Simmel, 22
  and the social, 145
dream of Daniel, 24
Duffy, Eamon
  Morebath, 21
Duncan, Carol
  rituals and the museum, 191

Durkheim, Emile
  and Catholicism, 168
  and the colour of religion, 23
  and faith in science and religion, 30
  on family holidays, 56
  on religion, 27, 38–9
  and time, 197n17
  and Varro, 38–9

Eagleton, Terry
  on culture, 80–1
  on the otherworldly, 163
Edomite watchman, 24, 65
Ely cathedral
  iconoclasm and ritual relief, 130–1
  seeing the unseen, 130–2
embodiment
  and disembodiment, 128–9
  and the face, 152
Enchantment of Sociology, The
  ambiguities and curiosities, 5
English society
  as post-Christian, 2, 194n2
Erickson, Victoria
  on Simmel and religion, 169
ethics
  and postmodernity, 46, 48
  and teaching sociology of religion, 60–1
evil
  and Baudelaire, 120, 161
  and Bauman, 177–9
  and boredom, 120, 161
  and fascination, 175
  and La Fontaine, 180
  forms of, 176–7
  and Foucault, 177
  and god, 161
  and God, 161, 177, 179–80
  and the Holocaust, 48, 161, 177–80
  and Huysmans, 120, 161
  and Lyman, 178–9
  and Neiman, 177, 179–80
  and popular culture, 176
  and prayer, 179
  as rumour, 180
  and St Augustine, 179
evil eye
  and the good eye, 161
  and Mark, 179
  sociological significance, 181

eye
  and acedia, 119
  and adultery, 118, 211n68
  and agency, 110–11
  and Alypius, 103–4, 124
  and Bourdieu, 111, 151,
      210n31
  and Christ, 140, 189
  as disciplinary, 107–8
  elective properties, 78
  'eyes of faith', 151, 153–4, 157
  of God and false gods, 66–7
  of God and Foucault, 69
  and healing, 121
  and Illich, 106–7
  and innocence, 148
  myth of the innocent eye, 151–2
  and Paul, 151
  and reflexivity, 111
  and religious sensibility, 175
  and St Augustine, 104, 189,
      222n125
  and Simmel, 109
  social implications, 8
  and Synnott, 111
  and Yeats, 107
  see also custody of the eyes; evil eye;
      period eye

face
  as avatar, 91
  and beauty, 152
  of Christ, 189–90
  and cyberspace, 91
  and embodiment, 152
  and Frank, 153–4
  of God, 139, 153–5, 188
  and Goffman, 68, 152
  and the Other, 49–50, 152–3
  seeing the unseen, 153–6, 186–7
  and Simmel, 141
  of Stephen, 187
  and Synnott, 216n79
famine fatigue, 119–20
Fenn, Richard
  on secular religion, 40
fieldnotes
  as liminal, 35
Fontaine, Jean La
  rumours of evil, 180

Foucault, Michel
  and 'as if', 67
  and the death of God
      and god, 68
  and evil, 177
  and the eye of God, 69
  and the gaze, 67–9, 109
  invisible visibility, 67, 86,
      206n36
  and St John Cassian, 32–3
  light and dark, 68
  and the Panopticon, 67–70
  and sexual abstinence, 118
  and spectacle, 68, 177
Frank, Georgia
  defining visuality, 108
  'eyes of faith', 153–4
  touching the unseen, 153

gaze
  adjectival properties, 144
  cinematic forms, 123–4
  and the *flâneur*, 83
  forms and sociology, 121
  and Foucault, 67–9, 109
  on letters, 127–8
  the male version, 123
  and the tourist, 111
  The Tourist Gaze, 147–8
  see also glance
Geertz, Clifford
  reflexivity and 'being there', 62
Generation X
  and Beaudoin, 10
Giddens, Anthony
  on addiction, 113
  and sexual desire, 122
  trust and late modernity, 64–5,
      204n97
glance
  and the gaze, 109
god
  and evil, 161
  the killing gaze, 68–9, 205n107
  as voyeur, 71
God
  absence, 48–9, 177, 179–80
  and His eyes, 66–7, 69, 139–40
  seeing His face, 139, 153–5
  see also death of God

Goffman, Erving
  actual and virtual identity, 98
  'as if' and his world, 36
  and civil inattention, 65
  co-presence and cyberspace, 90–1
  as cynic, 12
  on the face, 68, 152
  and MacIntyre, 52
  and the moral career, 59
  and 'passing' and covering,
    125–6
  and self consecration, 40
  and self image, 187
  and *Stigma*, 59, 125–7
  the world safe from sociology, 11
good and evil
  Orwell, 70
Goodness
  and Anscombe, 53
  and Murdoch, 53–4

Habakkuk's vision, 66
Halbwachs, Maurice
  on commemoration, 20
  memory and perception, 131
  seeing the unseen, 131
Heaven's Gate, 93–4, 207n64
hermeneutics
  and seeing, 111
Hervieu-Léger, Danièle
  parish as the site of memory, 21
Hine, Christine
  ethnography and the Internet, 92
Holocaust
  and Bauman, 48, 161, 177–8
  forms of evil, 176–7
Huysmans, J.-K.
  on the beauty of chastity, 188
  and boredom, 115
  and the cathedral, 197n19
  and *The Crucifixion*, 189
  and doors, 23
  and evil, 120, 161
  and healing of the eyes, 121

icon painter
  and the photographer, 84–5
  prayer and petition, 84–5
iconoclasm
  and Ely Cathedral, 130–1

icons
  and Besançon, 156–7
  defined, 156
  as doors, 157
  as images of the Divine, 188
Idiot, The
  and Holbein's Christ, 189
idols and idolatry, 66–7, 130
Illich, Ivan
  on the eye, 106–7
images
  and advertising, 112
  Berger and de-spiritualisation, 81
  and Bourdieu, 86
  of the heavenly, 182–3
  and Jervis, 87–8, 188
  and Judaism, 106
  and photography, 85–6
  and reflexivity, 122
  and religious context,
    206n20
  and ritual setting, 82
  and temptation, 113
  of the unseen, 153–5
Imaginary Friends
  as a parable of the virtual, 75–6
  sociologist's prayer, 25
  and sociology, 25–7
Internet
  and co-presence, 90–1
  and ethnography, 91–2
  and the forbidden, 74
  military origins, 90
  netiquette, 90
  and reflexivity, 92
  and religious orders, 97–8
  and the virtual, 29
  and virtuous regard, 76
  see also religion and
    the Internet

James, William
  and inner seeing, 62
  science and living religion, 96
  on the seen and the unseen, 159
Jenks, Chris
  ideas and the visual, 152
Jervis, John
  on image and allegory, 87–8
  on the truth of images, 188

Kempis, Thomas Á
  witness of inner life, 186
Khare
  knitting the seen and unseen, 190

Latour, Bruno
  and the angels, 184
  seeing 'as if', 184
letters
  and the gaze, 127–8
Lewis, C.S.
  Shadowlands, 9
lieu de mémoire, 19
light
  and dark, 161
  and faith, 158–61, 186–7
  and Foucault, 68
  Simmel on Rembrandt,
    171–2
Limerick
  misty recollections, 14–16
liminal
  and boredom, 118–19
  choices and the virtual, 28
  and fieldnotes, 35
  and the liminoid, 100
  and pilgrimage, 149
  and Shields, 100
liminoid, 190
  and liminality, 3, 100
liminoid virtualities
  and 'as if', 183
  as fourth form of the virtual,
    defined, 100–1
  and pilgrimage, 149
  and the seen and the unseen,
    105–6
  and Simmel, 169
  and the tactile, 154
liquid modernity
  and Bauman, 4, 10, 45, 51,
    66, 89
Lord of the Rings
  theological resonances, 88
Lurie, Alison
  Imaginary Friends, 25–7,
    75–6
Lyman, Stanford
  and acedia, 119
  sociology and evil, 178–9

MacIntyre, Alasdair
  critiques of Weber and Goffman, 52–3
  and nostalgia, 53
  traits of virtue, 54–5
Macmillan, James
  crises of Christianity, 2
Maffesoli, Michel
  and the cathedral, 33
  tribes and the 'social divine, 33
Maines, David
  sociology's narrative moment, 58
Mandelson, Peter
  and the Millennium Dome, 18–19
Martin, Richard
  sociology as virtual religion, 34–5
Mauss, Marcel
  sociology of prayer, 6–7
Mead, Margaret
  idealised fieldwork, 35
memory
  'as if', 131–2
  and Comte, 19
  and cyberspace, 96–7
  Orwell and manipulation, 70
  and the parish, 21
metaphorical religion, 40
Millennium Dome
  and Mr Mandelson, 18–19
  and *Seeing Salvation*, 190–1
Miller, William Watts,
  Durkheim and time, 197n17
  milieux de mémoire, 19–20
  secular religion, 39, 196n8
mirror memory, 19–21
Mirzoeff, Nicholas
  visual culture, 78
Mitchell, W.J.T.
  and cultural studies, 77
  definition of visual culture, 77
  significance of Benjamin, 81–2
  syllabus of visual culture, 77
  visual culture and the field, 79
mobile phones
  as camphones, 103
  dangerous powers, 74
Möllering, Guido
  Simmel and trust, 63
Morebath, 21
Morgan, David
  definition of visual piety, 159

Mulvey, Laura
  the male gaze, 123
Murdoch, Iris
  and goodness, 53–4

Narayan, Kirin
  ascetic images, 96
Neiman, Susan
  evil and the absence of God, 177,
    179–80
Nora, Pierre
  lieux de mémoire, 19
  milieux de mémoire, 19–20
  mirror memory, 19–21
novices
  and sociological training,
    34–5, 157

O'Connor, Flannery
  Wise Blood, 140–1
O'Neill, Onora
  paradox of trust, 63
  as social capital, 64
Orwell, George
  Nineteen Eighty-Four,
    69–70
O'Toole, Roger
  Weber on art, 168

Pascal, Blaise
  on boredom, 115
  on habit and conversion, 182
Paul
  on the all seeing eye of God, 69
  eyes of understanding, 151
  and the flesh, 112
  the heavenly city, 10
  on hope, 33
  the mirror of the self, 153
  on the seen and unseen, 9–10
  on the unseen God, 76
period eye
  and Baxandall, 133–4
photograph
  and Barthes, 83
  and Bourdieu, 86–7
photographer
  and the icon painter, 84–5
  as predatory, 84
  and the self, 87

photography
  and Bourdieu, 86–7
  and images, 85–6
  and Sontag, 84–5
pilgrim
  forms of seeing, 153
  journeying, 148–9
  and the tourist, 51, 147
pilgrimage
  and the 'eyes of faith', 153–4
  and forms of liminality, 149
  and the innocence of the eye, 148
  Lough Derg, 149
  virtual forms, 97
Plummer, Ken
  on pornography and witness, 121
  on the rise of narratives, 57
  tales and blindness, 61
Poor Clares
  Internet witness, 97
pornography
  and Aitkenhead, 121–2
  and the voyeur, 121
positivist religion
  Comte's church of humanity,
    19, 30–1
  and Ireland 31
postmodernity
  and ethics, 46,48
  and liquid modernity, 4,10, 45,
    51, 66, 89
  and religion, 47
  and virtual religion, 28
prayer
  and Comte, 185, 196n4
  and Mauss, 6–7
  and Nietzsche, 185
  and recognition of evil, 179
  and seeing the unseen, 185
  and Simmel, 174–5
  the sociologist's petition, 25, 191
  and Winch, 185
Protestant Ethic, the
  and Bauman, 51, 167
  and Calvinists, 164–5
  and Carroll, 162, 166
  and Catholicism, 163–8
  and sociology's identity, 167,
    218n36
  and visual piety, 165–66

Protestantism
  and Catholicism, 162–8
  and civil religion, 37–8, 40
  and Eagleton, 163
  and visual culture, 99–100, 167
  and visual piety, 162, 167
  Weber's choice, 162

Raposa, Michael
  acedia and sloth, 211n72
  boredom as ambiguous, 117
  liminality and boredom, 118–19
  routine and ritual, 182
Rappaport, Roy, 23
Ratzinger, Joseph
  angels and art, 183
  art, image and faith, 11
  icons, 188
real religion
  as Catholicism, 18
  as theology, 3, 27, 39
reflexivity
  and 'as if', 144–5
  and Bourdieu, 56, 60
  and the eye, 111
  and Geertz, 62
  and images, 122
  and the inside of religion, 23
  and the Internet, 92
  religion and ethics, 60–1
  and the sociological gaze, 105–8,
    191–2
  visual dimensions, 3, 7–8
Reformation
  and memory, 20–1
  and Morebath, 21
religion and the Internet
  Brasher, 92, 208n91
  Catholicism, 95, 97–8, 208n91
  Dawson, 98
  Heaven's Gate, 93–4, 207n66
  and religious orders, 97–8
  virtual church services, 94–5
religious capital
  and 'as if', 137–8
  and Bourdieu, 136–87
  and Iannoccone, 137
  and seeing the unseen, 137–8
  and vocations, 137, 195n16,
    214n15–17

Rose, Gillian
  conversion to Christianity, 50, 202n23

St Mary's Church
  Shrewsbury, 1, 194n1
Sarup, Madan
  on self, identity and postmodernism, 58
Satanism
  and La Fontaine, 180
  and Huysmans, 120, 161
  and popular culture, 176
Saward, John
  on the angels, 183
  on beauty and holiness, 184
'Science as a Vocation'
  and the Edomite Watchman, 24, 65
  and identity of sociological novices,
    36–7
  and theology, 12
  and virtual religion, 13
secular religion
  Fenn, 40
  Varro, 29–30
  Watts Miller, 39, 196n8
secularisation
  death of a concept, 2, 194n8
Seeing Salvation
  and Davie, 191
  and the Millennium Dome, 190–1
seen and the unseen
  'as if', 144–5
  and the angels, 182–4
  and von Balthasar, 117
  and blindness, 139–41, 143–4
  and the cathedral, 150
  and the cathedral door, 22
  choirboy's witness, 154
  and Christ, 76, 139–40
  and the colour of religion, 175
  and cyberspace, 72
  as defined, 10
  in Ely cathedral, 130–2
  and the face, 153–6, 186–7
  and Goffman, 125–7
  Halbwachs, 131
  and hermeneutics, 111
  and images, 153–5
  and Islamic women, 126–7
  and James, 159
  and Khare, 190

seen and the unseen – *continued*
  and liminoid virtualities, 100–1,
    105–6, 183
  in the medieval world, 149–50
  Paul, 9–10
  and the pilgrim, 149
  and prayer, 185
  and religious capital, 137–8
  and the religious habit, 186
  and St Augustine, 118, 140,
    159, 179
  and sociology, 8, 77, 144–5
  and the spectator, 120
  Syrian ascetics, 110
  see also voyeur
Séguy, Jean
  metaphorical religion, 40,
    201n96
Shadowlands, 9
Shields, Rob
  liminoid virtualities, 100–1
  on the virtual, 99–100
Simmel, Georg
  actuality of religion, 171
  on art and the soul, 174
  and blaséness, 114
  and the blind, 141
  on the colour of religion, 110,
    171–2, 175
  on the door, 22
  and Erickson, 169
  on the eye, 109
  and the face, 141
  on faith, 172–4
  on Fra Angelico, 183
  and the glance, 109
  and liminoid virtualities, 169
  on prayer, 174–5
  redemption of the tragedy of culture,
    171, 173
  on the religious person, 175
  on Rembrandt, 171–2
  and the soul, 12
  and spirituality, 12
  and trust, 63
  visual estrangement, 73
  and yearning for God, 172–4
sociology
  and acedia, 119, 157
  and the cathedral, 22–3, 197n17

  and dilemmas of the ocular, 106
  and the gaze, 105–8, 121
  and Goffman, 11
  as imagined, 36
  and the seen and the unseen, 8
  suspicion of the visual, 7
  and Sztompka, 57
  and tales, 4, 44, 57–9
  and theological afflictions, 168
  and theology, 5, 195n15
  see also sociology as a
    virtual religion
Sociology and Liturgy
  and opacity, 5
  and re-presentations, 184
  virtuous dissimulation, 187
sociology as a virtual religion
  first form, 9, 17–18, 26–7, 34–5,
    37, 75, 163
  and novices, 34–7, 167
  Richard Martin, 34–5
  and Weber, 13
Sontag, Susan
  on image and identity, 87
  on photography, 84–5
Spacks, Patricia Meyer
  inwardness and boredom, 117
spectacle
  Debord, 110
  and the Eucharist, 132
  and Foucault, 68
  and tourism, 147
spectator
  and moral indifference, 120
  and gender, 123, 212n93
  and the tourist, 147–8
Stark and Finke
  belief and the study of religion, 23
surveillance, 66–71
Synnott, Anthony
  the eye and I, 111
  and the face, 216n79
Sztompka, Piotr
  two forms of sociology, 57

tales
  of seeking 'us', 58–9
  and the self, 58
  of sexuality, 59–60
  and sociology, 4, 44, 57–8

temptation
and addiction, 113
and boredom, 113–14
and desire, 112–13
and images, 113
and inward blindness, 112
Tester, Keith
on compassion fatigue, 119–20
and Weber's theology, 217n6
theology
and sociology, 5, 195n15
and Weber, 12, 163, 217n6
time
and Durkheim 197n17
trust
'as if', 63
and Bauman, 63
and Bok, 62
and Giddens, 64–5, 204–5n97
and the glance, 109
and lies, 62–3
and O'Neill, 63–4
and Simmel, 63
sociological properties, 44
Turner, Victor
and the innocence of the eye, 148
Lough Derg as 'archaic', 149
pilgrim and the tourist, 147
on pilgrimage, 149
see also liminal; liminoid

Urry, John
The Tourist Gaze, 147–8

Varro, Marcus
Cicero's appraisal, 30
and Durkheim, 38–9
religion and secularisation, 29–30
and St Augustine, 38, 199n52
and virtual religion, 38
Vattimo, Gianni
and the 'lapsed', 11
Vauchez, André
on cathedrals, 21–2
veiling
and Islamic women, 126–7
vicarious religion, 39, 201n93
vice
and acedia 116, 119, 210–11nn51, 72
of gluttony, 113

and lust, 113
and temptation, 113
and Weber, 119
virtual
'as if', 77
and cultural memory, 16
and cyberspace, 29, 75–6,
91–2, 135
and ethnography, 92
Imaginary Friends as parable,
75–6
pilgrimage, 97
and the real, 39
and Shields, 99–100
and social identity, 98
and sociology, 11, 196n30
and vicarious religion, 39
virtual and cyberspace
third form, 29, 75–6, 135
virtual liturgy
second form, 27–9, 94–5
virtual reality
'as if', 89
defined, 90
and ethics, 91–2
lure, 73–4
virtual religion
and acedia, 116
and Beaudoin, 28
and Bergeron, 27–8
and Big Brother, 71
and English society, 37
as expression of civil religion, 37
and false memory syndrome, 41
and Maffesoli, 33
and metaphorical religion, 40
and self-consecration, 40, 47
as sociology's false consciousness, 106
three forms, 26–9, 75–6
and Weber, 13, 160
and Varro's civil theology, 38
see also liminoid virtualities; sociology
as a virtual religion; virtual and
cyberspace; virtual liturgy
virtue
and acedia, 116
and MacIntyre, 54–5
and sociology of sport, 55
virtue ethics
and Catholicism, 53

virtue and vice
  as antinomies, 118, 211n66
  and discernment, 153
visual culture
  and allegory, 87–9
  Barnard's forms, 109
  and Benjamin, 81–2
  and cultural studies, 80
  defined, 77
  in disciplinary limbo, 77–8
  and Jenks, 152
  and Jervis, 87–8, 188
  and the medieval world, 149–50
  and Mirzoeff, 78
  and Mitchell, 77, 79–82
  and other forms of culture, 80–1
  and Protestantism, 99–100, 167
  and the social field, 79
  syllabus, 77
  and tourism, 148
  visualising existence, 78
visual piety
  as defined, 159
  and the *Protestant Ethic*, 165–6
  and Protestantism, 162, 167
visuality
  and Frank, 108
vocation
  sacerdotal disposition, 6, 195n16
  and sociology, 198n40
  and Weber, 12–13, 27, 198n40–1
voyeur
  and Alypius, 124
  and the cinematic gaze, 123–4

and disembodiment, 124–5
embodiment and disembodiment,
  128–9
as god, 71
and pornography, 121

Wacquant, Loïc
  on Bourdieu and reflexivity, 56
Waksler, Frances Chaput
  'as if' and Goffman, 36
Weber, Max
  and aesthetics, 160
  and art, 168
  and Bauman, 48, 50–1, 167, 178
  and blindness, 166
  and Catholicism, 166
  and the Edomite watchman, 24, 65
  inner-worldly pilgrims, 50–1
  and McIntyre, 52–3
  and theology, 12, 163, 217n6
  and the vice of sloth, 119
  and virtual religion, 13, 160
  and vocation, 12–13, 27, 198n40–1
  and the Wild West, 56
Winch, Peter
  on prayer, 186
Wright, Alex
  on the decline of academic theology,
  2, 194n3
Wuthnow, Robert
  definition of civil religion, 38

Yeats, William Butler
  on the eye, 107